unforgettable journeys

DK EYEWITNESS

unforgettable journeys

SLOW DOWN AND
SEE THE WORLD

Contents

Introduction
6

ON FOOT
8

BY ROAD
86

BY BIKE
148

BY WATER
250

BY RAIL
192

Index
312

Acknowledgments
318

Camping at the majestic Tre Cime di Lavaredo after a day's hike

Introduction

What's your idea of an unforgettable journey? Watching a country unfurl outside a train window, scaling the peak of a sky-grazing summit or simply seeing the world float by from the sun-kissed deck of a boat? Whatever it is, there's one thing that's true: often it's the journey, rather than the destination, that matters most.

When you're battling your way against the flow of other walkers on a city street, pushing onto a crowded commuter train or stuck in traffic on a gridlocked road, it's hard to remember that getting from A to B can be pleasurable. The modern world is constantly on the move, with everyone striving to get anywhere fast, but when you slow down and take the scenic route, you're guaranteed experiences that would otherwise pass you by. Sampling a freshly fried delicacy from a roadside stall, talking to carriage companions, sleeping under the stars – these are the little details that make up a trip of a lifetime.

In *Unforgettable Journeys*, we've picked the world's best adventures, from cruising around Alaska and Antarctica to train journeys in Zambia and Zimbabwe. Of course, the big-hitters are covered – riding the Orient Express, driving Route 66 and walking the Camino de Santiago – but we also take you off the beaten path, cycling around Botswana, kayaking through Finnish lakeland and scaling the cirques of La Réunion on foot. We've organized the book by types of transport, so whether you're an avid hiker, cyclist or driver, or love to be on the water or on the rails, we've got you covered.

We're certain that you'll find inspiration while leafing through this book, but it's your own experiences that will stay with you forever. So don't just turn the page – pack your bags, and get out and explore the world.

ON FOOT

Walking is so much more than getting from A to B: it's about connecting to the past and following in the footsteps of pilgrims and adventurers; escaping the crowds and striking out on your own. Something new lies around every corner, whether it's pretty villages, native wildlife or superlative views. All of this from the simple, almost meditative, act of placing one foot in front of the other.

AT A GLANCE
ON FOOT

NORTH AMERICA pp12–23

Great lakes, colossal mountains, mighty rivers and the Grand Canyon – explore them all on North America's stunning trails.

CENTRAL AND SOUTH AMERICA pp24–31

Trace the ancient Ruta del Maya across the Yucatán Peninsula and follow Incan trails down South America's Andean spine.

KEY TO MAP

.... Long route
● End point

Previous page *Hiking through the Himalayas on the Manaslu Circuit, Nepal*

10

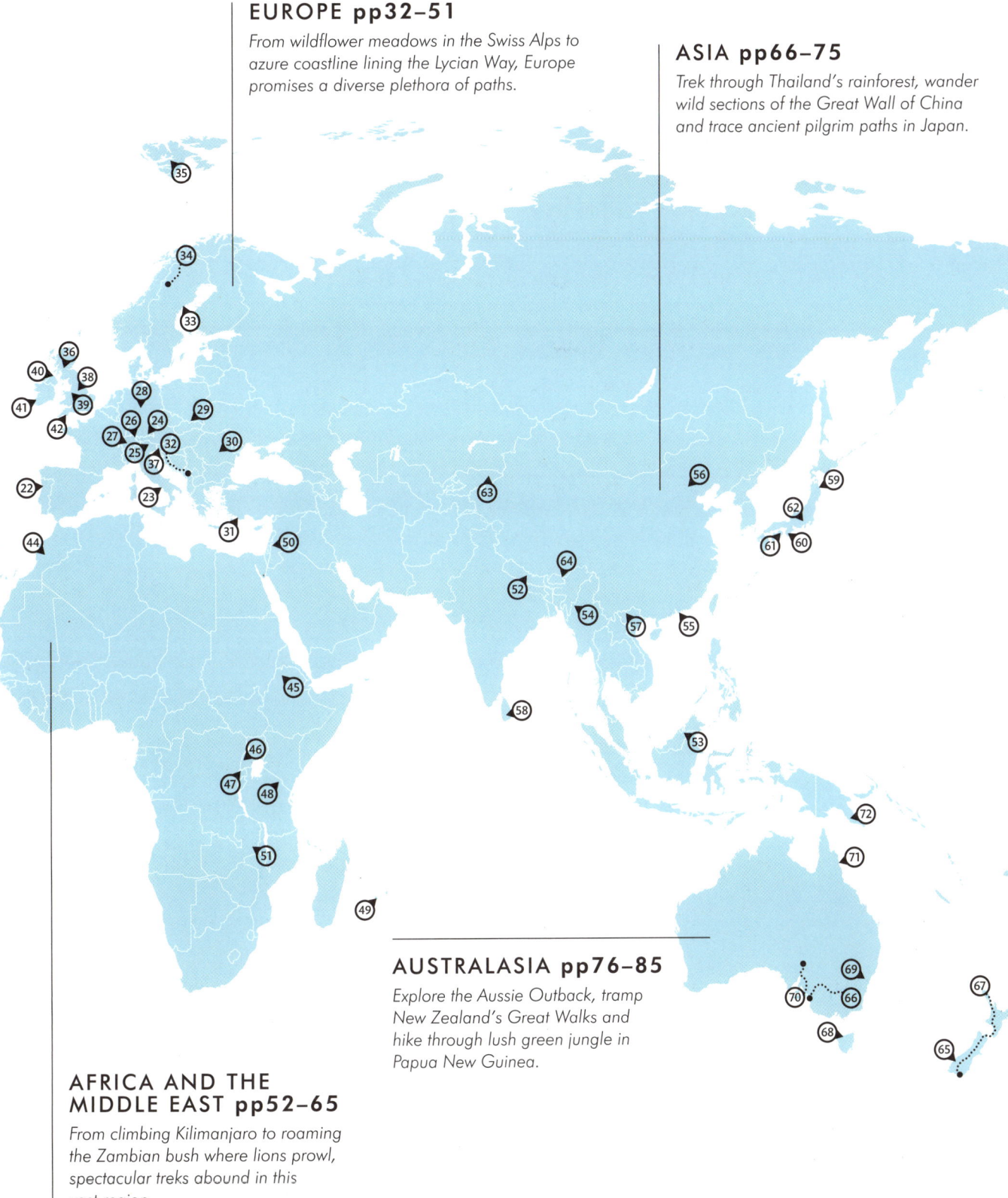

EUROPE pp32–51

From wildflower meadows in the Swiss Alps to azure coastline lining the Lycian Way, Europe promises a diverse plethora of paths.

ASIA pp66–75

Trek through Thailand's rainforest, wander wild sections of the Great Wall of China and trace ancient pilgrim paths in Japan.

AUSTRALASIA pp76–85

Explore the Aussie Outback, tramp New Zealand's Great Walks and hike through lush green jungle in Papua New Guinea.

AFRICA AND THE MIDDLE EAST pp52–65

From climbing Kilimanjaro to roaming the Zambian bush where lions prowl, spectacular treks abound in this vast region.

11

ON FOOT
NORTH AMERICA

Appalachian Trail

LOCATION US **START/FINISH** Springer Mountain/Mount Katahdin **DISTANCE** 3,528 km (2,192 miles) **TIME** 5–7 months **DIFFICULTY** Challenging; mountainous terrain **INFORMATION** www.appalachiantrail.org

Linking the soaring peaks and misty valleys of the South with the vast forests and clapboard villages of New England, the Appalachian Trail – the world's longest hiking-only footpath – is a mammoth challenge that only the hardy will complete.

Black bears and moose, the scent of smoky campfires and slopes blanketed in fiery maple await on the gargantuan Appalachian Trail, a multi-sensory – and multi-seasonal – experience. Conceived in 1921 by conservationist Benton MacKaye, this trail – the king of American wilderness routes – was completed in 1937. Today, over 2 million people take to the trail each year, but fewer than 25 per cent of hikers tackle the entire route at once.

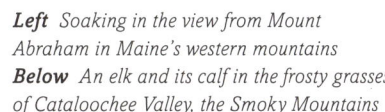

> Fewer than 25 per cent of hikers tackle the entire route at once

Most thru-hikers start in Georgia's rugged Blue Ridge Mountains in March or April, following the warm weather as it creeps north to reach Mount Katahdin in Maine before mid-October, when the leaves start to erupt in autumn colour. One of the most popular sections of the trail navigates the Great Smoky Mountains, the country's most visited national park, on the border between North Carolina and Tennessee. Wispy fog explains their "smoky" epithet and veils herds of elk, fire lookout towers and the Appalachian's highest peak – Clingmans Dome. As spring matures, thru-hikers cross the mountains into Tennessee, where clumps of delicate bluets and other wildflowers shadow the trail. In Virginia, everything suddenly changes – overlooks, such as McAfee Knob, reveal more pastoral scenes where forest blends with farmland.

Left *Soaking in the view from Mount Abraham in Maine's western mountains*
Below *An elk and its calf in the frosty grasses of Cataloochee Valley, the Smoky Mountains*

WATCH *the leaves turn from green to gold in the forests of* **Vermont** *and* **New Hampshire** *from September*

Mount Katahdin

HAVE A PADDLE
and a picnic at scenic
Delaware Water Gap

UNITED STATES

SPOT BLACK BEARS
and look for bear tracks in
Shenandoah National Park

Springer Mountain

HIKE *the mist-filled valleys and peaks of* **Great Smoky Mountains National Park**

It's not all empty landscapes though. In West Virginia, stroll through the heart of Harpers Ferry, a small town made up of 19th-century red-brick and clapboard homes that tumble down the slopes towards the Potomac and Shenandoah rivers. This was the site of John Brown's Raid in 1859, when the abolitionist made a failed attempt to initiate a rebellion of enslaved people.

The weather turns hot and humid as you pass into the mid-Atlantic states in midsummer. Maryland features some of the trail's gentlest terrain, while Pennsylvania lives up to its "Rocksylvania" nickname, with its boulder-strewn sections. Relieve the humidity and ease weary limbs in the aptly named Boiling Springs, a town sprinkled with spas and fizzing thermal waters – the most famous is dubbed "The Bubble". In New York's Harriman State Park, slip through the "Lemon Squeezer", a narrow crack between giant rocks, before crossing the spectacular Bear Mountain Bridge over the Hudson River.

Temperatures become comfortable and mild by the time the trail leads into New England. At Falls Village, watch the Housatonic River tumble over a 15-m- (50-ft-) high pile of granite slabs, while densely

> Relieve the humidity and ease weary limbs in the aptly named Boiling Springs

14

ON FOOT
NORTH AMERICA

forested hills stretch out in all directions from the top of Mount Greylock. During the fall foliage season from September to October, Vermont and New Hampshire's oceans of maple, birch and beech turn red, gold and amber. Here, the weather cools again and the way becomes rougher and steeper, with true alpine conditions on the White Mountain tops. Maine presents the most challenging terrain of all. In Mahoosuc Notch, giant boulders block the path and there are countless unbridged streams. Thankfully, the dangerous crossing over the Kennebec River has a free canoe ferry service during hiking season. Then, finally, Mount Katahdin looms on the horizon. It's a steep, gruelling climb to the top, where a simple, weather-beaten sign proclaims the trail's northern terminus. Take in your achievement and absorb the view – nothing else will have seemed quite so beautiful.

A WALK IN THE WOODS

Travel writer Bill Bryson attempted to hike the Appalachian Trail in the 1990s, recording his experiences in *A Walk in the Woods* (1998). Bryson was accompanied by "Stephen Katz", an overweight, recovering alcoholic (who may or may not be a real person). Like the vast majority of hikers, the hapless couple failed to walk the whole thing, though they did complete a respectable 1,287 km (800 miles). In 2015 the book was adapted into a movie starring Robert Redford and Nick Nolte.

Left *Autumn sets the forest aflame all along the Potomac River, Maryland*
Above *Mount Cammerer's fire lookout tower, one of the many found on the trail*

15

ON FOOT
NORTH AMERICA

The Narrows

LOCATION US **START/FINISH** Temple of Sinawava/Big Spring **DISTANCE** 16 km (10 miles) **TIME** 1 day **DIFFICULTY** Moderate
INFORMATION www.nps.gov

Tramping into The Narrows, found within Zion National Park, is an unusually intimate wilderness experience – hikers must wade along the submerged path, which is hemmed in by giant walls of multicoloured sandstone.

A short but exhilarating route, The Narrows navigates the tightest section of Zion Canyon, a craggy gorge that is just 6- to 9-m (20- to 30-ft) wide but 610-m (2,000-ft) high. Starting at the Temple of Sinawava, a natural amphitheatre of red sandstone cliffs, the paved Riverside Trail leads to the mouth of the gorge. There's no path from here; instead, you must walk into the shallow Virgin River. The water is cool and deliciously refreshing on weary legs, but there are slippery, uneven rocks to negotiate on the relentless plod upstream. Other noises gradually fade away until all that's left is the constant gurgling of the shallow but fast-flowing water.

After around two hours, the river runs into the Orderville Canyon, formed by a tributary creek. The impossibly tight walls here have been smoothed and rounded over the millennia like melted wax, and are scoured with tiny gouges. As you wade further upstream, the cliffs seem to change colour, turning deeper shades of red, amber and brown. Finally, the gorge opens up a little at Big Springs, a pebbly cove where fresh water tumbles into the river and the hike ends. Here, you can rest on the riverbank before wading back in, and doing it all over again.

Wading through the water in The Narrows, Zion National Park

ON FOOT
NORTH AMERICA

Camping beside Lake Marjorie, one of the many lakes on the John Muir Trail

John Muir Trail

LOCATION US **START/FINISH** Happy Isles/Mount Whitney
DISTANCE 340 km (211 miles) **TIME** 3 weeks
DIFFICULTY Challenging; mountainous terrain
INFORMATION www.nps.gov; permit required

Traversing the finest mountain scenery in California – if not the US – the John Muir Trail takes in the snow-capped Sierra Nevada, gem-coloured lakes and an otherworldly arid landscape far above the treeline.

Negotiating a series of vertiginous ups and downs, the John Muir Trail is a challenging hike. Walkers must tackle the "Golden Staircase" – a steep 457-m (1,500-ft) ascent via 50 or more jaw-dropping switchbacks – and the final climb up Mount Whitney, where the moonscape summit seems to overlook the whole of California. There are few guesthouses to provide creature comforts along the way; instead, hikers must camp beside the Sierra Nevada's alpine lakes, but this is all part of the trail's charm.

  Jumping into a snow-fed lake after a sweaty hike is far more energizing than a shower, and it's hard to resist the glistening depths of Lower Cathedral Lake, Thousand Island Lake or Garnett Lake. After drying off and setting up camp, settle down to stargaze to the soundtrack of rustling winds and screeching hawks. In the morning, the sun rises over jagged peaks, and deer and bighorn sheep clamber up the rocky slopes. With scenes like these, it's easy to see why John Muir fought so hard to protect this stretch of wilderness.

JOHN MUIR

Pioneering naturalist and author John Muir was born in Dunbar, Scotland, in 1838. He emigrated to the US with his family when he was 11 years old, but saw Yosemite Valley for the first time in 1868. He spent the rest of his life fighting for its preservation, writing the essays that helped establish Yosemite National Park in 1890.

17

Snow-capped Denali, overlooking the snaking McKinley Bar Trail, painted red with arctic blossom

McKinley Bar Trail

LOCATION US **START/FINISH** Wonder Lake Campground Road (loop) **DISTANCE** 16 km (10 miles) **TIME** 6 hours **DIFFICULTY** Moderate **INFORMATION** www.nps.gov

This Denali National Park hike is best walked in June, when wildflowers bloom and the peaks are still framed by snow. Easily tackled in a day, the trail begins on tundra smothered with brush and Arctic blossom, and pitted by hidden ponds and bogs. To the south lies the jagged ridge of the Alaska Range, including North America's highest peak, Denali itself. The mountains form a giant snow-topped wall, glistening in the sunlight as you walk closer. Icy snowmelt streams gurgle across the plain, and the path continues along wooden boardwalks that skim the wettest, spongiest patches. Gradually, the trail fades into spruce woods, and soon a dense forest of spiky emerald blocks the mountains from view. Suddenly, the path emerges from the trees – ahead lies the McKinley River Bar, a gravel bank threaded by swift-running water. Before returning to the trailhead, there's time to bathe your feet and look for the tracks of the bears who also roam this trail.

Colorado Trail

LOCATION US **START/FINISH** Denver/Durango **DISTANCE** 782 km (486 miles) **TIME** 4–6 weeks **DIFFICULTY** Easy to challenging **INFORMATION** www.coloradotrail.org

This trail gives hikers a taste of Colorado's wild, rugged interior, little changed since the Ute people roamed the Rocky Mountains centuries ago. Most walkers start in Denver and tramp south, saving the steep San Juan Mountains for last. The first stretch to Kenosha Pass snakes through the South Platte River valley up to vast meadows sprinkled with spring wildflowers. Deeper into the Rockies, the air becomes fresher, the creeks faster and colder – groves of Ponderosa pine and Douglas fir cling to the slopes. Deer and elk graze on the high meadows, while bighorn sheep and marmots skitter across the trail. Later, the path crosses the cattle country of Cochetopa Valley, home to cows, cowboys and wide-open country. The final section through the San Juan Mountains is the most challenging but rewarding – vast alpine panoramas unfold ahead and the trail rolls down to Durango, where well-earned Western-style hospitality awaits.

another way

The Colorado Trail is also open to mountain bikers. The initial segment from the Denver trailhead at Waterton Canyon is ideal for beginners, while experienced riders should aim for the steep San Juan Mountain section between Molas Pass and Durango.

ON FOOT
NORTH AMERICA

⑥ Pacific Crest Trail

LOCATION US **START/FINISH** Campo/Monument 78 **DISTANCE** 4,625 km (2,650 miles) **TIME** 4–6 months **DIFFICULTY** Challenging **INFORMATION** www.pcta.org

Running all the way from Southern California to the Canadian border, this epic trail takes in all the landscapes of the American West – snow-capped Sierras, sun-bleached deserts and mist-wrapped volcanoes. A half-year-long hike, the trail transports walkers through the seasons too.

As late-April's emergence of spring flushes into California, walkers skirt the edge of the parched Mojave Desert. Tramping through the summer, dedicated thru-hikers conquer the High Sierras, where saw-toothed peaks rise like giant waves from the valley floor. By September, they'll have clambered over great ridges of Oregon and tackled the rain-lashed snaggletoothed North Cascades of Washington State. On the cusp of autumn, you'll reach a Canadian border fringed by honey-gold larches – and new paths that press ever northwards into winter.

⑦ Kalalau Trail

LOCATION US **START/FINISH** Ha'ena State Park/Kalalau Beach **DISTANCE** 35 km (22 miles) **TIME** 2 days **DIFFICULTY** Challenging **INFORMATION** www.kalalautrail.com

Far from the bustle of sun-soaked Waikīkī Beach, Hawaii's Kalalau Trail leads walkers into a timeless Polynesian world of misty sea cliffs, turquoise bays and primeval jungle. There are no resorts or souvenir shops – just the untrammelled Nāpali coast of Kauai. Most walkers set aside a couple of days to complete this route, which starts with a steady climb circling the base of fang-like Makana Mountain. Tantalizing glimpses of the Pacific Ocean are granted at intervals as the trail plunges through dense scrub and spiny pandanus. Undulating switchbacks lead through an abandoned coffee plantation and over towering high cliffs, dropping down to Pu'ukulua ("Red Hill"), a ridge of dark red earth. Many choose to spend the last night camped out on untouched Kalalau Beach, under a sky full of stars, the only sound the gentle lapping of Pacific swells.

Hiking the Pacific Crest Trail high above California's sparkling Echo Lakes

LEGENDS OF NĀPALI

Nau and Paka were two students at the Nāpali hula school. Dating was forbidden but the students fell in love. One night, they were discovered by the head teacher, Kilioe. Paka hid in a cave while Nau ran up the mountain, but Kilioe caught and killed them both. Unique to Kauai, the naupaka flower has grown here ever since, an enduring symbol of their love.

West Coast Trail

The pretty Tsusiat Falls, located near a campsite along the West Coast Trail

LOCATION Canada **START/FINISH** Pachena Bay/Gordon River **DISTANCE** 75 km (47 miles) **TIME** 5–7 days **DIFFICULTY** Challenging **INFORMATION** www.westcoasttrail.com; open May–Sep; permits required

Thousands of intrepid hikers attempt this remote coastal hike every year, though many fail to complete it. Those who do reach the finish are left with incredible tales to tell and an incredible sense of self sufficiency.

Once called the Dominion Lifesaving Trail, this route along the southwestern edge of Vancouver Island was built in 1907 to aid the rescue of sailors shipwrecked along this fog-riddled section of the wild Pacific Ocean. But, even before this, the local First Nations began etching out trading paths and paddling routes here some 4,000 years ago.

Hikers will have been preparing for this journey for months, if not years, in advance. The arduous trail winds through dense and storm-inflicted rainforests, thick and muddy bogs, and pebble beach crescents for short, much-needed breaks. Expect slippery wooden boardwalks, high ladders and moss-covered boulders. Rivers will need crossing. Clothes will refuse to dry. Nights will be cold and damp. And plenty of rainfall and strong winds will try to deter you from reaching the end.

Why then, would you choose such a gruelling trek? First, there's the opportunity to feast on freshly caught crab while sitting around a beach campfire, to witness huge whales breaching out in the cool waves and to ride thrilling cable cars across raging rivers. But, on top of all this, a primal instinct awakens here. One of survival, endurance and sheer will, but also a feeling of belonging to this remarkable and pristine part of our incredible planet.

ON FOOT
NORTH AMERICA

⑨ # East Coast Trail

LOCATION Canada **START/FINISH** Topsail Beach/Cappahayden **DISTANCE** 336 km (209 miles) **TIME** 3–4 weeks **DIFFICULTY** Easy to challenging
INFORMATION www.eastcoasttrail.com

An epic coastal footpath like no other, the East Coast Trail hugs the Avalon Peninsula on Canada's easternmost shoreline. Traverse the rocky and wind-ravaged headlands, watching whales swimming between icebergs and spotting puffins navigating the fjord cliffs.

A relatively new network of paths created in the mid-1990s, this trail is currently made up of 25 individual but connected paths and continues to expand up and down the coast of the Canadian province of Newfoundland and Labrador. Taking in historic lighthouses, ecological reserves and almost constant vistas of the vast waters of the Atlantic, hikers of all levels can take on this rewarding adventure, choosing sections of the trail that can take anywhere from hours to weeks to complete. One such section is the Sugarloaf Path, a moderate one-way day hike that begins in Quidi Vidi Village.

This quaint fishing community, tucked around a natural harbour, is known for its candy-coloured cottages and microbrewery that uses iceberg water to make its refreshing beers. Hikers ascend steeply along the path from here, taking in perfect views of the surrounding cliffs and St John's – the capital of the province. The trail closely follows the coastline up to barren Sugarloaf Head, into deep woodlands, and out onto exposed shrubby meadows. Logy Bay, where bobbing boats, whales and seals share the rough ocean waves below, marks the end of the Sugarloaf Path, but the East Coast Trail beckons on.

> Logy Bay, where bobbing boats, whales and seals share the rough ocean waves below

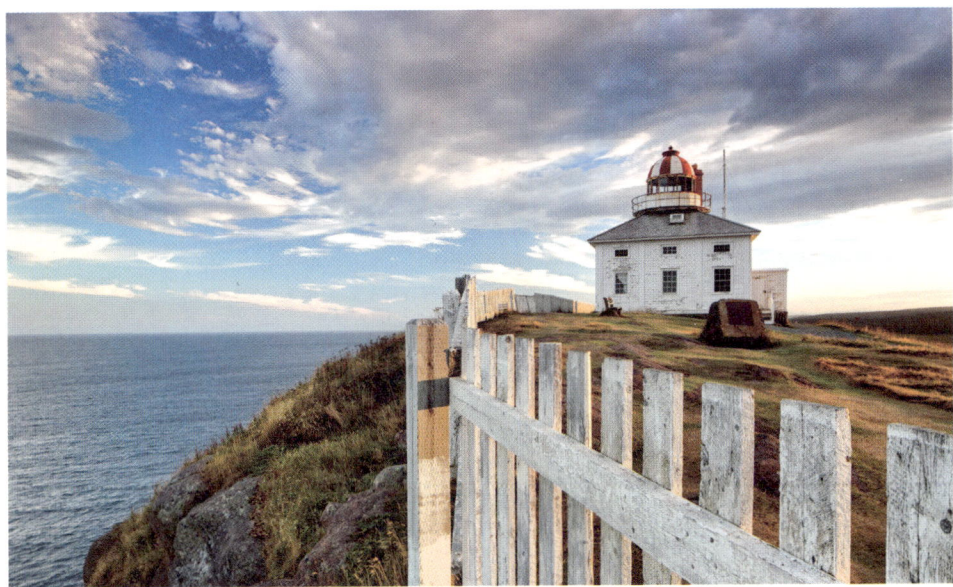

Cape Spear Lighthouse, built in 1835, one of the many historic lighthouses on the East Coast Trail

21

ON FOOT
NORTH AMERICA

Coastal Hiking Trail

LOCATION Canada **START/FINISH** North Swallow River/Hattie Cove **DISTANCE** 60 km (37 miles) **TIME** 5–9 days **DIFFICULTY** Challenging **INFORMATION** www.pc.gc.ca; registration mandatory at the park kiosk

Weaving along an undeveloped shoreline of the spectacular Lake Superior in Ontario's Pukaskwa National Park, the Coastal Hiking Trail chases a faint and ancient path once used by First Nations tribes many millennia ago. Be prepared to share the steep, rough terrain with the timber wolves, lynx and other reclusive creatures who roam the isolated boreal forests and boulder-strewn landscapes of this stunning part of Canada.

Crossing over the slick lichen-covered granite slabs that are part of the massive Precambrian rock formation known as the Canadian Shield, the trail has only a few cairn markers – small, man-made stone piles – to lead the way by day. And after dark, walkers must camp on deserted lake-side beaches. Welcome to the wilderness.

Thunder Bay at the head of Lake Superior on the Coastal Hiking Trail, Pukaskwa National Park

Half Dome

LOCATION US **START/FINISH** Happy Isles (loop) **DISTANCE** 26 km (16 miles) **TIME** 10–12 hours **DIFFICULTY** Challenging **INFORMATION** www.nps.gov; permit required

A hike to the round, smooth summit of Half Dome is one of Yosemite National Park's greatest challenges, despite the route's brevity. Starting on the leafy banks of the fast-flowing Merced River, the trail steadily gets trickier. After passing the Vernal Falls, a thin ribbon of water plunging off a cliff, and the wider Nevada Falls, hikers climb through forests of fir and spruce. Giant mountains rise up all around, towering above this ocean of green trees.

Then, suddenly, it's there – Half Dome. The path runs onto the northeast ridge of this barren hulk of weathered granite. From here, the slopes of the final summit seem almost sheer, but two metal cables allow hikers to clamber the last 122 m (400 ft) to the top without rock-climbing equipment. It's an exhilaratingly steep scramble over the smooth rock surface, but the flat top of Half Dome is the perfect place to catch your breath, before heading back down to earth.

THE LEGEND OF TIS-SA-ACK

The local Ahwahnechee name for Half Dome – Tis-sa-ack – is derived from the legend of a woman who journeyed with her husband to Mirror Lake. Upon arrival, Tis-sa-ack was so thirsty that she drank the lake dry and her enraged husband beat her. Shocked by their behaviour, the Great Spirit turned them both into granite and Tis-sa-ack became Half Dome.

Hiking through yellow aspen on the Jenny Lake Trail, Grand Teton National Park

12

Jenny Lake Trail

LOCATION US **START/FINISH** Jenny Lake Trailhead (loop) **DISTANCE** 11 km (7 miles) **TIME** 3–4 hours **DIFFICULTY** Moderate **INFORMATION** www.nps.gov

The trail around Jenny Lake at the heart of Grand Teton National Park cuts through tranquil forest glades, providing mesmerizing glimpses of the saw-toothed Teton range at intervals. It's best to tackle this half-day route in the morning, and to hike the lake counter-clockwise, so that you can catch the Tetons glittering in the new day's sun.

Even when the peaks aren't visible through the trees, the forest has its own charms. Long patches of thimbleberries interrupt the cottonwood, alder and aspen. These raspberry-like fruits are black bears' favourite treats, so look out for their tracks. These aren't the only animals that call the park home. River otters, muskrats and beavers make themselves busy in the lake and on its shores, while coyotes and mule deer hide among the trees. In the early morning, moose gather at the two aptly named Moose Ponds, on the south side of the lake, to bathe. But, again and again, the Cathedral Group – the tallest mountains in the Teton range – steal the scene.

13

Bright Angel Trail

LOCATION US **START/FINISH** Bright Angel Trailhead (loop) **DISTANCE** 30 km (19 miles) **TIME** 2 days **DIFFICULTY** Challenging **INFORMATION** www.nps.gov

Following a natural fault used for millennia by the Havasupai people, hiking the rim-to-river Bright Angel Trail offers a chance to get to grips with the Grand Canyon's gargantuan proportions. The trail starts by traversing seemingly endless switchbacks, framed by soaring cliffs. Gorgeous multi-hued views emerge at every turn as you zigzag down through the rust-colored Redwall Limestone zone of the canyon. Finally, the trail flattens out as it crosses the shale-smothered Tonto Platform to reach Indian Garden, a lush oasis engulfed in cottonwood trees, and Garden Creek, a gully of plunge pools, water-sculpted rocks and glistening cottonwoods.

Then it's down again, through almost black canyon walls of Devil's Corkscrew to Pipe Creek, which is lined with prickly pear, willows and brittlebush. For the final, blisteringly hot section, you clamber over sand dunes before reaching a silver bridge across the churning waters of the Colorado River. On the other side lies Bright Angel Campground, where you can recharge before tackling the uphill climb tomorrow.

another way

For a wilder experience, hike the North Kaibab Trail – the least visited but most difficult of the three trails at the Grand Canyon. You'll pass through every eco-system to be found between Canada and Mexico on this route, from fir trees and aspen at the rim, to desert vegetation at the base.

ON FOOT
CENTRAL AND SOUTH AMERICA

The O Circuit

LOCATION Chile **START/FINISH** Torre Central campground (loop)
DISTANCE 118 km (73 miles) **TIME** 9 days **DIFFICULTY** Challenging; mountainous terrain **INFORMATION** www.parquetorresdelpaine.cl; trekking without a guide is only permitted Oct–Apr

Circling Patagonia's iconic Torres del Paine National Park, the O Circuit takes in all the highlights of this magnificent region: lumbering glaciers, rugged granite mountain peaks and wind-blasted forests. Most visitors choose to hike the truncated W section of the route, but the O Circuit rewards the intrepid.

Watching the sunrise over the mountains surrounding Lago Pehoé, Torres del Paine

KEEP your eyes peeled for pumas around **Torre Central**

TAKE A DAY out to kayak on the waters beneath the calving snout of **Glacier Grey**

ABSORB the views of **Los Cuernos**, the most photogenic peaks of the Paine Massif

Watch out for huemul – a rare, native species of deer – around **Lago Pehoé** and the **Vallée del Francés**

Torres del Paine National Park

ARGENTINA

CHILE

Tracing a wide loop around the Paine Massif range that dominates Torres del Paine National Park, the nine-day O Circuit is a breathtaking introduction to Patagonia. Each day, the scenery changes. Ochre steppes (grassy plains) fold into groves of wind-contorted beech trees. Teal-coloured lakes grow from their banks to become soaring granite peaks. The forceful River Paine becomes the motionless Lago Dickson, with its amphitheatre of hanging glaciers, where the distant fizzle and pop as the ice creaks ever downwards punctuates the air.

Despite being a loop, the O Circuit is far from flat. A steep, lung-emptying climb brings you to John Gardner's Pass, one of the region's finest vantage points. Down below, the Southern Patagonian Ice Field stretches onwards, stained in ribbons of mineral black and cobalt blue. Closer still, Glacier Grey sits silently at your feet, with bergs the size of apartment blocks crumbling into the greedy, milky waters of Lago Grey.

It's from this pass that the Circuit joins the W – a five-day trail and playlist of the park's greatest hits, including the Vallée del Francés, with its dramatic hanging glacier. But the park's ultimate gift is offered on the final day. A steep scramble up into the eastern spur of the mountains and there they are: the three torres, or towers, after which the park is named. Caressed by the dawn, these peaks cast their orange-hued reflection into the gleaming waters of Lago Torres below. The silence of this moment will stay with you as you clamber back down to reality.

Coffee-coloured guanaco – the wild relative of the alpaca – grazing on the steppe in Torres del Paine National Park

25

ON FOOT
CENTRAL AND SOUTH AMERICA

Overlooking the Lago Quilotoa from the end point of the Quilotoa Traverse

⑮ Quilotoa Traverse

LOCATION Ecuador **START/FINISH** Sigchos/Quilotoa **DISTANCE** 30 km (19 miles) **TIME** 3 days **DIFFICULTY** Moderate **INFORMATION** Acclimatize in Quito beforehand

At 3,800 m (12,460 ft) above sea level, the biting air is thin in Andean Quechua territory – but it's the view from the rim of the Quilotoa crater that will really take your breath away. At your feet, the mineral-enriched turquoise of the wind-rippled Lago Quilotoa gleams, formed during its namesake volcano's last riotous eruption in 1280.

To reach the lake, you'll first need to tackle the Quilotoa Traverse, a 30-km (19-mile) dirt trail that's not for the faint of heart. Beginning in the town of Sigchos, the route clambers in and out of a series of gaping canyons as it ticks off a list of remote Andean market villages. Here, Quechua farmers – trailed by herds of llama – live in the shadow of volcanoes and beside the lake's sparkling shimmer. At each picturesque waypoint, locally owned guesthouses pamper weary hikers with hot showers and hearty Andean dishes – and often, to help you rise early, a dawn rooster chorus.

⑯ La Ruta de Maya

LOCATION Guatemala **START/FINISH** Cruce dos Aguadas/Tikal **DISTANCE** 50 km (31 miles) **TIME** 3 days **DIFFICULTY** Easy **INFORMATION** Stay at campsites in the jungle

The mysterious Maya civilization built a mighty empire across Central America, their majestic cities masterpieces of art and architecture. Deep in the Guatemalan jungle lies one of their greatest achievements: the now-ruined metropolis of Tikal. Once a Mayan seat of power, by the 19th century it had become lost to the sands of time, swallowed by the jungles of the Petén Basin.

A similar fate befell El Zotz, the first stop on this three-day trek tracing the Maya's footsteps across Guatemala. Besieged by dense jungle, it's easy to see how this seemingly impenetrable city lay undiscovered until 1977. Trekking further into the wilderness, past screaming howler monkeys and snuffling wild boar, you almost stumble across crumbling temples overgrown with creepers and vines. Then, suddenly, you emerge at Tikal, where moss-covered temples and ornate carvings are being reclaimed by humanity once again.

ON FOOT
CENTRAL AND SOUTH AMERICA

⑰ Kaieteur Falls Trek

LOCATION Guyana **START/FINISH** Pamela/Kaieteur **DISTANCE** 30 km (19 miles) **TIME** 4 days **DIFFICULTY** Challenging **INFORMATION** guyanatourism.com

Five times the height of Niagara Falls, Kaieteur – the world's largest single-drop waterfall – is a thundering, rainbow-framed rush of water that gushes out of the jungle and plunges into the tea-coloured Potaro River below.

Most travellers discover the falls by helicopter, but putting sole to soil unlocks more adventure. Companionship is provided by Guianan Cock-of-the-Rocks – mohawked, marmalade-hued birds. On the last day, thighs must be braced for the final stage of the trail – nicknamed "Oh My God" on account of the steep gradient – but once you reach the top, the view of Kaieteur's cascading curtain of water is more than worth it.

another way

Can't spare four days? What about four hours? Hikers can skip the start and join the last section from Tukiet, which ascends the steepest section of the trail before arriving at the falls.

⑱ Chapada Diamantina Trek

LOCATION Brazil **START/FINISH** Vale do Capão/Andaraí **DISTANCE** 60 km (38 miles) **TIME** 5 days **DIFFICULTY** Challenging **INFORMATION** Take a local guide

In the sun-baked interior of northeastern Brazil, Chapada Diamantina National Park is an adventurer's paradise. Hiking the deep canyon is the best way to appreciate its craggy features, worn by wind and rain over a billion years ago. There are many routes, but for the ultimate experience, tackle the Grand Circuit, which weaves its way through forest-fringed plateaux, and past waterfalls and caves.

Starting from Capão in the north, the steep trail climbs up to the Pai Inácio plateau, through a landscape of gnarled scrub and meadows with castle-like plateaux looming on the horizon. Descending to the Vale do Pati, the deep gorge opens up. Here, underground lagoons beckon hikers down side routes, but the best spot for a dip is saved till last – Cachoeirão, a sparkling waterfall cascading some 270 m (886 ft) into the drenched forest floor below.

The unstoppable, thunderous flow of the Kaieteur Falls, tumbling into the winding Potaro River

ON FOOT
CENTRAL AND SOUTH AMERICA

STAY in sustainable campsites and lodges, such as **Mountain Lodges of Peru**

END the trail at the iconic Inca fortress of **Machu Picchu**

HIKE past the imposing, folded peak of **Nevado Salkantay**

SPOT animals in both highland montane landscapes and lowland rainforest

PERU — Salkantay Trek

Machu Picchu

Mollepata

⑲ Salkantay Trek

LOCATION Peru **START/FINISH** Mollepata/Machu Picchu **DISTANCE** 74 km (46 miles) **TIME** 5 days **DIFFICULTY** Challenging; mountain passes at high altitude pose a considerable hurdle **INFORMATION** At least 2 days' acclimatization in Cusco is essential preparation for the hike

Taking in cinematic scenery, Quecha communities and Machu Picchu, the Salkantay Trek is a more challenging but lesser-travelled alternative to the Inca Trail.

The trek takes you off the beaten path through some of the most breathtaking and diverse landscapes in Peru, past beautiful valleys, snow-capped mountains, lush rainforests, stunning waterfalls and tiny Quecha villages. Starting northwest of former Inca stronghold Cusco, the ancient footpath clambers into the Cordillera Vilcabamba mountain range, flowing beneath jagged Andean peaks. An indefinable mysticism defines every step as you climb steadily towards the highest point at Nevado Salkantay, a mountain believed by the local Quechua people to be inhabited by *apus* (gods). After two days of overcoming the challenges of this high-altitude terrain, you'll make a welcome descent into oxygen-rich territory and steamy cloud forest, the air thick with darting hummingbirds and the sweet fragrance of orchids. On the last day, either one final hike or a shuttle bus brings you up the last mountain where the lost city of Machu Picchu perches precariously between two peaks like a citadel in the sky.

Hiking the Salkantay Trail through mountainous terrain towards Machu Pichu

another way

The nine-day trek from Choquequirao to Machu Picchu connects the iconic ruins of Machu Picchu with those of Choquequirao, a barely visited Inca site believed to be three times larger than the world-famous Machu Picchu citadel.

The ruins of 15th-century Machu Picchu, the best preserved of the Inca citadels

ON FOOT
CENTRAL AND SOUTH AMERICA

Above Thatched dwellings in a Wiwa village in the Sierra Nevada de Santa Marta *Left* Teyuna's oval-shaped stone terraces at the end of the Lost City Trek

⑳ Lost City Trek

LOCATION Colombia **START/FINISH** El Mamey/Santa Marta
DISTANCE 50 km (31 miles) **TIME** 4–6 days **DIFFICULTY** Challenging
INFORMATION www.colombia.travel; official guide required

This sweaty, steep pilgrimage requires both fitness and a willingness to forgo home comforts, but the pay-off is the exploration of an archaeological site of unparalleled position and beauty.

In 1972, a couple of Colombian *guaqueros* (looters) hunting for tropical bird feathers in the forests of the Sierra Nevada de Santa Marta mountains pulled back some tangled roots and found the ruins of a forgotten city. They had discovered Teyuna, a township once home to 2,000 Tairona people dating from AD 650 – some 650 years older than Machu Picchu in Peru.

Today, travellers brave the hothouse humidity of the tropical jungle, which easily hits 90 per cent, to reach the remains of this ancient city. A Wiwa guide – a direct descendant of the Tairona people who built the Lost City – leads the way to this sacred site. Rollercoaster sandy paths weave through Wiwa villages, where the fruits of cocoa and coffee plantations can be sampled, and zigzag back and forth across the Buritaca River, whose tannin-coloured pools are perfect to plunge into after a hot and clammy hike. Along the way, there are glimpses of tarantulas and snakes slinking away into the undergrowth, as well as the flash of tropical birds darting in and out of the thick forest.

On the final day, hikers rise early for the last sticky ascent to the Lost City, enshrouded in a tunnel of trees. More than a thousand ancient stone steps climb ever upwards until, at last, you see it. Ahead, the great tiers of Teyuna's oval terraces floating over the tree canopy like a castle in the clouds.

ON FOOT
CENTRAL AND SOUTH AMERICA

(21) # The Shackleton Crossing

LOCATION South Georgia **START/FINISH** King Haakon Bay/Stromness Bay **DISTANCE** 51 km (32 miles) **TIME** 3 days **DIFFICULTY** Challenging **INFORMATION** www.gov.gs

This route recreates the life-or-death crossing by Ernest Shackleton, the great 20th-century polar explorer, across a stunningly remote South Atlantic island.

South Georgia forms a sub-Antarctic sliver of ice and snow, its nearest inhabited neighbour, the Falkland Islands, 1,390 km (864 miles) away. But when Shackleton landed here in May 1916 after an epic 16-day open-boat journey across the roughest waters on earth, this inhospitable island promised salvation. His ship *Endurance* was sunk by an Antarctic ice pack, the rest of the crew stranded on Elephant Island – Shackleton and five colleagues struck out to South Georgia to seek help from whalers. Shackleton, Frank Worsley and Tom Crean then trekked 51 km (32 miles) from King Haakon Bay across the mountainous uncharted interior to Stromness whaling station, where they plotted the rescue of their comrades. More than a century on, few have retraced this route. The trek is brutal, marked by blizzards and mountainous ascents. But unlike Shackleton, you'll have the benefit of thermal clothing, tents and skis, not to mention an experienced guide following a properly mapped route through some of the most dramatic scenery and wildlife on earth.

SIR ERNEST SHACKLETON

Anglo-Irish explorer Sir Ernest Shackleton (1874–1922) first ventured to Antarctica on Robert Falcon Scott's 1901 *Discovery* expedition. He returned in 1908 on the *Nimrod* but was forced to turn back before reaching the South Pole: "A live donkey is better than a dead lion," he later remarked. After the *Endurance* expedition, Shackleton returned to Antarctica for a fourth time, but died en route in 1922. He is buried at Grytviken on South Georgia.

Descending through deep snow on a rope line overlooking Fortuna Bay, South Georgia

ON FOOT
EUROPE

(22)
Camino de Santiago

LOCATION Portugal to Spain **START/FINISH** Porto/Santiago de Compostela
DISTANCE 265 km (165 miles) **TIME** 14–15 days **DIFFICULTY** Easy to moderate **INFORMATION** www.oficinadelperegrino.com

Equipped simply with a backpack, walking stick and scallop-shell pilgrim's badge, follow the Way of St James on a mindful journey through the timeless landscapes and ancient villages of Portugal and Northern Spain. A thousand years of pilgrims have prepared your path.

> Salt-tinged ocean breezes blunt the heat of the southern sun

Cheerful greetings of "Buen Camino" reverberate along every stretch of the Way, whose spiderweb paths weave right across the Iberian Peninsula all the way through France, Spain and Portugal. But it's only on this Portuguese coastal section of the route that the incessant lapping of waves counts your pace.

After obtaining your Pilgrim's Passport at Porto's cathedral, leave behind this bustling Portuguese city and set out on a two-week trek to Santiago de Compostela and the tomb of St James. The main part of the journey begins by the sea in the city of Matosinhos, where endless beaches of golden sand stretch northwards and salt-tinged ocean breezes blunt the heat of the southern sun. Symbolic scallop shells mark the straight seaside path from here to Vila de Conde and its atmospheric medieval shipyard.

No two days are the same. Beaches on one day give way to boardwalks overlooking bird-filled coastal wetlands on the next. Soon the Way turns inland, and smooth flat paths steepen to dramatic headlands, where lighthouse beacons warn sailors of treacherous rocks and ledges just beneath the waves. Away from the ocean, you'll climb dusty upland trails that follow country roads. From grape-garlanded vineyards and green pastures you'll tumble downhill as the route returns to the sea at humble fishing ports.

Left Vila Praia de Âncora, Portugal
Below Scallop-shelled stone marking the Way **Right** Vineyards lining the path

33

Left *Looking out at the cathedral of Santiago de Compostela, the site of the tomb of St James* **Above** *Stone marking the end of the Camino de Santiago*

WHO WAS SANTIAGO?

St James the apostle met his fate in AD 44 when he was martyred by beheading in Jerusalem. Through the Middle Ages, Christian armies evoked his avenging sword in battles to retake Spain from Islamic rule. Santiago's tomb in Galicia became one of the world's most famous pilgrimage destinations when the imposing cathedral of Santiago de Compostela was erected in the 12th century. Today the name of the patron saint of Spain and Galicia remains on the lips of hundreds of thousands of pilgrims each year.

The hospitality of people along the Camino is legendary – aiding pilgrims is a way of life for those who stay put as well as those who walk. As the days accumulate, every pilgrim experiences at least one act of grace or kindness to relay – a shared snack here, an offer of directions there.

In the evenings, wayside hospices grant a room for the night. At these cosy and sometimes ancient hostels, walkers kick off their boots in favour of sandals and sit down to a dinner of steaming *caldeirada* stew, brimming with fish, potatoes and vegetables – a powerful restorative after a full day's hiking. Away from the road, lively camaraderie of fellow pilgrims buoys the spirits. After-dinner conversation turns to the delights of the day's walking – perhaps the sight of a succession of rainbows from a headland, or a glimpse of a dozen purple herons rising at sunset to nest in marsh-side trees.

At Caminha, a ferry takes pilgrims across the Río Miño to Spain, where anticipation builds for the final week-long leg of the journey. The city of Santiago de Compostela beckons, but first come the joys and challenges of the wild Galician coast. When the shoreline turns rocky along the broad estuaries of the Rías Baixas, the path ascends to high coastal ridgelines, where the sky feels closer than the sea. But soon the rising cliffs give way to sloping hillsides as the path

ON FOOT
EUROPE

descends once more. A landscape of kiwi- and grape-draped pergolas unfolds as walkers continue inland towards the gracious Renaissance city of Pontevedra.

The remaining three days grow ever more picturesque, as pilgrims cross pretty medieval stone bridges through quaint villages, and weave through cool forests and meadows awash with wildflowers. The final stretch from Padrón retraces the oxen path that delivered St James to his final resting place. Half an hour from Santiago, the majestic cathedral towers thrust above the horizon. You have arrived, at last, at the end of the Way. Each pilgrim's certificate marks forever a journey shared with thousands through the ages.

> Pilgrims cross pretty medieval stone bridges through quaint villages

another way

The French Route is the busiest Camino de Santiago variant. From a mountain pass in France, the 800-km- (500-mile-) long trek crosses the tablelands of Castilla y Léon and the rugged Galician hills.

TREAT YOURSELF *to a luxurious night at the* **Hostal dos Reis Católicos***, built by royalty in 1499 for noble pilgrims*

SAVOUR *the heady spiced flavours of the celebrated Albariño wines of the* **Rías Baixas**

PHOTOGRAPH *the Cubist jumble of pastel houses in the Spanish fishing village of* **A Guarda**

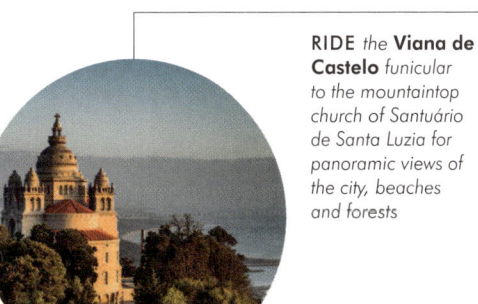

RIDE *the* **Viana de Castelo** *funicular to the mountaintop church of Santuário de Santa Luzia for panoramic views of the city, beaches and forests*

Santiago de Compostela

SPAIN

PORTUGAL

Porto

Il Sentiero degli Dei

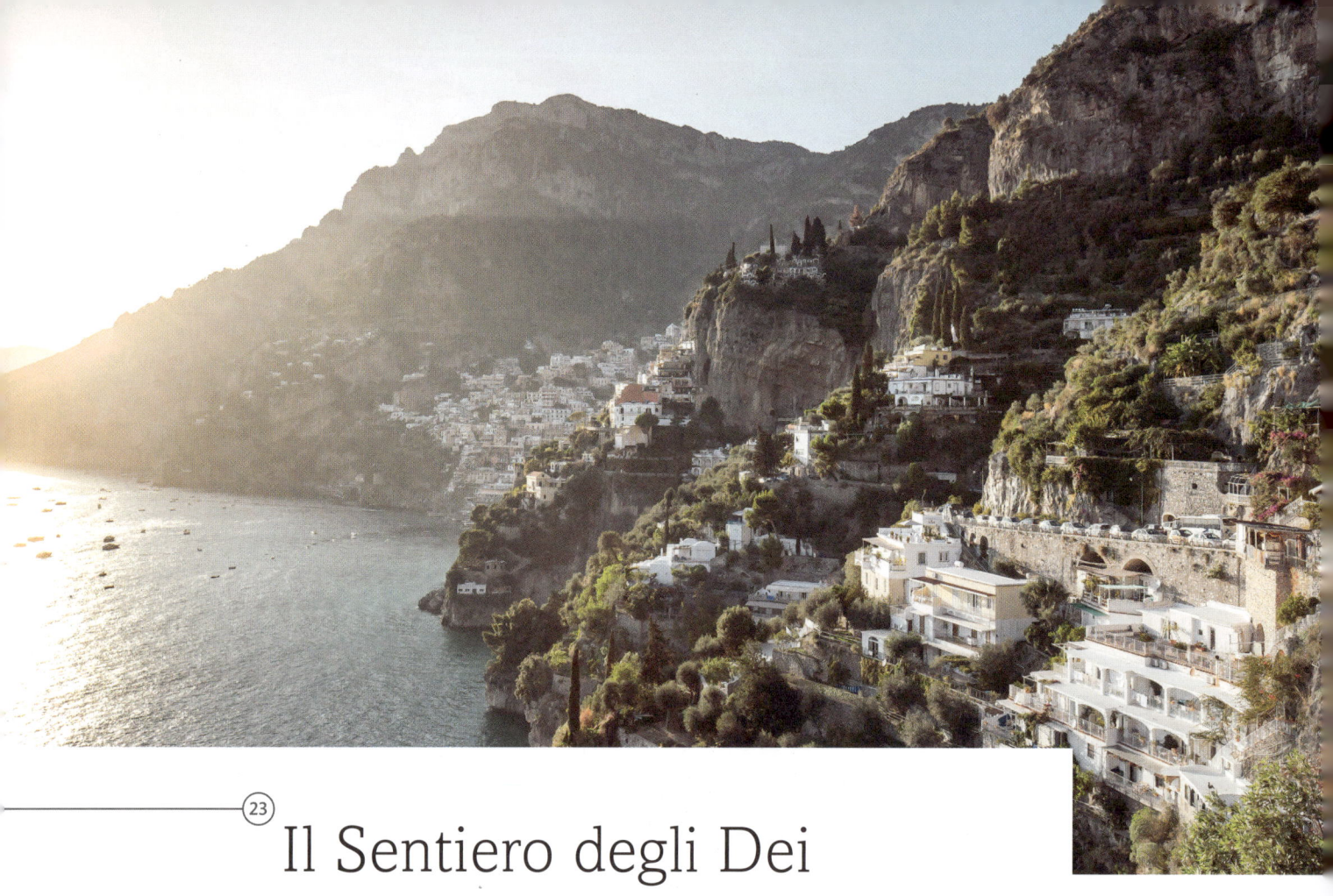

The spectacular Il Sentiero degli Dei, winding along the sunny Amalfi Coast

LOCATION Italy **START/FINISH** Agerola/Nocelle **DISTANCE** 8 km (5 miles)
TIME 3 hours **DIFFICULTY** Easy, but not suitable if you suffer from vertigo
INFORMATION www.incampania.com/en/location/path-of-the-gods

Hugging the sun-kissed cliffs of the Amalfi Coast, the Sentiero degli Dei offers spectacular views of the azure Mediterranean Sea, stretching from the sleepy town of Praiano to the chic island resort of Capri.

The sweeping vistas that open up before you as you snake your way along the Sentiero degli Dei are certain to leave an everlasting impression. The pathway's very name (it translates as "The Path of the Gods") couldn't be more apt, conjuring up mythological landscapes of dramatic cliffs plunging into deep blue waters – a place where heaven meets earth. Italian journalist and writer Italo Calvino described it as "that road suspended over the magical gulf of the mermaids still furrowed today by memory and myth".

Connecting the villages of Agerola and Nocelle, the path was once a busy mule track linking the coast to the villages inland. The walk, which takes around three hours, traces a rugged stretch of coastline. Dramatic views unfold at every corner, making it easy to imagine how this landscape so inspired writers and poets, from Goethe to D H Lawrence. Aromatic herbs and endemic plant species scent the air and, in summer, it's common to see farmers leading mules laden with sacks of fresh figs and lemons. Below, the waves form frothy white strokes, while boats bob up and down in the secluded sandy coves.

The path ends at Nocelle, a sleepy village built as a coastal defence post. Remember to look back: some of the most impressive views of the heavenly coastline can be enjoyed from here.

ON FOOT
EUROPE

Trans-Alpine Crossing

LOCATION Germany to Italy **START/FINISH** Tegernsee/Sterzing **DISTANCE** 115 km (71 miles) **TIME** 7 days **DIFFICULTY** Moderate **INFORMATION** www.tyrol.com

Follow this centuries-old path through the central Alps, where mountain valleys tell of Bavarian and Austrian tradition and rivers tumble towards the Dolomites.

Looping past ice-sheathed mountains, glacial valleys and dreamlike lakes, the Trans-Alpine Crossing takes hikers on a journey through some of Europe's most epic mountain scenery. The way-marked route begins at Tegernsee in Germany, before following a lesser-known path across the Zillertal Valley in Austria, leading to Italy's northernmost town. There are few roads here, and even fewer villages, but this is not an expedition that requires fluency in mountaineering skills. The route is all about enjoying the spectacular landscape – from razor-edged mountains to valleys blanketed by wildflowers – as well as the simpler things in life. At times, hikers are stopped by ruddy-cheeked farmers proffering chestnuts and cheese, and before night falls, innkeepers stoke fires, plump bedspreads and pour big glasses of wine – the path will have to wait until tomorrow.

Below Two cows grazing beneath a snowy mountain in the Bavarian Alps, Germany
Below left Hiking to Tegernseer Hütte, a mountain inn perched above Tegernsee

ON FOOT
EUROPE

Circuiting the Tre Cime di Lavaredo, with the mountains providing a dramatic backdrop

25 Tre Cime di Lavaredo

LOCATION Italy **START/FINISH** Rifugio Auronzo (loop) **DISTANCE** 9 km (5 miles) **TIME** 4 hours **DIFFICULTY** Easy **INFORMATION** www.drei-zinnen.info

Tracing the base of the Tre Cime di Lavaredo – three majestic pinnacles that soar hundreds of feet into the air – this walk gently meanders up and down, dropping and rising here and there. It's an easy route but that makes the cosy *rifugi* (mountain huts) along the way no less inviting. Stop off at the popular Rifugio Locatelli, which buzzes with hikers who pause here to refuel on hearty Dolomite dishes and to soak up unobstructed views of the three silver-grey peaks jutting into the sky at jagged angles.

The walk is best enjoyed on summer mornings, when marmots and chamois have awoken from their winter slumber and the sweet smell of alpine flowers scents the air. But whenever you choose to tread the trail, the craggy silhouettes of the three peaks will take your breath away.

26 Appenzell Whisky Trek

LOCATION Switzerland **START/FINISH** Appenzell (loop) **DISTANCE** 84 km (52 miles) **TIME** 7 days **DIFFICULTY** Moderate **INFORMATION** www.saentismalt.com

Northeastern Switzerland wasn't always a land of whisky but today the air is heavy with grain and barley. It lingers across the Sitter river from the painted houses in Appenzell's town square to where the air is thin, high above in Switzerland's lesser-known Alpstein massif. This is all thanks to Brauerei Locher, a family-run brewery and distillery that has been using local barley and the soft spring water gushing from the mountains to formulate Säntis Malt – an unlikely, if exquisite, single malt – since 1886. Other enterprising Alpstein families soon followed suit and the Appenzell Whisky Trek was born.

There's little better than nursing a warming nightcap after a day spent in the mountains and this is the raison d'etre for this 27-stop snakes-and-ladders tour. Each *berggasthaus* (inn) promises unique, cask-aged drams in wildly different tastes and colours. In an unlikely marriage of alpinism and alcohol, the week-long trail also takes in the classic Swiss tropes: rolling grass, snow-fuzzed summits, belt-loosening lunches and lung-busting views. Really, it's enough to make you want to yodel.

> There's little better than nursing a warming nightcap after a day spent in the mountains

ON FOOT
EUROPE

㉗ The Eiger Trail

LOCATION Switzerland **START/FINISH** Eigergletscher station/Alpiglen **DISTANCE** 6 km (4 miles) **TIME** 3 hours **DIFFICULTY** Easy **INFORMATION** www.jungfrau.ch; open mid-Jun–Sep

While the ascent of the North Face of the Eiger remains reserved for those more comfortable with a rope and carabiner than trainers and backpack, seeing the mountain's dramatic rock face up close is easy for entry-level alpinists.

A downhill scramble skirting the base of the rock wall, this summer trail only takes a morning, but in that time it delivers killer views – look out for the summits of Jungfrau and Mönch – and an undiluted dose of Switzerland's Alps. This is the Switzerland of pop culture, a fantasy-rich landscape of snowy peaks and u-shaped valleys, ragged as a seismogram and populated by bell-jangling cows, lederhosen-clad farmers and proud cheese-makers.

Wooden Alpine buildings in a verdant valley, overlooked by the soaring Eiger mountain

㉘ Rennsteig Trail

LOCATION Germany **START/FINISH** Hörschel/Blankenstein **DISTANCE** 169 km (105 miles) **TIME** 6 days **DIFFICULTY** Moderate **INFORMATION** www.germany.travel

Two stony peaks edged with wildflowers soar above Thuringian Forest like manicured fists made by giants. A medieval castle, all stone turrets and Rapunzel towers, pokes its head out of the trees in the distance. A timber-frame village, part-hidden by creases and folds in the forest, appears beneath a great streak of pink as flushed as the trekkers puffing towards day's end.

Hiking the Rennsteig Trail, the six-stage ridgeway track through the Thuringian and Franconian forests in central Germany, changes your perspective on the country. Days can start by a secret dragon gorge near Eisenach or by the peaceful lakes of Ebertswiese, breathing in the scent of jasmine, and then end with a bang – on a cedar and spruce ridge, with sweeping views across to Sleeping Beauty-style Wartburg Castle. More than anything, this journey encapsulates the essence of slow travel: even in peak season, from May to September, the trail is silent and serene and there's a sense that this part of Germany is still waiting to be truly discovered.

ON FOOT
EUROPE

(29)
Tatra Mountains

LOCATION Poland to Slovakia **START/FINISH** Kuźnice (loop) **DISTANCE** 17 km (10.5 miles) **TIME** 8.5 hours **DIFFICULTY** Moderate
INFORMATION Best May to September, when dry

Skirting the mountainous border between Poland and Slovakia, this circular hike takes in the Tatras' most spectacular scenery, from craggy cliffs to pristine pine forest.

This day hike begins in Kuźnice, the southern edge of the chalet-dotted Polish city of Zakopane. Fringed by evergreen pines, the wide cobblestone track narrows as you pass a simple, timber-built monastery, the Hermitage of Brother Albert, while the views widen and unfurl. Hala Kondratowa, a historic mountain hut, makes the perfect place to pause, smell the carnations, and drink in the sweeping vista of golden brush, forest-veiled valleys and soaring rocky peaks.

From the hut, it's a steep ascent on slippery sheets of rock to reach Giewont's summit, but the panoramas improve with every step. Beyond lies the most scenic part of the hike, as the windswept path levels out into a rugged ridge walk. Ride the crest of the mountain all the way to the big-ticket peak of Kasprowy Wierch. Polish pinnacles dominate on the left, with Slovakian summits to the right; markers along the path indicate where the border lies.

Before descending through the alpine forest into Kuźnice, stop at the summit and soak up the panoramic views one last time – you've earned it.

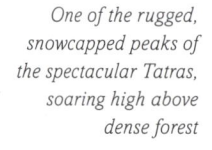

One of the rugged, snowcapped peaks of the spectacular Tatras, soaring high above dense forest

ON FOOT
EUROPE

A stony path winding through craggy Zărnești gorge in the Piatra Craiului National Park, Romania

Carpathian Mountains

LOCATION Romania **START/FINISH** Sinaia/Zărnești
DISTANCE 50 km (30 miles) **TIME** 4 days **DIFFICULTY** Moderate **INFORMATION** www.romania.travel

Explore Europe's last great wilderness on this four-day hike through the heart of Romania's captivating Carpathian Mountains.

Emerald forests, medieval castles and wildflower-dusted mountains: these are some of the sights you'll be treated to along this Transylvanian trail. Starting above Peleș Castle in the chocolate-box town of Sinaia, the trail zigzags up into the forest, offering glimpses of rolling Prahova Valley through the trees.

Quaint *cabanas* (mountain huts) provide overnight shelter as you delve deeper into nature. Traversing forest paths and sleepy streams, you'll pass unusual rock formations, and lucky hikers may catch sight of the Carpathian Chamois, a rare species of goat-antelope known for its black fur and white head.

Heading towards Zărnești, the picturesque town which ends your hike, pause in the fairy-tale village of Bran, famed for its 14th-century castle. From here, the limestone cliffs of Piatra Craiului National Park give way to the soaring cliffs of Zărnești Gorge, lined with caves, chasms and climbing spots galore.

DRACULA'S CASTLE

Bran Castle is colloquially known as "Dracula's Castle", yet there's no evidence that *Dracula* novelist Bram Stoker ever knew about it. Regardless, it's a site worth visiting for its 14th-century architecture, the display of royal art and furniture, and the exhibition on Romanian peasant culture.

ON FOOT
EUROPE

Gelidonya lighthouse on the Lycian Way, overlooking the Five Islands in the bay below

Lycian Way

LOCATION Turkey **START/FINISH** Ölüdeniz/Geyikbayırı **DISTANCE** 540 km (335 miles) **TIME** 29 days **DIFFICULTY** Moderate **INFORMATION** www.cultureroutesinturkey.com

Designed by British amateur historians Kate Clow and Terry Richardson in the 1990s, this twisting coastal trail weaves around the Tekke Peninsula in southwest Turkey and is named after the Lycian League, a 2,500-year-old civilization.

Over the course of a month, the Lycian Way takes in crescent after crescent of brilliant-blue bays, scaling vertiginous cliffs that fall away into glass-clear waters. Red-and-white waymarkers lead trekkers along a mix of old mule paths and Roman roads, passing brilliant beaches and hillside Lycian tombs. The highlight for some may be the staggering remains of Pinara's amphitheatre, but for many it will be sitting with an ice-cold beer in hand, overlooking the Med, at the end of a day spent on the Way.

Via Dinarica

LOCATION Slovenia to Macedonia **START/FINISH** Bled/Skopje **DISTANCE** 1,930 km (1,200 miles) **TIME** 2–4 months **DIFFICULTY** Challenging; mountainous terrain **INFORMATION** www.via-dinarica.org

Stretching like a spine across the Western Balkan Peninsula, the Dinaric Alps knit together eight nations to form one of Europe's most challenging hiking trails. Along the Via Dinarica, soaring mountain peaks meet plunging river valleys, and placid glacial lakes meet boisterous beach resorts.

For cross-country hikers, the summer-long journey begins in June in the lake-dotted landscape of Slovenia's Julian Alps, before heading south into Croatia, where the winding, coast-hugging mountain paths come with premium sea views. The Adriatic fades into the distance as the karst field plateaus and primeval forests of Bosnia and Herzegovina take over. But not for long – once lush Sutjeska National Park folds across the border into Montenegro, mountains tumble down to an idyllic Montenegrin scene of long sandy beaches and crystal-clear waters. Seagulls make way for sheep as the trail diverts inland and up into the Albanian Alps and North Macedonia's Sharr Mountains, where the leaves start to turn orange, red and gold, marking both the end of summer and this adventure.

> The Lycian Way takes in crescent after crescent of brilliant-blue bays

ON FOOT
EUROPE

33 High Coast Trail

LOCATION Sweden **START/FINISH** Hornöberget/Örnsköldsvik **DISTANCE** 130 km (80 miles) **TIME** 5–7 days **DIFFICULTY** Moderate **INFORMATION** www.hogakusten.com

Brace yourself: this long-distance, UNESCO-worthy hike along the world's highest coastline rewards the intrepid. On paper, the route peaks at 286 m (938 ft) above sea level, but that underestimates all the natural drama ahead – deep evergreen forests, vertiginous viewpoints, wistful sandy beaches and soul-stirring cliffs.

Fortunately, this Baltic Sea odyssey is divided into 13 bite-sized walkable sections, each between 15 km (9 miles) and 24 km (15 miles) in length, but varying in difficulty. Pick and choose from one or two days absorbing the trail's highlights — country lanes in Nordingrå, the Slåttdalsskrevan Canyon in Skuleskogen National Park and the dramatic Höga Kusten suspension bridge — or gear up for the whole seven-day marathon across a roadless wilderness, made particularly spectacular during the wildflower bloom of midsummer. Whichever you choose, the High Coast Trail will not disappoint.

34 Kungsleden Trail

LOCATION Sweden **START/FINISH** Abisko/Hemavan **DISTANCE** 425 km (264 miles) **TIME** 1 month **DIFFICULTY** Moderate **INFORMATION** www.svenskaturistforeningen.se

From the frostbitten doorway of the cabin, the land rises steadily up the valley, undulating over puffy snow drifts, before it suddenly opens up onto a vast plateau studded with dwarf pine. Look closer and tracks begin to emerge: a wolf, wolverine, or perhaps even a bear cub, fresh from hibernation, and on the hunt for crowberry hidden by the latest flurry.

This scene is typical of the Kungsleden, or King's Trail, Sweden's longest walking route, which snakes its way above the Arctic Circle in Swedish Lapland. Landscapes smothered by vast swathes of birch and needle forest swallow you up as you cross Europe's most sparsely populated region. Along the way, there are barren summits and wild moorland, Sami reindeer herders and nights spent in cabins, illuminated by the brilliant midnight sun or kaleidoscopic aurora borealis.

A reindeer in Sarek, one of the four national parks crossed by the Kungsleden Trail

Trollsteinen

The ethereal Northern Lights dancing above snow-cloaked Svalbard

LOCATION Norway **START/FINISH** Longyearbyen (loop) **DISTANCE** 10 km (6 miles) **TIME** 8 hours **DIFFICULTY** Moderate to challenging **INFORMATION** www.visitnorway.com

A walk through Svalbard's magical arctic terrain, with its dazzling snowy peaks and dramatic glaciers, immerses hikers in the intrepid tradition of polar explorers of yore.

This trek starts by scaling the jagged trail along Sarkofagen, the craggy mountain slicing through the luminescent Longyearbreen and Larsbreen glaciers. Leaving the storied Longyearbyen base camp, the path unwinds upwards through an icy wilderness to Trollsteinen, or "The Troll Rock", an enchanting tower formation, 850 m (2,800 ft) above sea level. Depending on snowfall and snowmelt, your guide will add microspikes or snowshoes to your hiking boots before you set off across the ice. Over your shoulder you'll catch glimpses of the turquoise Adventfjord, framed by the furrowed brow of the fjord's mountains, and the warm lights of the toy-sized town of Longyearbyen, a reminder that creature comforts are close by, keeping watch over the frozen fjord. On the far side of Larsbreen, Trollsteinen is just visible – an ancient beacon beckoning walkers onwards. The frosty bleached beauty of the glacier begins softly as you crunch across a flat, white expanse, but the sharp ascent of Trollsteinen is challenging. Walking on a pale knife edge, the view of Longyearbyen, perched alongside the Arctic water, grows in beauty with every step. At the summit, look down on the stunning glacial and fjord scenery, illuminated in the pastel light that characterizes this wintery world.

ON FOOT
EUROPE

(36)

West Highland Way

LOCATION UK **START/FINISH** Milngavie/Fort William
DISTANCE 154 km (96 miles) **TIME** 1 week **DIFFICULTY** Moderate **INFORMATION** www.westhighlandway.org

Stride through yawning vales, scale untamed wind-lashed uplands and tramp serene lochside paths. This classic Scottish walk promises both rain and rarefied beauty in equal measure.

Scotland's first long-distance walking route's bonnie views grace the silver screen for good reason. Cobbled together from old drovers' trails, coaching paths and military roads used during the Jacobite Uprisings, the West Highland Way passes through windy, wild landscapes of lochs, moors and pine forests.

The weather is predictably unpredictable, so strap on your boots, zip up your waterproof coat and hit the route between April and October to avoid the worst of it. En route, you'll cross the ravishing Rannoch Moor; skirt along the banks of Loch Lomond, keeping an eye out for the alleged cave hideout of outlaw Rob Roy McGregor; stop for a dram of whisky at Glengoyne Distillery; warm up at Scotland's oldest pub, the Drover's Inn; and pit your calves against the Devils Staircase path. Come evening, no-frills guesthouses, youth hostels and campsites are the only places to rest your head. No matter: the focus of this walk isn't comfort, it's the vast countryside vistas.

another way

The Rob Roy Way, an 80-mile (128-km) footpath running from Drymen to Pitlochry, which is named after the 17th-century folk outlaw Rob Roy McGregor, is a lesser-known route that passes through equally stunning Highland landscapes.

Blackrock Cottage and Buachaille Etive Mor, landmarks on the West Highland Way

Julian Alps Peak Walk

LOCATION Slovenia **START/FINISH** Bled (loop) **DISTANCE** 60 km (37 miles) **TIME** 5 days (plus 1 day if climbing Mount Triglav) **DIFFICULTY** Moderate to challenging **INFORMATION** www.slovenia.info; the dry, warm summer months (May–Sep) are best for hiking

This alpine adventure through Slovenia's Triglav National Park takes in sweeping mountain scenery, thick fir-tree forests, gorgeous glacial pools and enchanting waterfalls.

Starting at postcard-perfect Bled, take a stroll around the lake and visit the medieval Bled castle, perched on a precipice overlooking the cyan-blue lake. The route then leads away from the lake up through the fir forests to the Pokljuka high plateau. Shelter in welcoming, wooden mountain huts during your four nights in the Julian Alps (you'll need to book in advance in summer). Ascents climb through bright, flower-filled and airy alpine meadows, and are followed by dark descents through dense and wild woodlands.

Lake Bled, with the tiny, tear-shaped Bled Island in its centre, surrounded by forests and mountains

ON FOOT
EUROPE

The further you go, the bigger the climbs and the greater the vistas, from rocky ravines and canyons carved out by aqua-blue rivers to secret caves and caverns lined with creeping moss. At over 2,850 m (9,350 ft), the eponymous Mount Triglav juts self-consciously out of the landscape from every angle; it's climbable, if you've the time and inclination.

The trail opens up as it enters the Valley of the Triglav Lakes, a spectacular smattering of alpine glacial pools, then narrows into a steep, high-stepped path leading up to Savica Waterfall. One of Slovenia's biggest tourist draws, the falls burst out of the sheer rock face before tumbling down into the mighty Lake Bohinj, the largest lake in Slovenia.

Finally, it's time to put your feet up. Take the cable car up to the 1,532-m (5,026-ft) peak of Mount Vogel for a spectacular panoramic view of the Julian Alps before hopping on a bus for the 30-minute journey back down to Lake Bled.

| Ascents climb through bright, flower-filled and airy alpine meadows, and are followed by dark descents |

another way

Short on time during your trip to Lake Bled? Take a one-day hike to the gorgeous Vintgar Gorge. A wooden walkway leads along the sheer canyon walls and rumbling rapids to an arresting 13-m- (43-ft-) high river waterfall.

SLEEP in charming mountain huts and wake up to glorious panoramic views

LOOK for fossilized ammonites (Jurassic-era molluscs) in the rocks around the **Triglav Lakes**

TAKE a boat trip out to the pilgrimage church in the middle of **Lake Bled**

CLIMB up to the spectacular **Savica Waterfall**, one of Slovenia's most popular attractions

AUSTRIA
ITALY
Bled
SLOVENIA

ON FOOT
EUROPE

Above A traditional thatched cottage in Thornton-in-Craven, Yorkshire
Left Crossing a stile on the Pennine Way

Pennine Way

LOCATION UK **START/FINISH** Edale/Kirk Yetholm
DISTANCE 431 km (268 miles) **TIME** 16–18 days
DIFFICULTY Moderate; some steep summits and boggy terrain **INFORMATION** www.nationaltrail.co.uk

Stretching from the Peak District to the Scottish Lowlands, the Pennine Way might just be the finest long-distance walk in England, with its gently rolling dales, brooding moorland and historic sights.

Unfurling through a wild landscape criss-crossed by moss-covered dry-stone walls and speckled with woolly sheep, the Pennine Way is one of Britain's best-loved walks. Completing this challenging ramble in full usually takes around three weeks, but you can also do the route in sections, dipping in and out of the untamed scenery to your heart's content.

The route is at its best (and busiest) in summer, when the grassy meadows and rippling slopes are splashed with wildflowers. But try not to discount the other seasons – they each offer their own allure. In spring, the plaintive cry of the curlew echoes across the landscape and newborn lambs frolic in fresh fields. The sweeping moorland, home to plump red grouse, glows with purple heather in autumn, while winter brings its own bleak beauty, with swathes of snow blanketing the high fells. Whatever the season, the rugged charm of this rewarding route remains the same.

another way

The 135-km (84-mile) Hadrian's Wall Path intersects the Pennine Way. This coast-to-coast trail takes in Roman settlements and forts as it follows this line of stone and turf ramparts from Wallsend on the River Tyne to Bowness-on-Solway on the west coast.

Wales Coast Path

LOCATION UK **START/FINISH** Queensferry/Chepstow **DISTANCE** 1,400 km (870 miles) **TIME** 6–7 weeks **DIFFICULTY** Moderate **INFORMATION** www.visitwales.com

The first path in the world to follow a country's coastline in its entirety, the Wales Coast Path takes in low cliffs, lighthouse-primed peninsulas and windswept estuaries as it sweeps around this small but mighty land.

The sweeping curve of Caernarfon Bay, just one of the breathtaking views on the Wales Coast Path

Take a moment to capture the dazzling view of Caernarfon Bay as you round the dunes that roll out from Newborough Forest towards tidal Llanddwyn Island. Dolphins surf against the force of the Menai Strait current. Cormorants, shags and gulls soar over the waves. The shoulders of the Snowdon mountain range, cast in myth and shadow, tempt you to linger for an extra day or two. This is but a glimpse of the Wales Coast Path, an epic trail several millennia in the making, with more than a lifetime's worth of sights to savour.

Of course, it all begins and ends with beautifully preserved castles, of which Wales has an abundance. Bookending the trail are Chepstow's historic bastion and Flint's 13th-century fortress, but there are an equal number of impressive viewpoints, rocky headlands and coves to discover. Stunning beaches come at every turn — Pembrokeshire is home to 58 alone — the natural wonders that inspired Dylan Thomas, Lewis Carroll and Wales's patron saint of lovers, St Dwynwen. Looking out at the shoreline lit by the day's last rays, it's not hard to see why.

ON FOOT
EUROPE

The Giant's Causeway, shrouded in legends involving everything from camels to the eponymous giant

④ Causeway Coast Way

LOCATION UK **START/FINISH** Portstewart/Ballycastle **DISTANCE** 53 km (33 miles) **TIME** 2–3 days **DIFFICULTY** Easy **INFORMATION** www.causewaycoastway.com

It's probably Northern Ireland's most photographed natural attraction, but no pictures can prepare for the unique sight of the Giant's Causeway. Thousands of basalt hexagons slant into the North Atlantic, the outer rocks permanently darkened by foaming surf.

Just part of the mammoth Ulster Way, a 1,000-km (625-mile) circuit of Northern Ireland, the Causeway Coast Way is an easy walk that takes in craggy cliffs, secluded beaches, and the seaside towns of Ballycastle and Portstewart. Highlights along the way include the vertigo-defying Carrick-a-Rede Rope Bridge and crumbling Dunluce Castle, which squats on a basalt outcrop. But it is the Giant's Causeway, marking the very tip of Northern Ireland, that steals the show.

④ Dingle Way

LOCATION Ireland **START/FINISH** Tralee (loop) **DISTANCE** 179 km (109 miles) **TIME** 8–9 days **DIFFICULTY** Moderate **INFORMATION** www.thedingleway.com

The lush countryside of the Emerald Isle offers a number of long-distance walking trails, but for diverse landscapes and unadulterated Celtic charm, this loop is tough to beat.

Some of the Dingle Way follows quiet roads, but coastal views quickly distract from the tarmac underfoot. The stretch to Dunquin offers your best chance to take in the expanse of the North Atlantic, with the craggy humps of the Skellig Islands visible in the distance. The dramatic mountains found in this corner of southwest Ireland, too, are impressive. Mount Brandon is the trickiest part of this trail, but on clear days it rewards those who manage the scramble to its summit with a glorious vantage point.

And, of course, much of the enjoyment of this journey comes from the moments when you aren't walking. The path winds through picturesque villages where many of the pubs and B&Bs are pure Irish stereotype, complete with garrulous locals, impromptu singalongs and brimming pints of the black stuff. The weather can't be guaranteed at any time of the year, but as you tramp the final stretch back to Tralee, you can be sure that a warm welcome awaits.

FUNGIE THE DOLPHIN

The Dingle Dolphin, or Fungie as he was christened by local fishermen, was first spotted in the waters off the town's coast in 1983. He has been swimming playfully alongside the boats that leave Dingle Harbour ever since.

ON FOOT
EUROPE

㊷ Two Moors Way

LOCATION UK **START/FINISH** Wembury/Lynmouth **DISTANCE** 187 km (117 miles) **TIME** 1 week **DIFFICULTY** Moderate **INFORMATION** www.twomoorsway.org

This coast-to-coast trail takes in some of England's wildest terrain – a seemingly desolate land of barren fields, windswept shrubs and enigmatic monoliths. The last of these were created by early Bronze Age dwellers, at a time when the moors were well-wooded and dotted with human settlements. It's hard to imagine this verdant scene as you follow in the footsteps of Sherlock Holmes, who careered across the bogland at Fox Tor Mire in Arthur Conan Doyle's *The Hound of the Baskervilles*.

As you leave Dartmoor, the landscape mellows into the pretty villages and bluebell woods of the Teign Valley. But not for long. Exmoor – with its shaggy ponies, rolling hills of gorse and heather and deep, wooded valleys – lies ahead.

Exmoor ponies, grazing on the scrubby moorland by the sea

㊸ Laugavegur Trail

LOCATION Iceland **START/FINISH** Landmannalaugar/Þórsmörk **DISTANCE** 79 km (49 miles) **TIME** 5 days **DIFFICULTY** Moderate **INFORMATION** www.inspiredbyiceland.com; open Jul–Aug

Iceland was hewn by nature to make hikers smile. The whole island is riddled with routes, but the longest and most famous is the Laugavegur Trail. With its troll-haunted valleys, bubbling pools and glacial fingers clawing their way down the mountainside, walking this five-day route is akin to being plunged into a witches' cauldron – especially if you encounter the sporadic white-out blizzards and gale force winds.

Snug hiking huts dot the trail between the Landmannalaugar geothermal springs and the Þórsmörk nature reserve. The latter – an area supposedly peopled by trolls and fairies – makes a fitting climax to this legendary route.

another way

Þórsmörk nature reserve – which translates as "Thor's Forest" after the hammer-wielding thunder god – is riddled with enough of its own hiking trails to keep boots happy for a month. Be sure to visit the Singing Cave and Trollakirkja (Troll's church).

51

ON FOOT
AFRICA AND THE MIDDLE EAST

(44)

Atlas Mountains

LOCATION Morocco **START/FINISH** Imlil (loop) **DISTANCE** 15 km (9 miles) **TIME** 3 days **DIFFICULTY** Moderate to challenging; mountainous terrain **INFORMATION** www.visitmorocco.com

Despite being only a couple of hours away from Marrakech, the wild peaks and canyons of the Atlas Mountains are a world away from the madcap pace of city life. On the red-stained trails that criss-cross this mountain range, hikers discover Berber Morocco.

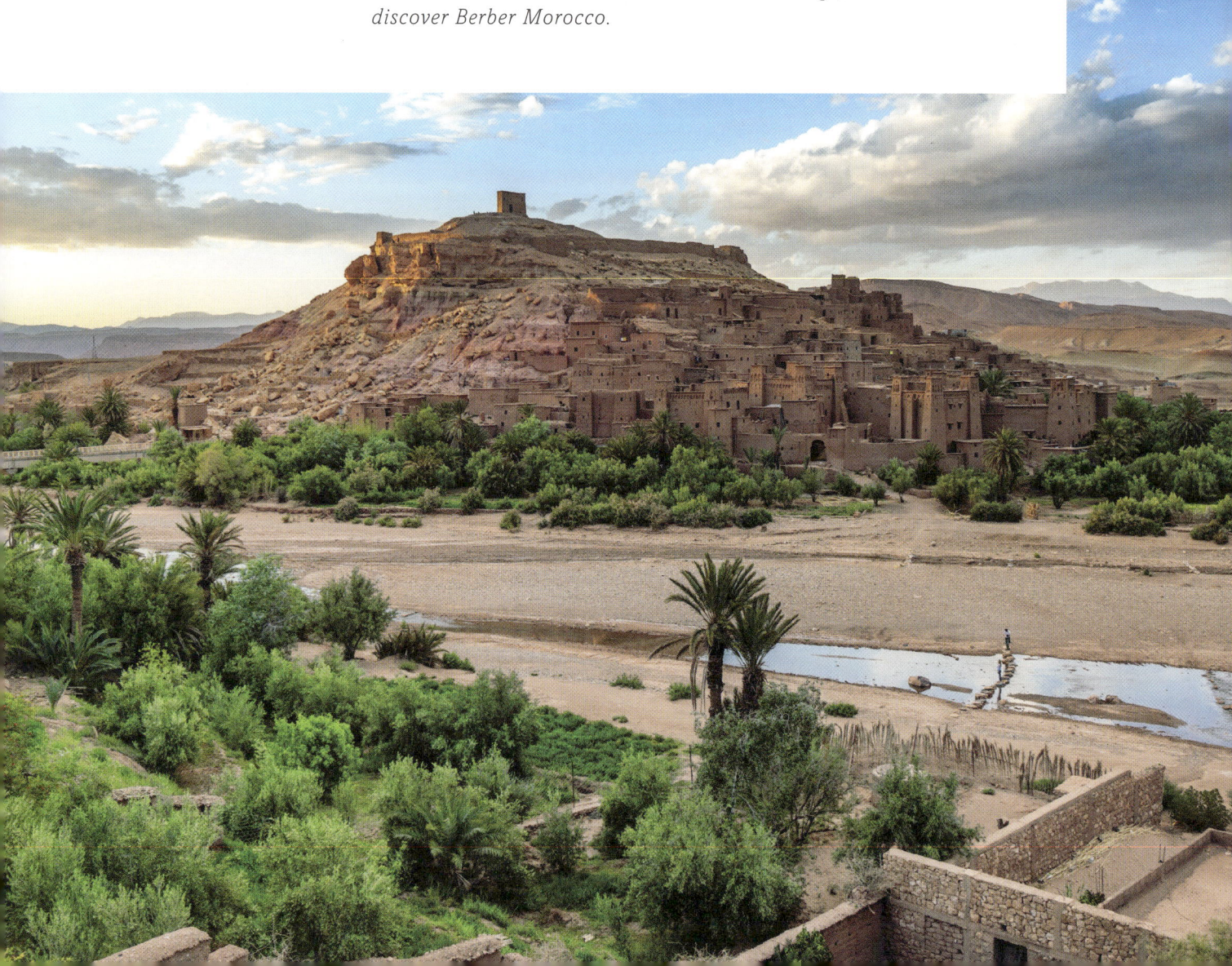

Rugged, russet, majestic – the Atlas Mountains form a dramatic barrier between the sea and the Sahara as they stretch the 2,500 km (1,553 miles) from Morocco to Tunisia. This is the ancient land of the Berbers, whose sun-scorched flat-roofed villages cling to mountainsides and pepper the foothills. These hospitable nomads guide walkers through this craggy, captivating landscape and invite visitors into their villages for sweet mint tea.

> Hikers are in heaven, and are faced with a dizzying choice of treks

Hikers are in heaven, and are faced with a dizzying choice of treks. The Atlas are not one homogeneous range of peaks: within Morocco, the mountains are divided into the Anti-Atlas, Middle Atlas and – the best known – High Atlas. Known by Berbers as "Idraren Draren" (Mountains of Mountains), the High Atlas is North Africa's highest mountain range and as such is both the most challenging and the most rewarding.

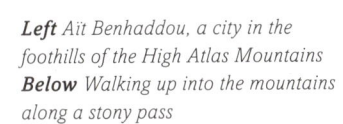

Left Aït Benhaddou, a city in the foothills of the High Atlas Mountains
Below Walking up into the mountains along a stony pass

ON FOOT
AFRICA AND THE MIDDLE EAST

Spreading from the Atlantic coast is the Anti-Atlas range, where a gruelling trek from Igherm to the top of 2,531-m- (8,304-ft-) high Jebel Aklim grants magnificent views of the High Atlas beyond, as well as Jebel Siroua, an extinct volcano. If you're looking for wild and rustic, it's here on these rough, barren tracks. These dusty ochre mountains have few people and fewer places to stay, so camping under the stars is in order. After a few days in the wilderness, laid-back Taroudant's hammams and souks call out to tired walkers.

Further north is the Middle Atlas range, where the trails are gentler and the fertile green plains are home to some surprising sights. Built by the French, the town of Ifrane looks like something out of the Alps, with chalet-style housing and a small skiing area (the Atlas are covered in snow well into May). Nearby is the Ifrane National Park, the largest forest in Morocco and a tranquil place to wander through cedar, juniper and oak woods, looking out for Barbary macaques.

> If you're looking for wild and rustic, it's here on these rough, barren tracks

Right A man standing outside the town of Tafraoute in the Anti-Atlas range *Below* A terracotta street in the kasbah Aït Ben Haddou

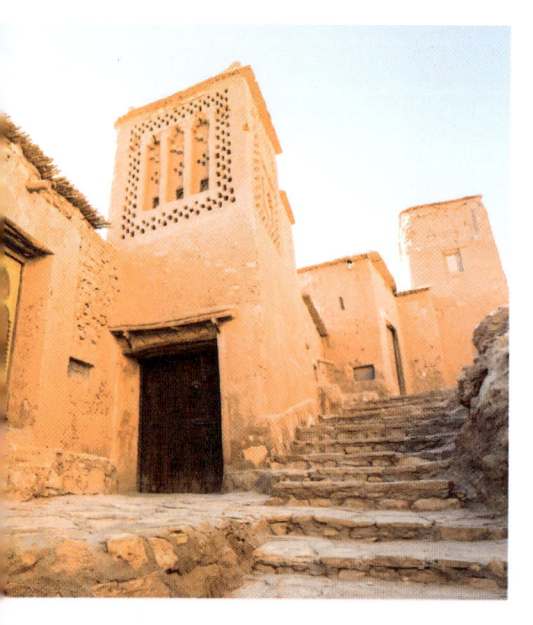

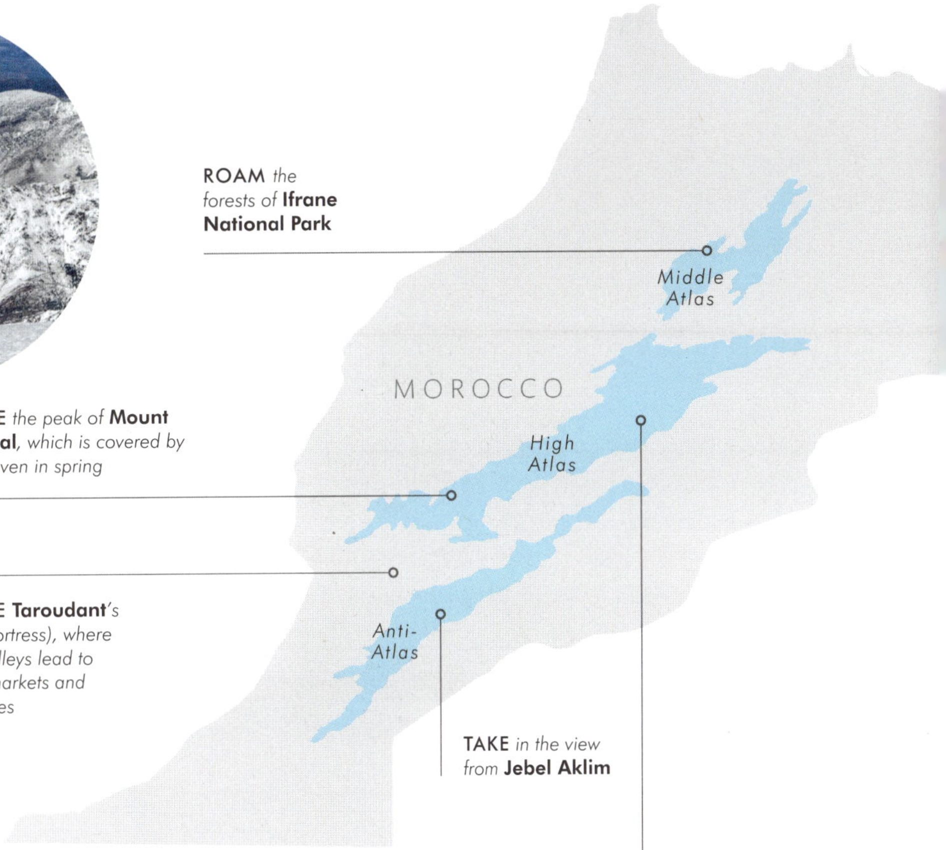

ROAM the forests of **Ifrane National Park**

SCALE the peak of **Mount Toubkal**, which is covered by snow even in spring

EXPLORE Taroudant's kasbah (fortress), where winding alleys lead to bustling markets and tiny squares

MOROCCO

Middle Atlas

High Atlas

Anti-Atlas

TAKE in the view from **Jebel Aklim**

SAVOUR Berber cuisine, including tagines and couscous

Serious trekkers have their eye on the Atlas's main prize – the 4,167 m (13,671 ft) peak of Mount Toubkal – the highest mountain in North Africa. Imlil's picturesque terraces of terracotta houses mark the starting point of this ascent into the High Atlas. Despite its height, the climb is a non-technical trek and the slow three-day ascent through fertile orchards, golden fields and Berber villages means that walkers can slowly acclimatize to the increasing altitude.

On the penultimate day, mule tracks covered in scree and boulders usher walkers to place one foot in front of the other as the air gets thinner and thinner, and snow starts to appear on the ground. After the five-hour trudge, the simple Refuge du Toubkal appears like an oasis. Here, walkers refuel with a hearty tagine and warm up by the open fire, while exchanging stories with their fellow travellers. Rising just before dawn, the early light shows the way to the summit, where the sunrise slowly transforms the silhouettes of the other peaks into the endlessly rippled landscape of the Atlas.

Whatever part of the Atlas Mountains that you choose to walk, it won't be just the altitude that takes your breath away.

another way

The Tizi-n-Test pass, at 2,092 m (6,861 ft), is one of the two great roads through the Atlas Mountains. With its treacherous hairpin bends, vertiginous height and lack of safety barriers, it's not for the faint-hearted.

55

ON FOOT
AFRICA AND THE MIDDLE EAST

Above left
Watching the sunset in the Simien Mountains

Above right
An aerial view of the Simien Mountains

Simien Mountains

LOCATION Ethiopia **START/FINISH** Debark/Adi Arkay **DISTANCE** 137 km (82 miles) **TIME** 10 days **DIFFICULTY** Challenging; some steep climbs at high altitude **INFORMATION** www.simienpark.org

Africa's answer to the Grand Canyon, the Simien Mountains are a vast cauldron of rock spires, precipices and gorges, deep ravines and soaring mountains. Climb any one of these peaks to soak up epic views.

Described by the Greek epic poet Homer as "chess pieces of the gods", the peaks of the Simien Mountains National Park in northern Ethiopia have an otherworldly beauty. You'll need to be fit to truly enjoy them – some of the ascents are unforgiving, reaching a dizzying altitude of over 4,500 m (14,764 ft) – but the views are worth the climb.

The hike up Imet Gogo, a 3,900-m (12,795-ft) peak at the end of a narrow ridge, reveals spectacular mountain panoramas, but to gain the ultimate bragging rights, walkers must tackle Ras Dashen – Ethiopia's highest peak. It's a torturous route, with rough and rocky terrain, false peaks and a summit-day ascent of 1,300 m (4,265 ft). Your reward is the dramatic vista of the Simien Mountains in hues of terracotta, gold and mauve from the so-called "Roof of Africa."

As you return back down to earth, the gentle blanket of green and gold hills in the lowlands reveal a true portrait of Ethiopian life. The aroma of roasting coffee beans wafts from the mud huts that dot the valleys like freckles. Lucky walkers will be invited to join a traditional Ethiopian coffee ceremony, where the woman of the house roasts, grinds, boils and pours coffee for family and friends, who come together to discuss the issues of the day.

ON FOOT
AFRICA AND THE MIDDLE EAST

The Rwenzori Mountains

LOCATION Uganda **START/FINISH** Kilembe (loop) **DISTANCE** 48 km (30 miles) **TIME** 6 days
DIFFICULTY Challenging; steep, rocky and boggy terrain
INFORMATION www.rwenzoritrekking.com

To trek the remote Rwenzoris is to enter a mystical land that few visitors venture into – a solitude that only adds to the mountains' air of mystery.

Stretching 120 km (74 miles) along the Congolese border, the Rwenzori mountain range is home to six peaks, the highest being snow-capped, oxygen-starved Mount Stanley, which reaches 5,109 m (16,762 ft). Leave that to technical climbers and head instead to 4,620-m (15,150-ft) Weismann Peak for a six-day hike through verdant wilderness.

The name Rwenzori means "rainmaker" and you'll need to pack some wellington boots in your kit bag to be able to negotiate the peak's deep and squelchy bogs. But the high precipitation is precisely what makes the Rwenzoris so special, encouraging surreal plant life that includes giant lobelia and heathers, huge ostrich plume plants, everlasting flowers and dense humid jungle. The fauna, too, is just as beguiling, with chimpanzees, colobus monkeys, rhinoceros chameleons and countless species of exotic birds calling these mountains home.

WHAT'S IN A NAME?

As long ago as AD 150, Greek astronomer and geographer Ptolemy described the Rwenzoris as "Mountains of the Moon", believing the range to be the legendary source of the Nile. Not until 1888 were they put on the map of Africa as the "Ruwenzoris" (with an Anglicized spelling) by colonialist explorer Henry Morton Stanley.

Climbing up a ladder in the Rwenzoris, passing giant lobelia and mossy slopes

ON FOOT
AFRICA AND THE MIDDLE EAST

(47)
Rwanda Gorilla Trekking

LOCATION Rwanda **START/FINISH** Volcanoes National Park **DISTANCE** Varies depending on location of troops **TIME** 1 day **DIFFICULTY** Easy to challenging **INFORMATION** www.volcanoesnationalparkrwanda.com; best in June–Sep and Dec–Feb

After hours spent trekking through Rwanda's wild jungle – looking out for the slightest sign of a gorilla all the way – few experiences on earth match the electric magic of finally meeting our hairy cousins in their natural habitat, in this "Land of a Thousand Hills".

Mountain gorillas in the undergrowth of Volcanoes National Park

DEM. REP. OF CONGO

UGANDA

Volcanoes National Park

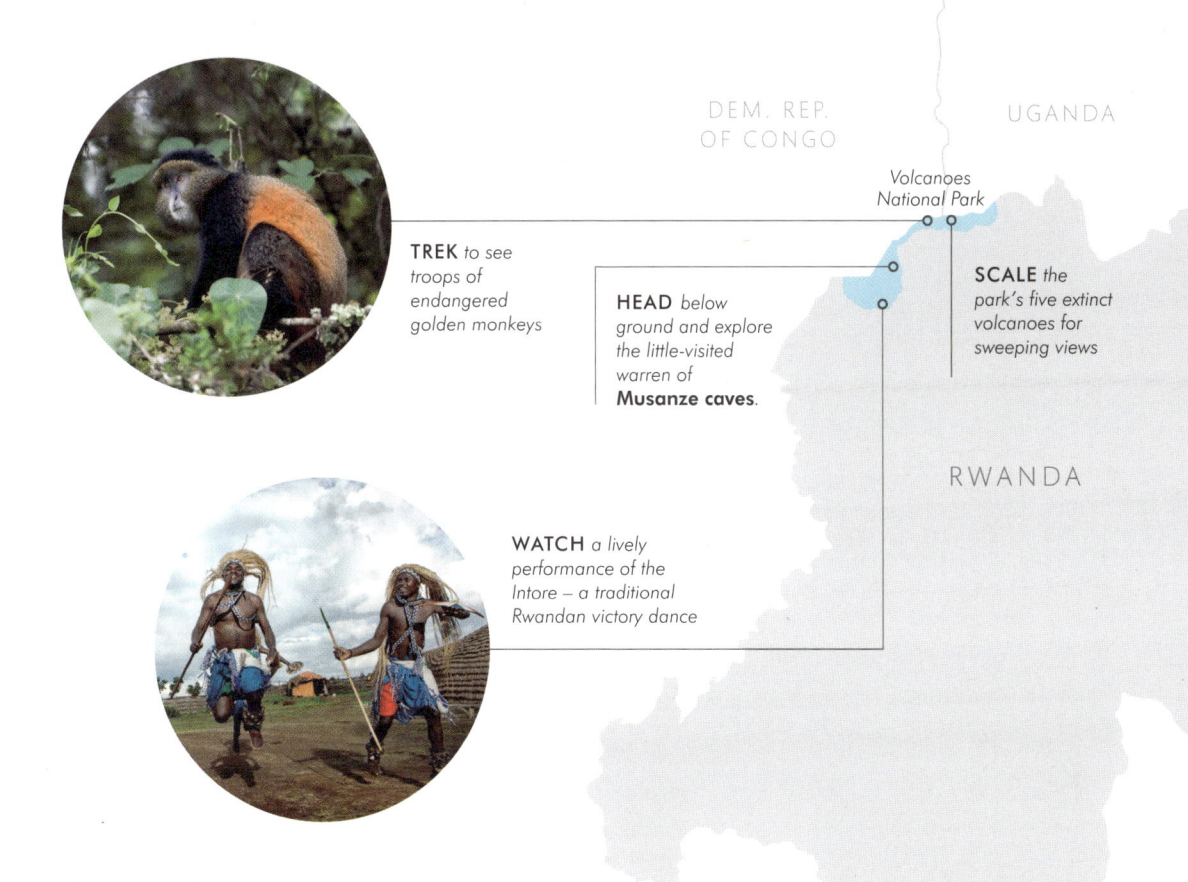

TREK to see troops of endangered golden monkeys

HEAD below ground and explore the little-visited warren of **Musanze caves**.

SCALE the park's five extinct volcanoes for sweeping views

WATCH a lively performance of the Intore – a traditional Rwandan victory dance

RWANDA

The squelch of mud under foot, the smell of damp leaves in your nostrils and the rough graze of a wooden walking pole in your palm. You walk with pricking ears until you hear it – the unmistakable sound of a broad chest being hammered echoing from the bowels of the forest. Viewing mountain gorillas is billed as one of the top wildlife experiences on the planet and, of the three countries where they're found, Rwanda is the most renowned thanks to the ground-breaking work of American primatologist Dian Fossey, who conducted her research here.

The gorillas are found within the mist-laced rainforests of Volcanoes National Park in the Virunga Mountains, a two-hour drive northwest of the Rwandan capital, Kigali. Currently, 18 troops live within the park (ten are habituated and visited by tourists, eight are studied by researchers) and the trek to find them can take anything from 40 minutes to seven hours, all the while building anticipation. And then, for one whole hour, you can watch their relationships unfold: the females teaching youngsters to forage for bamboo shoots, the infants suckling, and toddlers avoiding the grumpy glances of the mammoth silverback. Permits are very expensive, but the majority goes back into the conservation and protection of the endangered species, and locking eyes with one of these great apes will send shivers of recognition and joy through you for weeks afterwards.

Capturing a close-up of a mountain gorilla amid the lush foliage of the Virunga Mountains

59

ON FOOT
AFRICA AND THE MIDDLE EAST

Mount Kilimanjaro

LOCATION Tanzania **START/FINISH** Machame Gate/Mweka Gate **DISTANCE** 62 km (37 miles) **TIME** 6–7 days **DIFFICULTY** Challenging **INFORMATION** www.tanzaniatourism.go.tz

Kilimanjaro may be one of the most popular mountains to conquer, but don't underestimate the difficulty of the climb.

Towering above Tanzania's elephant-strewn savannahs, Africa's tallest summit holds special sway over hikers as the highest single free-standing mountain in the world. Its snow-capped peak seems like a miracle when gawked at from the sunbaked plains and, as a result, all manner of myths and legends have been woven around Kilimanjaro. The Chaaga tribesmen believe that mountain dwarfs called Wakonyingo live in caves beneath its slopes.

Six routes scale Kilimanjaro, ranging from the "'Coca-Cola'" Marangu trail, so called because it's the easiest, to Umbwe – the hardest. Most people choose the "whisky-difficult" Machame route, which passes through five climatic zones in as many days: from the lush banana plantations spread across the lower slopes, to the lunar-like scree near the summit, where mists sweep in and out as fast as ocean tides.

For the final ascent, start climbing under the cloak of night, with the stars shining bright as spilt sugar above. Reaching the summit in time for sunrise, the cold is forgotten as the first rays pinken the cloud tops: you've climbed one of the world's Seven Summits.

Camping in the shadow of Mount Kilimanjaro, its cone circled by mist

ON FOOT
AFRICA AND THE MIDDLE EAST

(49)

Tour des Cirques

LOCATION Réunion **START/FINISH** Cilaos (loop)
DISTANCE 56 km (35 miles) **TIME** 5 days
DIFFICULTY Challenging; rugged terrain
INFORMATION www.gr-infos.com/grr1.htm

Officially called the GR11, this epic hiking trail weaves its way through the mountainous heart of Réunion – a lost world of jagged peaks, cavernous valleys, razor-sharp ridges and thundering waterfalls.

A mere fleck in the Indian Ocean, the little-known French island of Réunion sits with Madagascar to the west and Mauritius to the east. With its turquoise lagoons, coral reefs and spectacular beaches, it has all the tropes of a tropical island paradise, but towering high above the coastal plains, another world exists. Here, three collapsed craters form Réunion's colossal cirques – Cilaos, Mafate and Salazie – each with their own microclimate, varied landscape and unique charm.

Accessible only by foot, Mafate is the most remote of the three cirques on the GR11 route. The sense of isolation here is palpable, eerie even, as you pass the vast plains of wiry tamarind trees, their gnarled branches draped in moss and mist. The dusky silence is broken only by the distant calls of a *paille-en-queue* – the white-tailed tropicbird – soaring overhead as you set up camp beneath the encroaching night sky.

LE MÉTISSAGE

Characterized by a period of French rule, a plantation economy and slavery, Réunion still remembers the painful events of the colonial era. But rather than divide the islanders, this history has culminated in a multicultural society that celebrates diversity and difference – which the Réunionese proudly call *le métissage*, or the mixing.

Right The town of Cilaos, separated from Mafate by a mountain pass
Below A grocery store in the small village of Hell-Bourg, once a popular spa resort in the Cirque de Salazie

61

ON FOOT
AFRICA AND THE MIDDLE EAST

The setting sun bathing Petra's rock-carved Ad Deir (The Monastery) in a red-hued glow

EAT fresh fruit from family orchards at a homestay in **Orjan** or **Rasoun**

TAKE A DIP in the rock pools of the **Three Wadis**

STARGAZE from **Feynan Eco-Lodge**, one of Jordan's many sustainable stays

The Jordan Trail

LOCATION Jordan **START/FINISH** Um Qais/Aqaba **DISTANCE** 650 km (400 miles)
TIME 40 days **DIFFICULTY** Moderate **INFORMATION** www.jordantrail.org

To walk along Jordan's rocky spine is to travel slowly through myriad layers of culture, history and faith. That such a journey is also breathtakingly beautiful, particularly in the multicoloured palettes of spring and autumn, is what makes this experience completely unique.

Walking in Jordan is not new; this is a landscape carved by footsteps. The Jordan Trail is the latest iteration of pedestrian passage here, using old pathways of pilgrims, traders and Bedouin nomads who have roamed these mountains for millennia. From start to end, each region is markedly different, and the trail is broken down into eight smaller segments for those unable to tackle the Biblical 40 day-stages in one go.

From the town of Um Qais in the north, walkers traverse rolling green hills and canyons, passing olive groves and oak forests between sprawling villages. The biggest danger anywhere is simply that of being overfed; hospitality is an innate part of local culture, and you can expect to be regularly greeted and offered sugary tea along the way.

The trail passes dramatic, deep gorges and high, dry outlooks, before wending its way into Petra. This ancient city is the last remnant of the Nabatean civilization, and tells that remarkable story through its network of cave-houses, ruined palaces and towering façades carved directly into sandstone.

In the south of Jordan, the red sands of the vast Wadi Rum valley stretch to the horizon, punctuated only by towering granite peaks bursting out of the desert. The trail ends at the lapping shoreline of the Red Sea, where a cool swim in azure waters is the perfect way to finish.

Zambian Safari

A family of African elephants in South Luangwa, just one of the park's 60 species of mammals

LOCATION Zambia **START/FINISH** South Luangwa National Park (loop)
DISTANCE Varies; usually 3–8 km (2–5 miles) a day **TIME** Varies; 3–4 days recommended **DIFFICULTY** Easy **INFORMATION** www.zambiatourism.com

For animal lovers, there is nothing more exhilarating than seeing wild animals in their homeland. One of the best places for a wildlife-watching journey is Zambia's South Luangwa National Park, where the walking safari was born.

Imagine standing in hushed silence watching a herd of elephants drinking from the river and rumbling softly to each other, completely oblivious to your presence. Or quietly following the tracks of a leopard that lead you to its kill, an unlucky impala dangling in a tree. The leopard has vanished, but you have that spine-tingling sensation that something, somewhere is watching you. Moments like these are what walking safaris are all about.

Renowned British conservationist Norman Carr first started walking safaris in South Luangwa in the 1960s. Carr's vision of safeguarding animals by empowering local communities is still upheld and the park was declared the world's first Sustainable National Park by the United Nations in 2017. It's a beautiful place, dominated by the Luangwa River, which twists and turns along its eastern border, leaving oxbow lakes and lagoons in its wake. Camps here are intimate, full of character, with a simple back-to-nature vibe and everything you need, from comfy beds and hearty meals to hot showers and cold G&Ts. Your route depends on

ON FOOT
AFRICA AND THE MIDDLE EAST

ZAMBIA

South Luangwa National Park

MALAWI

MOZAMBIQUE

ZIMBABWE

WATCH huge flocks of beautiful carmine bee-eaters, the colour of rosé wine, fluttering around riverbanks in September

SLEEP in a simple fly-camp, with just a mosquito net between you and the stars

LET YOUR GUIDE show you their world and learn all about Africa's extraordinary wildlife

DEVOUR tasty feasts that are usually cooked on just an open fire, accompanied by earth-baked bread

STAYING SAFE

Your safety is paramount to your guide and ranger. Help them by following some simple rules. Walk in single file behind the guide. Stay quiet so that your guide can hear any helpful sounds or alarm calls. If you come across dangerous animals, stay calm, obey instructions – and never run. If you run you act like prey.

where you stay. You might return to one bush camp each night or you could embark on a "mobile safari", hiking from one camp to another.

Walking safaris focus not just on big game but on all creatures great and small, including bugs and birds. Your senses go into overdrive as you follow your guide through the bush – you smell, see and hear so much more than you would on a game drive. The whiff of fresh dung, the sight of pin-sharp hairlines on a lion's paw-print, the shriek of a tree squirrel indicating the presence of predators – everything tells a tale as you immerse yourself in nature at its best.

another way
Most national parks in Zambia offer walking safaris, including the popular Lower Zambezi bordering Zimbabwe and North Luangwa, a raw and remote area with only a couple of camps.

Watching a giraffe from a safe distance, accompanied by an armed ranger

ON FOOT
ASIA

(52)

Manaslu Circuit

LOCATION Nepal **START/FINISH** Arughat/Besisahar
DISTANCE 177 km (110 miles) **TIME** 2–3 weeks
DIFFICULTY Moderate **INFORMATION** Various Nepalese and international companies offer organised treks of Manaslu

Hike the Nepalese Himalayas, cross plunging gorges on swaying suspension bridges and enjoy the hospitality in cosy local teahouses – the Manaslu Circuit promises a Himalayan adventure without the crowds.

Mention Nepal, and you think of the Himalayas, and, inevitably, Everest Base Camp. But steer clear of this busy route and make for the Manaslu Circuit, far quieter and less commercialized, but spectacular. You'll have the views all to yourself on a breathtaking fortnight's hike circumnavigating Manaslu, the world's eighth-highest mountain at a staggering 8,163 m (26,781 ft).

Leaving Arughat, the path hugs the valley walls of the Budhi Gandaki, climbing into Buddhist country at Nupri, where crimson-robed monks sweep around snow-dusted temples. Higher into the mountains the air thins as the views grow ever more expansive – the mountains' majesty unfurls like a lotus flower, and silent spectral snow leopards pad the forested slopes.

At each day's close, a cosy teahouse lodge or tent brings sanctuary. Foot-sore travellers swap stories and refuel with *daal bhaat* (lentil curry) and a fortifying Himalayan staple, apple pie. The ultimate reward comes at snow-trapped Larkya La Pass. From Manaslu to the peak of Annapurna II, you'll gaze across a time-frozen torrent of glaciers, ample inspiration to carry you home.

another way

For an extended Himalayan adventure, add a few extra days to trek the Tsum Valley. This mysterious, remote Buddhist region's highlight is the ancient, spectacularly sited Mu Gompa monastery, cradled in the high mountains.

Crossing the suspension bridge over the woods between Lho Gham and Samagaon village, on the Manaslu Circuit

ON FOOT
ASIA

Wading through a tree-shaded river in Borneo's Gunung Mulu National Park

Headhunter's Trail

LOCATION Borneo **START/FINISH** Camp 5, Gunung Mulu National Park/Limbang **DISTANCE** 11 km (7 miles) **TIME** 24 hours **DIFFICULTY** Easy **INFORMATION** mulupark.com

Follow in the path of Borneo's once-feared Kayan warriors, navigating the thick jungle of Gunung Mulu National Park along a former headhunting trail that promises gentle hiking and astonishing scenery.

This steamy but mostly easy trail sets out on a four-hour ramble along jungle paths, dodging serpentine hanging vines, picking past carnivorous pitcher plants and crossing rock-strewn streams on swaying rope bridges. Gibbons swing lankily through the canopy, pythons curl menacingly around trunks, and hornbills flit by in a flash of colour. Keep an eye out too for armoured pangolins scuttling around on two legs and sun bears foraging for honey. After the half-day hike, a canoe ferries walkers three hours downriver. Home for the night is an Iban longhouse, where dinner is cooked traditionally in bamboo stems.

Navigating the forests and rivers on this overnight trek, it's easy to imagine the Kayan doing the same as they embarked on headhunting expeditions. These days, the Kayan people preserve their traditional culture by more peaceful means, in ornate tattoos, stretched earlobes, music and mythology.

> Pythons curl menacingly around trunks, and hornbills flit by in a flash of colour

ON FOOT
ASIA

Wat Phra That Doi Kong Mu, Mae Hong Son's hilltop temple at the end of the walk

54 Mae Hong Son

LOCATION Thailand **START/FINISH** Mae Hong Son (loop) **DISTANCE** 10 km (6 miles) **TIME** 2 days **DIFFICULTY** Moderate; some mountainous terrain **INFORMATION** www.tourismthailand.org

Not for nothing is the province of Mae Hong Son, with its alpine meadows and spectacular mountain backdrops, known as the "Switzerland of Thailand". It's cooler up here in the hills than on the stifling Thai lowlands, but hiking through the jungle is still hot and sweaty work; luckily, tumbling waterfalls promise hikers cooling dips.

Further relief is found in Huay Hee, home to the Karen people. An evening beside the campfire is the perfect tonic to the chilly mountain evenings and the smell of rich Burmese curries and *ngapi* (fermented shrimp paste) transports you across the border to neighbouring Myanmar, where the Karen have their roots. After a night spent in a homestay here, rise at dawn and head back to Mae Hong Son's gleaming white hilltop temple. As the sun rises, the mists slowly lift from the town and valley below – what a view.

55 The MacLehose Trail

LOCATION Hong Kong **START/FINISH** Pak Tam Chung/Tuen Mun **DISTANCE** 100 km (62 miles) **TIME** 6 days **DIFFICULTY** Challenging; steep terrain **INFORMATION** www.hiking.gov.hk

Hong Kong is so much more than just an urban jungle. Away from the flickering-neon noir scenes, bustling markets and gleaming skyscrapers lies a wild world of mountains, valleys and forests, criss-crossed by one of Asia's great coast-to-coast hiking trails.

The MacLehose Trail begins by circling the spidery eastern coastline of the New Territories. Striking hexagonal columns of rock betray the volcanic origins of High Island, before the trail turns inland, ascending steep mountains and plunging down deep valleys. It's tough on the knees, but a feast for the senses, with monkeys chattering in the trees above and heart-stopping views – an unbeatable cityscape unfolds as you emerge from the jungle to crest Lion Rock. At sundown, a campsite barbecue awaits, before your adventures begin anew tomorrow.

MURRAY MACLEHOSE

Governor of Hong Kong from 1971 to 1982, Sir Murray MacLehose was a keen hiker and established the territory's country parks, of which the trail spans eight. A colourful character, MacLehose had in a past life trained Chinese guerrilla fighters in World War II. He came very close to never making it to Hong Kong – his career survived an early scare after he left a confidential telegram, from Harold Wilson to Lyndon B. Johnson, lying around in a bank.

ON FOOT
ASIA

(56)
Huanghuacheng

LOCATION China **START/FINISH** Huanghuacheng (loop) **DISTANCE** 11 km (7 miles) **TIME** 1 day **DIFFICULTY** Moderate; some steep sections and stairs **INFORMATION** www.cnto.org.uk; entry charge for Great Wall

This snaking route takes in a blissfully unpeopled section of the Great Wall as it folds over the arid mountain crests northwest of Beijing. The best time to tackle it is in late spring, when the surrounding slopes are carpeted in the golden drifts of wildflowers that give the path its name, "Huanghua Cheng" or "Yellow Flower Wall".

There are no crowds for good reason – this is one of the most challenging sections of the wall to walk. There are no handrails or tidy stairs. Instead, hikers skirt tufts of grass growing from broken towers, and scramble over loose brickwork as they pass the 12 beacon towers along the route. After hours hiking in the dry Beijing heat, it's tempting to race down the final section, but loose footing demands caution. The closing stretch towards the Huanghuacheng Reservoir rewards your hard work with a surreal glistening vista of Ming-dynasty ramparts disappearing underwater.

A section of China's iconic Great Wall leading to the Huanghuacheng Reservoir

A family walking through the impossibly green rice terraces near Lao Chai, Sa Pa

(57)
Sa Pa

LOCATION Vietnam **START/FINISH** Sa Pa Town (loop) **DISTANCE** Varies **TIME** Varies **DIFFICULTY** Moderate to challenging **INFORMATION** www.trekkingsapa.com

Tier upon tier of rice terraces reflecting the vast sky like shards of a shattered mirror, while the conical straw hats of farmers bob up and down as they go about their work: it's pastoral views like these that draw walkers to Sa Pa. This implausibly pretty region is couched amid the craggy mountains of Hoang Lien National Park in northwest Vietnam.

Prepare to get muddy as you tramp through this camera-worthy landscape, which is home to eight different ethnic minority groups, including the Dao, Hmong and Giay. Tourism has been fully embraced here and you can give back to these communities – and immerse yourself in their different cultures – by hiking with a local guide, visiting markets and staying in homestays. There are countless routes, but try to visit Heaven's Gate, where bright light shines through a mountain arch, the cascading Love Waterfall, and the undulating terraces of Muong Hoa Valley.

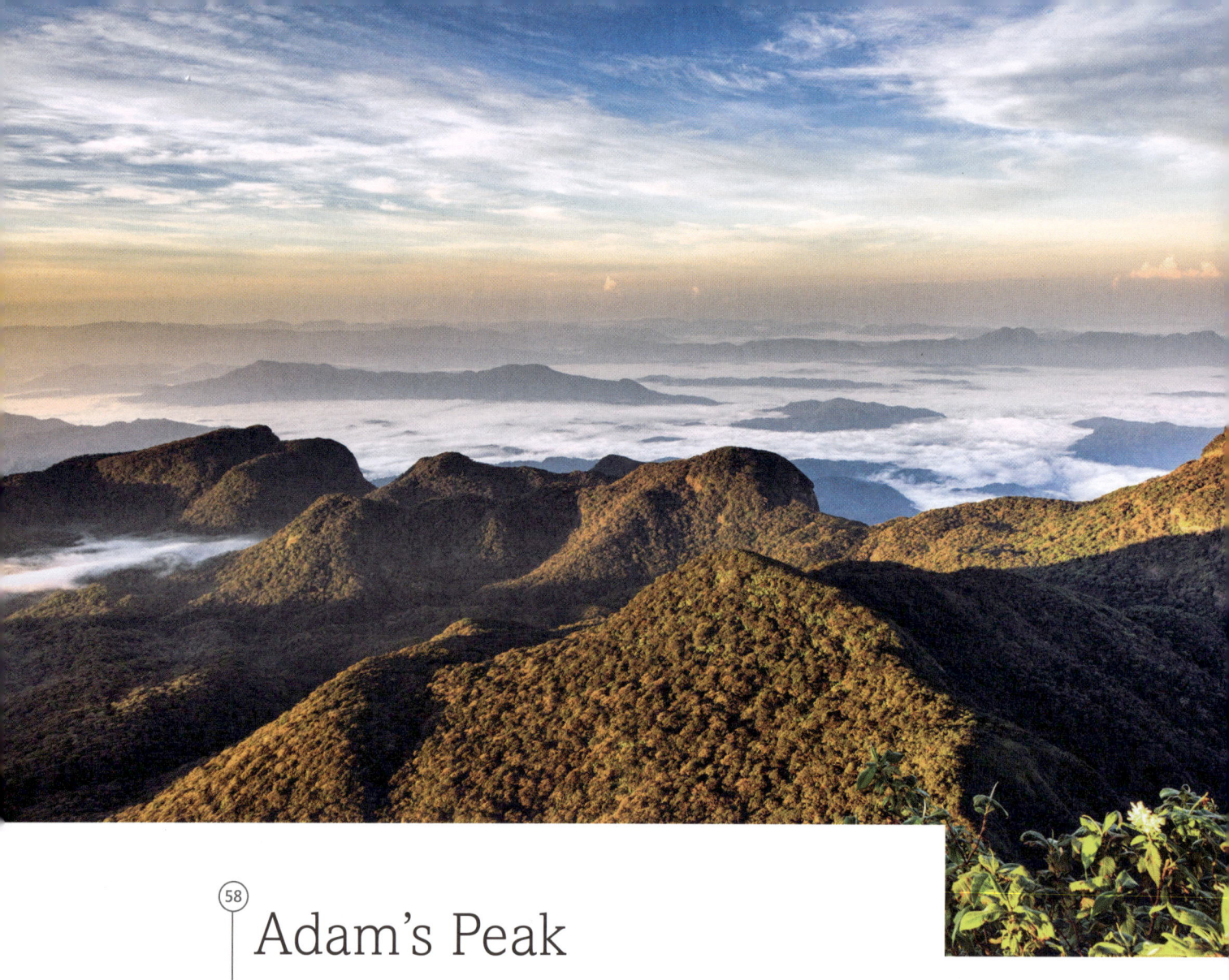

Sunrise over Adam's Peak, with clouds stretching into the distance

Adam's Peak

LOCATION Sri Lanka **START/FINISH** Dalhousie/Adam's Peak summit **DISTANCE** 7 km (4 miles) **TIME** 2–4 hours **DIFFICULTY** Moderate; steep steps **INFORMATION** www.srilanka.travel

The nocturnal ascent of Adam's Peak is a unique mix of wild hike and religious pilgrimage, with crowds of both devotees and walkers gathering to watch dawn break over the sacred summit.

Known locally as Sri Pada ("Sacred Footprint"), Adam's Peak is revered by all of Sri Lanka's faiths thanks to an impression on a rock at its summit. While Buddhists believe the mark to be an imprint of the Buddha's foot, Hindus associate it with Shiva, Muslims with Adam, and Christians with St Thomas. Nonetheless, the peak retains an emphatically Buddhist flavour and, from December to May, thousands of devotees climb this mountain.

> A cup of sweet, milky tea is a surprisingly effective pick-me-up

ON FOOT
ASIA

The ascent begins in the dead of night. A seemingly endless sequence of steps (over 5,000 in total) ushers you irresistibly upwards, while all around you is the mountain itself, huge and mysterious in the darkness. Lights strung out along the path relieve the blackness, while impromptu tea shacks offer oases of rest and refreshment along the way. A cup of sweet, milky tea is a surprisingly effective pick-me-up, as is the chance to chat with pilgrims and travellers.

As you approach the weather-lashed monastery clinging to the summit, the prayer-flag-festooned steps become increasingly narrow, crowded and knee-crackingly steep. Here, everyone waits for dawn. Most people gather on the eastern side, facing the rising sun, but the western side is quieter and offers the chance to see the surreal, perfectly triangular shadow of the peak. This sight is said to be a meteorological incarnation of the Buddhist Triple Gem, and further evidence of the Peak's unique and mysterious power.

The illuminated path snaking its way up to the summit of Adam's Peak

another way

A longer, more challenging and less-frequented path leads to the summit from the Ratnapura side of the mountain, via Palabaddale. Guesthouses in Ratnapura can arrange a guide.

OFFER a prayer to Saman, the resident mountain god, at the striking **Japanese Peace Pagoda**

◀ Dalhousie

STOP for rest, refreshment and a chat with local pilgrims at one of the numerous tea shacks dotting the steps

Adam's Peak summit

RING one of the temple bells at the mountaintop monastery to signal your safe arrival at the summit

SRI LANKA
Adam's Peak

71

ON FOOT
ASIA

59 Michinoku Coastal Trail

LOCATION Japan **START/FINISH** Hachinohe/Soma **DISTANCE** 1,000 km (620 miles) **TIME** 7 weeks **DIFFICULTY** Easy **INFORMATION** tohoku.env.go.jp/mct

Sheer sea cliffs, island-studded bays and fishing villages clustered around harbours: in this beautiful part of northeastern Tohoku, nature's bounty is evident, but so is its power – the area was devastated by the Great East Japan Earthquake and Tsunami of 2011. The Michinoku Coastal Trail opened in 2019 and, as walkers traverse the craggy coastline, they have the chance to contribute directly to communities relying on tourism income for their recovery, as well as to simply enjoy the breathtaking seascapes.

To the north, Ama women, who fish by free-diving, harvest abalone, sea urchins and oysters in the grey waters. Further south, the imposing sea cliffs of Kitayamazaki drop down to Jodogahama (Jodo Beach). And near the end of the trail, islands cluster along the ria coastline, from sacred Kinkasan – where deer wander freely – to Tashirojima – where cats outnumber people.

THE PATH TO RECOVERY

Many communities along the Michinoku Coastal Trail are still rebuilding after the 2011 disaster. You can learn more about what happened, and the recovery, at several museums and memorials along the coast, including the Kesennuma City Memorial Museum and the Iwate Tsunami Memorial in Rikuzentakata.

Pilgrims climbing up to Nachi Taisha on the Nakahechi trail of the Kumano Kodo

60 Kumano Kodo

LOCATION Japan **START/FINISH** Takijiri-oji/Kumano Nachi Taisha **DISTANCE** 68 km (42 miles) **TIME** 4 days **DIFFICULTY** Moderate **INFORMATION** www.tb-kumano.jp

One of the world's only UNESCO-listed pilgrimage routes, the Kumano Kodo's ancient trails criss-cross the Kii Hanto, Japan's largest peninsula. As you walk in the footsteps of centuries of pilgrims, you may find yourself drawn down a mysterious side road, revealing at its end a tiny Oji shrine – sometimes little more than a stone lantern hung with sacred Shinto ropes – which has been placed along the path by mountain ascetics to guide and protect weary travellers.

The most popular trail is the Nakahechi, which ends at Nachi Taisha, where a breathtaking waterfall plummets down a sheer rock face. On the way, the path passes under a 33-m- (108-ft-) tall torii (sacred gate), which dwarves even the ancient trees growing patiently beside it, before reaching Hongu Taisha – the Grand Shrine – the most sacred of the Kumano Kodo's shrines.

ON FOOT
ASIA

61 Shikoku Henro

LOCATION Japan **START/FINISH** Ryozen-ji, Naruto/Okubo-ji, Sanuki **DISTANCE** 1,150 km (715 miles) **TIME** 6–8 weeks **DIFFICULTY** Varies **INFORMATION** www.shikoku-tourism.com/shikoku-henro

The 88-temple pilgrimage around Shikoku traces the journey of Kobo Daishi, an 8th-century monk, through some of the island's most dramatic and beautiful scenery. Along the way, walkers dressed in pilgrim's clothes – a loose white top, conical sedge hat and rosary beads – and carrying wooden staffs, are offered cups of tea, snacks, lifts and even home-cooked meals. These acts of kindness towards *henro-san* (pilgrims) let locals participate in the spiritual journey themselves, so refusing an *osettai* (small gift) is considered bad form.

On more remote stretches of the trail, *osettai* will be few and far between. In places the path leads along windswept cliffs, over precipitous mountain passes, through dappled forests or past rippling fields of rice. In these quiet and beautiful surroundings, the centuries fall away, and it's easy to imagine Kobo Daishi forging his own path to enlightenment.

62 Mount Fuji

LOCATION Japan **START/FINISH** Fifth stations of trails (loop) **DISTANCE** 8–20 km (5–12.5 miles) **TIME** 1 day **DIFFICULTY** Moderate; some steep sections **INFORMATION** www.fujisan-climb.jp

Immortalized in art and poetry, the snow-capped cone of Mount Fuji resting serenely among the clouds is one of Japan's most iconic sights. Ascending Japan's highest mountain, at 3,776 m (12,389 ft), sits near the top of many travellers' lists. Though the climb is possible in a day, the real prize is watching the *goraiko*: the sunrise as seen from the summit, with golden light spreading over the clouds like honey.

The Yoshida Trail is the most popular of the mountain's four ascents – and the busiest. Gotemba is much quieter, but being on the west, misses out on views of the sunrise if you don't reach the summit in time. For the best of both worlds, climb up east-facing Subashiri, which is fairly quiet until the eighth station, when it joins the camaraderie of the Yoshida Trail.

> The real prize is watching the *goraiko*: the sunrise

The perfectly symmetrical Mount Fuji, viewed through the cloud from a smaller peak

ON FOOT
ASIA

Right The blue waters of Lake Issyk Kul, circled by the South Shore Panorama Trail
Below Two traditional yurts, where walkers can spend the night

63 South Shore Panorama Trail

LOCATION Kyrgyzstan **START/FINISH** Bokonbayevo (loop)
DISTANCE 33 km (20 miles) **TIME** 3 days **DIFFICULTY** Moderate
INFORMATION www.southshorekg.com

With stunning mountain views and Kyrgyz nomadic culture, this hike from the southern shore of Lake Issyk Kul shows you the best of Kyrgyzstan. It's a true back-to-nature experience – you might not see a soul for days, save for the golden eagles wheeling overhead.

Issyk Kul is the second-largest saline lake in the world, set at an altitude of over 1,600 m (5,250 ft) and surrounded by the Tian Shan mountains. On its northern shore, the unpretentious spa resort of Cholpon-Ata is a popular destination for Kygyz holiday-makers, but hikers make a beeline for the wilder south shore. From here, a network of trails traces the lake shore and strikes out into deep gorges, scree-scattered valleys and steep mountain passes. Best walked from June to September, the South Shore Panorama Trail takes hikers through summer pastures grazed by nomadic herders' livestock, up to awe-inspiring viewpoints. All around, the jagged snow-capped peaks of the Teskey Ala-To range dip down into yurt-dotted fields; to one side is Issyk Kul, impossibly deep and dark in the centre; and above is an expanse of cloud-speckled sky.

The spectacular landscapes may steal the show, but warm Kyrgyz hospitality will linger just as long in your memory, whether sleeping in a traditional yurt, soaking in a steaming hot spring or listening to epic Kyrgyz tales by starlight.

ON FOOT
ASIA

(64)
Rigsum Gompa Trek

LOCATION Bhutan **START/FINISH** Trashi Yangtse (loop)
DISTANCE 45 km (28 miles) **TIME** 3 days **DIFFICULTY** Moderate
INFORMATION www.bluepoppybhutan.com

Lamas, butterfly-filled meadows and hilltop dzongs framed by fluttering prayer flags. Untouched by mass tourism, eastern Bhutan is a salve for those seeking quiet.

Bhutan may be known as the "Land of the Thunder Dragon", but rather than fiery fury, this trek offers blissful silence and spirituality. Set in the rarely visited eastern province, this circular route crosses the lost valley of Trashi Yangtse and traces sites associated with Guru Rinpoche, revered founder of Tibetan Buddhism. The trail cuts through terraced rice fields and across rivers on swaying bridges, along the way passing locals gathering firewood, farming or guiding basket-laden horses to market.

Nearing Dechen Phodrang, a red-robed lama guides hikers to a cave once visited by Rinpoche, and then deeper into the forest to see an imprint of the guru's hair and the pool where he once bathed. Then onwards to meadows visited by blue butterflies, and ancient forests of hemlock and walnut, still purportedly roamed by bears. Hikers climb ever upwards until finally, there it is: the red-roofed hilltop *dzong* (fortress) of Rigsum Gompa, a prayer-flagged temple dedicated to the gods of Compassion, Power and Knowledge. Inside the butter lamp-lit halls, you may start to feel light-headed – perhaps from the incense, the altitude or something altogether more holy.

GURU RINPOCHE

Guru Rinpoche was a Buddhist master who lived during the 8th century. His life is shrouded in myth and mystery: from his birth as an eight-year-old child who appeared in a lotus blossom, to being doused in fire for teaching a local king's daughter tantra, only to be found alive and in meditation when the smoke cleared.

Young monks dressed in red robes at Dechen Phodrang, a monastery that is passed on the trek to Rigsum Gompa

ON FOOT
AUSTRALASIA

Milford Track

LOCATION New Zealand **START/FINISH** Te Anau Downs/Milford Sound
DISTANCE 53.5 km (33 miles) **TIME** 4 days **DIFFICULTY** Easy to moderate
INFORMATION www.doc.govt.nz; permits required

The most famous of New Zealand's "Great Walks", the undulating Milford Track dips in and out of luxuriant beech forest, arcs high above majestic fjords and flows between soaring peaks. Showing off the sheer diversity of the South Island's scenery, this walk is both enduringly popular and utterly spellbinding.

In 1908, *The Spectator* magazine named this the "world's finest walk", and with good reason. Milford Track is a hiking – or, as Kiwis would call it, "tramping" – adventure that leads through the wild scenery of Fiordland National Park. Think overgrown forests, finger-shaped fjords and lofty peaks. The fact that the track is inaccessible by car is part of its appeal – this is a chance to strike out alone and explore a truly remote wilderness.

> This is a chance to strike out alone and explore a truly remote wilderness

Keen hikers will be itching to get going, but remember that a prebooked permit is needed to tackle the route. Valid for specific dates, a permit allocates hikers a set four days to traverse the route, as accommodation is limited. While this means that you'll need to hike to schedule, it doesn't mean you'll have to rush – there's plenty of time to take in the view.

The trail is bookended by two spectacular bodies of water – Lake Te Anau and Milford Sound – and requires boat trips at both ends. Start with a water-taxi ride across pristine Lake Te Anau from Te Anau Downs, itself a remote pier requiring a car ride from the nearby town of Te Anau. The boat speeds across crystalline waters to Glade Wharf, little more than a wooden pier set at the wild hinterlands of the lakehead. The cruise hints at the alpine grandeur to come, with snowy peaks rising into opaque mists from the lake's northwestern end.

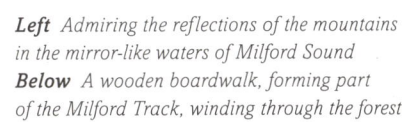

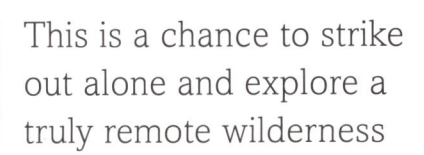

Left *Admiring the reflections of the mountains in the mirror-like waters of Milford Sound*
Below *A wooden boardwalk, forming part of the Milford Track, winding through the forest*

ON FOOT
AUSTRALASIA

From the end of the pier, the trail winds along a valley floor thick with red and silver beech trees, mounds of spongy emerald moss, fronds of dangling lichen, and blankets of filigreed ferns. The tempestuous weather patterns and heavy rainfall over the fjordlands help give rise to an astounding diversity of plantlife, providing an ever-changing backdrop as you stroll. The track itself is a wide gravel trail, with smaller sections composed of wooden boardwalks, though as the terrain becomes more mountainous it morphs into dirt paths.

As night descends, independent walkers can hunker down in bare-bones huts with simple kitchens, while those looking to treat themselves can book onto a guided tour, with access to privately maintained cabins that have hot showers, soft beds and basic cooking facilities. Wherever you choose to rest your head, at night the world goes silent and an expanse of stars twinkles over the mountaintops, with the Milky Way on full glittering display on moonless nights. Near Clinton Hut – the no-frills accommodation option for the first evening – a glimmering grotto of glow worms mirrors the night sky, casting an incandescent emerald gleam over the surrounding forest.

WHAT ARE THE GREAT WALKS?

Though New Zealand is criss-crossed by dozens of hiking trails, its Department of Conservation maintains ten that are officially listed as "Great Walks", allowing hikers to access some of the country's most spectacular and remote scenery. The most popular is the South Island's Abel Tasman Coast Track, a 60-km (37-mile) tramp along golden beaches and beside rushing rivers. The 82-km (51-mile) Heaphy Track is the longest, while the Paparoa Track, along the South Island's west coast, is the newest, added in 2019.

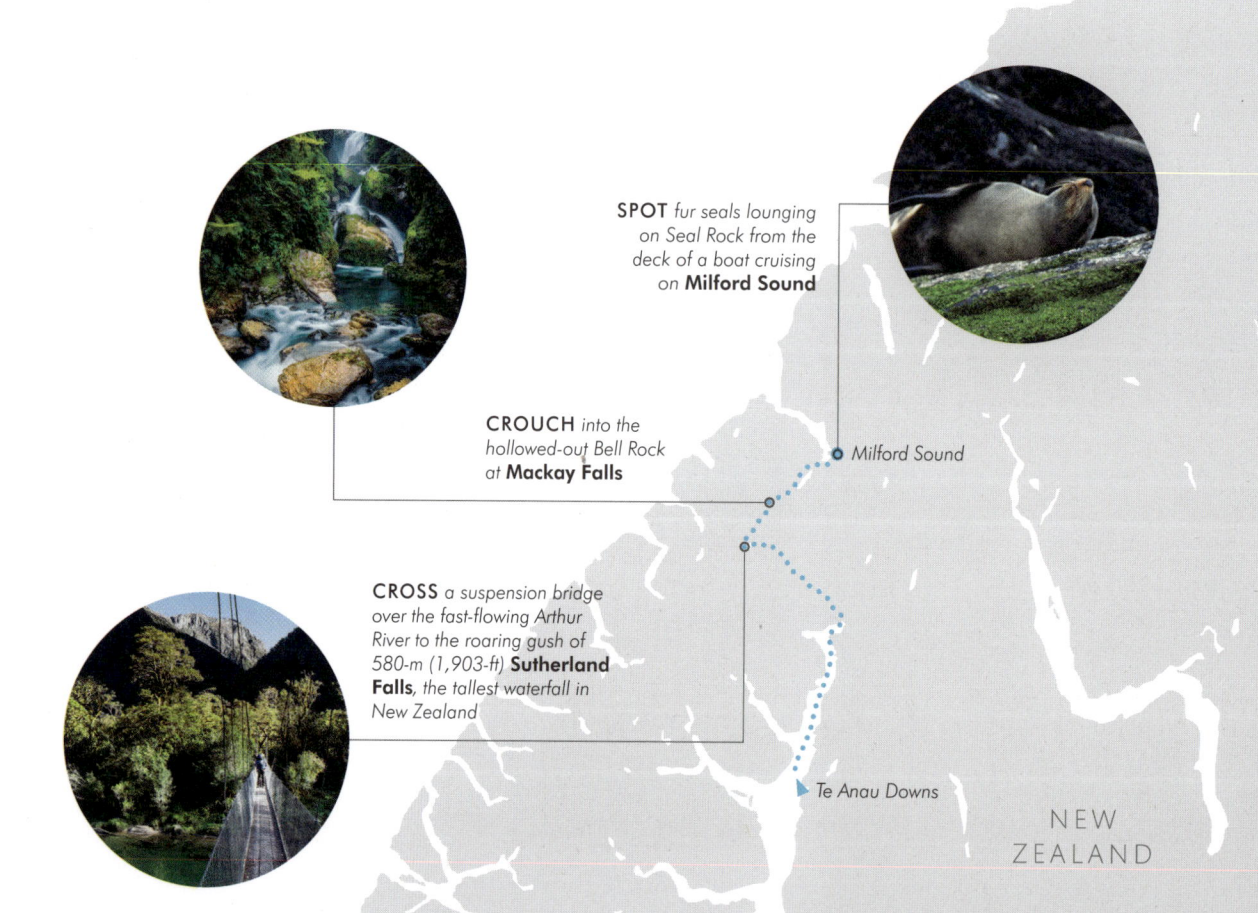

SPOT fur seals lounging on Seal Rock from the deck of a boat cruising on **Milford Sound**

CROUCH into the hollowed-out Bell Rock at **Mackay Falls**

CROSS a suspension bridge over the fast-flowing Arthur River to the roaring gush of 580-m (1,903-ft) **Sutherland Falls**, the tallest waterfall in New Zealand

Milford Sound

Te Anau Downs

NEW ZEALAND

Above Hiking along the rocky path that crosses the Mackinnon Pass, the highest point on the Milford Track *Below* Two eye-catching kea parrots, perching atop a lichen-covered rock

The dense forest gradually gives way to wide slopes covered by alpine tussock grass, growing in thick tufts out of the glacial rock. Cutting through this windswept landscape, the now rocky path edges round hulking mountainsides that offer expansive views across the peaks of Nicholas Cirque. You're likely to spot wild kea parrots, with their signature olive-green plumage and curved black beaks, as you make for the bleakly beautiful Mackinnon Pass, the highest point on the walk. Before you lies a sweeping vista of soaring, snow-capped mountain peaks that cascade effortlessly down into lush green valleys.

From here, the path descends back to the verdant forest floor and the final section of the walk. First looping through a forest of moss-covered birch trees, the track then flows alongside the peacock-green waters of the Arthur River on its winding journey into Lake Ada and heavenly Milford Sound. Found along the way is Mackay Falls, whose powerful torrent has, over centuries, carved out the intriguing Bell Rock, a hollowed-out boulder big enough to climb around in.

The final stretches of smooth, wide track lead to Sandfly Point, where the trail ends at another simple pier. Boats carry tired hikers across Milford Sound, where dark-green peaks rise from glassy waters, making for an enchantingly beautiful end to an epic journey.

Murray Valley Trail

Murray River sweeps through a crimson landscape in its final stage northeast of Adelaide

LOCATION Australia **START/FINISH** Corryong/Murray Mouth **DISTANCE** 1,000 km (620 miles) **TIME** 6 weeks **DIFFICULTY** Moderate **INFORMATION** www.mda.asn.au

This source-to-sea hike follows the riverbank of the Murray, Australia's longest river. Beginning in the Australian Alps, the route ends in a vast sandy delta, passing through a stunning riverine landscape along the way.

Where the Murray emerges from the Australian Alps there's little to suggest that this is inland Australia's mightiest body of water. By Corryong, at the start of this trail, the river has gained size and momentum. Tracking northwest across New South Wales and Victoria the waterway surges all the way to the ocean at Murray Mouth, all the while shadowed by this epic hiking trail.

Along its course, historic towns such as Echuca and Swan Hill break up the sand cliffs and eucalyptus forests, once the river's only companions. Flooded river red gums at Barmah and Gunbower islands, the sunset screech of corellas and cockatoos as they fly overhead, old steam-powered riverboats and riverside wooden architecture – walking the Murray combines landmarks from two centuries of European settlement with quintessentially Australian scenery.

And what is more Australian than the Outback? Deep into the crimson earth – known here as the Mallee – the river flows between high cliffs and deserted shores, before turning south in search of the sea. As the river nears the Great Australian Bight – the arc of ocean that caresses the country's southern shore – the landscape changes. Here, sand islands, lightly haired by coastal shrubs and serenaded by seabirds – mark the river's and the journey's end.

ON FOOT
AUSTRALASIA

Te Araroa – The Long Pathway

LOCATION New Zealand **START/FINISH** Cape Reinga, North Island/ Bluff, South Island **DISTANCE** 3,000 km (1,864 miles) **TIME** 3–6 months **DIFFICULTY** Challenging **INFORMATION** www.teararoa.org.nz

This epic trail truly lives up to its name, taking in the entire length of New Zealand, from the windswept far-north Aupouri Peninsula to the seaport of Bluff at South Island's tip.

The beauty of Te Araroa is that it takes in every landscape imaginable, from sugar-sanded coast and deep dense forest, to sheep-dotted farmland and multi-hued volcanic moonscapes of bright mineral lakes. From Cape Reinga's far-flung northern reaches, the route snakes south along myriad interconnected trails, roads and tracks, which are way-marked but not maintained as one cohesive path, so walkers will encounter all manner of terrain. You'll tramp sandy beaches and forested ridgelines, slog through muddy fields and beside steaming volcanic craters. The trail takes hikers through sleepy villages and remote wilderness – some nights bring a comfy hotel bed, and others a bare-bone mountain hut or a campsite under the stars. You'll need to be prepared for anything, but in exchange you're rewarded with constant Kiwi hospitality.

This months-long expedition requires planning, patience and steadfast stamina. But once you finish, you'll join the ranks of those who can say they have literally walked across New Zealand.

VOLCANIC HIKING

The Tongariro Alpine Crossing, a subsection of Te Araroa that can be walked as a stand-alone route, passes through an active volcanic zone. There are three active volcanoes in the area and dozens of cones and craters, all formed by eruptions from at least 12 vents over more than 275,000 years. Seismographic and volcanic activity are closely monitored by GNS Science, but the Department of Conservation, which maintains the trail, recommends that hikers remain vigilant, check conditions before setting out and heed all warnings in place.

Camping out on Aupouri Peninsula with views of remote Cape Reinga

ON FOOT
AUSTRALASIA

ADMIRE the murals that adorn the walls of small-town **Sheffield**

WATCH the sun setting over the **Derwent River**, one of Tasmania's prettiest waterways

ENJOY the quiet beauty of **Dover** in the island's deep south

Tasmanian Trail

LOCATION Australia **START/FINISH** Devonport/Dover
DISTANCE 480 km (299 miles) **TIME** 3 weeks **DIFFICULTY** Challenging **INFORMATION** www.tasmaniantrail.com.au

To walk across Tasmania is to experience Australia's greenest corner. It's a relentlessly beautiful three-week trip between the island's northern and southern shores, and one that passes through Tasmania's culinary and historical heartland.

Tasmania is the size of Ireland, Switzerland or the US state of West Virginia. Crossing such a territory on foot is a serious undertaking, requiring endurance and a reasonable level of fitness. If you don't fancy tackling the whole trail, the way can be split into shorter, more manageable sections. Whichever way you choose to hike this route, its rewards are constant and often spectacular.

Setting off from Devonport, a coastal town on the Bass Strait and the trail's northern gateway, there's a gradual sense of leaving civilization behind. Slowly the sound of city traffic recedes into the background, as a landscape of vineyards unfolds all around. The Central Highlands are the most strenuous section, and the two river crossings – impassable after heavy rains – add to the adventure. But for the most part, this rolling hill country is a world of small, stone-built settlements, dating back to the earliest days of European arrival, of orchards and of bespoke culinary experiences – farm visits, wine tastings and the like. After weeks of rambling, the smell of the sea announces journey's end, in the pretty hamlet of Dover, one of Australia's southernmost towns.

> Two river crossings – impassable after heavy rains – add to the adventure

Above The view from Mount Field, at the edge of Tasmania's Central Highlands
Left A Tasmanian pademelon, a nocturnal herbivore that spends daylight hours sheltering in the rainforest

ON FOOT
AUSTRALASIA

(69)

Grand Canyon Track, Blue Mountains

LOCATION Australia **START/FINISH** Evans Lookout (loop) **DISTANCE** 7 km (4 miles) **TIME** 3–4 hours **DIFFICULTY** Moderate to challenging **INFORMATION** www.nationalparks.nsw.gov.au

Many trails criss-cross the Blue Mountains, the spectacular massif west of Sydney, but none compare to the Grand Canyon Track. This short hike distils to its essence all the drama and beauty of the mountains, weaving under vertiginous sandstone cliffs and through shaded rainforest along fern- and wattle-fringed trails.

Evans Lookout, in the Blackheath area, is the best place to start and finish – a panoramic vista of sandstone buttes and forest-clad valleys rippling towards the far horizon. The sound of water is a constant on this journey – meandering creeks splash through the quiet forest, Beauchamp Falls cascades just off the main trail with a distant thunder, and there's the sense of rain falling in the forest long after it has ceased elsewhere.

Walking the Grand Canyon Track through the rainforest of the Blue Mountains

A grey kangaroo in the dusty red landscape of Flinders Ranges

(70)

Heysen Trail

LOCATION Australia **START/FINISH** Cape Jervis/Parachilna Gorge **DISTANCE** 1,200 km (746 miles) **TIME** 2–3 months **DIFFICULTY** Challenging **INFORMATION** www.heysentrail.asn.au

Viewed in its entirety, this is an epic expedition, a long-distance hike unlocking the diverse natural beauty of the Australian interior. Along the early stages of the thru-hike, the wild South Australian coast sets the scene with deserted yellow beaches and a soundtrack of wave-lashed cliffs and gusting winds. Further north, farmlands and forests give way to vineyards and the German-style villages of the Barossa Valley, one of Australia's oldest and most celebrated wine-growing regions. The landscape gradually gets drier – green-blues of the coast yielding to the red-brown of the interior. With one last glimpse of the ocean at Spencer's Gulf, the trail turns inland, marching deep into the Outback, past cattle stations and nearly abandoned villages, all the way into the Flinders Ranges, Australia's most beautiful desert massif.

ON FOOT
AUSTRALASIA

71 Mount Sorrow Ridge Trail

LOCATION Australia **START/FINISH** Cape Tribulation/Mount Sorrow **DISTANCE** 7 km (4 miles) **TIME** 4 hours **DIFFICULTY** Challenging **INFORMATION** www.parks.des.qld.gov.au

This sea-to-summit walk crosses from one melancholy epithet (Cape Tribulation) to another (Mount Sorrow). Despite its name, the trek is a joy, if you take it slowly: steamy tropical conditions and a steep climb from sea level to 680 m (2,231 ft) mean that pacing yourself is essential. The first stretch is a gentle climb; the last, a gruelling ascent into the clouds.

Often deserted, the glorious patch of sand at Cape Tribulation is where the paved road ends and the trail begins. Casting a shadow over the beach's inland edge, magical rainforest – dense and dripping with humidity – marks the spiritual homeland of the Kuku Yalanji people and the start of your hike. Keep an eye out for wildlife amid the undergrowth, from the giant southern cassowary to the tiny arboreal Bennett's tree-kangaroo. After the final sharp climb to Mount Sorrow, the view across the rainforest canopy to the Pacific Ocean beyond is a splendid reward.

THE CASSOWARY

At over 2 m (6.5 ft) tall, the world's second-heaviest bird is taller than most adults. The cassowary has a blue and purple head with a horn-like protrusion, and its blue droppings can spread the seeds of 70 species of rainforest trees. Fewer than 6,000 (possibly as few as 1,500) remain in the wild, along the coast of tropical far north Queensland.

72 Kokoda Trail

LOCATION Papua New Guinea **START/FINISH** Owers' Corner/Kokoda **DISTANCE** 96 km (60 miles) **TIME** 1 week **DIFFICULTY** Challenging **INFORMATION** www.kokodatrackauthority.org

Steeped in a history rich in heroics and tragedy, the Kokoda Trail is at once pilgrimage, following Track Campaign trails used during World War II, and an intensely rewarding hiking trail through the highlands of Papua New Guinea. It's an adventurous, demanding multi-day trek that can be completed in four days – though 16 hours is the record – or as many as 12, depending on time constraints and fitness. Don't expect carefully manicured hiking paths – the trail follows ancient byways, crossing creeks and rivers, and scrambling up muddy hillsides and vertiginous forest-green foothills of the Owen Stanley Range to the lofty heights of 2,490-m- (8,170-ft-) high Mount Bellamy.

Clambering up lush slopes from Nauro village on the Kokoda Trail

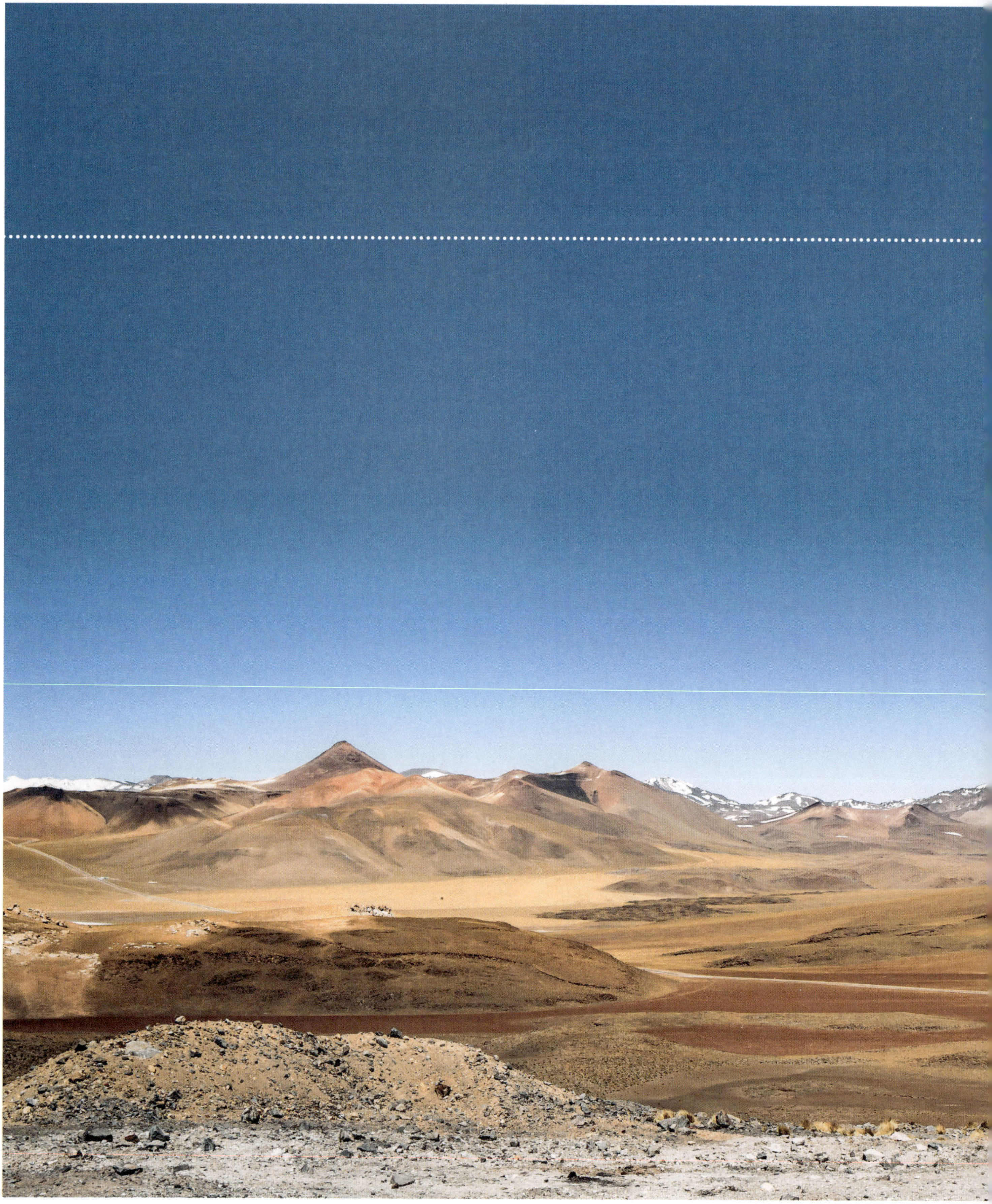

BY ROAD

"Nothing behind me, everything ahead of me, as is ever so on the road." Jack Kerouac's words encapsulate the possibilities promised by getting behind the wheel. Contrary to preconceptions, drivers need not be disconnected from their surroundings – make detours, stop often and talk to everyone you encounter along the way. This is your chance to get to the real heart of a country and its people.

AT A GLANCE
BY ROAD

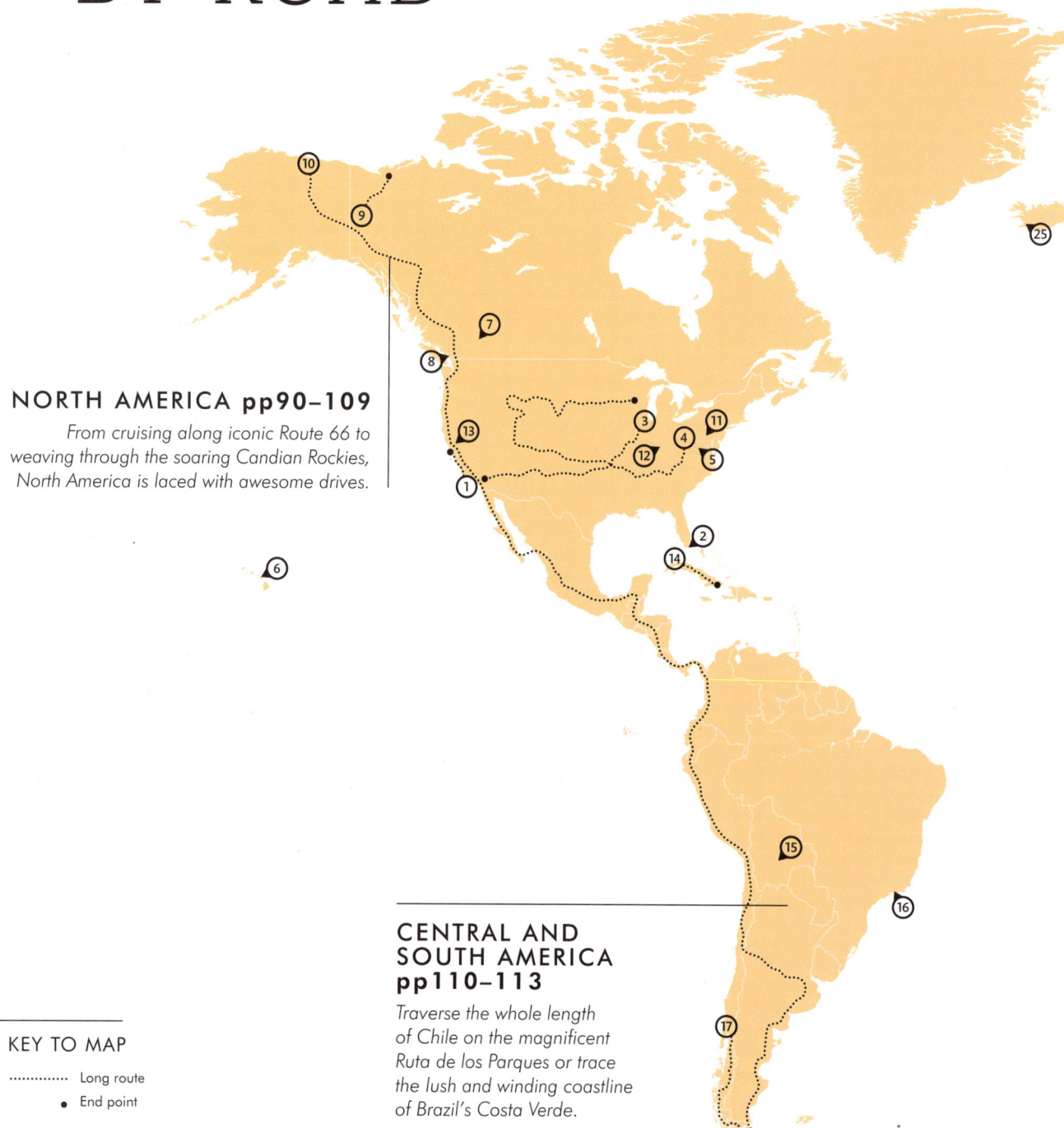

NORTH AMERICA pp90–109
From cruising along iconic Route 66 to weaving through the soaring Candian Rockies, North America is laced with awesome drives.

CENTRAL AND SOUTH AMERICA pp110–113
Traverse the whole length of Chile on the magnificent Ruta de los Parques or trace the lush and winding coastline of Brazil's Costa Verde.

KEY TO MAP
·········· Long route
• End point

Previous page *Two motorbikes driving through the Atacama Desert, Chile*

88

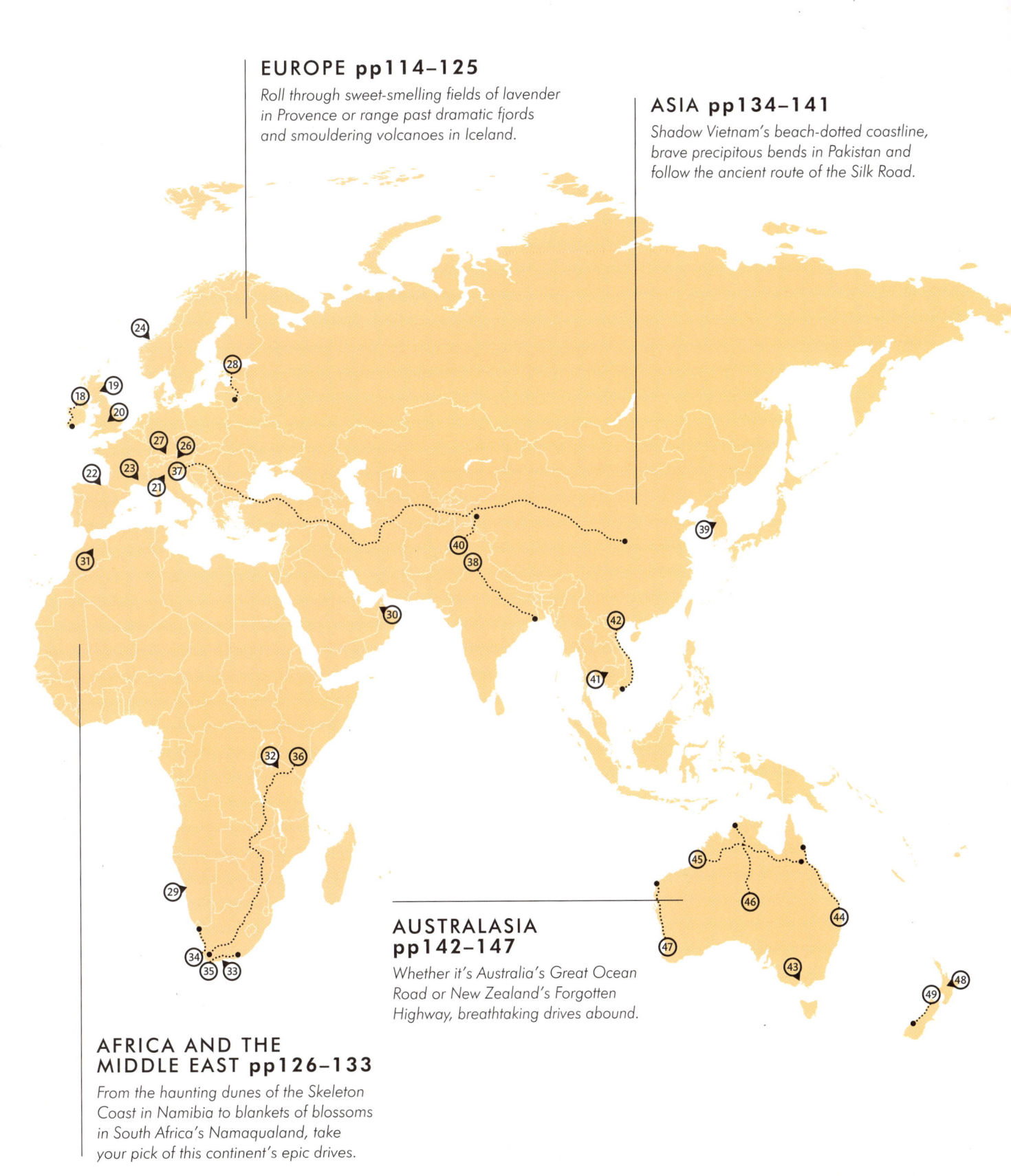

EUROPE pp114–125
Roll through sweet-smelling fields of lavender in Provence or range past dramatic fjords and smouldering volcanoes in Iceland.

ASIA pp134–141
Shadow Vietnam's beach-dotted coastline, brave precipitous bends in Pakistan and follow the ancient route of the Silk Road.

AUSTRALASIA pp142–147
Whether it's Australia's Great Ocean Road or New Zealand's Forgotten Highway, breathtaking drives abound.

AFRICA AND THE MIDDLE EAST pp126–133
From the haunting dunes of the Skeleton Coast in Namibia to blankets of blossoms in South Africa's Namaqualand, take your pick of this continent's epic drives.

89

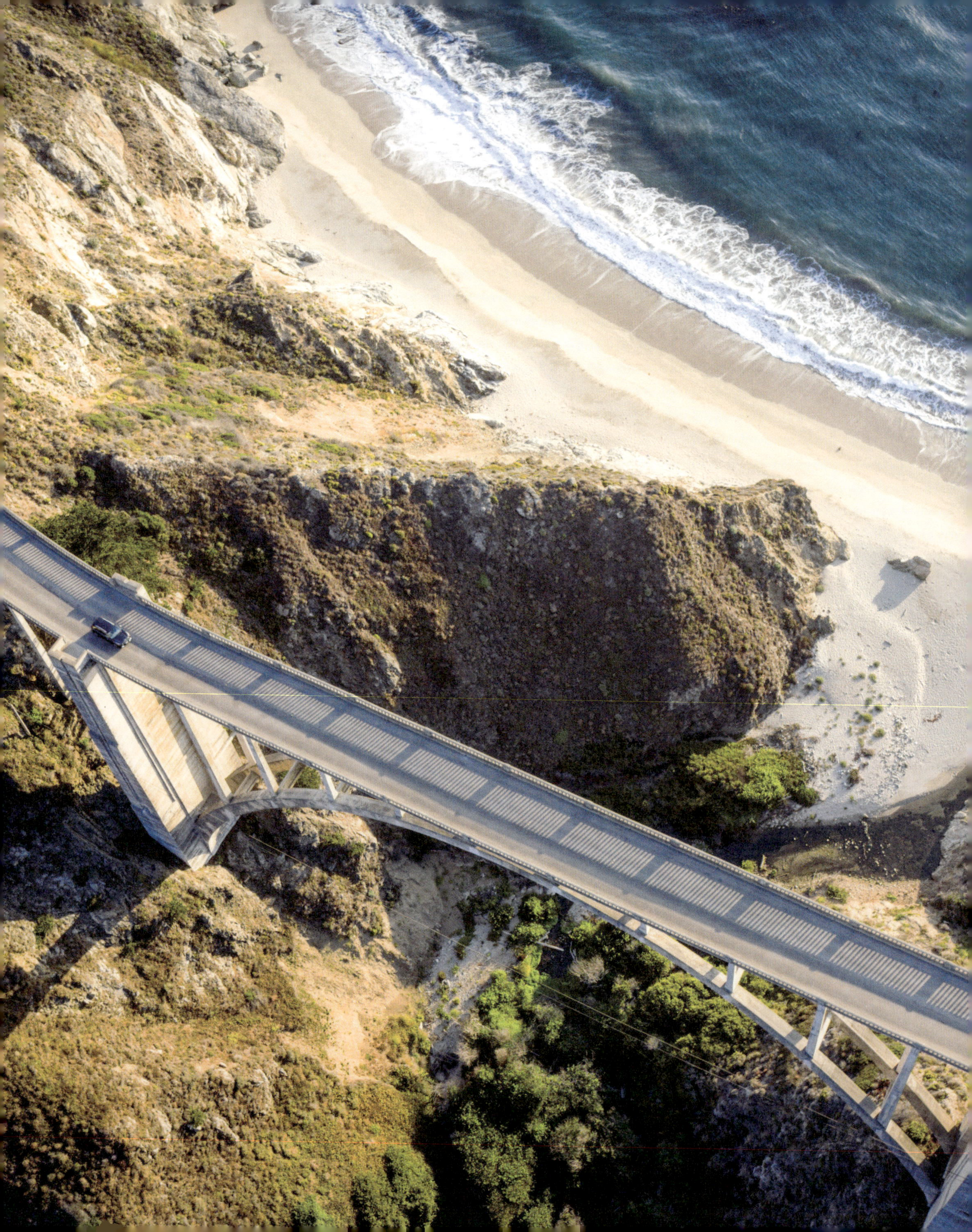

Driving through Big Sur across the picturesque Bixby Bridge

BY ROAD
NORTH AMERICA

① Pacific Coast Highway

LOCATION US **START/FINISH** Los Angeles/San Francisco
DISTANCE 732 km (455 miles) **TIME** 1–6 days **ROAD CONDITIONS** Good **INFORMATION** www.visittheusa.com/trip/pacific-coast-highway-road-trip

Stretching between LA and San Francisco, the Pacific Coast Highway has some of the most enchanting oceanside scenery in the world, blending surf beaches, towering cliffs, rustic towns and a host of wildlife, from otters to elephant seals.

A drive along the Pacific Coast Highway is the stuff of classic road-trip dreams: cruising alongside the glittering ocean, soaking up the warmth of the sun and feeling the kiss of salty sea air on your face. The coast opens up almost as soon as you leave LA, with the arid hills and canyons of Malibu seeming to crumple into the vastness of the ocean. Soon, the mountains begin to fall away, signalling your arrival at Santa Barbara, an affluent seaside city of Spanish colonial-style buildings with red-tiled roofs and white stucco walls. The highway hugs the city's palm-lined beaches along a gently curving bay, continuing past more tempting stretches of sand to Gaviota, where you can bathe in soothing hot springs.

> The highway hugs the city's palm-lined beaches along a gently curving bay

91

BY ROAD
NORTH AMERICA

From Gaviota, you cut inland through a mostly dry landscape of rolling hills, where detours to the small Danish town of Solvang and the Santa Ynez wine country offer a break from the endless blue of the Pacific. You hit the coast again at Pismo Beach, "clam capital of the world", crammed with classic American diners cooking up the delicious mollusks in chowders and stews, or deep-fried. To the north, the turrets and domes of Hearst Castle glitter in the sun, clearly visible from the highway. Perched in the hills a short drive inland, this was once the opulent home of newspaper tycoon William Randolph Hearst. Nearby, at Piedras Blancas, huge elephant seals with rubbery noses loll on the sand, their deep bellows echoing across the beach.

If you thought the scenery was good so far, just wait for the next stretch of road through Big Sur. Here, the coastal mountain ranges seem to collapse into the ocean, the highway wriggling high above jagged-edged cliffs and through dense redwood forests. The road

| At Piedras Blancas, huge elephant seals with rubbery noses loll on the sand |

Right One of Pismo Beach's many seafood restaurants
Below A hillside vineyard in Santa Ynez

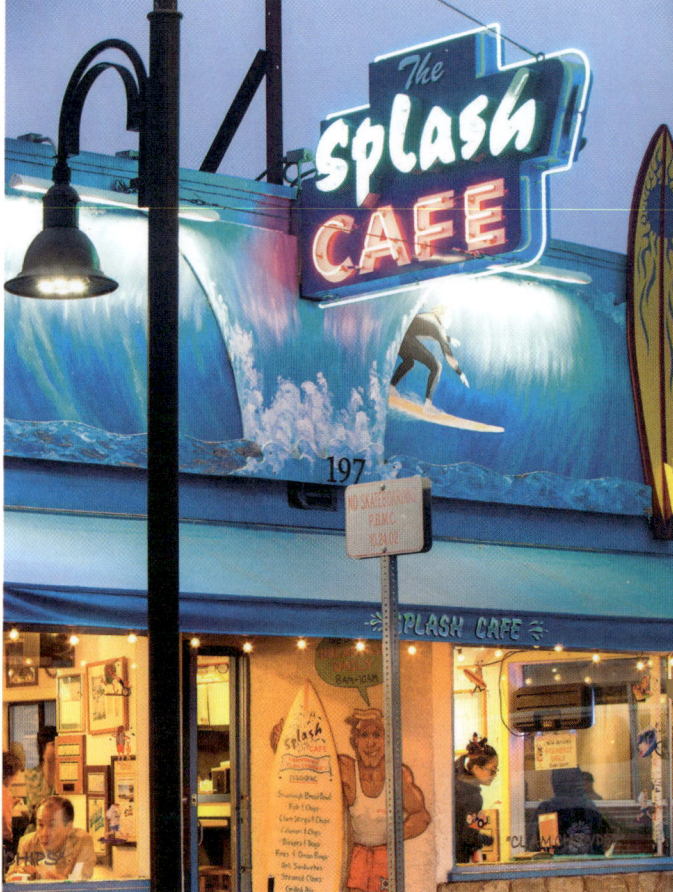

CATCH the surf at **Half Moon Bay**

EXPLORE the forested gullies and remote beaches of **Big Sur**

SEE elephant seals lounging at **Piedras Blancas**

MAKE a pilgrimage to the **Santa Ynez** wine region, inspiration for the movie Sideways (2004)

another way

If you don't fancy driving, go by train on Amtrak's daily Coast Starlight service. Linking LA with Seattle, it follows the Pacific Coast for most of its route and is especially scenic north of Los Angeles and Santa Barbara.

winds its way through a patchwork of state parks, which are laced with appealing hiking trails and pretty cascades, and pristine beaches where whales and otters frolic off the coast. Big Sur ends with a bang at Point Lobos State Natural Reserve, graced with trails rich in birdlife and craggy granite pinnacles reaching into rugged blue coves.

North of Point Lobos, the highway cuts through the rocky promontory and gnarled cypress trees of the Monterey Peninsula. This area is peppered with charming seaside towns, including Carmel, with its ornate 18th-century Spanish Mission, and sleepy Pacific Grove, known for its wooden Victorian architecture and winter flocks of orange-and-black monarch butterflies. Monterey itself is dripping with history, from Spanish adobe homes to Steinbeck's Cannery Row, a restored area of weathered tuna factories now housing shops and a huge aquarium.

The final stretch of highway passes cooler, storm-wracked beaches, artsy Santa Cruz and surfing hotspot Half Moon Bay, eventually hitting San Francisco on its quieter western side. The road here winds through a final bank of hills before suddenly dropping down to the Golden Gate and its famous russet-red bridge, often shrouded in fog. It's the end of this journey – though the road goes on, north over the bridge, to Oregon, and to Canada beyond.

CALIFORNIA'S SPANISH MISSIONS

This drive passes some of California's most famous Catholic Missions. Starting in 1769, early Spanish colonizers built a chain of 21 missions from San Diego to Sonoma, nine of them established by padre (and now saint) Junípero Serra. These include the Mission San Diego de Alcalá and Carmel Mission, where Serra is buried.

BY ROAD
NORTH AMERICA

②
Overseas Highway

COUNTRY US **START/FINISH** Key Largo/Key West **DISTANCE** 182 km (113 miles) **TIME** 1–4 days **ROAD CONDITIONS** Excellent **INFORMATION** www.fla-keys.com

Linking mainland Florida with a quirky subtropical island chain, the Overseas Highway cruises over giant causeways and bridges to fun-loving Key West.

The Overseas Highway began life as a railway, but the line was abandoned after the the Labor Day Hurricane of 1935. Today, the route is one of the US's most interesting roads. Your journey begins in Key Largo, a pancake-flat landscape of quiet creeks and dense, emerald-green mangroves, just a short hop from mainland Florida. From here, the highway soars over vivid aquamarine channels and the sea falls away on both sides to the horizon – only tiny patches of green mark out islands in the distance, making it feel as if you're driving into the heart of the ocean. Dark shadows flicker below, as sharks and manta rays slip between the concrete pillars of the highway.

South of Key Largo is Islamorada, a string of narrow, low-slung coral islands famed for fishing and fine seafood. Workaday Marathon island – a bustling pit stop of simple stores and conch shacks – is up next, followed by the epic Seven Mile Bridge. On the far side, Bahia Honda serves up the islands' best beaches, while Big Pine Key is home to delightfully tame deer. The final section of highways winds through ever busier islands to Key West, the end of the line and the home of sportfishing enthusiasts and raucous bars. Here, the tropical sun plummets into the deep dark blue, shooting radiant fingers across the evening sky.

The Overseas Highway, passing through mangrove trees in the Florida Keys

Travelling west on Route 66 through the Mojave Desert at sunset

Route 66

COUNTRY US **START/FINISH** Chicago/Los Angeles **DISTANCE** 3,940 km (2,448 miles) **TIME** 1–2 weeks **ROAD CONDITIONS** Good **INFORMATION** www.national66.org

Few journeys are as iconic as a road trip across America on Route 66, the original transcontinental highway.

Steeped in legend, the "Mother Road" is an enduring symbol of the classic American West. Although Route 66 was officially decommissioned in 1985, its path can still be traced via a blend of county roads, interstate highways and scenic byways. The route begins in Illinois, slicing southwest through rich farmland. It then crosses the swirling waters of the Mississippi at St Louis, before skirting the densely wooded Ozarks in Missouri. Heading into Oklahoma, Route 66 offers a hefty dose of 1950s nostalgia, lined with diners, quirky Americana and rustic red barns. Vast fields of corn and wheat dominate the Texas Panhandle, while New Mexico brings wilder, more mountainous terrain. Retro architectural icons pepper the deserts of Arizona and California's Mojave, giving a taste of the West Coast cool that awaits in the LA basin, where you're greeted by the stirring sight of the shimmering Pacific beyond.

GET YOUR KICKS

Established in 1926, Route 66 soon became America's most famous highway – as eulogized by Nat King Cole's 1946 hit "(Get Your Kicks on) Route 66". It was removed from the US Highway System in 1985, but revival associations soon emerged, and today the route is kept alive by sporadic "Historic Route 66" markers.

BY ROAD
NORTH AMERICA

④
TransAmerica Trail

LOCATION US **START/FINISH** Ripley/La Crescent
DISTANCE 8,000 km (5,000 miles) **TIME** 25 days minimum
ROAD CONDITIONS Mostly off-pavement travel (dual-sport motorcycle or a 4WD vehicle required) **INFORMATION** www.transamtrail.com

America's biggest motorbike adventure, the TransAmerica Trail snakes across the mountains, plains and deserts of the US on mostly empty dirt roads. It's a gargantuan ride that rewards endurance and skill with star-filled skies and rarely seen vistas.

Riding through the spectacular desert landscape in Utah

TAKE *in the otherworldly landscapes of* **Craters of the Moon National Monument**

La Crescent

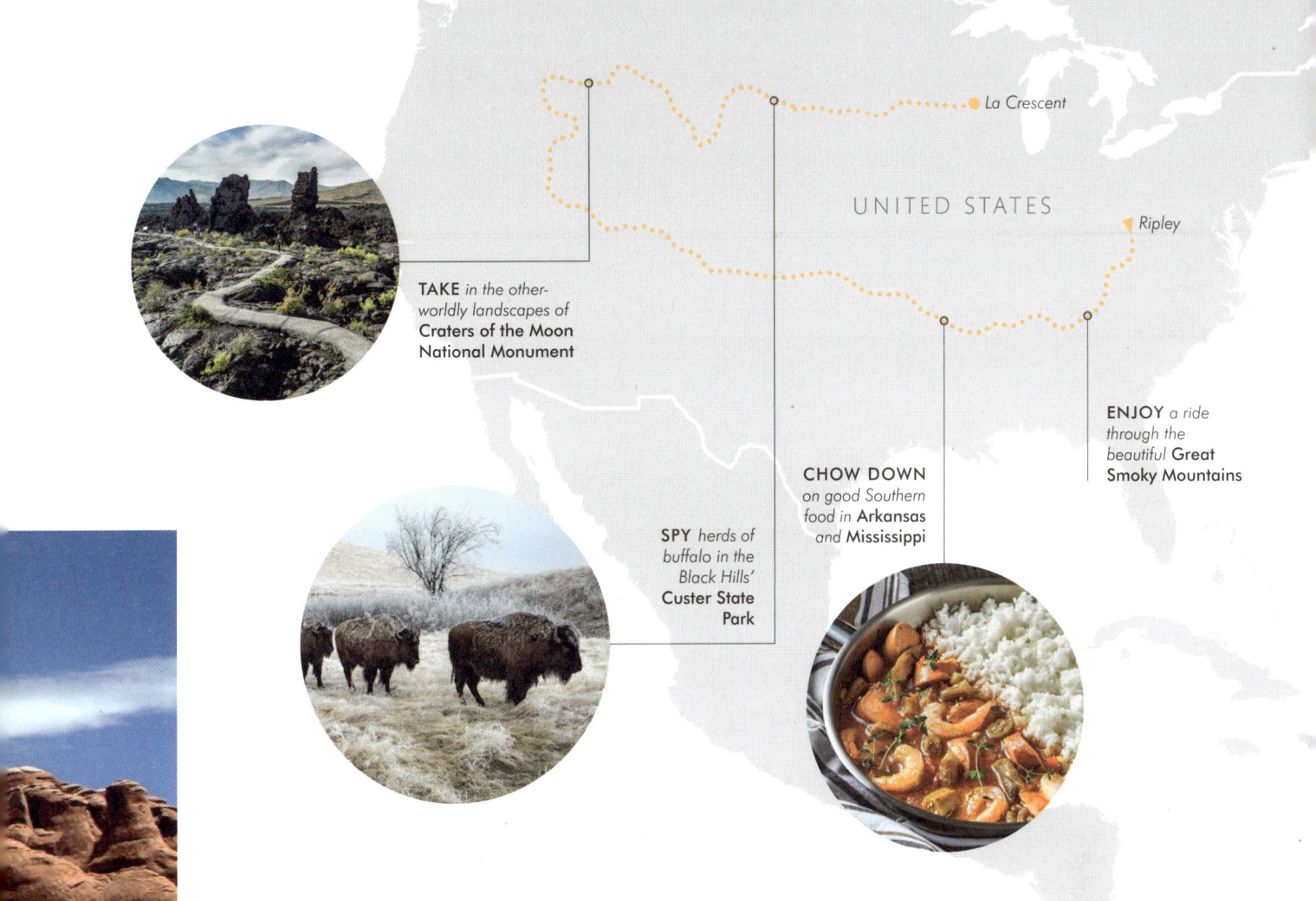

UNITED STATES

Ripley

ENJOY *a ride through the beautiful* **Great Smoky Mountains**

CHOW DOWN *on good Southern food in* **Arkansas** *and* **Mississippi**

SPY *herds of buffalo in the Black Hills'* **Custer State Park**

Riding the TransAmerica Trail means getting off the highways and connecting with the country's rural byways and backlands. Trees smothered in creeping green kudzu plants, apple orchards, wildflowers, junkyards and farm stalls – it's the small things that make this journey so unique. There are streams to ford and twisting trails through dense forests; red clay dirt roads in Mississippi, home to herds of white-tailed deer that scamper through the trees; and catfish pounds and water-logged rice fields over in Arkansas. At times you'll pass small farming towns and villages, as well as the odd wind-blown gas station and roadside shack selling fresh fruit and even barbecue, but often you'll be alone for miles, travelling down long, straight roads across the Great Plains, or circling sapphire-blue lakes and climbing craggy peaks in the Rockies. Utah is especially awe-inspiring, with vast stretches of arid badlands, broiling hot deserts and shimmering salt flats. In Idaho, potato farms really do run to the horizon, and you'll also pass through the desolate lava landscape of Craters of the Moon. Old barns, grain towers and pumpjacks dot the landscape out West, along with huge herds of slow-moving cattle and sprinting pronghorn. The trail is at its most magical at dawn or dusk – snow-topped mountains glisten, while fields of wheat and straw gleam gold, the whole horizon blazing with pink and red.

97

Blue Ridge Parkway

Above The Blue Ridge Parkway, fringed by golden forest in autumn
Below Mabry Mill, a watermill in Virginia

LOCATION US **START/FINISH** Rockfish Gap/Oconaluftee **DISTANCE** 755 km (469 miles) **TIME** 3–7 days **ROAD CONDITIONS** Good, some tight bends on stretches **INFORMATION** www.blueridgeparkway.org

Driving the serpentine Blue Ridge Parkway is best in the autumn, when the trees that cover the Appalachian Mountains erupt in a blaze of gold, copper and ruby-red.

There are traces of the American East's history and traditions scattered all along the Blue Ridge Highway – old gristmills, weathered wooden barns and no-frills roadside shacks serving up barbecued pork – but nature is the real star here.

At first, the highway meanders through northern Virginia where the Blue Ridge – part of the Appalachian Mountains – is sometimes reduced to a narrow ledge not much wider than the road. The central section is much less dramatic: the land is heavily farmed, and you share the highway with local traffic, especially around the city of Roanoke.

The most captivating part of the highway is the final segment in North Carolina. Here, the road is an asphalt ribbon slicing through the forest, snaking past glittering waterfalls and into a rugged landscape rich in Cherokee folklore. As you reach the top of a ridge, wide vistas open up across those famous hazy blue ridges: vast swathes of hickory, dogwood and birch, and groves of mountain ash bursting with vivid orange berries.

BY ROAD
NORTH AMERICA

6

Hana Highway

LOCATION US **START/FINISH** Kahului/Hana
DISTANCE 84 km (52 miles) **TIME** 2–4 hours
ROAD CONDITIONS Well-maintained, but lots of tight bends **INFORMATION** www.gohawaii.com

Few road trips can match the rugged beauty of Maui's northeast coast, with its mist-shrouded cliffs and jungle-smothered peaks.

Leaving Kahului, the road to Hana starts tamely enough, wriggling along a flat plain between dense sugar-cane plantations and white-sand beaches. The real twists and turns begin after Twin Falls – a winding road of blind corners, one-lane bridges and steep drop-offs. Tiny stalls, such as the Halfway to Hana Stand, tempt drivers to pause with their warm banana bread, handmade jewellery and fragrant flowers. Groves of "rainbow trees", with multicolored bark, stand guard over the road as it snakes around Honomanu Bay, before sweeping across the Ke'anae headland.

From here, drivers cut inland to a panoramic overlook over the farms of the Wailua Valley, the ocean and snaggletooth mountains looming above. Beyond the old stone bridge across the Upper Waikani Falls, the road becomes shrouded in a dense canopy of tropical trees and vegetation. Eventually, the car emerges into the light, passing small stores, homes and farms as the road continues into Hana itself – a small town looking out on the ocean, seemingly at the very end of the world.

"RAINBOW TREES"

Maui is home to groves of multi-hued rainbow eucalyptus. The bark of these "rainbow trees" shows shades of light blue, lavender, green, orange and red. Native to the Philippines, Indonesia and Papua New Guinea, the trees are thought to have been introduced to Hawaii in 1929 and have thrived here ever since.

Upper Waikani Falls, also known as the Three Bears Falls due to their differing heights

BY ROAD
NORTH AMERICA

Jasper

MARVEL at the **Athabasca Falls**, *transformed into striking ice formations during the winter months*

HIKE *up the trail from the Bow Summit parking area for a bird's eye view of the stunning* **Peyto Lake**

STAY *at the historic lakefront* **Num-Ti-Jah Lodge**

Lake Louise

CANADA
Icefields Parkway

(7) Icefields Parkway

LOCATION Canada **START/FINISH** Lake Louise/Jasper **DISTANCE** 232 km (144 miles) **TIME** 2 days **ROAD CONDITIONS** Winter tyres required Nov–Apr **INFORMATION** www.icefieldsparkway.com; National Park pass required, purchase at park kiosks

Every curve of this route unveils astonishing scenery: jewel-coloured lakes, sweeping evergreen valleys and ancient glaciers. So fuel up, put on several layers of clothing and head out on an incredible adventure.

Following the double-lane Highway 93 North, the Icefields Parkway winds through two national parks – Banff and Jasper – in the Canadian Rocky Mountains, where peaks easily reach a staggering 3,800 m (12,467 ft). Accessible for most of the year, this superb stretch of road has plenty of lay-bys to take in jaw-dropping views, or to reach hiking trails to thundering waterfalls and picnic spots alongside turquoise lakes. The alpine environment here harbours elusive cougar and regal elk, and mountain goats casually trotting along absurdly dangerous cliffs. Make sure to keep a watchful eye out for bears foraging along the edges of the highway.

Besides the wildlife and the splendid grandeur of the Rockies, this route's star attraction is the Columbia Icefield, one of the largest masses of glacial ice on earth, resembling a frozen river slowly inching down for over 25 km (15.5 miles) between walls of sky-high mountains. Hundreds of metres deep, this mighty flow feeds several large glaciers that in turn supply major rivers, crucial to surrounding ecosystems. Between Jasper and Lake Louise, the Icefield Discovery Centre has exhibits on the icefield, and offers further exploration via snowcoaches, sturdy all-terrain tour buses equipped with huge snow tyres.

Driving through the snow beside the monumental Rocky Mountains in Banff National Park

BY ROAD
NORTH AMERICA

Sea to Sky Highway

Above Admiring the view from the top of Whistler's ski slopes **Above right** *The Sea to Sky Highway skirting along Howe Sound*

LOCATION Canada **START/FINISH** Vancouver/Whistler **DISTANCE** 120 km (75 miles) **TIME** 2 hours **ROAD CONDITIONS** Winter tyres required Oct–Mar **INFORMATION** www.tourismvancouver.com

While it may only take a few hours to drive, there are so many points of interest along the Sea to Sky Highway that it's best to take it slow, soaking up the fjords, forests and frosty scenes.

The Sea to Sky Highway – as Highway 99 is known – begins with a bang. Leaving behind the glittering high-rises of Vancouver, the first glimpse of Canada's bountiful natural assets is granted by Lions Gate Bridge. Spanning high across the Burrard Inlet, the bridge offers drive-by views of pods of orcas swimming in the briny waters below.

Carrying on past the snug seaside village of Horseshoe Bay, the highway traces the rocky edge of Howe Sound, a sparkling deep-blue ocean fjord. Park up at Porteau Cove Provincial Park to go scuba diving in the frigid waters, scouring shipwrecks for clever octopuses and other marine life. Back on the road, a massive granite dome, named the Stawamus Chief, comes into view. Rock climbers spider up its sheer face as drivers glide below. The highway then briefly descends into the former mill town of Squamish – the perfect place to grab a bite to eat. Refuelled, roll down your windows as you continue north to feel the cool forest breeze.

In its last scenic stretch, the highway wends its way gently up to the famed ski resort town of Whistler, passing through a subalpine landscape of glacier-fed lakes and wide meadows where deer and black bears are often spotted. After setting off at sea level, the road is now a little closer to the sky.

BY ROAD
NORTH AMERICA

⑨
Dempster Highway

LOCATION Canada **START/FINISH** Dawson City/Inuvik **DISTANCE** 740 km (460 miles) **TIME** 4 days **ROAD CONDITIONS** Challenging; closed during the spring and autumn break-up and freeze-up of the Peel and Mackenzie rivers **INFORMATION** www.dempsterhighway.com

The only Canadian road that crosses the Arctic Circle, this historic gravel highway stretches unrelentingly north through an extraordinary subarctic realm.

The Dempster Highway roughly traces an old Canadian North-West Mounted Police winter dog sled route that was used for patrolling during the rowdy gold-mining days of the 1890s. From Dawson City, the road veers through the wide Klondike River Valley, the original source of the gold rush. Nowadays, the only gold seen here is in autumn when the valley's tundra landscape transforms into a fiery mosaic of yellows, reds and oranges.

This is not a road for the casual driver. There are rivers to cross – either by ferry or an ice bridge during the long winter months – and tyres often explode under the pressure of the road, with hardly any passersby to stop and help. Hours pass by in a meditative state as the lonely road crosses vast swathes of open tundra. But there are signs of life – mobs of prehistoric-looking musk oxen roam under the midnight sun, cunning grey wolves trail behind herds of caribou, and beluga whales share a chirpy chat in the Mackenzie River.

JACK LONDON

The Klondike River was fictionalized in several of American writer Jack London's novels, including *The Call of the Wild* (1903) and *White Fang* (1906). London joined the Klondike Gold Rush trail in 1897 when he was just 21. He died at the age of 40 due to complications from scurvy developed in the goldfields.

Caribou crossing the snow-covered Dempster Highway as they migrate to their wintering grounds

Pan-American Highway

LOCATION US to Argentina **START/FINISH** Alaska/Tierra del Fuego
DISTANCE 30,000 km (19,000 miles) **TIME** 9 months–2 years
ROAD CONDITIONS Variable; challenging in the far south
INFORMATION Check travel advice for individual countries

Stretching from the Arctic Circle to the tip of South America – and passing through at least 14 different countries, two continents and countless different landscapes along the way – the Pan-American Highway is quite simply the most epic road trip on earth.

Polar bears and sloths, tropical beaches and Arctic tundra, ghost towns and megacities. The world's driest non-polar desert, longest continental mountain range, highest capitals, and most southerly city. An array of UNESCO World Heritage Sites, including the pre-Columbian pyramids at Teotihuacán, the engineering triumph of the Panama Canal, and the mysterious geoglyphs of the ancient Nazca Lines. How can any other road trip compete with the superlative Pan-American Highway?

BY ROAD
NORTH AMERICA

Left Snowy Alaskan scenery along the first stretch of the Pan-American Highway
Above The mysterious Nazca Lines at the side of the road in Peru

Despite its name, the highway is actually a network of interconnected roads, with innumerable options for detours, side trips and diversions, making no two journeys along the route the same. Remarkably, given its length, only two sections of the highway are not drivable. The lawless Darién Gap – the thick, mountainous jungle that separates southern Panama from northwestern Colombia – must be bypassed by boat or plane, and the choppy Strait of Magellan dividing mainland Patagonia from the Tierra del Fuego archipelago has to be crossed on a car ferry. Otherwise, the rest of the journey is by road.

Most people attempting to drive the whole route set off from Prudhoe Bay, which sits at the northern tip of Alaska, inside the Arctic Circle. Cities as varied as Los Angeles, Mexico City, Medellín, Quito, Lima, Santiago and Buenos Aires provide plenty of distractions on the way south, but the ever-shifting landscape is the biggest draw. The first international border crossing takes you into the Yukon, the westernmost part of Canada, a rugged, sparsely populated wilderness. Down in Mexico, the route passes through the thickly forested hills of Chiapas, a state rich in indigenous cultures and colonial-era architecture. Later, in Costa Rica, it bisects the dry savannah of Guanacaste province, before cutting through the lush, biodiverse rainforests of the Zona Sur region.

THE HISTORY OF THE HIGHWAY

A continuous overland route between North and South America was first proposed by the US in the late 19th century. The initial plan was to build a railway, but instead governments agreed to build a highway (or, rather, a series of highways) in 1937. The first section was completed in Mexico in the 1950s.

105

Alaska

GET A TASTE of the Arctic in **Alaska**

SPOT bears, gold-rush relics and the Northern Lights in the **Yukon**

VISIT Los Angeles, Hollywood's glitzy home

CALL IN at **Mexico City**, which blends the modern with the historic

EXPLORE an alien landscape of volcanoes, salt flats and geysers in Chile's **Atacama Desert**

TRAVEL along Ecuador's majestic **Avenue of the Volcanoes**

STOP OFF in **Buenos Aires**, Argentina's elegant, engaging capital, the "Paris of the south"

EXPERIENCE one of the world's last great wildernesses in **Patagonia** and **Tierra del Fuego**

Tierra del Fuego

106

BY ROAD
NORTH AMERICA

If the idea of spending so much time on the road makes you balk, stick to Central America, taking in the diverse nations between Mexico and Colombia. But it'll be a challenge in itself to stop and leave it at that, when South America lies just beyond the next bend in the road, luring you onwards. Who can resist Ecuador's Avenue of Volcanoes – a series of valleys between two branches of the Andes featuring seven peaks over 5,182 m (17,000 ft) – or Chile's Atacama Desert – an otherworldly land of salt flats, high-altitude geyser fields, huge sand dunes, pre-Hispanic ruins, and flamingo-filled lakes?

Eventually, many months or even years after setting off from Alaska, drivers pull into the isolated city of Ushuaia on the Beagle Channel, barely 1,000 km (620 miles) north of Antarctica. Down at the port a sign proudly proclaims that you have reached "El Fin del Mundo" – The End of the World. While this may not be strictly true – there are actually a couple of small settlements slightly further south in the Chilean part of Tierra de Fuego – the city certainly feels like a fitting finale to the Pan-American Highway.

another way

There are myriad ways to customize your journey: one option is to continue south from Santiago in Chile and connect with the Carretera Austral (Southern Highway); another is to branch north from Buenos Aires in Argentina, travel through Uruguay and head to Brazil.

Below Driving through the Atacama Desert, Chile
Right Colourful church spires in Ushuaia, at the southern tip of the highway

107

BY ROAD
NORTH AMERICA

Union General Sickles' headquarters at the Gettysburg National Battlefield Park, Pennsylvania

⑪ Civil War Battlefields

LOCATION US **START/FINISH** Gettysburg/Appomattox **DISTANCE** 520 km (323 miles) **TIME** 1 week **ROAD CONDITIONS** Good **INFORMATION** www.battlefields.org

This route takes in some of the most important memorials to the Civil War. Driving south through the pastures and cornfields of Pennsylvania, it's hard to imagine the desperate fighting that took place in 1863 at Gettysburg, and in 1862 at Antietam National Battlefield, site of the bloodiest one-day battle in US history. After passing through handsome Harpers Ferry – the site of John Brown's failed attempt to start a rebellion of enslaved people in 1859 – the route crosses into Virginia, where you can trace the paths of the Confederate and Union armies from the battlefields of Bull Run to Richmond, the Confederate capital. The final stretch of the trip runs deep into rural Virginia, past farms and groves of oak-hickory and pine. It ends where the war did: at the simple Appomattox Court House where Confederate General Lee surrendered in 1865.

⑫ Kentucky Bourbon Trail

LOCATION US **START/FINISH** Louisville/Lexington **DISTANCE** 241 km (150 miles) **TIME** 4 days **ROAD CONDITIONS** Good **INFORMATION** https://kybourbontrail.com

The rich aromas of smoky wood and corn mash, dense forests of oak and hickory, and tempting no-frills barbecue shacks – welcome to Kentucky bourbon country. This tour of the state's finest distilleries begins in Louisville, home of the iconic Jim Beam, before continuing on to historic Bardstown, the "Bourbon Capital of the World". Here lie the grand red-brick premises of Barton 1792 Distillery, homely Heaven Hill and elegantly contemporary Lux Row, which are all open for tastings (assuming there's a designated driver on hand). Further south, Maker's Mark Distillery sits in a sylvan landscape of gurgling creeks and shady lanes, providing a rustic contrast to the Spanish Mission-style Four Roses and scenic Wild Turkey distilleries in nearby Lawrenceburg. The final stretch of the tour passes through prime horse country, with a stop at Woodford Reserve Distillery before arriving at Lexington, America's horse-racing capital. Your journey ends here, with a final taste of bourbon – and fine Kentucky hospitality – at "brew-distillery" Town Branch.

WHAT IS KENTUCKY BOURBON?

Bourbon is American whiskey, usually defined as being made from sour mash comprising 51–80 per cent corn, with other grains making up the rest. "Straight" bourbon must be aged in brand-new charred oak barrels for a minimum of two years.

BY ROAD
NORTH AMERICA

⑬ Napa Valley Tour

LOCATION US **START/FINISH** Domaine Chandon/Charles Krug Winery **DISTANCE** 20 km (13 miles) **TIME** 1–3 days **ROAD CONDITIONS** Excellent **INFORMATION** www.napavalley.com

This short drive through the heart of Napa takes in the most famous wineries in the valley, all wrapped in endless fields of vines. Your tour begins with a pop at Domaine Chandon, the sparkling wine specialist in Yountville. The vineyard is set in beautifully landscaped grounds, with outdoor tasting rooms that look like sculpted wood tunnels. From here, you drive through the heart of the bright, sunlit Napa Valley, surrounded by vineyards and low-lying, emerald-green hills. The Robert Mondavi Winery resembles an elegant Spanish Mission, with low-slung buildings made to look like adobe. Nearby, and in stark contrast, film director Francis Ford Coppola's Inglenook Estate features a grand European-style chateau completed in 1887. Continuing north through ever more dense fields of grapes, you'll pass the Louis M Martini Winery with its stylish, modern premises, and Beringer Vineyards, home to Rhine House, a classic German-style chateau. The trail ends, fittingly, at the vast Charles Krug complex, Napa's oldest winery.

another way

Hike or bike the Napa Valley Vine Trail, an ambitious 47-mile (76-km) trail through the heart of Napa Valley, from Vallejo to Calistoga. Some of its ten sections have been built, but others are in various stages of construction; check www.vinetrail.org for the latest updates.

⑭ Cuban Drive

LOCATION Cuba **START/FINISH** Havana/Santiago de Cuba **DISTANCE** 804 km (499 miles) **TIME** 7–10 days **ROAD CONDITIONS** Good, but some potholes **INFORMATION** www.infotur.cu

Hit the road in a vintage convertible to take part in the rainbow parade of *yanqui* motors on Cuba's highways. The road trip begins in candy-coloured Havana, zipping east past glittering seas and powder-soft sands to the pulse of Afro-Cuban samba. It then plunges inland towards the lush Península de Zapata, rich in wildlife and revolutionary history, before tracing the coastline to Punta Perdiz, where the coral reef invites exploration below the waterline. Back in the driving seat, follow the snaking road past dusty villages, up through the university town of Santa Clara, and down the spine of the island. As the tarmac chips away under your tyres, Sierra Maestra's cloud-draped peaks rear up on the horizon, and the highway wriggles through a series of sharp bends before revealing the jaw-dropping sight of pristine beach after pristine beach, all the way to Santiago.

Two vintage convertibles cruising past the colourful architecture of downtown Havana

109

BY ROAD
CENTRAL AND SOUTH AMERICA

⑮
Che Trail

LOCATION Bolivia **START/FINISH** La Higuera/Vallegrande
DISTANCE 61 km (38 miles) **TIME** 1 day **ROAD CONDITIONS**
Steep and mountainous **INFORMATION** www.minculturas.gob.bo;
guide required to visit the memorials in Vallegrande

Trace the doomed final footsteps of Cuba's hero, Ernesto "Che" Guevara across the remote Bolivian countryside, where the truth of his death was once buried underground.

This journey is a drive through an important, but tragic, chapter in South America's history. It starts with death – the 1967 shooting of Che Guevara, who was killed in this desolate corner of Bolivia by the army after he failed to spark a revolution here. It's easy to dwell on this tragic event as you traverse the landscape of gorse and cacti, while ominous condors watch from overhead.

La Higuera's one-roomed schoolhouse, the site of the shooting, is the first stop on this trail. Outside, a large bust of Che stands sentinel, its stoic expression set against the cries for justice painted onto the walls of the hamlet's 17 adobe houses. A short drive down the valley, in the town of Vallegrande, impassioned murals lead to the hospital's laundry room, where Che's body was washed before burial. The room is now a makeshift shrine, the walls daubed with haphazard graffiti exalting the revolutionary leader. More artwork emblazons the dusty road that leads to the final stop: a mausoleum built over Che's unmarked grave. Here, there is time to pause and consider the life of an icon and a revolutionary.

CHE GUEVARA

Born Ernesto Guevara, "Che" was angered by the poverty he saw on a trip across South America. He became committed to overthrowing capitalism across the continent, and in 1953, he joined the successful guerrilla campaign to topple Cuban dictator Fulgencio Batista, becoming, in the process, a symbol of revolution.

The bust of Che Guevara standing guard in La Higuera, the site where he was shot

BY ROAD
CENTRAL AND SOUTH AMERICA

Above left Praia do Aventureiro, a beach on the island of Ilha Grande **Above right** Praça da Matriz in the town of Paraty

(16)
Costa Verde

LOCATION Brazil **START/FINISH** Itaguai/Santos **DISTANCE** 485 km (303 miles) **TIME** 2 days **ROAD CONDITIONS** Well-paved road; check for landslides and floods in Dec **INFORMATION** www.visitbrasil.com

Often called Brazil's most beautiful coastal route, the winding road that shadows the Costa Verde seems a world away from the country's traffic-clogged cities.

If you put your foot down and drove non-stop, you could motor along the BR101 highway, which shadows the Costa Verde, in about eight hours. But why do that, when this aptly named "Green Coast" is so packed with scenic wonders? Either start in the port city of Santos and head north to the outskirts of Rio, or vice versa, and take your time – Brazilian-style – soaking up the scenery slowly over a couple of days.

Looming high above the winding highway, the lush Atlantic Forest spills over granite peaks. Ceiba trees are draped with bromeliads and flowers embroider the overgrown banks. Whitewashed colonial churches stand guard over sleepy villages and roadside stalls sell sizzling grilled fish. Hundreds of offshore islands sprinkle the coastline, some of which are uninhabited, while others – such as Ilha Grande – are the haunt of jet-set millionaires. The unmissable highlight of the Costa Verde, however, is the historic port of Paraty. Situated midway along this stretch of coast, Paraty's cobblestoned lanes are lined with cafés and boutique *pousadas* (guesthouses), making it an idyllic spot to rest before hitting the road again, and heading back to the city hubbub.

BY ROAD
CENTRAL AND SOUTH AMERICA

SPOT *a remarkable hanging glacier in* **Parque Nacional Queulat**

HIKE *the world-renowned routes at* **Parque Nacional Torres del Paine**

FINISH *off in the friendly frontier town of* **Puerto Williams**

CALL IN *to* **Punta Arenas**, *a centre for sheep-ranching, gold-mining and shipping in the 19th century*

Puerto Montt

CHILE

ARGENTINA

Puerto Williams

(17)

Ruta de los Parques

LOCATION Chile **START/FINISH** Puerto Montt/Puerto Williams **DISTANCE** 2,736 km (1,700 miles) **TIME** 3–5 weeks **ROAD CONDITIONS** Varies; some sections are unpaved and require a high-clearance vehicle **INFORMATION** www.rutadelosparques.org

Sweeping through 17 national parks, the aptly named Ruta de los Parques (Route of Parks) takes in Andean peaks, icy fjords, lush forests and remote frontier settlements on its way from Patagonia to Tierra del Fuego.

The far south of Chile is a sparsely populated, awe-inspiring wilderness. Launched in 2018 following a massive donation of private land to the Chilean state, the Ruta de los Parques showcases the best of the region, and offers a great opportunity to support local initatives in sustainable tourism and wildlife conservation.

The route starts in the city of Puerto Montt and then follows the spectacular Carretera Austral (Southern Highway) through a diverse landscape of snow-topped mountains, smouldering volcanoes, great ice fields, expansive steppes and dense coniferous forests. At the southern end of the highway, the Chilean landmass fragments into an archipelago of islands and peninsulas, necessitating a magical ferry journey through iceberg-strewn fjords.

At the other side of the crossing is Puerto Natales, gateway to the trekking paradise of Parque Nacional Torres del Paine, and the beautiful city of Punta Arenas. Before you know it, you've reached the Strait of Magellan, where a ferry is again required to reach starkly beautiful Tierra del Fuego, home to Puerto Williams, the southernmost town on earth. Perched on the Beagle Channel, this is the end of the road.

Snow capped mountains around Lake Pehoe in Parque Nacional Torres del Paine

BY ROAD
EUROPE

⑱ Wild Atlantic Way

LOCATION Ireland **START/FINISH** Malin Head/Kinsale **DISTANCE** 2,600 km (1,600 miles) **TIME** 3 weeks **ROAD CONDITIONS** Entirely asphalted, but many narrow, winding, one-track sections, and challenging in poor weather
INFORMATION www.wildatlanticway.com

Tracing its way along Ireland's western coast, this epic road trip runs almost the entire length of the country. The views are dramatic, with Atlantic waves tumbling against sheer, craggy cliffs, while the towns and tiny villages that dot the route offer pockets of celebrated Irish charm.

Fanad Head lighthouse on the craggy north coast of County Donegal

TAKE IN the sheer crags of **Sliabh Liag**, the highest sea cliffs in Europe

SAMPLE the nightlife of **Galway** during festival season

SPOT whales and dolphins aboard a glass-bottomed boat tour from **Letterfrack Pier**

TRAMP down Hag's Head at the **Cliffs of Moher** for the best views of the shore

Malin Head

IRELAND

Kinsale

SIP a white-topped pint of Guinness in one of **Kinsale**'s cosy traditional pubs

A wind-buffeted peninsula where grass-carpeted rocks taper into the ocean, Malin Head is Ireland's northernmost tip and the starting point of your journey. From here, the road picks through the rugged headlands of Donegal, where megalithic monuments loom at every bend. The Way traces southward, along Ireland's "Surf Coast", with huge swells lashing beaches, such as Strandhill and Enniscrone. For those less keen to don a wetsuit and catch a wave, the region's pub-packed towns offer a cosier alternative..

As Sligo and Mayo fade from the back windscreen, the Way cuts sharply westward into Connemara. This district's name comes from the Gaelic meaning "inlets for the sea", and its coastline is laced with pretty coves and golden sandy bays. But the mellow scenery doesn't last long as the road rolls onwards into Clare and Kerry, passing dizzying cliffs and the sprawling karst landscape of the Burren, on its way to Ireland's most westerly point. Accents grow thicker and more musical, and the tiny seaside towns ever more colourful and picturesque around you. Here, the Way meanders gently along the southerly coast of Cork, threading past historic castles and fringed by rolling green fields until it reaches Kinsale. With its rainbow-hued houses and narrow streets, this gourmet hotspot is the perfect place to end your Irish adventure.

Boats moored in Kinsale's picturesque harbour, surrounded by rolling green hills

The Scottish Highlands

Above The road through Glencoe
Below The town of Stirling, overlooked by its historic castle

LOCATION UK **START/FINISH** Perth/Stirling **DISTANCE** 640 km (400 miles) **TIME** 5 days **ROAD CONDITIONS** Good; heavy snow is a risk from Jan–late-Mar **INFORMATION** www.visitscotland.com

Summer is the best time for a meandering road trip around the Highlands, when the last snows have vanished from the high tops and days are long. Set off on a drive through ever-changing landscapes that are by turns gently green and breathtakingly dramatic.

Bidding farewell to the tidy lowlands of Tayside at the city of Perth, the high road to the north tracks the River Tay upstream through beech forest and birchwoods. Striking the Grampian Mountains, the tarmac slants along the River Spey, beneath the conifer-cloaked slopes of the Cairngorm massif.

From Inverness – the capital of the Highlands – the road curves along the silvery Beauly Firth before plunging into heathery countryside, where red deer roam and red kites wheel overhead. Back inland, the Five Sisters ridge looms on the horizon like giant knuckles, on the way to the Great Glen. This mighty rift valley sweeps you back to the west coast and Ben Nevis, Britain's highest peak, which towers above the seal-haunted Atlantic inlet Loch Linnhe. At the head of the fated valley of Glencoe – in 1692 the scene of an infamous massacre of a clan who had failed to pledge timely allegiance to the new King William III – the road turns to sweep across a vast expanse of lochans, trickling burns and peat bog stretching to the eastern horizon. There's a stark transition from this desolate terrain with its big skies to gentler landscapes as the road wends its way through the green hills of the Trossachs to Stirling and its mighty castle, once known as "the key to the kingdom of Scotland".

BY ROAD
EUROPE

(20)

Cotswolds

LOCATION UK **START/FINISH** Stratford upon Avon/Winchcombe
DISTANCE 100 km (64 miles) **TIME** 1 day **ROAD CONDITIONS**
Good **INFORMATION** www.cotswolds.com

This rambling journey takes you through one of the most picturesque corners of England, with honey-hued villages, winding narrow roads and rolling green fields.

The Cotswolds' villages are often described as "chocolate-box" because they resemble the picture-perfect scenes depicted on confectionary packaging. Decide for yourself whether these much-touted settlements deserve so much acclaim on this drive through the Cotsworld Hills. Leaving Stratford upon Avon behind – birthplace of England's great bard, William Shakespeare – the road rolls along the River Avon, through the Vale of Evesham, where springtime lambs gambol in grassy pastures. But the Cotswolds really begin at Chipping Campden, the first of the area's golden-stone settlements. There's Great Tew, a quintessentially quaint village of ivy-covered thatched cottages set in rose-filled gardens, and Stow-on-the-Wold, which has been a hub since medieval times, as well as countless pretty hamlets. The age-old clutter of half-timbered shops, oak-beamed pubs and inns of Winchcombe provide the grand finale of your tour through England's loveliest villages.

> A quintessentially quaint village of ivy-covered thatched cottages

Sheep beside St James' Church, Chipping Campden

BY ROAD
EUROPE

㉑ Via Emilia

LOCATION Italy **START/FINISH** Parma/Ravenna **DISTANCE** 176 km (109 miles) **TIME** 2 hours **ROAD CONDITIONS** Good **INFORMATION** www.emiliaromagnaturismo.com

As you motor along the ancient Via Emilia, you can almost smell the sweet aromas of the region's culinary treats wafting through the air. Leaving behind the town of Parma, famous for its nutty prosciutto, the route meanders through rolling vineyards before reaching Reggio Emilia, the charming Renaissance city that is the birthplace of Parmigiano Reggiano. The road continues east, revealing sleepy traditional villages in between the foodie cities. Picturesque Modena packs a punch with its rich balsamic vinegar and sparkling Lambrusco wine, while the lively trattorias of Bologna serve up some of Italy's most succulent fare, including mouth-watering *tagliatelle al ragù*. The ancient city of Ravenna heralds the end of this road trip, where churches and monuments, bursting at the seams with spectacular 5th- and 6th-century mosaics, are a feast, this time for the eyes alone.

A typical shop selling traditional produce, including pasta, cured meats and parmesan, in Bologna

㉒ The Basque Circuit

LOCATION Spain **START/FINISH** Bilbao (loop) **DISTANCE** 387 km (240 miles) **TIME** 5 days **ROAD CONDITIONS** Some narrow, twisting roads **INFORMATION** www.tourism.euskadi.eus

On this drive through the diverse landscapes of the Basque Country, you'll grip the wheel with white knuckles on spiralling mountain pavements one minute, and glide along stately coastal corniches above dashing resorts the next.

Leaving the modern architecture of Bilbao in the rear-view mirror, you climb through wooded highlands to the mountain stronghold of Vitoria-Gasteiz. Vultures circle above the limestone massifs as you zoom into Navarre and down into the valley of Pamplona – the medieval capital of the Basque Kingdom. Towering evergreen oaks and lithe birches line the deeply forested mountains, where the hairpin turns leading to the coast make the AP-15 road one of the top technical driving challenges in Europe.

The rollercoaster descent ends in sumptuous San Sebastian, whose epicurean bars are worth every drop of adrenaline. Ready to hit the road again? Sinuous bluff-top roads along the Basque coast sport plenty of scenic spots where you can get out of the car to let the sun warm your face. Don't miss the chance to watch championship surfers ride the famous left-hand break to the sandy beach in Mundaka, before zigzagging along small inland roads to return to Bilbao.

another way

At the opposite end of Spain from the Basque Circuit is the Pueblos Blancos drive. Some of Spain's most dramatic mountain scenery marks the road from Ronda through Algodonales and Zahara de la Sierra, then west to Arcos de la Frontera.

The Atlantic Ocean Road, snaking between islands in a series of bridges

(23) Provence

LOCATION France **START/FINISH** Orange/Les Saintes Maries-de-la-Mer **DISTANCE** 240 km (150 miles) **TIME** 1 week **ROAD CONDITIONS** Excellent **INFORMATION** www.arlestourisme.com

France's deep south is magical in late summer, when the hills are filled with the scent of pine and the vines are heavy with plump purple grapes. The final product of these serried ranks of green and gold vines can be sampled in Châteauneuf-du-Pape, at the heart of the wine region that bears its name. But it's not all vineyards and wineries; this is a route of contrasting parts.

Near Cavaillon, fertile plains give way to the steep foothills of the Petit Luberon. The route then winds its way beneath the limestone mini-sierra of the Alpilles to Arles – forever associated with Vincent van Gogh who immortalized the surrounding patchwork quilt of sunflower fields in paint. The biggest change of scene comes when the road plunges into Camargue – a unique pocket of wilderness stalked by bulls, horses and flamingos – before finally arriving on the shore of the Mediterranean at Les Saintes Maries-de-la-Mer.

(24) Atlantic Ocean Road

LOCATION Norway **START/FINISH** Vevang/Kårvåg **DISTANCE** 8 km (5 miles) **TIME** 3 hours **ROAD CONDITIONS** Winding, blind bends **INFORMATION** www.nasjonaleturistveger.no

Resembling the mighty sea serpent Jörmungandr from ancient Norse mythology, the Atlantic Road links the tiny islands and skerries of Eide and Averøy to the mainland via eight curving bridges. In summer, the twisted route glitters with golden light, while in storm season, wrathful waves crash onto the roadway.

Hailed as the construction of the 20th century, this spine-tingling 8-km (5-mile) stretch of County Road 64 leaves the mainland at the tiny village Vevang and plunges out into open water. The journey's untamed oceanic beauty builds in intensity with every bridge until Storseisund – the longest and most gravity-defying arch, where the road soars skyward before plummeting down towards Kårvåg, a savage stretch of water where many a ship has been lost. With these ocean views, it's no wonder that County Road 64 has become known as the Atlantic Ocean Road.

Iceland's Ring Road

The aurora borealis over Dettifoss waterfall in Vatnajökull National Park

LOCATION Iceland **START/FINISH** Reykjavík (loop) **DISTANCE** 1,332 km (828 miles) **TIME** 1–2 weeks **ROAD CONDITIONS** 4WD required **INFORMATION** www.guidetoiceland.is

Forget visions of a bland motorway: this two-lane road circles otherworldly landscapes home to mythical beasts, wild reindeer and Game of Thrones *settings galore.*

Precipitous waterfalls, shaggy-fringed horses, black-sand beaches studded with diamond-bright ice chunks, and whales cavorting in blue seas – all are on show on this epic road trip. Connecting the inhabited fringes of the island, Iceland's Ring Road – or Route One – is riddled with so many alluring detours that the length of a trip can easily double. Driving here is akin to being led through a fairy tale, where travellers voyage through ice-gnarled peaks, ragged fjords and grumbling volcanoes. Explore Grjótagjá, a hot spring inside a cave that featured in *Game of Thrones*, and pit your windpipes against the roar of Dettifoss, Europe's most powerful waterfall. You might even spy a giant lake monster at Egilsstaðir, home of the legendary Lagarfljot Worm.

There's plenty more to enjoy beyond the nature, including gorging on langoustine at the annual

BY ROAD
EUROPE

SET ASIDE a few days for first-rate humpback sightings at **Húsavík** – Iceland's whale-watching capital

BUBBLE away in the hot waters of **Lake Myvatn** geothermal nature baths

ADMIRE views of the capital city of **Reykjavík** from the top of **Hallgrimskirkja** church

ICELAND

Reykjavík

TAKE a detour to the beautiful town of **Seyðisfjörður**, home to a thriving art scene

lobster festival in Höfn and studying up on Snorri Sturluson, the famous Viking poet, in Reykholt. This route also gives travellers a chance to mingle with Icelanders, whether wandering tiny hamlets like Vik, sharing prayers beneath Hofskirkja's turf-roofed church, or partying in Akureyri, the capital of the north.

another way

The 306-km (190-mile) Golden Circle loop, taking in Iceland's three main natural attractions – Geysir Geothermal Area, Gullfoss Waterfall and Þingvellir National Park – can easily be added to the Ring Route as a half-day detour from Hveragerði.

Surveying the dramatic black-sand beach at Reynisfjara, just outside Vik

121

BY ROAD
EUROPE

Grossglockner High Alpine Road

LOCATION Austria **START/FINISH** Heiligenblut/Fusch an der Glocknerstrasse **DISTANCE** 48 km (30 miles) **TIME** 1 hour each way **ROAD CONDITIONS** Paved road; open early May–early Nov **INFORMATION** www.grossglockner.at

One of Europe's most spectacular paved roads, this looping route climbs upwards in a never-ending succession of serpentine hairpins above some of the Alps' most breathtaking scenery.

Snaking its way across the Hohe Tauern National Park in a series of 36 hairpins, the Grossglockner High Alpine Road climbs to an altitude of over 2,500 m (8,200 ft) on its route between the village of Heiligenblut in Carinthia and Fusch an der Glocknerstrasse in Salzburgerland.

Named after the Grossglockner mountain, which towers over the surrounding landscape, the current road opened in 1935 – but this route is actually much older. Since the Celts and Romans, people have crossed between Villach and Salzburg to trade; before the road, this alpine crossing was long, arduous and often fraught with danger.

Today, the journey is far more relaxing. As you drive slowly upwards, the landscape unfolds in a series of magnificent panoramas. Snow-streaked mountains compete with lush meadows flecked with brightly coloured alpine flowers. Inquisitive marmot scurry across these meadows, majestic alpine ibex scale impossible heights and the huge shadow of a lammergeier soaring overhead darkens the road.

Opportunities to stop and linger abound, whether to take photographs, enjoy delicious Austrian cuisine at roadside restaurants or strike off on a short, well-marked hike. Then it's back behind the wheel to take in more epic scenery.

The coiling bends of the Grossglockner High Alpine Road, winding through Austria's alps

Clifftop Schloss Neuschwanstein, soaring over the bucolic Bavarian landscape

㉗ Romantic Road

LOCATION Germany **START/FINISH** Füssen/Würzburg **DISTANCE** 354 km (220 miles) **TIME** 3 days **ROAD CONDITIONS** Good **INFORMATION** www.romanticroadgermany.com

Take it slow on this scenic route, which is peppered with little-known medieval villages and Bavarian towns thronging with gingerbread-style houses.

Despite the name, this is not a trip solely for couples. Germany came up with this scenic itinerary in the 1950s to lift the public mood following World War II trauma. The legacy today is a spirit-raising road trip from the River Main to the northern Alps, winding through the historic southern heartlands of Bavaria and Baden-Württemberg, past as many 12th-century towns as the map can handle.

On the way, the grandeur of Schloss Neuschwanstein awes, as does fairy-tale Füssen, historic Munich and the lip-smacking wine lands of Würzburg – but often it's the smaller moments that will make you catch your breath, maybe in the shadow of a stately Baroque castle, or while gazing at flower boxes spilling from a half-timbered house. Set your own pace, but make sure that you drive the German way: in a high-powered coupé or sleek, electrified motor – all testament to this powerhouse of automotive history.

WINTER WONDERLAND

The Romantic Road is drivable year-round, but at its best in winter when the towns sparkle with festive lights and Weihnachtsmarkts (Christmas markets). Picture-postcard Würzburg scores high for festive nibbles, while the Advent Market in Rothenburg, a dreamscape of baubles and bells, dates to the 15th century.

Baltic Trail

LOCATION Estonia to Lithuania **START/FINISH** Tallinn/Vilnius **DISTANCE** 640 km (400 miles) **TIME** 4 days **ROAD CONDITIONS** Roads are generally well-surfaced, with no steep terrain; off main highways, some rural roads are single-lane
INFORMATION www.visitestonia.com; www.latvia.travel; www.lithuania.travel

Drive through this trio of Baltic states in summer to enjoy sunny beach days, long, light evenings and never-ending skies. Whatever the season, you'll be enchanted by the region's pine-scented forests and history-steeped cities.

Leaving Tallinn, with its turreted Toompea Castle, the route enters the primeval pinewood forests of Lahemaa National Park, where elk and roe deer graze and meadows blaze with wildflowers. The park is fringed by rocky bays dotted with age-smoothed boulders and, in summer, drifts of yellow pollen streak the surface of the glass-calm Baltic sea.

From here, the road unwinds across flat farmland, through Rakvere with its four-square castle, to pretty Parnu on the Gulf of Riga. A huge sandy beach made Parnu a fashionable resort during the tsarist era, and its streets are still lined with stylish villas built in its 19th-century heyday.

The road sweeps down the dune-lined coast to Riga, at the head of the Gulf. Latvia's capital has a treasury of Art Nouveau mansions, their elaborate façades adorned with stylized faces and swooping patterns.

After the coastal flatlands, the Daugava valley, with its chain of artificial lakes, offers a majestic change of scenery. The landscape continues to subtly alter as you roll eastwards: the hilly, birch-forested lakeland of Latgale becomes the wooded hills, silvery lakes and serpentine rivers of Aukstaitija National Park in Lithuania. It's hard to believe that this tranquil place is so close to Vilnius, the Lithuanian capital, whose maze of cobbled alleys marks the journey's end.

Waves lapping the shores of Tuja, on the Gulf of Riga in Latvia

BY ROAD
EUROPE

EXPLORE the pinewood forests of **Lahemaa National Park** on foot or by bike

WALK around the towers and ramparts of **Tallinn**'s Toompea Castle, the mightiest medieval stronghold in Estonia

Tallinn

ESTONIA

KAYAK in **Aukstaitija National Park**, Lithuania's lake district

LATVIA

ADMIRE Riga's collection of Art Nouveau mansions

DISCOVER Vilnius's Jewish heritage on a guided walk around the old town

LITHUANIA

Vilnius

Above Aerial view of the magical Skeleton Coast
Left A shipwrecked fishing vessel at the edge of the coast

BY ROAD
AFRICA AND THE MIDDLE EAST

EXPLORE *the caves along the three-day* **Ugab River Trail**

Terrace Bay

VISIT *the black rhinos at* **Ugab River Rhino Camp**, *administered by the Save the Rhino Trust*

TAKE *a 4WD tour of the towering dunes inside* **Dorob National Park**

NAMIBIA

Swakopmund

ADMIRE *the German-style architecture in* **Swakopmund**

(29)
Skeleton Coast

LOCATION Namibia **START/FINISH** Swakopmund/Terrace Bay
DISTANCE 460 km (285 miles) **TIME** 2–3 days **ROAD CONDITIONS** 4WD required **INFORMATION** www.namibitatourism.com.na

Known as Africa's "Bermuda Triangle", this fog-shrouded, wave-ravaged coastline of savage beauty is haunted by shipwrecks, seal colonies and even the odd desert elephant.

The Khoisan bushmen call the Skeleton Coast "The Land God Created in Anger", and with good reason – in this elemental moonscape of salt, sea and wind, life and death can turn on a grain of sand. The freezing Benguela current sweeps up from Antarctica and mingles with the warm desert air to conjure thick mists that cause ships to run aground. Tracing the edge of this world between worlds, the C34, then, is a route ripe for adventure. Fuel up on supplies and first-rate coffee at the German colonial town of Swakopmund and then bid civilization adieu.

Crackling across tracks of compacted salt and sand, mirages shimmer like spilt mercury on the horizon and headlights are needed even during daylight. The route passes by graveyards of rusting ocean liners, trawlers, galleons, clippers and gunboats, and, occasionally, the bleached bones of a whale carcass. There are few signs of life here, with the notable exception of the noisy – and smelly – Cape Cross seals, and the hungry jackals that prowl around them. The road ends at the entrance to Skeleton Coast National Park, but the desolate sands stretch on, to the edge of the horizon and beyond.

BY ROAD
AFTRICA AND THE MIDDLE EAST

Jebel Hafeet

LOCATION UAE **START/FINISH** Jebel Al Hafeet Street/Jebel Hafeet summit
DISTANCE 12 km (7 miles) **TIME** 40 minutes **ROAD CONDITIONS** Multiple blind bends **INFORMATION** www.visitabudhabi.ae

A smooth black asphalt ribbon laces up the jagged surface of the Jebel Hafeet, or "Empty Mountain", on the UAE-Oman border in a series of dramatic tarmac twists guaranteed to get heart rates racing.

Regularly pressed by high-performance tyres, the road zigzagging up Jebel Hafeet has co-starred in big-budget movies, as well as Porsche and Lamborghini advertising campaigns. Film fans make pilgrimages here, following in the tracks of Bollywood's *Race* and Hollywood's *6 Underground*, and supercar-spotting is act one on this tarmacked stage. The main attraction, however, is the curves.

Some 60 bends, from exhilarating hairpins to swift sweepers, must be navigated on the 12-km (7-mile) drive to the top of Abu Dhabi's highest peak. In just 20 minutes, the road climbs 1,240 m (4,070 ft), passing virile desert vegetation and Bronze Age beehive tombs along the way. At the summit, the panorama expands to sand-blurred horizons.

Accessible by car, motorbike and even bicycle, the uppermost observation deck hosts an eclectic congregation of petrolheads, serious cyclists, leather-clad bikers, picnicking families and selfie-takers, all worshipping the view. The facilities may be humble – a car park, play area, café and a scattering of wooden gazebos – but the vista is nothing short of humbling.

The winding road up to the top of Jebel Hafeet

Fès Southwards

LOCATION Morocco **START/FINISH** Fès/Merzouga **DISTANCE** 470 km (292 miles) **TIME** 7 hours **ROAD CONDITIONS** Good **INFORMATION** www.visitmorocco.com

Leave the city and head for the hills or – more accurately – dunes. The wiggling N13 road transports drivers into a lunar landscape broken up by palm groves and sandcastle-like settlements.

At first, the deep orange scrubland south of the city of Fès lulls drivers into a hypnotic state, with the tantalizing promise of the jagged peaks of the Atlas Mountains on the horizon. Near the town of Midelt, the road finally makes its serpentine way through the mountains, winding and twisting in the shadow of forbidding cliffs. It's not a route to rush, so sit back and enjoy the ride and the stark beauty of the mountains.

When you reach the lively oasis town of Erfoud some six hours later, it's tempting to park up and end the journey here, shopping in the town's colourful souks and exploring the ancient fortified village of Ksar Maadid. But if you stop, you'll miss out on one of Morocco's most surprising sights: Lac Dayet Srij. Surrounded by terracotta-coloured dunes, this glittering lake is home, from November to May, to graceful flocks of migratory desert birds, such as Egyptian nightjars, desert warblers, fulvous babblers and blue-cheeked bee-eaters. The surrounding sculptural sea of dunes – called Erg Chebbi – is equally beguiling and the small village of Merzouga, where this route ends, is the gateway to the erg's Saharan sands. The drive may be over but desert dreams continue on foot, sandboards and in 4WDs.

Above left Driving past the dunes at Erg Chebbi *Above right* Merchants in a souk

> It's not a route to rush, so sit back and enjoy the ride

BY ROAD
AFRICA AND THE MIDDLE EAST

32 The Serengeti

LOCATION Tanzania **START/FINISH** Seronera Airstrip (loop) **DISTANCE** 300 km (190 miles) **TIME** 1 week **ROAD CONDITIONS** 4WD required **INFORMATION** www.serengeti.com

During the Great Migration, 2,000,000 wildebeest storm across the Serengeti National Park's endless plains. However, droves of safari cars also flock to the park at this time, packed with visitors keen to witness one of nature's most spectacular events.

Come instead in February to discover a secret Serengeti without the crowds, driving north from the busy hub of Seronera towards the rolling Wogakuria Hills. At dusk, you may spot a leopard in the boughs of an acacia, stretching out its paws before setting off to hunt. An impala barks its alarm call, standing rigid, while warthogs run away and a hyena pops up from behind a *kopje* (boulder).

The golden savannah may seem empty as you head south but soon you'll see Serengeti's majestic maternity ward on the Southern Plains where, in February, about 200,000 baby wildebeest are born; cheetahs and lions – but few tourists – lurk nearby.

A zebra and her colt crossing the road in Serengeti National Park, Tanzania

The sweeping golden beach at Plettenberg Bay, a seaside town

33 Garden Route

LOCATION South Africa **START/FINISH** Mossel Bay/Storms River **DISTANCE** 300 km (190 miles) **TIME** 3–5 days **ROAD CONDITIONS** Excellent **INFORMATION** www.southafrica.net

Recognized by UNESCO for its rich ecosystems, and bathed in the second-mildest climate on earth (after Hawaii), South Africa's Garden Route doesn't just look like paradise – it feels like it too. The trip's starting point, Mossel Bay, is one of South Africa's most beautiful and historic coastal towns. Pull yourself away from here, but don't expect to be driving for long – whenever the road draws near to the coast, lookouts promise the sight of southern right whales frolicking offshore.

As suggested by the route's name, this road often feels like a perfectly imagined garden, albeit one where nature is in charge. There's even a town called Wilderness, where wild waves crash against cliffs. But it's not all about the coast. Between pretty towns like Knysna and Plettenberg Bay, the route cuts inland, passing wineries and snaking through forests. Tsitsikamma National Park, near journey's end, showcases all of Eastern Cape's splendour, with dense forest and deep gorges.

BY ROAD
AFRICA AND THE MIDDLE EAST

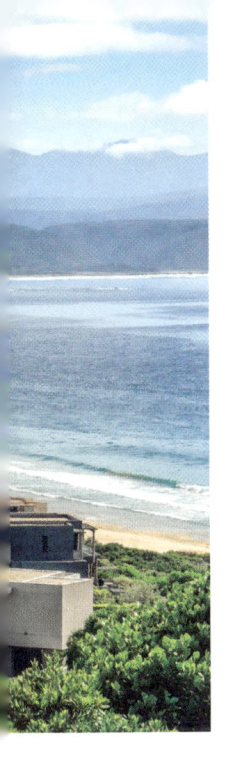

34 N7 Namaqualand Flower Route

LOCATION South Africa **START/FINISH** Cape Town/Port Nolloth **DISTANCE** 699 km (435 miles) **TIME** 3–4 days **ROAD CONDITIONS** Excellent **INFORMATION** www.southafrica.net

The miracle of flowers in the desert is one of Africa's most unlikely – and spectacular – natural wonders. For most of the year, more than 4,000 plant varieties lie sleeping beneath the earth; then, in August and September, rains bring the red-earth dust plains of Namaqualand to life, with flowers in colour palettes of astonishing variety suddenly carpeting the landscape.

They're best viewed on a drive north along the N7, with the blooms of West Coast National Park offering a precursor to what lies ahead. Long straight-road stretches of scorched, arid country are interrupted by fields of wildflowers, sudden and surprising, around Kamieskroon and Port Nolloth, and bloom all through Richtersveld National Park and Skilpad Wildflower Reserve.

Winding between the vivid blooms in Skilpad Wildflower Reserve

35 Route 62

LOCATION South Africa **START/FINISH** Cape Town/Port Elizabeth **DISTANCE** 850 km (529 miles) **TIME** 1 week **ROAD CONDITIONS** Excellent **INFORMATION** www.route62.co.za

You're never far from mountains or coast on this picturesque drive across Africa's southernmost reaches. The land here defies the stereotypes of the continent, and is green-hued and breezily cold in winter – the perfect conditions for producing some of South Africa's best food and wine. The rolling hills around Montagu are carpeted in orchards, while Calitzdorp and Robertson are surrounded by vineyards. Not only does this mean plenty of delightful scenery, but it also makes Route 62 the world's longest wine route.

It's not just foodies and oenophiles who are rewarded on this drive. You'll find gangly ostriches populating farms in Oudtshoorn and rare free-roaming white lions in the Sanbona Reserve, while pretty towns like Barrydale and Ladismith serve as trailheads into the region's rocky mountains. Blend all of this together and it's easy to see how this awesome route often tops lists of the best wine routes on earth.

SOUTH AFRICAN WINES

The first South African wine was bottled in Cape Town in 1659, and today the country has around 60 official wine-producing areas. The region's Mediterranean climate produces a February or March harvest, and popular grape varieties include Chenin Blanc and Riesling. Pinotage, a hybrid of Pinot Noir and Cinsaut, is a particular local favourite.

131

WATCH the epic populations of elephants, big cats and baobabs in Tanzania's **Tarangire National Park**

RELAX on the white-sand beach at Zambia's **Lake Tanganyika**

JOIN IN the buzz of **Cape Town**, southern Africa's coolest city

another way
From Zambia the road branches at Lusaka, taking a scenic detour through Botswana or Namibia to reach South Africa.

(36) Nairobi to Cape Town

LOCATION Kenya to South Africa **START/FINISH** Nairobi/Cape Town **DISTANCE** 5,725 km (3,558 miles) **TIME** 1 month **ROAD CONDITIONS** Varies **INFORMATION** The route passes through four border crossings – make sure that you have the requisite visas

Forging down through the continent past stunning landscapes in the path of legendary explorers, the drive from Nairobi to Cape Town is an African odyssey.

This trip from East Africa's safari heartland to the southern tip of the continent is at its best from May to October when the rains have passed, visibility is excellent, wildlife is easy to spot and road conditions are at their kindest. From potholed tracks to lightly trafficked city streets, the road itself carries no great appeal – it's the detours that make this journey spectacular. Main stopping-off points include Kenya's Amboseli National Park, framed by the backdrop of Mount Kilimanjaro; the world-famous Tarangire, Serengeti and Ngorongoro Crater, part of Tanzania's northern safari circuit; and Kruger National Park and Pilanesberg Game Reserve in South Africa, both brimming with wildlife. From the back roads of Tanzania to the deep rural heartland of Zambia and Zimbabwe, this drive rewards, with ample opportunity to meet locals at countless roadside markets and to sample regional fare at small restaurants along the way.

BY ROAD
AFRICA AND THE MIDDLE EAST

Driving through the bush in South Africa's Pilanesberg Game Reserve, home to a rich array of wildlife

BY ROAD
ASIA

(37) # Silk Road

LOCATION Italy to China **START/FINISH** Venice/Xi'an **DISTANCE** 10,460 km (6,500 miles) **TIME** 3 weeks **ROAD CONDITIONS** Varies; anything from well-maintained international highways to unmade mountain tracks
INFORMATION Caravanistan (www.caravanistan.com) provides up-to-date travel information on the Central Asian Silk Road, including the current status of border crossings

Linking East and West, Orient and Occident, Asia and Europe, the Silk Road embodies a world of contrasts, but at the same time weaves together diverse places and cultures in a way that emphasizes their similarities just as much as their differences.

Crossing Khaburabot Pass on the Pamir Highway in Tajikistan

There was never just one Silk Road. The term was dreamed up in the 19th century by a German geographer, Ferdinand von Richthofen, to describe the plethora of intercontinental trading routes criss-crossing Eurasia, linking the Mediterranean, Persia, Central Asia and China with the Indian subcontinent. What von Richthofen did, unknowingly, was inspire generations of writers and travellers to look at the East through a romantic lens. Even now, the phrase "Silk Road" conjures up images of camel caravans with precious goods making their way across empty deserts, mosques and madrassas bejewelled with turquoise and lapis lazuli, and exotic bazaars where you can buy anything from a bust of Lenin to a magic lamp.

> Even now, the phrase "Silk Road" conjures up images of camel caravans

Despite the numerous routes, the general consensus is that the Silk Road stretched between Venice and Xi'an. In places where the terrain was most difficult, it made sense to follow the path of least resistance over natural passes and between oases. The most popular route, therefore, was the Central Asian Silk Road, including what the poet James Elroy Flecker termed "The Golden Journey to Samarkand".

Below *A golden camel, a familiar sight on the Silk Road*
Right *The beautiful Shah Mosque in Isfahan, Iran*

135

BY ROAD
ASIA

For the first time in its history, the journey through Uzbekistan – at the heart of the Silk Road– is easy. Some 86 nationalities can visit without a visa; there are direct flight connections across Europe, the Middle East and Asia; and you can even travel between the UNESCO World Heritage Sites by high-speed train. But as ancient Silk Road travellers found, there's a great pleasure to be had in making your way independently, at your own pace, between the dazzling cities.

Driving along the tarmac-covered highways (which follow the same course as the ancient trading routes), you have the chance to stop whenever you fancy, to meet people, and to explore sites which have gone unchanged for centuries. In Navoi, for example, intricately decorated plaster and brickwork still adorn the façade of the Rabati Malik, a medieval caravanserai, or roadside inn, where Silk Road merchants and pilgrims would once have stopped to safely spend the night.

ULUG BEG

Just as goods and people travelled along the Silk Road, ideas spread, too. Emperor Ulug Beg (1394–1449) invited the Islamic world's greatest minds to work at his observatory in Samarkand, and together they created star charts of unparalleled precision. In fact, Ulug Beg's calculation of the length of the year was not improved upon until the invention of the computer.

Below *Mogao Caves in Dunhuang, China*
Right *A rug merchant Bukhara, Uzbekistan*
Bottom right *Boats on the canals of Venice, Italy*

Venice ▶

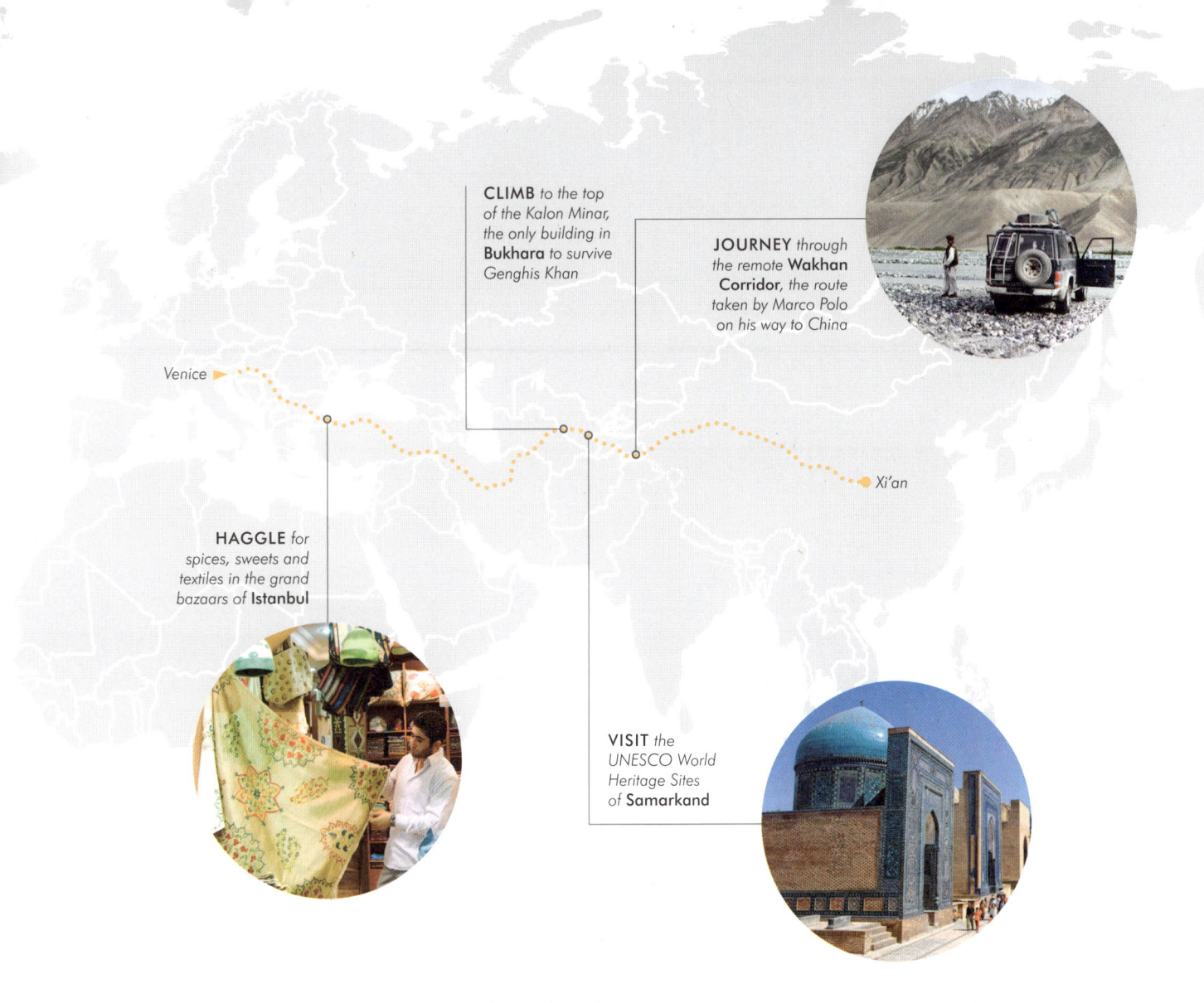

CLIMB to the top of the Kalon Minar, the only building in **Bukhara** to survive Genghis Khan

JOURNEY through the remote **Wakhan Corridor**, the route taken by Marco Polo on his way to China

HAGGLE for spices, sweets and textiles in the grand bazaars of **Istanbul**

VISIT the UNESCO World Heritage Sites of **Samarkand**

Xi'an

A dozen or so metres away is the Sardoba Malik, the domed reservoir which ensured that even here, in the remoteness of the desert, travellers would always have fresh water to drink. It's not uncommon, even in the 21st century, to pass by two-humped Bactrian camels grazing, women by the side of the road hawking piles of juicy winter melons or blood-red pomegranates, or a trader manhandling rolls of carpets onto the roof of a Lada, ready to sell them in the trading domes of Bukhara. There's always time to stop, drink tea and to barter enthusiastically with a smile.

Of course, Uzbekistan is the perfect place to see the Silk Road in miniature but, if time allows, you can drive the entire route. Along the way you'll see the dazzling palazzos of Venice, built by wealthy merchants with the profits of their Silk Road trade; the extraordinary Buddhist Mogao Caves of Dunhuang and Isfahan's tiled mosques; and pagodas, temples and Terracotta Warriors in Xi'an, the Silk Road's eastern terminus. It really is the journey of a lifetime.

another way

The Pamir Highway through Afghanistan, Uzbekistan, Tajikistan and Kyrgyzstan is a microcosm of the Silk Road. It's a nail biting drive through the world's most dramatic scenery, with everything from Zoroastrian fire temples to nomads' yurts along the way.

137

BY ROAD
ASIA

The splendid Golden Temple in Amritsar, the chief place of pilgrimage of Sikhism

38 Grand Trunk Road

LOCATION India **START/FINISH** Amritsar/Kolkata **DISTANCE** 2,092 km (1,300 miles) **TIME** 5–10 days **ROAD CONDITIONS** Good, 4WD not necessary **INFORMATION** Best time is mid-Dec–Mar

Connecting Kabul in Afghanistan with Chittagong in Bangladesh, the fascinating Grand Trunk Road is the modern incarnation of a trade route that dates back more than 2,500 years. The Indian section, which runs from the state of Punjab in the north to West Bengal in the east, is a testament to the country's religious and cultural diversity. From its start in Amritsar, home to the magnificent Golden Temple, the centrepiece of the Sikh faith, the road snakes southeast through Delhi, and then on to Agra, and India's jewel, the great Taj Mahal, Mughal emperor Shah Jahan's evocative mausoleum for his late wife. Beyond lie the Hindu holy cities of Prayagraj and Varanasi, both on the banks of the Ganges. Further east, in the state of Bihar, is the spiritual site of Bodhgaya, where the Buddha found enlightenment.

39 Seoul to Busan

LOCATION South Korea **START/FINISH** Seoul/Busan **DISTANCE** 467 km (290 miles) **TIME** 3 days **ROAD CONDITIONS** Good, but beware hairpin mountain roads **INFORMATION** International Driving Permit required

Bookended by South Korea's forward-facing capital, Seoul, and its life-affirming second city, Busan, this drive takes in mist-shrouded mountain valleys, pristine parkland and buzzing cities. Leaving Seoul behind, drive south through wooded hills to refined Gongju, erstwhile seat of power of the Baekje kingdom, and walk among the ruins of Gongsan-seong, its 5th-century mountain fortress. Ancient city streets give way to forested mountain trails in nearby Gyeryongsan National Park, while carved stone Buddhas and sumptuous food await in Daegu. Driving east, discover historical treasures in Gyeongju, a living museum to the ancient Silla kingdom, before ending your journey in Busan, with its hip galleries, a clifftop Buddhist temple and South Korea's best seafood.

KOREAN CUISINE

Korean cuisine has taken the world by storm, and you don't have to walk far in major cities such as London or New York to find a voguish restaurant promising Korean barbecue, bibimbap rice bowls or gochujang wings. Perhaps the biggest international breakout star from this ancient culinary tradition has been kimchi, a dish of fermented vegetables – especially cabbage and radish – said to boost immunity and gut health, and strengthen teeth and bones.

BY ROAD
ASIA

(40)
The Karakoram Highway

LOCATION Pakistan to China **START/FINISH** Islamabad/Kashgar **DISTANCE** 1,300 km (810 miles) **TIME** 3–4 days **ROAD CONDITIONS** Tough, 4WD recommended **INFORMATION** www.tourism.gov.pk

This Silk Road offshoot weaves across the three greatest mountain ranges on earth, snaking through the rugged peaks of the Himalayas, Karakorams and Hindu Kush. These are the epic folds and creases the first humans scrambled across 3,000 years ago, leaving petroglyphs; the ranges that Alexander the Great's troops marched through; and the valleys across which the Great Game – the 19th-century political tussle between the British and Russian empires – played out. The route is both feted and feared as the architectonic Eighth Wonder of the World and the scariest road in the world on account of the precipitous bends and unpredictable weather. Tracing the world's highest paved road requires skill, bravery and preparedness.

Karakoram Highway winding through mountains

Tuk-tuk passing through a temple gateway at Angor Wat

(41)
Angkor Wat by Tuk-tuk

LOCATION Cambodia **START/FINISH** Siem Riep (loop) **DISTANCE** Varies depending on temple **TIME** 1–3 days **ROAD CONDITIONS** Paved **INFORMATION** www.visit-angkor.org

Silhouetted against the pinkening dawn, the domes and crenulations of UNESCO-listed Angkor Wat are unmistakable. So heavenly is its beauty, that it's claimed the capital of the Khmer Empire was constructed in a single night by a divine architect. Made of not one temple, but 72, the medieval Hindu complex – the largest spread of religious monuments in the world – is being clawed back into the jungle by muscular tree roots that snarl and snake around the stones.

Walking this sprawling compound in the tropical humidity leaves visitors in an exhausted soup of sunscreen and sweat – by far the best way to explore Angkor Wat is by tuk-tuk. Hiring a local driver for one day, or three, removes the risk of getting lost and frees travellers to revel in the glory of this ancient complex, a sublime marvel of human creativity and ingenuity.

EXPLORE the caves and mountain pagodas of UNESCO-listed **Tam Cốc-Bích Động**

PULL OVER for **Mỹ Sơn** – a cluster of 4th- to 14th-century Hindu temples dedicated to the god Shiva

SOAK UP the sun on **Nha Trang's** world-class white-sand beach

42 Motorcycling in Vietnam

LOCATION Vietnam **START/FINISH** Hanoi/Ho Chi Minh City **DISTANCE** 2,770 km (1,720 miles) **TIME** 2–3 weeks **ROAD CONDITIONS** Varies **INFORMATION** www.vietnam.travel

Pack your saddlebags and set off on a south-to-north motorcycle trip through Vietnam – there's no better way to blend in with the bike-mad locals.

A warm wind laced with the aroma of fuel and frying chillies is your constant companion from Ho Chi Minh City to the capital Hanoi. The route follows the rather blandly labelled National Route 1A, wending through vibrant cities and taking in historical highlights such as UNESCO-listed Hôi An, a perfectly preserved 15th-century trading port, and the vast Cù Chi Tunnels, created by the Viet Cong as a hiding place during the Vietnam War. In between, lie time-lost villages, where farmers coax water buffalo to till their rice paddies, as well as natural wonders such as Phong Nha Khe Bang National Park – home to the Lord of the Rings-esque, moss-furred Hang Son Doong, the world's largest cave. And don't miss testing your tyres against the Hai Van Pass, a 21-km (13-mile) section of switchback coastal road best tried at sunset. Skirting (mostly) along the edge of the South China Sea, this stunning route showcases a country much changed since the Vietnam War.

another way

National Route 1A used to be the only option between Hanoi and Ho Chi Minh City, but new roads are steadily opening up. Other scenic routes range from 2,050 km (1,274 miles) to 4,180 km (2,597 miles), or 10 days to 6 weeks – maps are available.

BY ROAD
ASIA

Above Looking towards Lang Co Beach from Hai Van Pass
Left The motorbike-filled streets of Ho Chi Minh City

141

BY ROAD
AUSTRALASIA

(43) Great Ocean Road

LOCATION Australia **START/FINISH** Melbourne/Warrnambool **DISTANCE** 353 km (220 miles) **TIME** 3–4 days **ROAD CONDITIONS** Lots of bends **INFORMATION** www.visitgreatoceanroad.org.au

Following what may just be Australia's most beautiful stretch of coastline, the Great Ocean Road combines dramatic scenery with world-famous surf beaches, iconic Australian wildlife and a fascinating history.

There's something elemental about driving the Great Ocean Road and there's no bad time of year to do it. When it's warm, this road trip can feel like travelling through an idealized version of an Aussie summer, with wild waves crashing upon seemingly endless expanses of golden sand. This is especially true around Bells Beach, one of the world's elite surf beaches, as well as Jan Juc and Torquay. When the wind blows, it's easy to see why there have been so many shipwrecks along this stretch of coast and striking rock formations such as the Twelve Apostles and Loch Ard Gorge attest to the ocean's erosive power.

Wildlife animates so many stops along the way, from koalas right by the general store at Kennett River to the kangaroos at Anglesea. From June to September, humpback whales pass offshore, visible from many vantage points, especially around Warrnambool. Classic seaside towns, including Lorne, Apollo Bay and Port Campbell, break up the journey, offering a window on coastal Australian life, especially in summer. And the route is fast becoming a foodie trail, serving up everything from classic fish and chips to gourmet choices.

> When it's warm, this road trip can feel like travelling through an idealized version of an Aussie summer

The Twelve Apostles, towering over the golden beaches found on this stretch of Victoria's coastline

142

BY ROAD
AUSTRALASIA

Lush rainforest vegetation at Cape Tribulation, part of Daintree National Park

Queensland Coast

LOCATION Australia **START/FINISH** Gold Coast/Cape Tribulation **DISTANCE** 1,763 km (1,096 miles) **TIME** 2–3 weeks **ROAD CONDITIONS** Excellent **INFORMATION** www.queensland.com

Shadowing the peerless Great Barrier Reef for much of the way, a drive along Queensland's coast connects the glittering charms and seemingly endless beaches of the south to the wild tropical north.

The beauty of this route is that you steadily leave urban scenes behind. One after the other, the cosmopolitan cities of Gold Coast, Brisbane and Cairns are reduced to mere specks in your rear-view mirror. As you drive ever northwards, rainforests begin to hug the shoreline and tower over the road. Kangaroos and wallabies lunge across the tarmac and the occasional flash of a parrot or cassowary breaks up the dark green of the forest.

There's something to be said about beach fatigue – you come across so many endless golden stretches in this part of northeast Australia that you can start to become a bit tired of the sun and sand. But if you drive the route in this direction you arguably finish with the best: Cape Tribulation. Emerging from the rainforest, you step straight onto the white ribbon of sand. It's the perfect way to end your trip.

The Pentecost River making its serpentine way through the Kimberley region

BY ROAD
AUSTRALASIA

④⑤

Savannah Way

LOCATION Australia **START/FINISH** Broome/Cairns **DISTANCE** 3,700 km (2,300 miles) **TIME** 2 weeks **ROAD CONDITIONS** You can drive a version of the Way by 2WD in dry season (Jun–Oct), but a 4WD is necessary to follow the usual route at all times **INFORMATION** www.savannahway.com.au

This classic drive across Australia's Top End captures the remote essence of the Outback, crossing Aboriginal homelands, wildlife-rich tropical wetlands, coastal mangroves and red-rock cliffs.

There are few more beautiful road trips in Australia than the Savannah Way. Whether you take the 4WD-only Gibb River Road or the paved Route 1, the drama of the Kimberley region is everywhere. Right by Route 1, Purnululu National Park, with its sandstone ridges and palm-filled gorges, is an underrated Outback gem, and an easy detour. Next, the main Savannah Way skirts the southern reaches of Arnhem Land, a place of remote Aboriginal communities and art centres, and its 4WD trails pass sandstone rocks, knowns as "lost cities".

Tracing the southern shore of the Gulf of Carpentaria lies a land of mangroves and quiet towns. The route arcs down through a wildly beautiful landscape of cattle stations on its way to Pungalina-Seven Emu Wildlife Sanctuary – home to wallabies, dingos and some of Australia's rarest birds.

As it crosses the interior of Far North Queensland, the Savannah Way becomes entirely paved. After so many empty roads and tiny settlements, the city of Cairns will either look like an oasis of urban sophistication or a noisy, too-clamorous place.

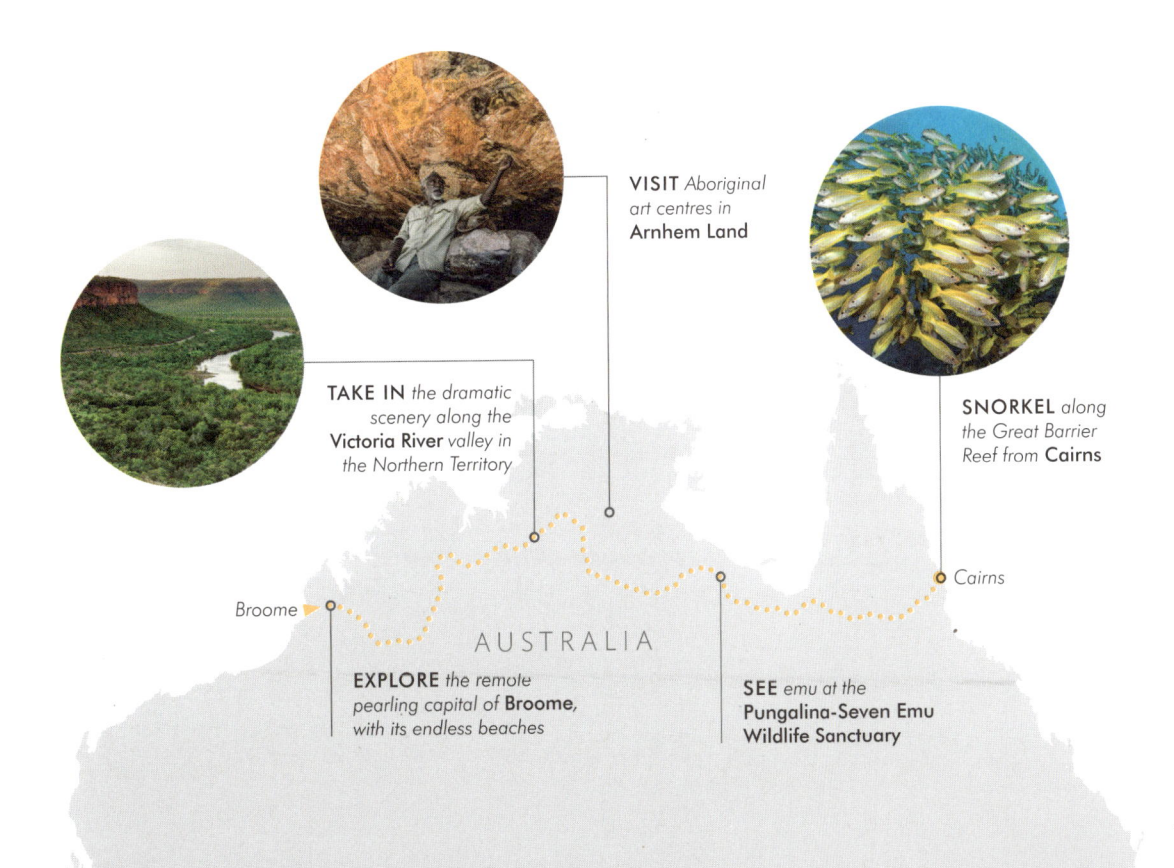

VISIT *Aboriginal art centres in* **Arnhem Land**

TAKE IN *the dramatic scenery along the* **Victoria River** *valley in the Northern Territory*

SNORKEL *along the Great Barrier Reef from* **Cairns**

Broome

AUSTRALIA

Cairns

EXPLORE *the remote pearling capital of* **Broome**, *with its endless beaches*

SEE *emu at the* **Pungalina-Seven Emu Wildlife Sanctuary**

145

BY ROAD
AUSTRALASIA

46 Alice Springs to Darwin

LOCATION Australia **START/FINISH** Alice Springs/Darwin **DISTANCE** 1,497 km (930 miles) **TIME** 1 week **ROAD CONDITIONS** Good **INFORMATION** www.northernterritory.com

Unfurling across almost half of Australia, from the Outback to the high tropics of the north, the long, lonely Stuart Highway travels through a vast and starkly beautiful landscape. Close to the desert town of Katherine, the chasms of Nitmiluk Gorge rise from the desert like red-rocked apparitions. Further south, near the isolated town of Tennant Creek, are the soulful Karlu Karlu – eye-catching fields of giant boulders that are of deep spiritual significance for the local Aboriginal people. At either end of this epic road trip are the Northern Territory's two largest cities. Alice Springs is the gateway to Australia's Red Centre (home to Uluru, Kata Tjuta and King's Canyon), while Darwin is a quintessentially tropical city, with a seafood-rich culinary scene and some fabulous museums.

> **KARLU KARLU**
>
> Karlu Karlu means "round boulders", a prosaic name that belies the site's significance. To the Aboriginal people of the area, the granite boulders are the saliva from Arrange, the Devil Man, who passed through the area and spat upon the ground. Other stories suggest that the rocks are the eggs of the Rainbow Serpent from local creation tales. Ownership of this sacred site passed back to the land's traditional owners in 2008.

The Pinnacles, a series of striking limestone formations within Nambung National Park

47 Coral Coast

LOCATION Australia **START/FINISH** Perth/Exmouth **DISTANCE** 1,268 km (788 miles) **TIME** 2 weeks **ROAD CONDITIONS** Single lanes **INFORMATION** www.australiascoralcoast.com

With world-class wildlife-watching, exceptional landforms and an Outback-meets-the-sea feel, the Coral Coast of Western Australia ranks among the world's most spectacular coastal drives – and is also one of the least known. Driving this remote stretch of wild coast is like taking a step back in time: this is how the Australian shore looked before Europeans landed here in the 18th century. Along the route, stirring Outback landforms alternate with snatched glimpses of lonely rocky headlands and empty white-sand beaches pounded by waves that have crossed half the globe. Typical of this unspoiled stretch of coast, and just a short detour off the road, are the otherworldly Pinnacles of Nambung National Park – huge limestone pillars eroded by sea, sand and wind. Peppered throughout is an array of wildlife, from noisy sea lions at Jurien Bay to gentle whale sharks in Shark Bay.

BY ROAD
AUSTRALASIA

㊽ Forgotten World Highway

LOCATION New Zealand **START/FINISH** Taumarunui/Stratford **DISTANCE** 151 km (94 miles) **TIME** 1–2 days **ROAD CONDITIONS** Winding, with a 12-km (7.5-mile) unsealed section **INFORMATION** www.newzealand.com

This backcountry road trip slices across the North Island's remote interior, following Highway 43 through the "Forgotten World" of the defunct Stratford–Okahukura railway line. From its outset at Taumarunui, the road meanders past lavender fields and grassy hills, which soon turn to lush rainforest with swaying palms and feathery ferns. At the halfway point is the quirky settlement of Whangamomona, which declared itself an independent republic in 1989. This testing route demands careful driving, especially at the Tangarakau River Gorge, where the highway drops to a single lane carved into a sheer shale cliffside. The best views are saved for last, as you crest the mountain saddles of Whangamomona and Pohokura, with Mt Taranaki providing a near-constant compass for the final stretch to Stratford.

㊾ West Coast Drive

LOCATION New Zealand **START/FINISH** Westport/Jackson Bay **DISTANCE** 470 km (292 miles) **TIME** 5–7 days **ROAD CONDITIONS** Good **INFORMATION** www.westcoast.co.nz

Where else in the world could you drive with endless ocean to one side, while to the other icy glaciers hide beyond tangled rainforest? Snaking down New Zealand's wild and windswept West Coast, this twisting route follows a section of State Highway 6 – the country's longest road – taking in the full gamut of Kiwi scenery on the way. Setting off from the former coal town of Westport, you'll hug the rugged coastline, winding past deserted beaches and the striking stacks of the Pancake Rocks, on to the old gold-mining town of Hokitika. As you sweep further south, the sugar-frosted Southern Alps rise up to your left, heralding the arrival of glacier country where you'll find the icy bulks of Franz Josef and Fox. From Haast, the highway turns inland to Lake Wanaka, but keep heading south to isolated Jackson Bay; here, you can watch the sunset over the ocean while devouring some of New Zealand's best fish and chips.

Mist rising over Lake Matheson, near Fox Glacier

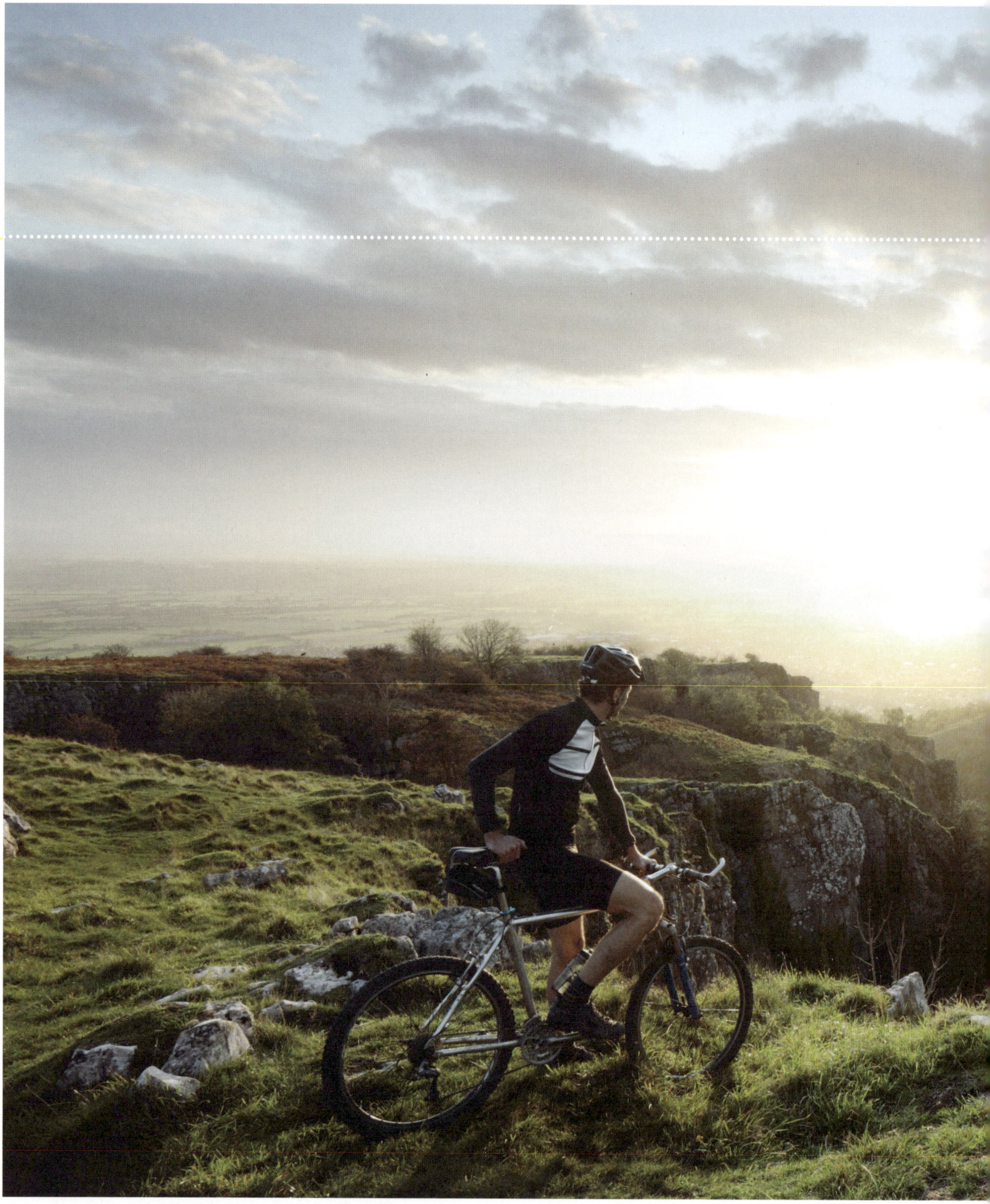

BY BIKE

There's a wonderful freedom to travelling on two wheels, revolving under your own steam along routes otherwise untrammeled. This centuries-old way of travelling is not only a great health kick and wonderfully green, it's also budget friendly. Whether you love speeding around tarmacked hairpin bends, bumping along rugged trails or cruising between vineyards, there's a cycling route for you.

AT A GLANCE
BY BIKE

NORTH AMERICA pp152–159
Whether it's pedalling along the eastern edge of Canada or slicing through America's Deep South, this continent is a cyclist's dream.

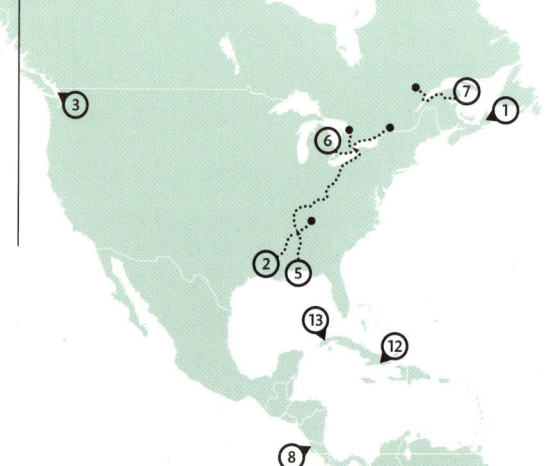

CENTRAL AND SOUTH AMERICA pp160–163
Wheel through lush valleys in Cuba, roll along a volcano-lined avenue in Ecuador or tackle Bolivia's infamous Death Road.

KEY TO MAP
- .... Long route
- • End point

Previous page *A cyclist admiring the view over Cheddar Gorge in the UK*

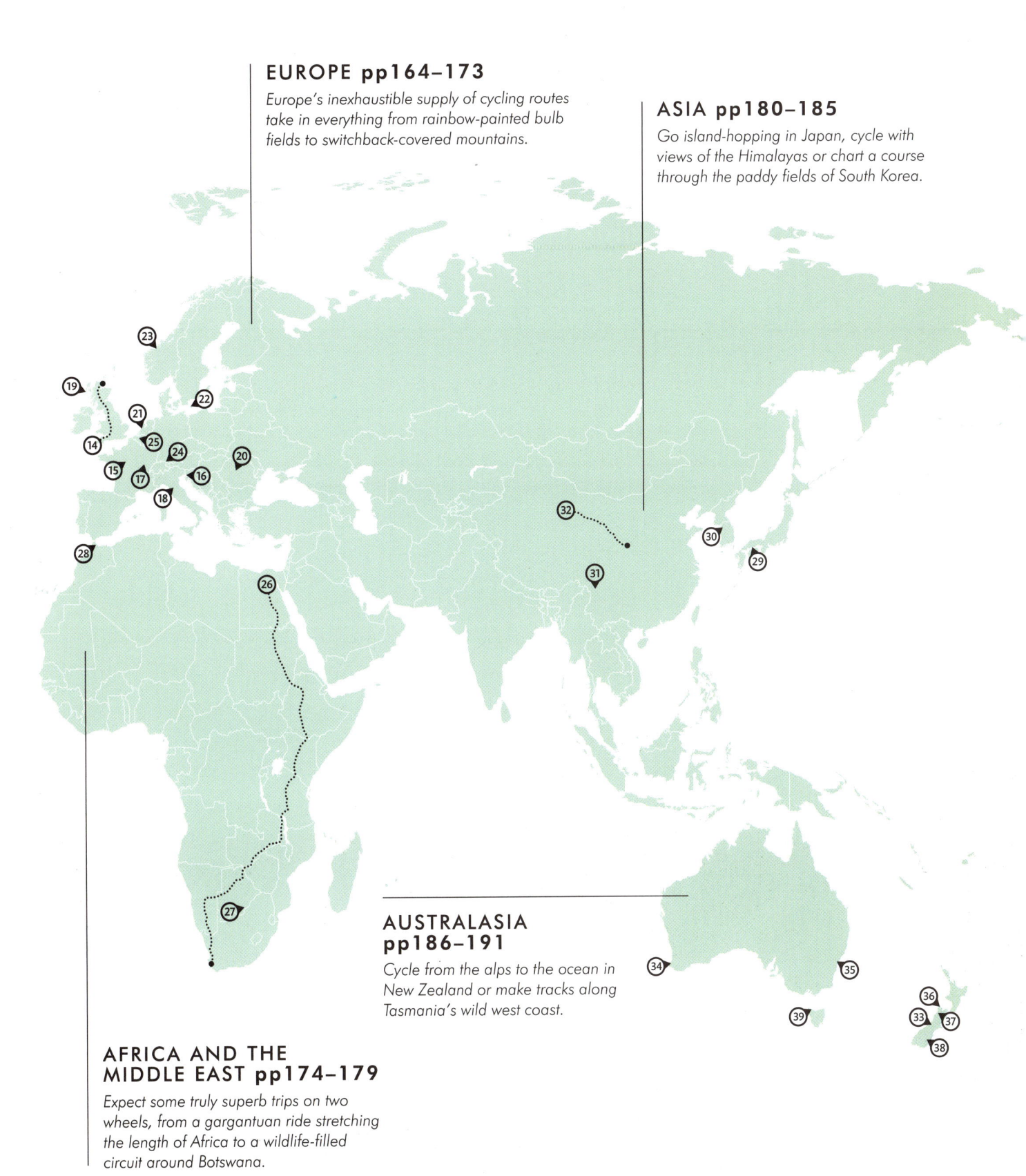

EUROPE pp164–173
Europe's inexhaustible supply of cycling routes take in everything from rainbow-painted bulb fields to switchback-covered mountains.

ASIA pp180–185
Go island-hopping in Japan, cycle with views of the Himalayas or chart a course through the paddy fields of South Korea.

AUSTRALASIA pp186–191
Cycle from the alps to the ocean in New Zealand or make tracks along Tasmania's wild west coast.

AFRICA AND THE MIDDLE EAST pp174–179
Expect some truly superb trips on two wheels, from a gargantuan ride stretching the length of Africa to a wildlife-filled circuit around Botswana.

151

BY BIKE
NORTH AMERICA

① Cabot Trail

LOCATION Canada **START/FINISH** Baddeck (loop) **DISTANCE** 298 km (185 miles) **TIME** 1 week **DIFFICULTY** Moderate; several steep ascents and descents **INFORMATION** www.novascotia.com

This astonishingly scenic trail is carved into the eastern edge of Canada, a place where emerald-green mountains dramatically collide with sparkling blue ocean. It's often driven by car, but choose to pedal two wheels instead of powering four and you'll gain a new perspective on this, the Gaelic heart of the country.

Constructed in 1932, the Cabot Trail is a paved, all-access road that showcases the spectacular landscapes and rich Gaelic history of the east coast of Canada. Dotting the stony shores of the trail, quaint fishing hamlets promise a bounty of local seafood, and the jovial rhythms of fiddles and flutes pour from cosy pubs – delightful reminders of the Scottish and Irish roots of this weathered land settled in the 18th century by pioneering families seeking a new life.

> Coyote, lynx and bobcat hunt around the tundra-like plateau of the highlands

The route loops along the mountainous north of Cape Breton Island, which belongs to Canada's Nova Scotia province. Cyclists can choose to take the trail clockwise, which is slightly less challenging with the wind at your back, or counter-clockwise, where, by revolving along the outside lane, you'll enjoy truly sweeping views along the coast.

As you descend into lake-speckled valleys, traverse the glacier-scarred territory of the Cape Breton Highlands, and hug the high shoreline bluffs full of secluded coves, there are plenty of wildlife-spotting opportunities. Moose, black bear and deer forage around the deep river canyons. Coyote, lynx and bobcat hunt around the tundra-like plateau of the highlands, and pods of whales can often be seen from the flat summit of MacKenzie Mountain, breaking the rough, white-tipped waves of the Atlantic Ocean.

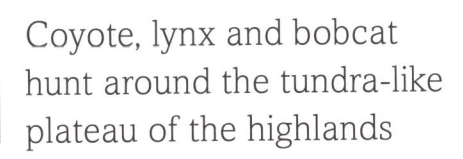

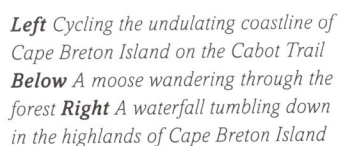

Left Cycling the undulating coastline of Cape Breton Island on the Cabot Trail
Below A moose wandering through the forest **Right** A waterfall tumbling down in the highlands of Cape Breton Island

BY BIKE
NORTH AMERICA

Autumn colours in Cape Breton Highlands National Park, viewed from Cape Smokey

THE TRAIL'S NAMESAKE

The trail was named after the Venetian explorer John Cabot, who sailed to Canada's east coast over five centuries ago. Where exactly he made his historic landfall in the summer of 1497 is hotly contested: some say Cape Bonavista in Newfoundland and Labrador, others Cape Breton Island in Nova Scotia.

CYCLE along a coastal path through gently rolling terrain to reach **White Point** for misty views of craggy sea stacks frequented by seals

SPOT pods of pilot whales in the cool waters around the little fishing village of **Pleasant Bay**

FOLLOW the **Skyline Trail** along an impressive headland cliff overlooking the coast

WALK along the pretty boardwalk of **Chéticamp**, a traditional fishing town rich in Acadian culture

SWIM in either salt water or fresh water at **Ingonish Beach**, where the fish-and-chip shacks are some of the best around

CANADA

Braddeck

154

A third of the Cabot Trail makes its way through the sprawling Cape Breton Highlands National Park, one of the most spectacular sections of the whole journey. Pedal through old-growth boreal forests that tumble down towards rust-coloured cliffs, and take in the endless mountain and ocean scenery. The park is laced with a selection of wooded hiking trails that are great for stretching sore legs after a long day in the saddle. Or stop by MacIntosh Brook, perched on the northern edge of the park, to take a reviving dip in the tranquil pool that's fed by a cascading veil waterfall. Wherever you are on the trail, the crisp, salty air blowing in from the ocean is wonderfully refreshing.

In the evenings, seek out the beachside eateries that line the loop for a steaming plate of freshly caught local lobster and a bowl of hot clam chowder. Then bed down under a thick duvet at a cosy inn or tuck into your sleeping bag at one of the many campgrounds dotted around the trail. As morning dawns, your slight muscle ache will be a tender yet wonderful reminder of yesterday's epic adventures, while the road stretching ahead will make you eager to get back in the saddle to see what's next around the corner.

Top *A lonely lobster shack sitting next to a red-and-white lighthouse at Neil's Harbour*
Above *One of the many picturesque campsites that can be found along the trail*

another way

The Cabot Trail is hugely popular as a driving route and can be done in a day, albeit a long one. Along the way, there are plenty of places to take in the gorgeous views – just be on the lookout for moose, motorcyclists and cyclists, especially around the hairpin turns.

BY BIKE
NORTH AMERICA

A charming rustic barn in French Camp, Mississippi, one of the stops on the Natchez Trace Parkway

② Natchez Trace Parkway

LOCATION US **START/FINISH** Natchez/Nashville **DISTANCE** 715 km (444 miles) **TIME** 1 week **DIFFICULTY** Easy to moderate **INFORMATION** www.natcheztracetravel.com

Cutting north through three states in the Deep South, this route follows an ancient trail once used by American Indians. Pedal through a landscape of creaking barns, tranquil forests, and grassy meadows that explode with colour in spring. On the way, glimpse the original trail at Sunken Trace, where a portion of deeply eroded dirt track, "sunk" below a dense forest canopy, has been preserved; it still echoes with the journeys of American Indians and early pioneers. Ride on to Tupelo, where Elvis Presley was born, before coasting down to Buzzard Roost in Alabama, which harbours a gushing natural spring of azure water. Finally, you reach Nashville, home of country music, spicy hot chicken and new adventures.

③ San Juan Islands Scenic Byway

LOCATION US **START/FINISH** Friday Harbor (loop) **DISTANCE** 71 km (44 miles) **TIME** 2–3 days **DIFFICULTY** Moderate; some challenging slopes **INFORMATION** www.visitsanjuans.com

Looping around sleepy San Juan Island – the main isle in the Washington state archipelago – this stunning route serves up a tantalizing blend of quiet forest roads, clapboard villages and sunny harbours studded with bobbing sailing boats.

From Friday Harbor, a village of weathered shingle houses, cycle through golden pastures, and strands of pine and spruce. At the historic resort of Roche Harbor, handsome double-gallery houses snake down to the water, while lavish yachts and boats cram the deep-blue bay. Along the west side of the island, pass Lime Kiln Point with its tiny lighthouse and dazzling views across to Canada; in summer, orca whales surface just off the coast. At the island's southern tip search for coloured sea glass below Cattle Point Lighthouse, before rolling back to Friday Harbor.

another way
Plenty of scenic hiking trails lace San Juan Island, from the 198-m (650-ft) summit of Young Hill, with stunning panoramas of Vancouver Island and beyond, to Lime Kiln Point State Park, where you can view whales, sea lions, otters and bald eagles from the rocky shoreline.

BY BIKE
NORTH AMERICA

④ Denali Highway

LOCATION US **START/FINISH** Cantwell/Paxson **DISTANCE** 217 km (135 miles) **TIME** 4 days **DIFFICULTY** Challenging **INFORMATION** www.alaska.org

This lonely highway cuts across the Alaskan wilds – a world of sapphire-blue lakes and rolling tundra backed by snow-capped mountains and glaciers.

The route begins at the old roadhouse at Paxson, where porcupines trot along the verge and moose roam in the distance. Tranquil Tangle Lake, its serene surface a mirror for the saw-toothed mountains, is soon followed by 1,245-m (4,086-ft) Maclaren Pass – the highest point on the highway – a wind-blown moorland that feels like the top of the world. Unfurling alongside the Nenana River, the final stretch leads downhill to Cantwell, where the soaring peaks of Denali National Park loom invitingly on the horizon.

The Nenana River, overlooked by the snowy peaks of the Alaska Range

⑤ Underground Railroad

LOCATION US to Canada **START/FINISH** Mobile/Owen Sound **DISTANCE** 3,230 km (2,007 miles) **TIME** 1 month **DIFFICULTY** Easy to challenging **INFORMATION** www.adventurecycling.org

Running from the port at Mobile in Alabama, to what would have been freedom in Ontario, the Underground Railroad traces a captivating path through historic towns, tranquil forests and sleepy swamps, past poignant monuments, and former safe houses and plantations.

Cycling the month-long route is a gargantuan undertaking, but one of the gentler sections runs between Milford and Xenia in southern Ohio. Here, the trail winds through rolling farmland and through shady tunnels of trees, following old rail tracks once used by those fleeing north. At points, the tumultuous history of this now-peaceful route is revealed by side trips to places like Springboro, a small city home to preserved safe houses. As you cycle, it's uplifting to think of all those who found their freedom by following the same route.

THE UNDERGROUND RAILROAD

The Underground Railroad was the informal network of routes and safe houses – which included everything from schoolhouses to private homes – used by those escaping slavery in the South before the Civil War (1861–1865). Though the North was free, many of those fleeing aimed to reach Canada, beyond the reach of those seeking to enslave them.

Waterfront Trail

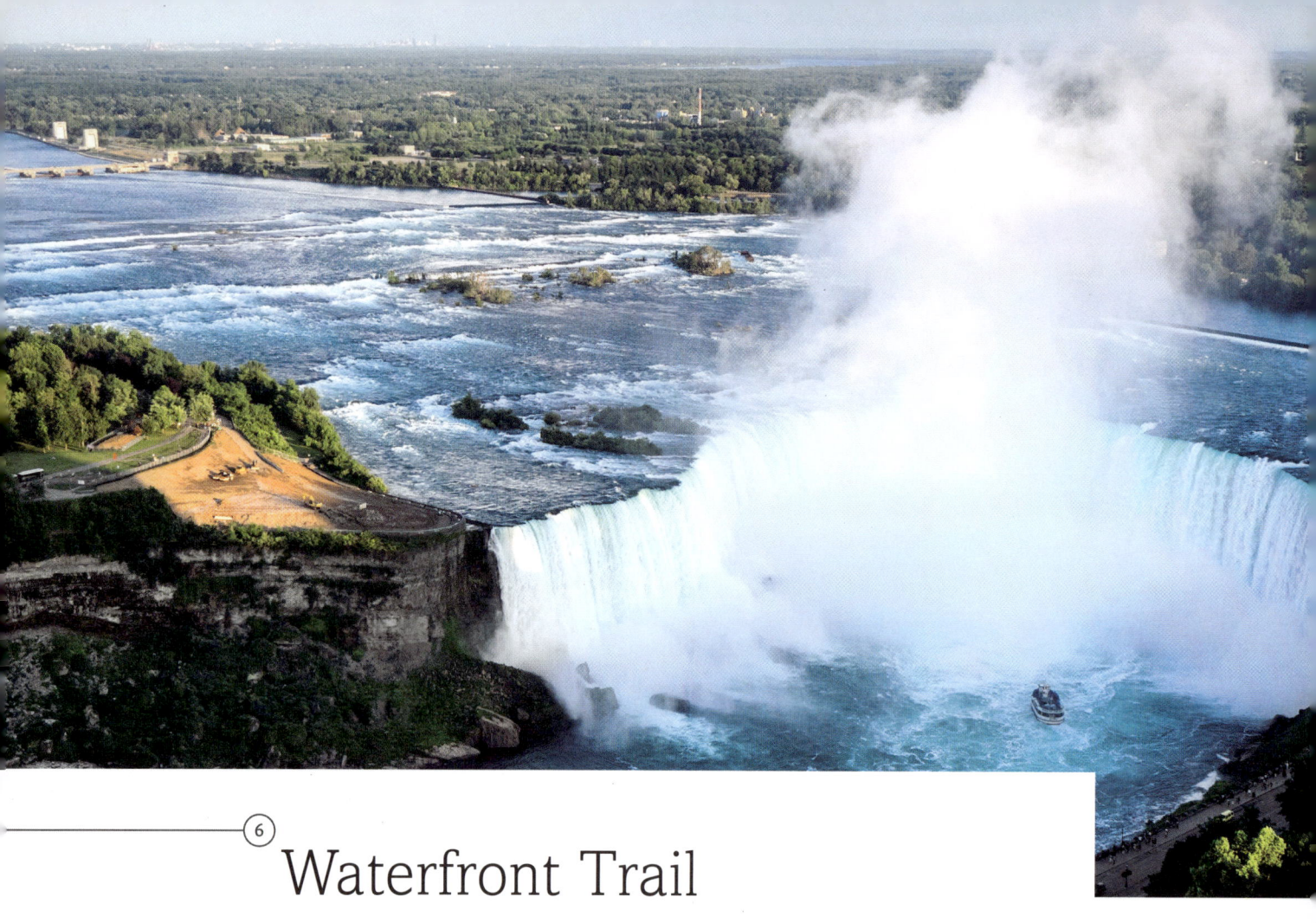

The powerful Horseshoe Falls, one of three waterfalls that comprise Niagara Falls

LOCATION Canada **START/FINISH** Grand Bend, Lake Huron/Ontario–Québec border **DISTANCE** 1,600 km (990 miles) **TIME** 3 weeks **DIFFICULTY** Easy
INFORMATION www.waterfronttrail.org

This epic trail wends its way around Ontario's Great Lakes to the border with Quebec, taking in everything from scenic port towns and historic lighthouses to pine-fringed wetlands and rolling vineyards along the way.

Clinging to the shoreline of the turquoise-tinged Great Lakes, the Waterfront Trail swaps city streets for pretty lakeside paths. Starting in Grand Bend, a vibrant beach town flanked by a sumptuous stretch of white-sugar sand, the ride heads southwards down the Essex County coast, painting a quaint picture of rural farmsteads on one side and historic lighthouses reflected in the water on the other. The bucolic scene shifts at the mouth of the Detroit River, when the trail bursts into bustling Windsor and sails right through the art-filled city's sculpture park. Lush countryside soon reclaims the route: grape-laden vineyards stretching up from the lake give way to wetland and forest on the approach to serene Point Pelee, a paradise for birders. From here, tiny beach communities appear around each bend all the way to thunderous Niagara Falls. A sharp turn, marked by historic Fort Erie, leads up to the famous cascades; before they come into sight, their rumble can be felt beneath your tyres. Winding around Lake Ontario, the trail passes big cities and secluded fishing hamlets. On the trail's last stretch along the St Lawrence river, the promise of perfect Montreal bagels and Québécois *je ne sais quoi* lures cyclists towards journey's end.

BY BIKE
NORTH AMERICA

La Route Verte

LOCATION Canada **START/FINISH** The Eastern Townships/Saguenay Fjord **DISTANCE** 5,000 km (3,106 miles) **TIME** 2–3 months **DIFFICULTY** Easy **INFORMATION** www.routeverte.org

Made up of hundreds of smaller routes, this well-marked, diverse network of interweaving trails has turned Québec into an oasis for cyclists.

French for "Green Path", Québec's Route Verte is ideal for picking your own adventure. Pedal off almost anywhere in the province and you'll find yourself following trails that loop around lakes, up rivers, over the foothills of mountains or into urban streets.

One of the earliest sections of this vast route runs from leafy Richmond to the pine-scented Saguenay Fjord. Here, you'll start by cutting through the Eastern Township's chequerboard of rolling green fields as your wheels revolve towards the city of Québec and reviving plates of tummy-lining poutine. Moving north, follow the St Lawrence River as it heads out to sea, before crossing its powerful flow (via ferry) at the pretty town of Rivière-du-Loup. Back on dry land, keep to the riverside as you roll around the coast of Baie-Sainte-Catherine towards your final stop, the tree-frosted Saguenay Fjord. Before you head inland, look right and – if you're lucky – spy beluga whales breaching the river's surface.

ORIGINS OF THE GREEN PATH

In 1994, Vélo Québec submitted an official proposal to the Québec government to create a provincial cycle network. The plan was approved one year later, but mapping and signposting the route took another 12 years to complete. It wasn't until 2013 that the 5,000th km (3,106th mile) was completed.

Below left Quebec City and the St Laurence River *Below* Cycling along the Route Verte

BY BIKE
CENTRAL AND SOUTH AMERICA

⑧
Nicoya Peninsula

LOCATION Costa Rica **START/FINISH** Playa Flamingo/Mal Pais
DISTANCE 186 km (116 miles) **TIME** 6–7 days **DIFFICULTY** Moderate
INFORMATION www.mtbproject.com

Running along the lush Pacific coast of Costa Rica's Nicoya Peninsula, this bike journey combines beach riding with blissfully empty country roads, gliding over white sands and through wildlife-rich tropical forest.

With coatis and raccoons padding alongside the trail and toucans and macaws squawking above, this cycle down Costa Rica's Pacific coast provides an exquisite introduction to the country's remarkable flora and fauna. Beginning at Playa Flamingo, the route runs south along the Nicoya Peninsula to Mal Pais, a popular surf village strung out beneath forested hills. Most of the trail runs along vast, empty tracts of sand, laced with turtle tracks and sprinklings of seashells. Huge waves pound the shore, with a handful of hardy surfers riding the breaks.

The route occasionally cuts inland, meandering along gravel trails and climbing gently undulating hills, rich in birdlife. Sometimes, even the odd sloth can be seen lounging upside down in the trees. At Tamarindo, ferries cross the estuary, pootling past gliding crocodiles. After days in the saddle, mellow villages such as Samara Beach provide welcome comforts, with hammocks rocking between swaying palms and shacks selling glistening cold beers. Most nights there will be no Wi-Fi or phone service – just the breaking of waves and a sky full of stars.

A palm tree-lined stretch of beach on the Nicoya Peninsula

BY BIKE
CENTRAL AND SOUTH AMERICA

Left The snow-capped peak of Volcán Cotopaxi
Above A basket vendor at Saquisili Market

⑨ Avenue of the Volcanoes

LOCATION Ecuador **START/FINISH** Tulcan/Cuenca **DISTANCE** 1,070 km (665 miles) **TIME** 18 days **DIFFICULTY** Challenging **INFORMATION** Mid-June to mid-September is Ecuador's dry season and the best time to embark upon this journey

Pedalling through rural Quechua communities and diverse terrain with a magnificent volcanic backdrop, every day of this ride offers a new opportunity to experience Ecuador's remote Andean highlights.

Running down two-thirds of the length of Ecuador, the Avenue of the Volcanoes is a string of over 50 volcanoes, many with their own namesake national parks. Popular with cyclists and practically devoid of vehicles, the gravel road connecting the peaks rises up into the Andes, granting million-dollar views across a horizon of vaulted volcanoes.

A kaleidoscope of scenery passes by each day, from the grassy, wind-blasted highlands to the hilly patchwork of fields and steamy cloud forest at lower altitudes. Deliciously empty and rugged landscapes are interrupted only by remote mountain settlements, often encircled by surreal, slow-lifting fog.

This journey is at its best from Cotopaxi National Park, where a herculean incline is followed by the first of many spellbinding viewpoints of the perfectly conical Volcán Cotopaxi. If luck prevails, the clouds will melt away to reveal this solitary giant of a volcano, which towers over landscapes that in any other circumstances would themselves be considered colossal. The final push reaches the fortified Inca ruins of Ingapirca, and then the city of Cueca. Here, even the hustle of urban life isn't enough to fade the vivid memories of life on the road, camping beneath vast night skies or snuggling into the warmth of a cosy *choza* thatched hut.

Riding along Bolivia's nerve-jangling Camino de la Muerte, or Death Road

10 Death Road

LOCATION Bolivia **START/FINISH** La Paz/Coroico **DISTANCE** 64 km (40 miles) **TIME** 5–6 hours **DIFFICULTY** Moderate **INFORMATION** Acclimatize to the altitude before trying the ride

Built in the 1930s, the Yungas Road plunges from the high-altitude city of La Paz to the tranquil town of Coroico, which clings to a mountainside some 3,600 m (11,800 ft) below. In the 1990s, hundreds of people died in accidents here every year, giving rise to the nickname Camino de la Muerte – Death Road. A bypass has since been built around the most dangerous segment, but intrepid cyclists – and many motorists – continue to travel down the original route.

The descent takes five to six hours and although the scenery is spectacular, your eyes must stay on the road. Some sections are just 3-m (10-ft) wide, with sheer vertical drops on one side. Oncoming traffic, waterfalls and swirling clouds of fog provide further challenges, but the sense of satisfaction of reaching Coroico in one piece is immense.

11 Route of the Seven Lakes

LOCATION Argentina **START/FINISH** Villa La Angostura/San Martín de Los Andes **DISTANCE** 110 km (68 miles) **TIME** 2 days **DIFFICULTY** Moderate **INFORMATION** Avoid winter when the road can be closed following heavy snowfall

Skirting seven crystalline lakes – each prettier than the last – the 110-km (68-mile) Ruta de los Siete Lagos takes you through one of the most beautiful parts of Patagonia. Leafy, evergreen trees create thick forests that tumble from hilltop to lakeside, overlooked by the crooked peak of Volcán Lanín. The shores of the jade-coloured waters provide picture-perfect rest stops, while simple wooden cabins offer a cosy place to hunker down after a day of pedalling. The steady tempo of a bike makes the ideal pace at which to soak up the majesty of the scenery, powered by invigorating lungfuls of fresh alpine air.

BY BIKE
CENTRAL AND SOUTH AMERICA

12 Santiago to Marea del Portillo

LOCATION Cuba **START/FINISH** Santiago de Cuba/Marea del Portillo **DISTANCE** 64 km (40 miles) **TIME** 2 days **DIFFICULTY** Moderate **INFORMATION** Decent bike rentals are rare in Cuba, so it is advisable to bring your own

A cycle along the bumpy but spectacular coastal road that edges Cuba's southeastern corner is at once idyllic and wild. Starting in Santiago de Cuba, the birthplace of the revolution, the route grinds ever upward, until the peak crests and the slope breezes into an easy, scenic road through verdant countryside. From here, the ride alternates between challenging hills and stony tracks, with tempting white-sugar beaches around every corner – there's plenty of time to plunge into the crystalline water for a refreshing swim. Roaming cattle, lounging lizards and goats standing stubbornly in the road steadily give way to swaying palms, signalling the outskirts of Marea del Portillo. Pull up at a beach bar and toast your arrival under the glow of the setting sun.

The slopes of Cuba's Sierra Maestra range reaching down to the Caribbean Sea

13 Valle de Viñales

LOCATION Cuba **START/FINISH** Viñales/Viñales National Park **DISTANCE** 32 km (19 miles) **TIME** 6 hours **DIFFICULTY** Moderate **INFORMATION** Decent bike rentals are rare in Cuba, so it is advisable to bring your own

Cycle back in time through Cuba's Valle de Viñales, a lush expanse of fields where age-old agricultural methods have survived unchanged for centuries. Royal palms sway overhead as you roll over a network of paved lanes and red-earth paths, past Jurassic *mogotes* (near-vertical hills) that rise up to 400 m (1,312 ft). The route crisscrosses bright-green tobacco fields, tilled by *guajiros* (farmers) coaxing lumbering oxen; nearby, workers perch in small wooden huts hand-rolling cigars. Respite from the heat comes in the form of roadside stalls selling *guarapo* (sugar-cane juice), providing a refreshing energy boost for the final push to the National Park office. There, a tiny bar makes a scenic vantage point from which to look back on your day's adventure in this timeless landscape.

MOGOTES

Valle de Viñales is framed by the bulging karstic *mogotes*, or sugarloaf mountains, of Sierra de los Órganos. Legend has it that the range was named by Spanish sailors, who thought the misty *mogotes* resembled church organs.

163

BY BIKE
EUROPE

(14) # Land's End to John O'Groats

LOCATION UK **START/FINISH** Land's End/John O'Groats **DISTANCE** 1,770 km (1,100 miles) **TIME** 16 days **DIFFICULTY** Challenging; a long ride, mostly on relatively flat terrain, with some steep climbs and long ascents **INFORMATION** www.sustrans.org.uk

This epic ride leads from the southernmost tip of England to the northernmost point of mainland Scotland, across rolling moors, green valleys and rugged hills, through market towns amid gentle farmland, and along misty, seabird-haunted coasts.

Cycling through the picturesque scenery of the Lake District

CELEBRATE the end of your journey with a dram of one of Scotland's renowned malt whiskies

John O'Groats

RIDE the **Nevis Range Mountain Gondola** for a breathtaking view of Ben Nevis from nearby Aonach Mòr

SPOT seals and seabirds on a Loch Linnhe wildlife cruise from **Fort William**

EXPLORE the lush greenery of a pocket of rainforest within the **Eden Project**

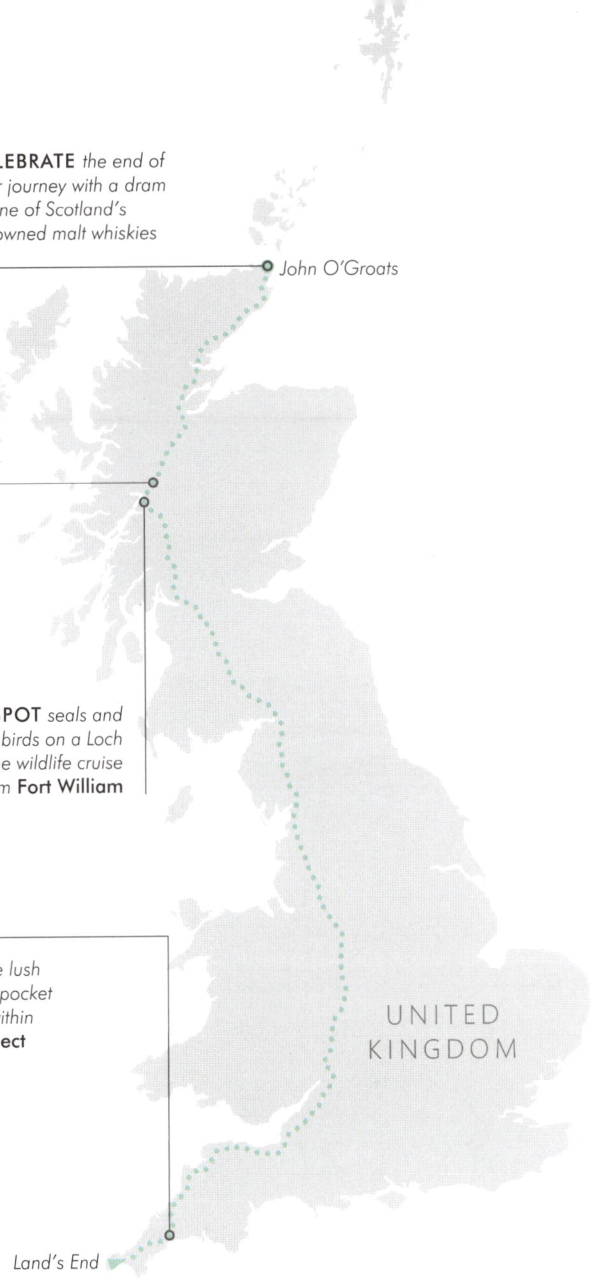

UNITED KINGDOM

Land's End

One of Britain's longest and most rewarding rides, this route takes you through every conceivable landscape that the island has to offer. Starting from the surf-pounded cliffs of Land's End, the weathered granite and white beaches of Cornwall give way to the close-cropped grassland of Bodmin Moor and Exmoor and the lush lowlands and apple orchards of Somerset. Things move up a gear as the route plunges into the tree-studded gorges of the Mendip Hills, before rolling downhill into the Marches – the borderlands between England and Wales – and onwards through the city-scapes of the West Midlands and Manchester. This urban sprawl gives way to the pastoral beauty of the Lake District, where signposts that for hundreds of miles have simply indicated "The North" finally concede that Scotland is next door – just past the 2,000-year-old Roman ramparts of Hadrian's Wall.

Skirting Glasgow involves busy urban roads, but the going soon gets wilder – and steeper – as you venture into the Highlands. Pine trees darken the slopes of the Great Glen and its chain of lochs, eventually bringing the first glimpse of the east coast and Inverness. You may spot dolphins as you round the Moray Firth, before heading northeast into the weird and bleakly beautiful Caithness Flow Country. This flat landscape of peat and heather makes for easy riding on the final stretch to John O'Groats. On arrival, take a well-earned rest and congratulate yourself: you've joined the élite band of successful "end-to-enders".

165

BY BIKE
EUROPE

(15)
La Loire à Vélo

LOCATION France **START/FINISH** Blois/Saumur **DISTANCE** 160 km (100 miles) **TIME** 5 days **DIFFICULTY** Easy **INFORMATION** www.loireavelo.fr

Following France's longest and loveliest river, this journey takes in beautiful medieval towns, willow-covered islands and grape-laden vineyards, but it's the castles that steal the show. Home to three kings – Louis XII, Francois I and Henri III – Blois' royal chateau is a fabulous confection of medieval, Gothic, Renaissance and Classical architecture. As you pedal along the shade-dappled trails from here, the feudal fantasy that is the Château de Chaumont soon comes into sight – an elegant, monochrome fortress, with white walls and grey turrets. So it continues, with a new set of ramparts looming into view above the Loire every day.

Once you've had your fill of castles, take advantage of the produce grown on the river's fertile valley. In lush Touraine, cherries and melons ripen and purple artichokes nod under the summer sun. No wonder they call this the "garden of France".

Cycling past the Chateau d'Amboise on the bank of the River Loire

(16)
Istrian Coast

LOCATION Italy to Croatia **START/FINISH** Trieste/Pula **DISTANCE** 250 km (155 miles) **TIME** 1 week **DIFFICULTY** Easy **INFORMATION** Accessible year-round

It may be small, but the attraction-packed Istrian peninsula spans three different countries. This trail begins in Italy's Trieste, an isolated port city that offers grand Neo-Classical architecture and even grander sea views. From here, the coast-hugging trail slithers southwards into Slovenia, sweeping through one impossibly pretty orange-roofed seaport after another, before giving you a (rather briny) taste of the Sečovlje Salina saltpans.

The two-wheeler trail continues into Croatia, passing up and over undulating hills, crossing fertile farmland and swerving around sandy coves, before making a beeline for picture-perfect Rovinj. Set on an oval isle that juts out into the Adriatic and topped by a towering white church tower, this quaint, colourful harbour town is an unmissable stop. One more day's ride will bring you into Pula, Istria's oldest town and the end of the road.

another way

Still have energy in your legs? Add on a day's cycling around the scenic Brijuni Islands. Ferries to the main island Veliki Brijun (famed for its dinosaur footprints) depart from Fažana, midway between Rovinj and Pula on the Istrian Coast.

BY BIKE
EUROPE

Golden leaves leading to an old-fashioned windmill in a vineyard near Santenay

⑰ Route des Grands Crus

LOCATION France **START/FINISH** Dijon/Santenay **DISTANCE** 64 km (40 miles) **TIME** 3 days **DIFFICULTY** Easy
INFORMATION www.beaune-tourism.com

One for cycling oenophiles, the Route des Grands Crus (Route of the Great Wine Localities) takes in some of France's finest wineries. It's a journey best made when the vines turn from green to gold and crimson as summer ripens into autumn.

Rolling south from the city of Dijon, the verdant terraces morph into the vineyards of the Côte de Nuits, where the vines are heavy with Pinot Noir grapes. Here, red wine is king and the commune of Nuits-Saint-Georges' very name is pronounced in reverential tones by sommeliers. Wheeling on to Corgoloin, follow the road into the Côte de Beaune, homeland of dry white wines. With the vineyards of Meursault and Montrachet stretching invitingly either side of the road, how could you not stop for a taste?

⑱ Tuscany

LOCATION Italy **START/FINISH** Florence (loop)
DISTANCE 190 km (118 miles) **TIME** 5 days
DIFFICULTY Moderate to challenging
INFORMATION www.viaggiareinbici.it

There's no better way to soak up Tuscany's vineyards than on two wheels. This circular route from Florence to Chianti, and back again, takes five days of vigorous cycling, but each turn of the pedal is worth it, as the road snakes its way through Tuscany's most recognizable landscapes.

Pedalling south from the Renaissance city of Florence, through the Tuscan hills, you'll find Tavarnelle Val di Pesa. This historic town is nestled in the wine-producing Chianti region – an undulating hillscape, carpeted with vineyards and olive groves. Ancient villages and historic fortresses pepper the horizon, as you wheel through medieval Gaiole and past the terracotta-coloured Castello di Brolio.

Breeze back to Florence, along the beautiful Via Chiantigiana, along quiet country lanes and white gravel tracks that criss-cross oak forest. On either side, gorgeous cypress-lined drives twist and turn to reach hillside estates. It's hard to resist making a detour up one of these vertiginous roads on the way back to the Tuscan capital.

◄ ►
L'EROICA

Every October, thousands of cyclists dressed in vintage clothing take to Tuscany's roads for L'Eroica. This non-competitive cycling event aims to protect the region's *strade bianche* (white gravel tracks) from being paved.

Left The road bending around Loch Bun Abhainn Eadarra on the Isle of Harris
Above Watching the sunset from Callanish stone circle on Lewis

Hebridean Way

LOCATION UK **START/FINISH** Vatersay/Butt of Lewis **DISTANCE** 298 km (185 miles) **TIME** 1 week **DIFFICULTY** Moderate; some steep ascents **INFORMATION** www.visitouterhebrides.co.uk; route is marked as the NCR 780

Ten islands, six causeways and two ferry crossings make up this cycling adventure. Take your time, enjoy the ride, and prepare to be dazzled by the enchanting seascapes, desolate mountains ranges and heart-wrenching history of the Outer Hebrides.

Begin on the tiny island of Vatersay, famed for its white sands and impossibly turquoise waters. With the prevailing wind at your back as you pedal north, a series of causeways and ferry crossings take you through the low-lying islands of Barra and Eriskay, across waterlogged South Uist and tiny Benbecula to the rusted-orange hillsides of North Uist and sandy Berneray. But it's Harris that will steal your heart. With every bend another idyllic seascape slides into view, backed by sweet-smelling wildflower meadows known as machair.

On to Lewis, where ancient standing stones speak of long-lost civilizations, while deserted crofters' cottages – scars of highland clearances – tell a more recent tale. Both are solemn reminders that, sooner or later, all things must pass, and upon arrival at the Butt of Lewis, so too must your journey.

GAELIC

First introduced by Celts from Ireland and mixed with Old Norse, Gaelic was once the language of Scotland. While it faces extinction on the mainland, Gaelic is still the language of daily life in the Outer Hebrides. But Gaelic culture is more than just a language; it's a rich and ancient heritage of music and song, storytelling and seafaring, community and kinship.

BY BIKE
EUROPE

⑳
Transylvania

LOCATION Romania **START/FINISH** Copșa Mare/Viscri **DISTANCE** 130 km (80 miles) **TIME** 4 days **DIFFICULTY** Moderate; regular climbs and descents **INFORMATION** www.romaniatourism.com

Transylvania isn't all about Dracula; this in-the-saddle adventure bypasses the mythology and explores the reality of this remarkable Romanian region, which is home not to vampires, but time-worn villages.

Set off in autumn and wheel along this scenic route, sweeping past village after village swaddled in a blanket of yellows, browns and oranges. Starting in tiny Copșa Mare, the path climbs up to a series of forested ridges, before diving back down into Mălâncrav – home to the largest Saxon population in Transylvania. Gold-hued haystacks, fruit-filled apple trees and quaint slope-roofed houses suggest a world little changed since the 14th century.

The path climbs skywards once more, through ancient oak forests towards the mist-covered medieval walled city of Sighișoara, a sea of implausibly pretty – and impeccably preserved – pastel-shaded buildings. From here, the trail flees the "big city" – first along flat tree-lined streets, then up through thickly forested hilltop trails – for sleepy Saschiz, a little village with a UNESCO-listed fortified church. Sweeping, sheep-dotted slopes mark the final stretch into the spectacularly beautiful Saxon village of Viscri. With hundreds of historic, renovated buildings ringed by rolling countryside, it is the perfect end to this traditional Transylvanian tour.

The stone buildings and fortified church at the centre of the medieval village of Copșa Mare

Bollenstreek

Cycling towards a traditional windmill through a golden field of rapeseed

LOCATION The Netherlands **START/FINISH** Bloemendaal aan Zee/Lisse
DISTANCE 30 km (19 miles) **TIME** 4 hours **DIFFICULTY** Easy; flat terrain
INFORMATION www.holland.com

Set off through the Netherlands' kaleidoscopic bulb fields in March or April to catch the spectacular floral display for which the country is famed.

This half-a-day cycle starts with a seascape painted in hues of blue and grey. As you ride inland from the seaside town of Bloemendaal aan Zee, and the rolling combers of the North Sea coast, dead-flat trails lead through the sandy heaths and huddled oak and beech coppices of the Zuid-Kemmerland National Park. When you join the LF1 Nordzeeroute cycle trail at Zeeweg, platoons of other cyclists suddenly appear: troops of hard-core lycra-clad endurance riders intent on completing this long-distance route across the Netherlands, and families cycling from Amsterdam to Haarlem on city bikes with kids in tow – literally – aboard toddler trailers. This disparate group tracks the sandy

BY BIKE
EUROPE

Expansive fields in the Bollenstreek, lined with colourful rows of tulips

shoreline of the Amsterdamse Waterleinduinen. Bikes aren't allowed to stray off the marked trail in this conservation area, nicknamed "the green heart of Holland", so dismount, lock up your bike and go, on foot, in search of red deer and other wildlife.

From the southern edge of this pocket of wilderness, there's an abrupt transition from windswept moorland and russet-brown heath to a tidy, typically Dutch gridwork of canals and reclaimed polder around the town of Noorwijkerhout. Crossing the Leidsevaart canal – an impossibly straight ribbon of water stretching from horizon to horizon – the trail is suddenly plunged into the dazzling colours and gorgeous scents of the Bollenstreek (Flower Strip) leading to Lisse. Purple crocuses peek first from chilly soil in March, followed by yellow daffodils and narcissus. Then it's time for deep blue hyacinths and irises. At the height of the season, in mid-April, tulips explode in a pyrotechnic display of rainbow colours beneath the delicate white and pink blossoms of Japanese cherry trees. It's a sight that will take your breath away.

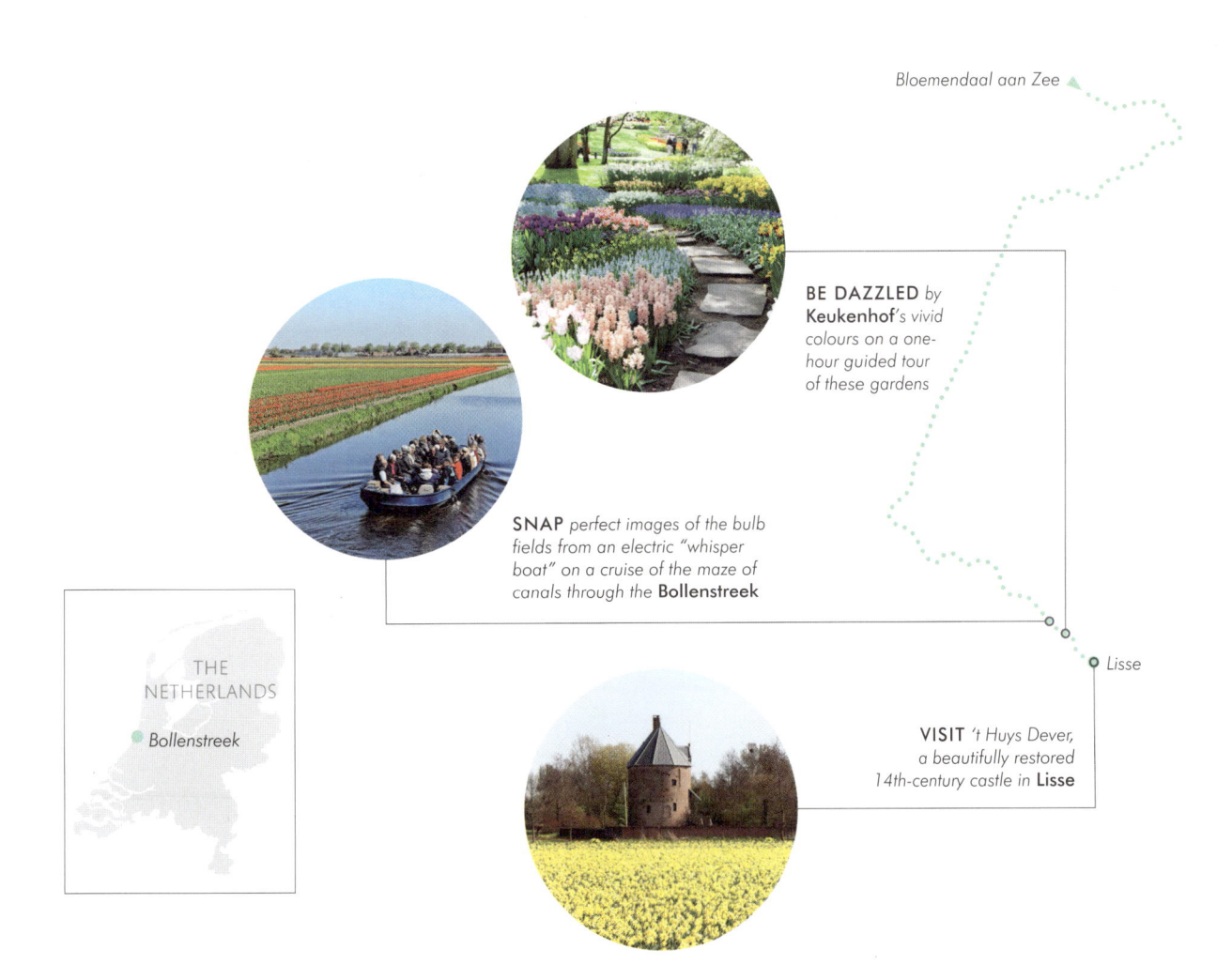

Bloemendaal aan Zee

BE DAZZLED by *Keukenhof*'s vivid colours on a one-hour guided tour of these gardens

SNAP *perfect images of the bulb fields from an electric "whisper boat" on a cruise of the maze of canals through the* **Bollenstreek**

THE NETHERLANDS
Bollenstreek

Lisse

VISIT *'t Huys Dever, a beautifully restored 14th-century castle in* **Lisse**

BY BIKE
EUROPE

Wildflowers on the outskirts of Svaneke, a small town on the eastern coast of Bornholm

㉒ Around Bornholm

LOCATION Denmark **START/FINISH** Bornholm Kunstmuseum/Dueodde Beach **DISTANCE** 40 km (25 miles) **TIME** 5 hours **DIFFICULTY** Moderate **INFORMATION** www.bornholm.info

Around 230 km (143 miles) of cycling trails traverse this Danish island, winding along steep seaside cliffs, through golden fields, past lighthouses and down to bone-white beaches backed with tall pines. The routes were constructed for practical purposes, but they've swiftly become a hit with visitors.

The most evocative journey takes in Bornholm's far-flung eastern perimeter, stopping off en route for a *smørrebrod* (open-faced sandwich) at the small town of Gudhjem. As the summer sun sends shimmers across the water, opportunities for sea bathing are endless. At the southern tip of the island lies Dueodde, where a dusky emerald coniferous forest opens out to soft, ivory sand and deep water. Is it any wonder that Bornholm is also called Solskinsøen (Sunshine Island)?

㉓ Trollstigen

LOCATION Norway **START/FINISH** Åndalsnes/Trollstigen Plateau **DISTANCE** 17 km (11 miles) **TIME** 1 day **DIFFICULTY** Challenging **INFORMATION** www.visitnorway.com

When the snow clears around May, the zigzagging Trollstigen – a mountain pass on Route 63 – opens up to adrenaline-seeking cyclists, who use this feat of engineering to climb from the fjord-front town of Åndalsnes to the top of Stigrøra mountain.

The hardest part of the ride comes at the end. After rolling over the bridge across the rushing and foaming Rauma River, riders tense with anticipation. Boulders – legend says they are trolls petrified by sunlight – loom eerily on either side of the track, and the thinning air, coupled with 11 dramatic hairpin turns, sucks any energy reserves dry. Thankfully, Stigfossen waterfall revives cyclists with a welcome spray before – finally – there's the precipitous Trollstigen Plateau. This steel and glass platform hovers 200 m (656 ft) above the pass, seemingly jutting out into the mouth of the abyss. The sense of achievement is nearly as overwhelming as the view.

another way

Intense training is required to be able to tackle the whole of Trollstigen from Åndalsnes, but those who haven't prepared need not be perturbed. Electric bikes are available from Hotel Aak, halfway up the pass, making Trollstigen accessible to all.

BY BIKE
EUROPE

㉔ Bodensee to the Königssee

LOCATION Germany **START/FINISH** Lindau/Schönau **DISTANCE** 418 km (259 miles) **TIME** 3 weeks **DIFFICULTY** Moderate **INFORMATION** www.bodensee-koenigssee-radweg.de

Here's the thing about Bodensee: it's so big, boundless and beautiful that Germany, Switzerland and Austria all fight for space along its bucolic shoreline. To keen, lycra-clad cyclists, though, it's the starting point for one of Central Europe's most striking long-distance rides, a route which crosses the Ammergau Alps from Southern Germany before trundling north to the Königssee. See it from the saddle yourself and you'll soon understand why this route represents Central Europe at its best: there are wild swimming spots, unspoiled mountain plateaus, stunning alpine panoramas and belly-hugging foodie pit stops with unmatched German hospitality.

The placid waters of Germany's Königssee, fringed by alpine forest and mountains

㉕ Flanders

LOCATION Belgium **START/FINISH** Ghent/Bruges **DISTANCE** 45 km (28 miles) **TIME** 2–3 hours **DIFFICULTY** Challenging **INFORMATION** www.visitflanders.com

This Belgian region may be best known for its tragic role in World War I, but nowadays Flanders is gaining a reputation for cycling. One of the most challenging rides is the legendary Oude Kwaremont, on the route between Ghent and Bruges. This 2-km (1-mile) ribbon of crudely cobbled asphalt climbs in an everlasting series of bumps and gear grinds. Well known to riders and tour competitors, the scramble is a bit of a shock to the system, but the ascent is one of Belgium's most rewarding. Considered alongside the region's other Holy Grail rides — the tricky Koppenberg, tormenting Kapelmuur and thigh-burning Kemmelberg — you'll quickly gather that cycling in Flanders is not for the faint-hearted.

FLANDERS IN WARTIME

From 1914 to 1918, Flanders saw more than a million fatalities as the Western Front of World War I. Learn more about the region during wartime at In Flanders Fields Museum in Ypres or at Tyne Cot, the largest cemetery for Commonwealth forces who died in Flanders' fields.

BY BIKE
AFRICA AND THE MIDDLE EAST

Tour d'Afrique

LOCATION Egypt to South Africa **START/FINISH** Cairo/Cape Town **DISTANCE** 12,000 km (7,500 miles) **TIME** 4 months **DIFFICULTY** Challenging, with every road and weather condition imaginable (with the possible exception of snow) **INFORMATION** https://tdaglobalcycling.com/tour-dafrique

There is no more epic ride than this one from Cairo to Cape Town – traversing the length of the African continent, it is the ultimate cycling challenge.

Whether riding the almost-annual race or undertaking the expedition alone, the Tour d'Afrique is the kind of journey that oozes adventure. From the clamour of Cairo to the clear blue skies of Cape Town, via every possible terrain in between, this ride takes you deep into the heart of the continent. Along the way, you'll discover an Africa that few visitors get to experience, far removed from the safari world of private planes and luxury lodges. At journey's end, you'll dismount dusty and exhausted, but you'll also take with you countless memories that will secure a very special place for Africa in your heart.

The scenery en route is continental in its variety and scope. Beginning in the hot, dry north, you follow the Nile Valley through Egypt and Sudan, with the forbidding sands of the Sahara Desert lying just beyond the fertile fringes of the river. As you pass down through Ethiopia, the character of the land changes – things become greener and the weather becomes more humid, with rain a constant possibility.

Along the way, you'll discover an Africa that few visitors get to experience

Right *Pausing for a rest in the highlands of northern Ethiopia*
Below *Elephants in front of Mount Kilimanjaro, Amboseli National Park, Kenya*

Cairo

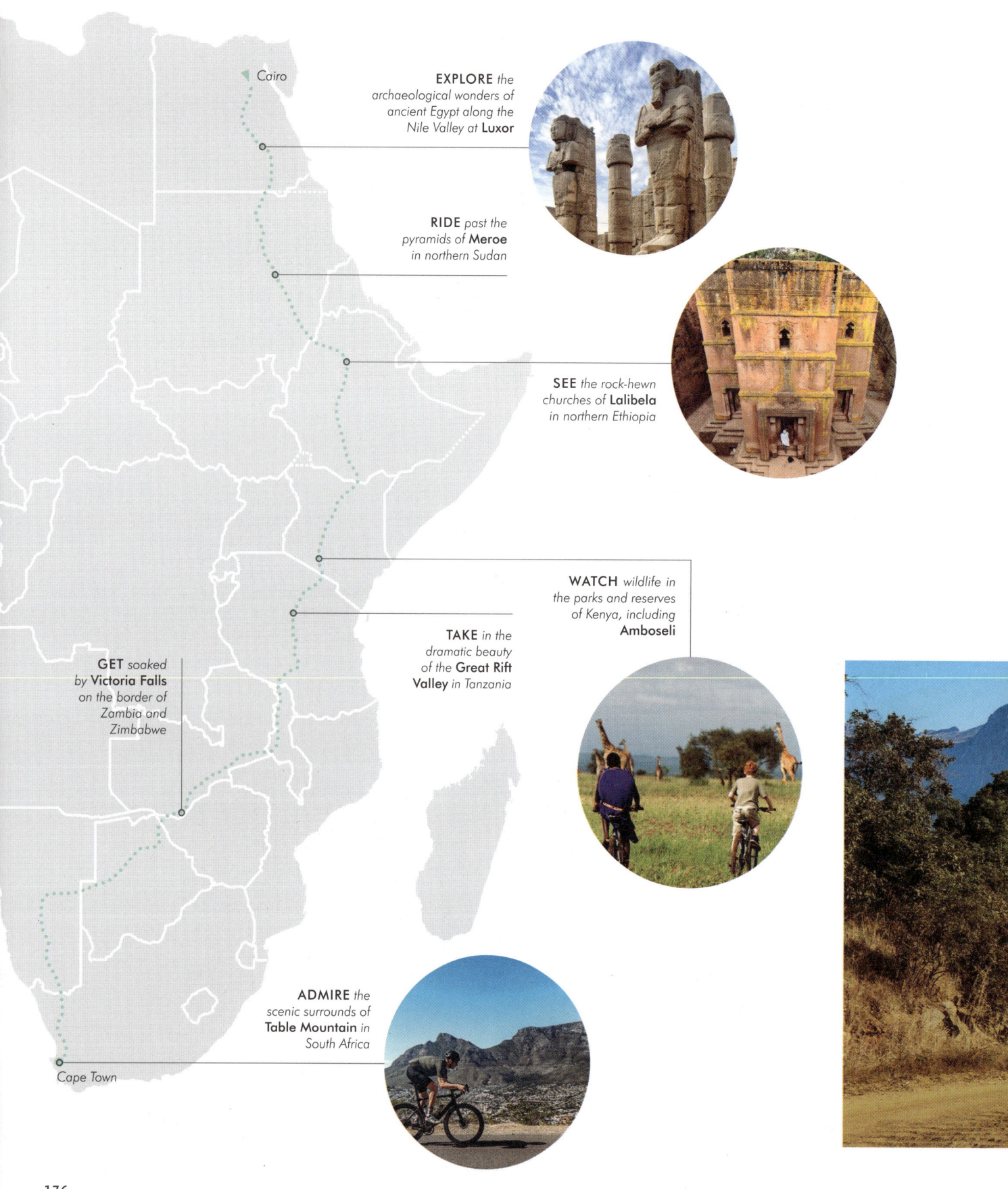

EXPLORE *the archaeological wonders of ancient Egypt along the Nile Valley at* **Luxor**

RIDE *past the pyramids of* **Meroe** *in northern Sudan*

SEE *the rock-hewn churches of* **Lalibela** *in northern Ethiopia*

WATCH *wildlife in the parks and reserves of Kenya, including* **Amboseli**

TAKE *in the dramatic beauty of the* **Great Rift Valley** *in Tanzania*

GET *soaked by* **Victoria Falls** *on the border of Zambia and Zimbabwe*

ADMIRE *the scenic surrounds of* **Table Mountain** *in South Africa*

Cape Town

BY BIKE
AFRICA AND THE MIDDLE EAST

Down into the south, the journey continues through the verdant tropics, past the glorious mountains of the Great Rift Valley and the wildlife-rich savannah grasslands across East Africa's heartland. South of the equator, down through Tanzania, Malawi, Zambia, Botswana and Namibia, the climate and terrain become drier by degrees, and the strain of the constant truck traffic with which you share the road is offset by the astonishing mosaic of cultures and languages. All roads lead to South Africa, where parched deserts give way to lush vineyards as you draw ever closer to Cape Town.

This is the kind of journey that requires careful planning. If the race itself – a semi-regular event at best – is not running, the entire trip is best accomplished in a team of riders to share the load when the going gets tough. Back-up helpers and vehicles are also recommended to assist in the many obstacles you'll encounter along the way, from flat tyres and equipment failures to bureaucratic visa complications and communication misunderstandings. But don't let any of this deter you: this is one of the greatest rides you'll have the chance to undertake, anywhere, ever.

another way
There are almost as many alternative routes as there are African countries – South Sudan and Uganda instead of Ethiopia and Kenya, for example, or Zimbabwe as a substitute for Botswana and Namibia. Much depends on security and open border crossings.

Below *The granite peaks of Mount Mulanje, Malawi* **Bottom right** *Members of the Masai community in Amboseli National Park, Kenya* **Right** *Franschhoek Wine Valley, South Africa*

BY BIKE
AFRICA AND THE MIDDLE EAST

Above Camping en route at the roadside *Right* A zebra crossing the road

Botswana Circuit

LOCATION Botswana **START/FINISH** Gaborone (loop) **DISTANCE** 1,791 km (1,113 miles) **TIME** 2 weeks **DIFFICULTY** Flat roads, but long distances between towns **INFORMATION** www.botswanatourism.co.bw

It's rare that you can visit an entire country by bicycle and barely climb a single hill, with traffic so light that you can go hours between glimpses of vehicles. Welcome to Botswana, a land as rich in wildlife as it is lightly populated with people.

Botswana might almost have been custom-made for cycling. Yes, traffic can be quite heavy between the cities of Gaborone and Francistown, but otherwise this is a journey of virtually empty roads lined with flat-topped acacias. The long stretches of tarmac between towns such as Nata, Maun and Ghanzi are rarely frequented by trucks or other vehicles. Instead, natural giants rule these roads, with elephants languidly crossing at will and great baobab trees silhouetted against the deep blue of a desert sky.

In some ways, Botswana is Africa for beginner cyclists, a gentle introduction without the busy cities or fear-inducing traffic. But you'll need to be fit enough to cover long distances between towns, and self-sufficient in food and water for those days when you have to camp by the roadside. The heat, too, can be fierce, while the rains can ruin your trip – avoid December to March or April. The sense of achievement is powerful: by journey's end, you'll have circumnavigated much of the Kalahari, the world's largest sand desert, on two wheels.

BY BIKE
AFRICA AND THE MIDDLE EAST

(28)
Rif Mountains

LOCATION Morocco **START/FINISH** Tetouan/Chefchaouen
DISTANCE 65 km (40 miles) **TIME** 1 week **DIFFICULTY**
Moderate to challenging **INFORMATION** www.visitmorocco.com;
a mountain bike is recommended

This ride through the Rif Mountains – homeland of the Berbers and overflowing with picture-perfect villages – is one of the most scenic cycling routes in the whole of North Africa.

The Rif Mountains are a microcosm of Morocco, and this ride will leave you in no doubt of the country's charms. It begins in Tetouan, one of Morocco's least known yet most beautiful towns, with a UNESCO World Heritage-listed medina (old town). At the other end of the route lies Chefchaouen, a smaller, enchanted version of Tetouan – blue-hued, clinging to the hillside and labyrinthine in its tangle of pretty lanes. The road in between bucks and weaves across the hills, passing many scenes of rural Berber life: hand-hoed agricultural fields, baking olive groves and donkey carts transporting goods to market. Follow the local rhythm by rising with the sun, riding in the fresh morning, then resting in the shade during the heat of the day. Arriving at sunset with tired legs, you'll find villages buzzing with life as everyone emerges into the relative cool of evening. After taking in the sights and sounds, hit the hay early to ensure that you're rested and ready to do it all over again the next day.

THE RIF MOUNTAINS

The Rif Mountains are part of the same geological range as the massifs of southern Spain. Wth a name that means "the coast" in the local dialect, they can seem as much of the sea as of the interior. Although deforestation is a major problem, forests of cedar and oak, fir and pine trees provide a habitat here for endangered populations of Barbary macaque.

The beautiful town of Tetouan in the foothills of the Rif Mountains

BY BIKE
ASIA

(29) # Shimanami Kaido

LOCATION Japan **START/FINISH** Onomichi/Imabari **DISTANCE** 70 km (44 miles) **TIME** 1–2 days **DIFFICULTY** Easy; the route is well maintained and clearly marked, with few steep inclines **INFORMATION** www.shimanami-cycle.or.jp

Running across the serene Seto Inland Sea, this leisurely bike ride takes you on an epic island-hopping adventure. Found all along the way are sparkling coastal vistas, dense, emerald-hued forests and laid-back fishing villages.

Kurushima-Kaikyo Bridge, spanning the Kurushima Strait

JAPAN

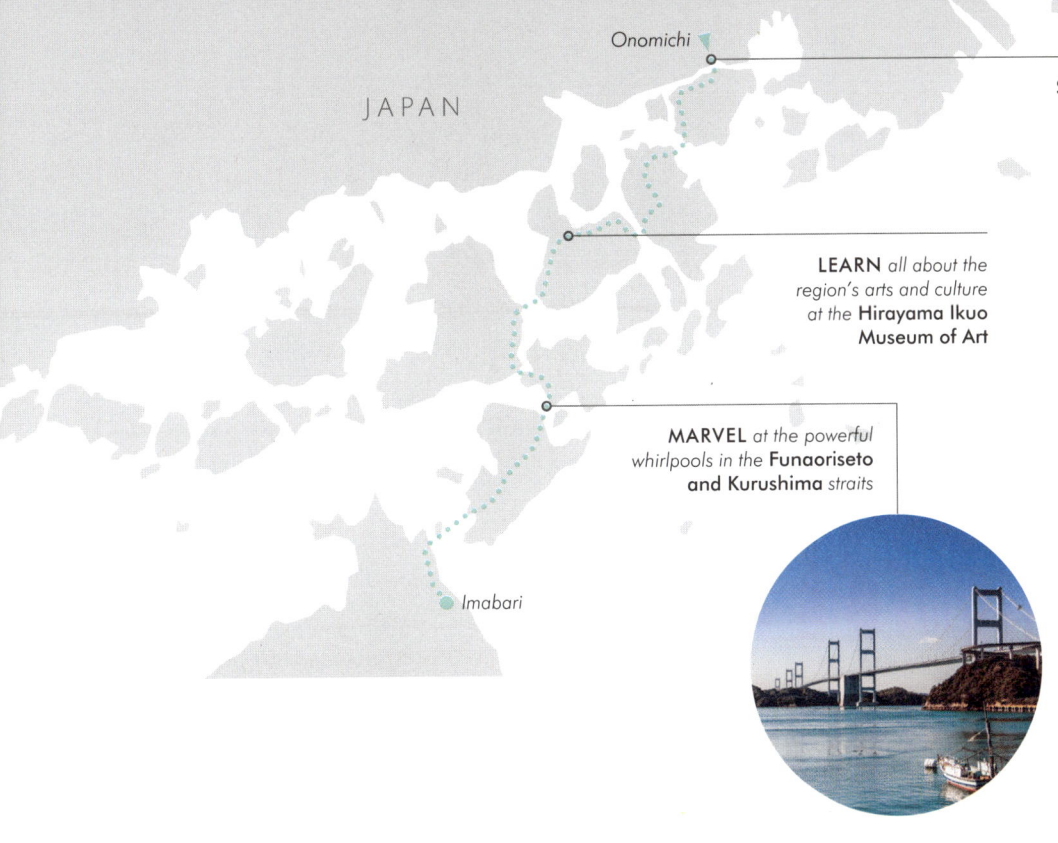

Onomichi

START *your trip at U2 in* **Onomichi**, *home to a bike-friendly hotel, stylish café and cycling shop*

LEARN *all about the region's arts and culture at the* **Hirayama Ikuo Museum of Art**

MARVEL *at the powerful whirlpools in the* **Funaoriseto** *and* **Kurushima** *straits*

Imabari

The wide, calm waters of Japan's Seto Inland Sea present a relaxing vista, speckled with pine-capped islets and lazily traversed by sightseeing boats. Part of Japan's oldest national park, this area has attracted artists, poets and pilgrims for centuries.

The scenic Shimanami Kaido cycle path crosses the Seto Inland Sea to connect the San'yo Coast of Honshu, Japan's largest island, with Shikoku, the fourth largest. Along the way, it hops across a further six islands – including castle-topped Innoshima and beach-lined Ikuchijima – via seven main bridges.

Though the route can be tackled in a day, a slower paces gives you more time to explore off the bike. Just a short ferry ride from Innoshima and Ikuchijima is the island of Iwagijima, where looming Mount Sekizen blushes pink with cherry blossoms in spring. Visit the observatory atop its summit for 360-degree views, best at sunset when the rosy light languidly spreads over the water, then hunker down at a *minshuku*. At these

> Indulge in home-cooked meals of fresh seafood and drift off to sleep to the sound of the sea

traditional family-run inns, you can experience the area's warm hospitality, indulge in home-cooked meals of fresh seafood and drift off to sleep to the sound of the sea.

While the whole route is spellbinding, the best is saved until last. Crossing the elegant Kurushima-Kaikyo bridge – spanning the Kurushima Strait from Oshima to Shikoku – the final stretch treats you to spectacular views across the islet-sprinkled sea, where swirling tidal whirlpools mirror the spinning wheels of your bike.

Following the coastline on the scenic Shimanami Kaido path

BY BIKE
ASIA

Four Rivers Path

LOCATION South Korea **START/FINISH** Seoul/Busan
DISTANCE 630 km (391 miles) **TIME** 1–2 weeks
DIFFICULTY Moderate; few climbs **INFORMATION** www.bikenara.co.kr

This dedicated cycling route is a deep-dive into the centre of South Korea. Passing over mountains and through lime-green paddy fields, the path follows the course of the country's greatest rivers all the way from Seoul in the north to Busan in the south.

Designed to protect South Korea's riverbanks from flooding and environmental damage, the Four Rivers Path follows the Han, Nakdong, Geum and Yeongsan rivers, which together cut a diagonal route across the county. Part of the pleasure of this route is its slick infrastructure, a reflection of the country's efficient approach to design. You'll never want for amenities – there are bathrooms, rest areas and repair shops all along the way. But the real joy of this ride is the effortless inland scenery.

As you pedal out of Seoul, the path follows the broad Han River along flat plains, passing through bike-only tunnels and over futuristic bridges, leaving the city's blazing neon and towering apartment blocks behind. For much of the way, you'll breeze right alongside the rivers, or even cycle directly over them on raised platforms, as you whizz by rice paddy fields.

Overnights in small towns like Mungyeong and Sangju offer the chance to sample traditional Korean cuisine, such as *bibimbap* (sauteed vegetables and kimchi on warm rice) and succulent barbecued meats, as well as to soothe aching muscles in one of the many *jjimjilbang* (bathhouses). Riding the Four Rivers Path is a great way to get to know South Korea.

The tail end of the Four Rivers Path, passing through Oncheoncheon Citizen Park in Busan

Traditional architecture in Lijiang's pretty old town

㉛ Tea Horse Road

LOCATION China **START/FINISH** Shangri-la/Dali
DISTANCE 430 km (270 miles) **TIME** 10 days
DIFFICULTY Challenging **INFORMATION** www.cnto.org.uk

A high-altitude ride at the base of the Himalayas, this route shadows the ancient Tea Horse Road trading route, which once connected China with south Asia.

This trail is shaped by its history as a route for trading tea for horses, and vice versa. The ride sets off from the mountain village of Zhongdian, better known as Shangri-la after the utopian paradise depicted in James Hilton's novel *Lost Horizons*. Here, tea is mixed with yak butter – the perfect calorific treat to help cyclists acclimatize to the heady 3,160 m (10,367 ft) altitude.

Traders rarely made it to the end of the road with all their goods and the small city of Lijiang – traditional home of the Naxi people – grew in prosperity due to its market. It's still a difficult stop to resist, with its ornate temples, lantern-strung buildings and easygoing nightlife. From here, the ride descends along country roads, through farmland and past orchards, to cobblestoned Shaxi, where you can stay in a traditional guest-house, complete with stables for muleteers. But the most fitting place to end your journey is where the Tea Horse Road always finished for traders – Dali. This city was where the Bai, an ethnic minority group, acted as the conduit between tea growers from the Xishuangbanna province and horse traders from Tibet.

THE TEA HORSE ROAD

Yunnan is believed to be one of the first places in the world to produce tea. From the 6th century, a series of trading routes connected this province to empires in south and central Asia, with whom the Chinese traded their tea for horses, giving the route its name. Trading ceased in the 20th century, when horses were replaced by cars.

183

Silk Road

LOCATION China **START/FINISH** Dunhuang/Xi'an **DISTANCE** 1,700 km (1,050 miles) **TIME** 3 weeks **DIFFICULTY** Moderate **INFORMATION** Be prepared for temperatures to vary dramatically between day and night

From gliding through the vast Gobi Desert to pedalling beside the austere Great Wall, tackling China's Silk Road by bike gets you up close to this ancient trail's epic landscapes, culture and history.

For 1,500 years, right up to the 14th century, the Silk Road was a vital artery connecting East and West, allowing goods and ideas to travel between China and the Mediterranean – raw materials, religious and philosophical texts, gunpowder, spices, ceramics and, of course, fabrics such as silk.

Just as merchants wouldn't try to cover all 6,500 km (4,000 miles) of the Silk Road back in its heyday, most modern travellers tackle just a portion of the route. The best way to appreciate the phenomenal journeys these traders undertook is to travel slowly by bike. Along the way, you'll have time to linger at ancient trading posts, admire awe-inspiring landscapes and experience local hospitality.

A lonely road cutting through the Rainbow Mountains near Zhangye

BY BIKE
ASIA

The journey from Dunhuang to Xi'an makes for a varied and rewarding cycle ride. Starting in the shifting sands of the Taklamakan and Gobi deserts, it passes through the remains of the lonely yet imposing Yumen Pass and, at Jiayuguan, the grand reconstruction of Jiayu Pass, the westernmost point of the Great Wall of China. The route then cuts southeast to Zhangye, where you can gaze at the undulating, multicoloured Rainbow Mountains and China's largest reclining Buddha. Further on, past the city of Lanzhou, the monumental carvings of the Bingling Caves lie waiting to be discovered.

Finally, you'll reach the great city of Xi'an, both the eastern terminus of the Silk Road and China's imperial capital for a staggering 2,000 years. As you weave your way into its historic centre, you'll be joining the ranks of countless others who, centuries before you, arrived here along this ancient trading route.

A traveller cycling along an unpaved road through the flat plains of the Gobi Desert

another way

There are trains between Xi'an and Dunhuang, making it simple to save on a few days' cycling if you're pushed for time. Lanzhou is three hours from Xi'an or eight hours from Dunhuang.

BROWSE street food and handicrafts at Shazhou Night Market in **Dunhuang**, the "City of Sands"

VENTURE into the **Bingling Caves**, where enormous statues were carved into a canyon on the Yellow River, near Lanzhou

DISCOVER Xi'an's ancient treasures, including the Terracotta Army of Emperor Qin Shi Huang

Dunhuang

CHINA

Xi'an

NEW ZEALAND

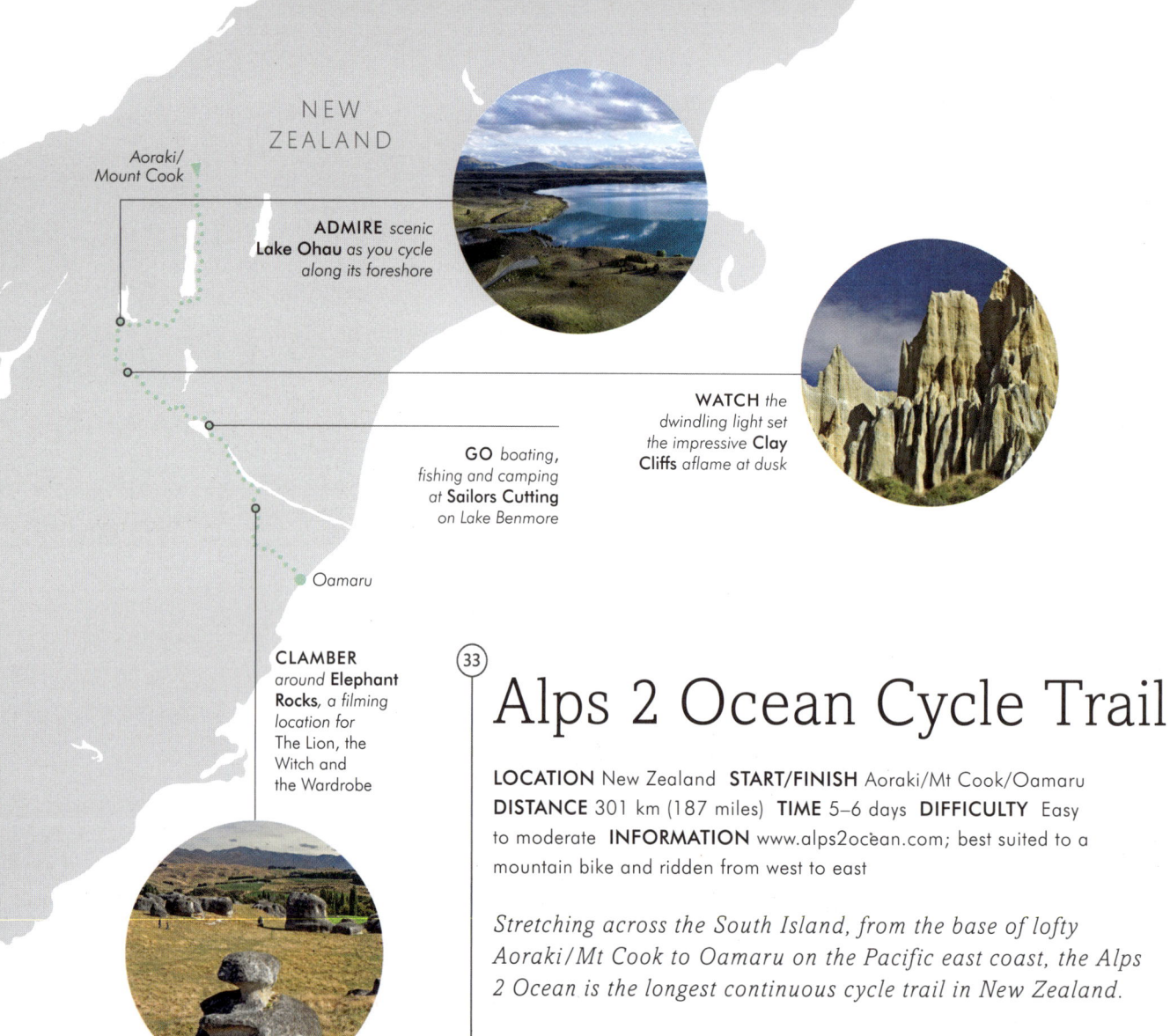

Aoraki/Mount Cook

ADMIRE scenic **Lake Ohau** as you cycle along its foreshore

WATCH the dwindling light set the impressive **Clay Cliffs** aflame at dusk

GO boating, fishing and camping at **Sailors Cutting** on Lake Benmore

Oamaru

CLAMBER around **Elephant Rocks**, a filming location for The Lion, the Witch and the Wardrobe

Alps 2 Ocean Cycle Trail

LOCATION New Zealand **START/FINISH** Aoraki/Mt Cook/Oamaru **DISTANCE** 301 km (187 miles) **TIME** 5–6 days **DIFFICULTY** Easy to moderate **INFORMATION** www.alps2ocean.com; best suited to a mountain bike and ridden from west to east

Stretching across the South Island, from the base of lofty Aoraki/Mt Cook to Oamaru on the Pacific east coast, the Alps 2 Ocean is the longest continuous cycle trail in New Zealand.

On its descent to the coast from the snow-capped Southern Alps, this glorious cycle route skirts glacial-fed lakes and meanders through the honey-coloured landscape of the wide Waitaki River valley. If you opt for the official start point from Aoraki/Mt Cook, you must book a helicopter to cross the Tasman River after just 7 km (4 miles) – to avoid this, there's an alternative starting point at Lake Tekapo. The well-signposted trail is easy to follow, and if you're an experienced cyclist you might tackle two of the nine sections in one day.

Changing constantly as the route unfolds before you, the landscape is unbeatable. Rolling along under the clear Mackenzie region sky, past lakes, creeks, beech forests and wetlands, you might not see another soul, but there's a long human history here. The region is rich in Māori heritage and it's well worth stopping at the Takiroa limestone shelter near Duntroon to see rock art thought to date to the 1400s. The final stretch to the pretty town of Oamaru ends at the harbour, by the sparkling waters of the Pacific. Here, one last natural wonder awaits as a closing reward: a colony of tiny blue penguins swimming ashore to their nest site under the dusky light of the setting sun.

BY BIKE
AUSTRALASIA

Above *Cycling alongside the turquoise waters of Lake Oahu*
Right *A blue penguin standing on the shore at Oamaru*

> Changing constantly as the route unfolds before you, the landscape is unbeatable

BY BIKE
AUSTRALASIA

34 Cowaramup to Margaret River

LOCATION Australia **START/FINISH** Cowaramup/Margaret River **DISTANCE** 13 km (8 miles) **TIME** 3 hours **DIFFICULTY** Easy **INFORMATION** www.margaretriver.com

In the far southwest of Western Australia, all roads lead to Margaret River – the centrepiece of one of Australia's most celebrated food and wine regions. This short cycle is a glorious ride, as well as a fine way to build up an appetite. It starts in Cowaramup, a classic small town with a quirky twist: locals know it as "Cowtown" because it holds the official world record for the largest number of people dressed in bovine costumes at once; unsurprisingly, there are plenty of opportunities to buy dairy produce here.

Once in the saddle, you traverse gently undulating hills that are littered with tempting side journeys to wineries and craft breweries. All offer cellar-door sales and the opportunity to stop in for tastings – if you overindulge, remember that there's no shame in calling for a taxi.

Mist veiling one of the many vineyards found in the Margaret River wine region

35 MS Sydney to Gong

LOCATION Australia **START/FINISH** Sydney/Wollongong **DISTANCE** 82 km (51 miles) **TIME** 1 day **DIFFICULTY** Easy to moderate **INFORMATION** www.msgongride.org.au

Organized by Multiple Sclerosis Australia, this charity ride is held on the first Sunday in November, but it's possible to cycle the route on your own at any time of year.

First, the group makes a speedy sweep along Botany Bay, the vast harbour where Captain Cook stepped ashore in 1770. Then, it's a tough climb up to Waterfall Train Station, where tired legs are rewarded with beautiful rainforest views. Brakes are put to the test on the steep descent from the station into the fragrant eucalyptus forests of the Royal National Park, before another uphill climb to the Otford Lookout. Mercifully, it's downhill all the way from here. As the route crosses the Pacific Ocean on the Sea Cliff Bridge, the teeth-gritting camaraderie that dominated the tougher sections builds to a relieved, good humour as the crowd of riders are able to sit back in the saddle and soak up the view.

another way

A shorter version of the ride, starting at Engadine, 58 km (36 miles) from Wollongong, avoids much of the southern suburbs of Sydney and most of the first climb to Waterfall Train Station.

BY BIKE
AUSTRALASIA

Cycling along the southern, coastal section of the rugged Heaphy Track

(36) Heaphy Track

LOCATION New Zealand **START/FINISH** Aorere/ Karamea **DISTANCE** 78 km (49 miles) **TIME** 2–3 days **DIFFICULTY** Moderate to challenging **INFORMATION** www.heaphytrack.com; open May–Nov only

The only multi-day ride through a National Park in New Zealand, this route meanders through Kahurangi's lush tropical rainforest, over rocky alpine terrain and across subalpine shrubland to palm-fringed beaches where the Heaphy River tumbles out into the Tasman Sea.

Kahurangi translates as "treasured possession" and it's not hard to see why this pristine landscape is so highly prized. Māori have long traversed the area, heading to central Westland in search of *pounamu* (greenstone). First designated as one of New Zealand's "Great Walks", today, the tussock grasslands and boulder outcrops of the Heaphy Track are prime mountain-biking territory. With countless comfortable huts to choose from each night, the biggest worry on this journey is that you might run over the palm-sized *Powelliphanta* land snails that come out after dark or on rainy days – keep your eyes peeled!

(37) Old Ghost Road

LOCATION New Zealand **START/FINISH** Lyell/Seddonville **DISTANCE** 85 km (53 miles) **TIME** 2–4 days **DIFFICULTY** Challenging **INFORMATION** www.oldghostroad.org.nz

This challenging off-road trail resurrects an old gold-mining link between the ghost town of Lyell and the mighty Mōkihinui Valley. It's a true adventure, an exhilarating ride through rocky and remote backcountry.

The first stretch is a gruelling ascent through dense beech forests to Ghost Lake hut, which rests on a panoramic craggy outcrop. With the highest point on the ride in the bag, this is the perfect place to call it a day. The narrow descent from here on the following day is heart-in-mouth stuff – the steep and exposed 4-km (2.5-mile) section of trail beyond Ghost Lake is the reason cyclists tackle the route south to north (uphill would be almost impossible).

The rest of the trail traverses thick bush, crossing vertiginous suspension bridges and shallow fords, before skirting the towering cliffs of the spectacular Mokihinui River gorge. With just a few huts for rest along the way, you need to be self-sufficient on the Old Ghost Road.

BIRDS ON THE OLD GHOST ROAD

Birdlife on the old dray trail is teeming. Efforts to eradicate predators – predominantly stoats, rats and possums – means that kākā, kea, whio (blue duck), kerer, toutouwai (robin), weka and even the rod (great spotted kiwi) are flourishing. Watch out though: wekas (also known as Māori hen) are prolific thieves of belongings.

BY BIKE
AUSTRALASIA

Otago Central Rail Trail

LOCATION New Zealand **START/FINISH** Middlemarch/Clyde
DISTANCE 152 km (94 miles) **TIME** 3–4 days **DIFFICULTY** Easy
INFORMATION www.otagocentralrailtrail.co.nz

The first of New Zealand's "Great Rides" – 22 cycle routes that today cover the width and breadth of the country – this pioneering rail trail sets an unswerving course through the hinterland of the historic Otago region.

The Otago Central Railway was originally built in 1879 so that a steam train could service the New Zealand gold rush. Today, there's just 64 km (40 miles) of working track left, between Dunedin and Middlemarch. The rest of the railway line has been transformed into an off-road cycleway that sweeps through the countryside, passing old mining towns and the occasional enticing pub or winery along the way.

The trail's former life is obvious as you wheel along railway bridges and soaring viaducts, and through deep, dark tunnels. Take time to admire the engineering challenge posed by the dramatic Poolburn Gorge. It took three years and 300 men to blast two long, dark tunnels through the schist rock, and to build the massive steel viaduct that you'll pedal across here. It's hard to imagine their hardship as you breeze along this (mostly) flat cycle path, before stopping for a rest at a railway station that has been turned into a hotel.

TAIERI GORGE RAILWAY

The only working section of the Central Otago Railway runs between Dunedin and Middlemarch once or twice a week. The rest of the time it stops at Pukerangi, 20 km (12 miles) from the trailhead. En route, the railway traverses its new namesake – the Taieri Gorge – crossing bridges and viaducts up to 47 m (155 ft) high.

Soaking up the mountain views while pedalling along the Otago Central Rail Trail

Wild West Coast

Stanley's curving bay, overlooked by Munatrik or "The Nut", an old volcanic plug

LOCATION Australia **START/FINISH** Stanley/Strahan **DISTANCE** 243 km (151 miles) **TIME** 1 week **DIFFICULTY** Moderate **INFORMATION** www.discovertasmania.com.au

The ride from Stanley to Strahan takes you through some of Tasmania's wildest and most beautiful country as it traverses the untouched rainforests and deserted beaches of the island's west.

This wild and wonderful cycle begins rather sedately in the historic settlement of Stanley on the island's north coast. Cycling south, the roads become quieter as they wind their way into what is Australia's largest temperate rainforest. Tasmania's forests have long been a battleground between conservationists and loggers and this one, thankfully, remains gloriously intact. The Western Explorer Highway cuts through the trees, although "highway" is something of a misnomer: much of the road is a serpentine track best suited to mountain biking. Birdsong is heard above the gentle whir of the wheels and the rustle of wildlife sometimes disturbs the bushes.

At Corinna, a remote former mining community has been transformed into a simple wilderness retreat, where you spend the night before crossing the Pieman River by ferry the next day. Or, better yet, take a boat excursion to the river's mouth. Here, you'll find one of Tasmania's most beautiful and quietest beaches, washed by wild seas. It's the perfect place to relax before taking to the saddle once more. South of the river, the route rejoins the paved road, near Zeehan, and continues all the way into Strahan. This pretty town has a vast, sweeping bay, deep rainforest and the remnants of one of Australia's most remote penal colonies.

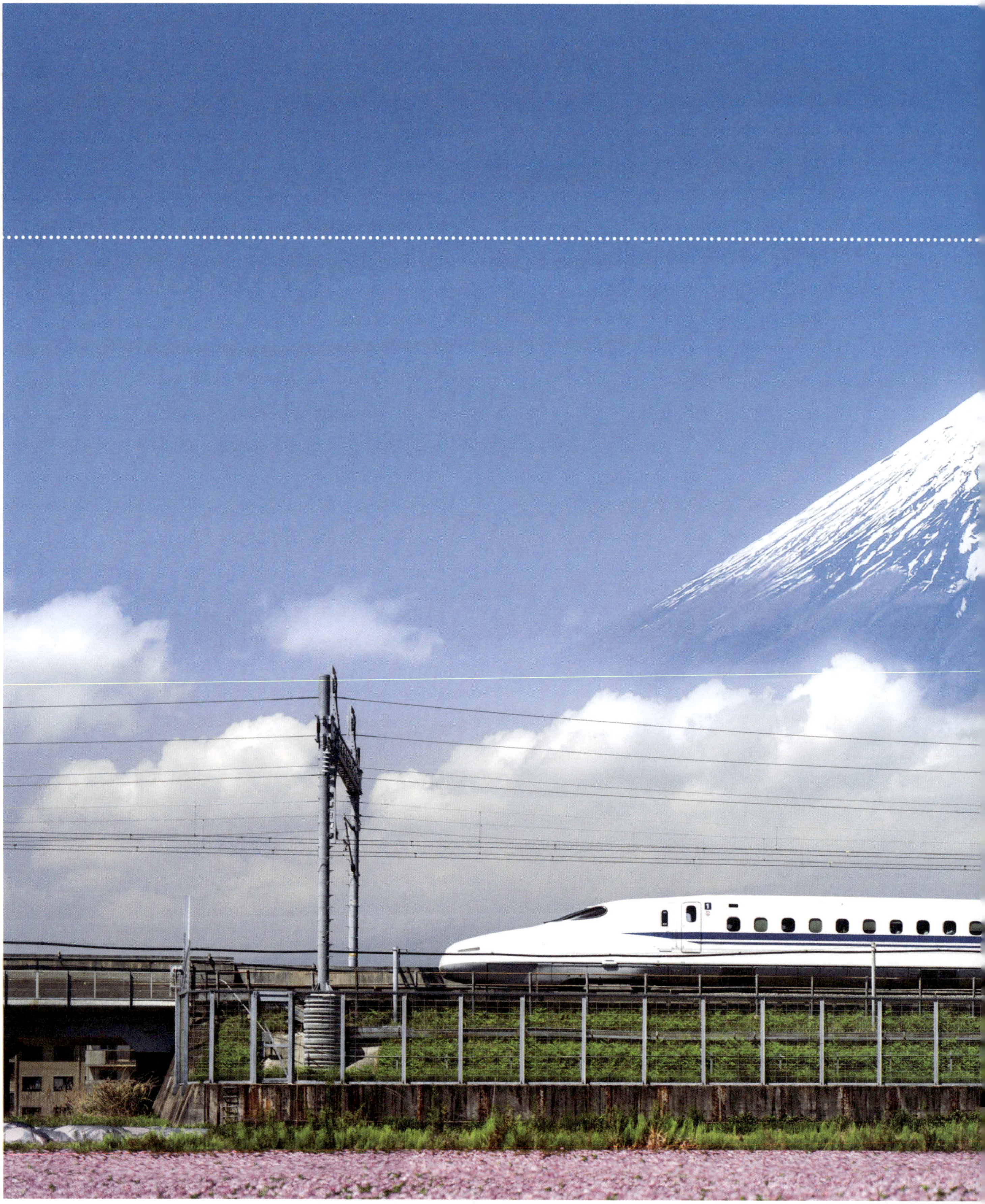

BY RAIL

Watching ever-changing landscapes flicker past your window; getting to know new-found companions; and being lulled by the rhythmic rocking of the rails: there's an undeniable magic to train travel. Whether you're cruising through Europe in carriages straight out of an Agatha Christie novel or zipping past Mount Fuji by bullet train, life on the rails truly lets you get under the skin of a country.

AT A GLANCE
BY RAIL

NORTH AMERICA pp196–205

Journey coast to coast across Canada, speed through Utah's otherworldly desert or roll through the flooded forests of Louisiana.

CENTRAL AND SOUTH AMERICA pp206–211

Train trips on this continent are awash with natural beauty – meander across windswept plains, wind through rainforest and forge between canyons.

KEY TO MAP
- .... Long route
- • End point

Previous page *A bullet train speeding through flower-filled fields beneath Mount Fuji*

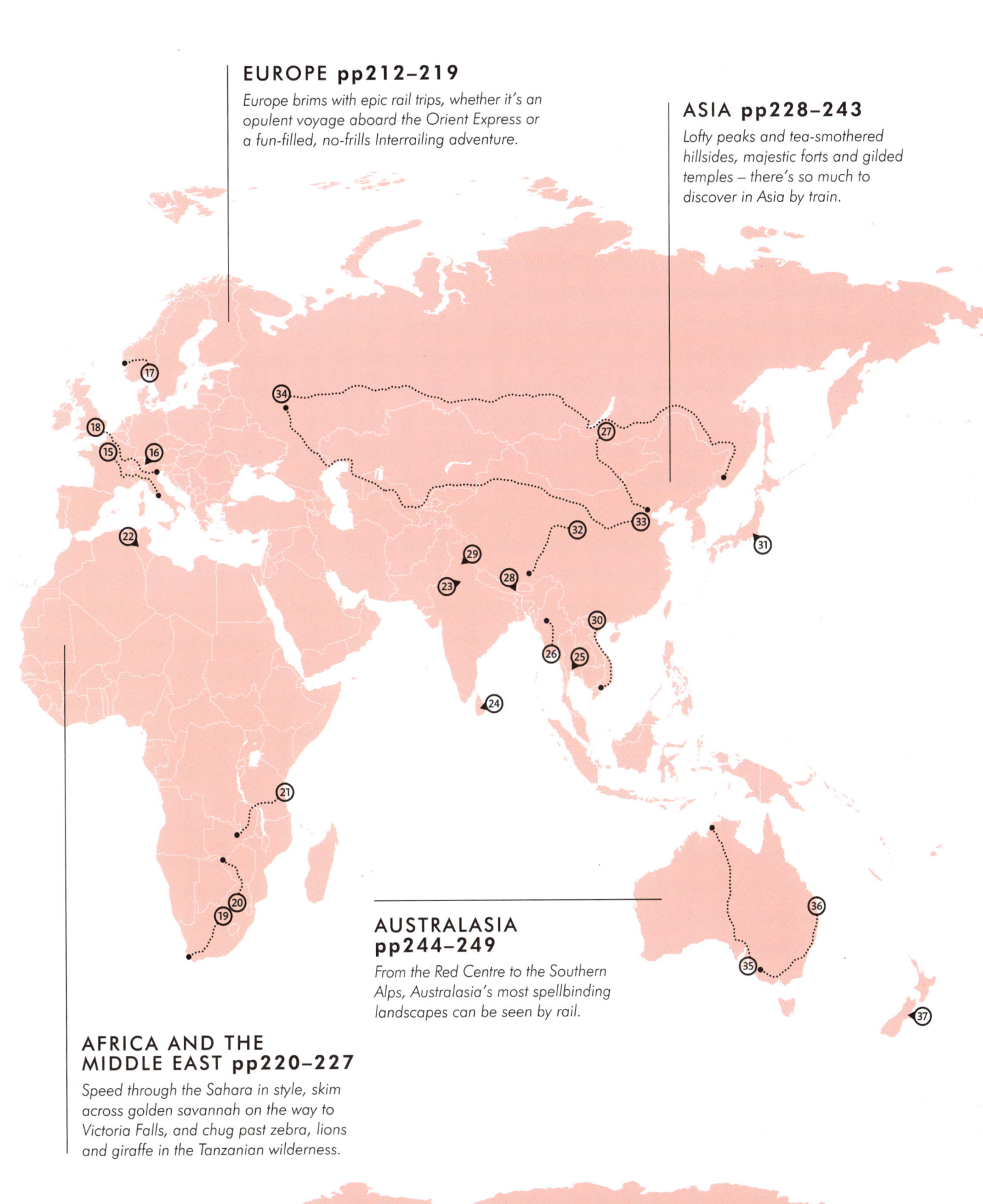

EUROPE pp212–219
Europe brims with epic rail trips, whether it's an opulent voyage aboard the Orient Express or a fun-filled, no-frills Interrailing adventure.

ASIA pp228–243
Lofty peaks and tea-smothered hillsides, majestic forts and gilded temples – there's so much to discover in Asia by train.

AUSTRALASIA pp244–249
From the Red Centre to the Southern Alps, Australasia's most spellbinding landscapes can be seen by rail.

AFRICA AND THE MIDDLE EAST pp220–227
Speed through the Sahara in style, skim across golden savannah on the way to Victoria Falls, and chug past zebra, lions and giraffe in the Tanzanian wilderness.

195

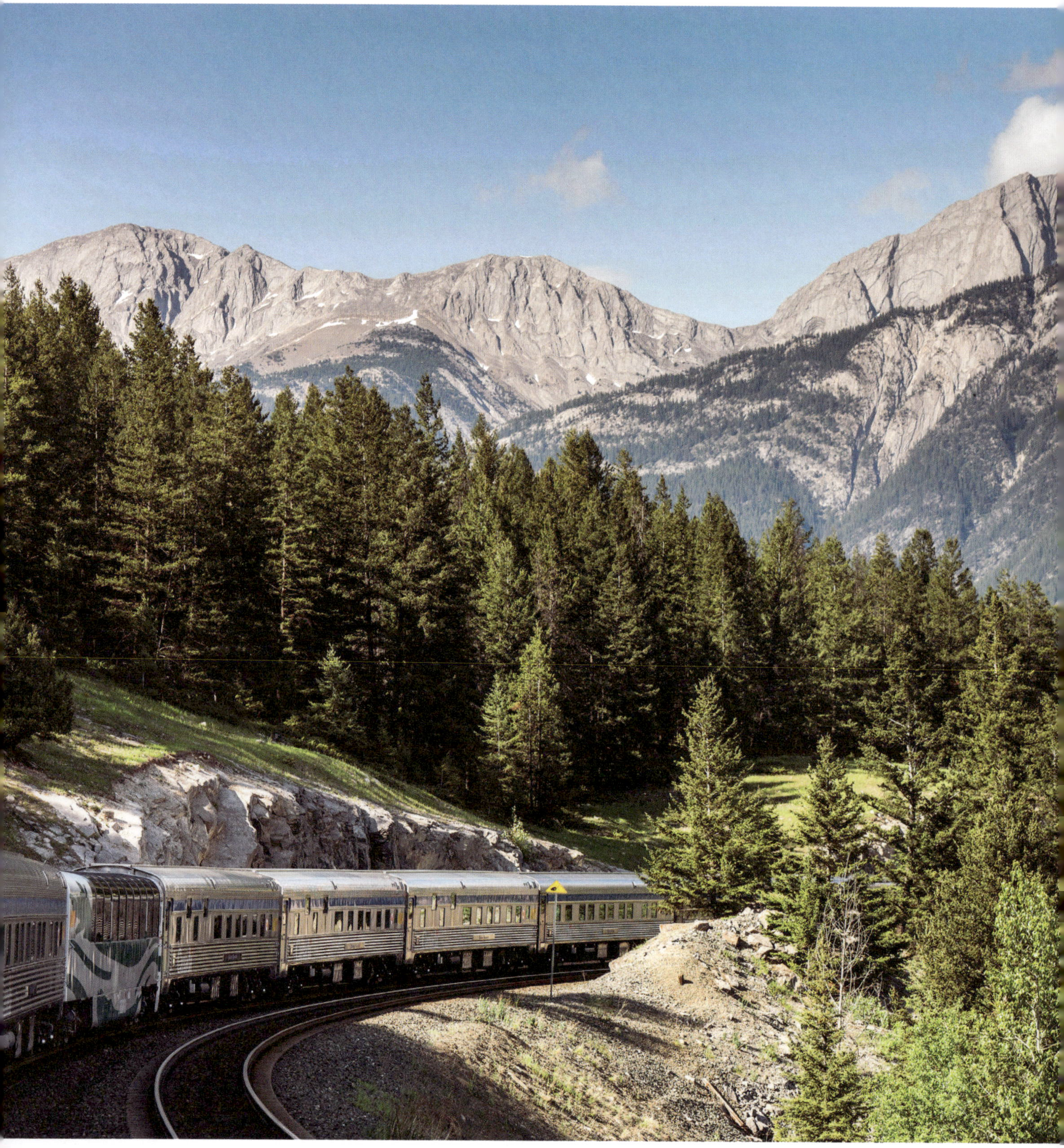

BY RAIL
NORTH AMERICA

The Canadian winding through the stunning landscape of the Canadian Rockies

① Coast to Coast

LOCATION Canada   **START/FINISH** Vancouver/Halifax
DISTANCE 6,350 km (3,946 miles)   **TIME** 5 days
INFORMATION www.viarail.ca

This grand cross-country train voyage cuts through some of Canada's most captivating landscapes – from dense forest to flower-flecked meadows to snow-capped peaks – with each day offering up an abundance of epic scenery.

Starting in cool and cultured Vancouver, on the country's west coast, this once-in-a-lifetime train journey stretches almost the entire length of Canada, heading for historic Halifax on the spellbinding east coast. It takes three different trains – the Canadian, the Corridor service and the Ocean – to traverse the whole route, which travels through a staggering five time zones and eight provinces over five days. Cruising in utter comfort and style, passengers can experience Canada's iconic and incredibly diverse natural beauty through a continuous corridor of ever-changing landscapes. Expect to pass by emerald-green subalpine forests, broad serpentine rivers, windswept arid canyons, sweeping snowy ridges and vast open pastures. There's even a sprinkling of urban charm throughout, from the cosmopolitan allure of Toronto to the French-influenced culture and architecture of Montréal.

> This once-in-a-lifetime train journey stretches almost the entire length of Canada

EXPERIENCE *the easygoing atmosphere of east-coast* **Halifax**

DISEMBARK *from the train at* **Kamloops,** *a 19th-century fur trading post, complete with prickly pear cacti and rattlesnake burrows*

SPEND *a night or two in French-speaking* **Montréal**

CANADA

Vancouver

Halifax

GET OUT *and enjoy the mountain town of* **Jasper,** *the centre of the world-renowned Jasper National Park*

TAKE *the time to experience* **Toronto,** *the country's biggest and perhaps liveliest city*

One of the most spectacular parts of the journey takes place aboard the Canadian – which runs between Vancouver and Toronto – as it weaves around the monumental peaks of the Canadian Rockies. These lofty pinnacles are carefully approached as the train begins to curl through a staccato of mountain ranges, each more sizeable and craggy than the last. Passing in and out of lengthy dark tunnels that perforate the shale and limestone rock, the train creeps along, clinging precariously to the mountainside. The surrounding landscape is dwarfed in comparison to these massive, perennially snow-covered crowns. Between them, immense ice sheets flow at a snail's pace into teal and jade-coloured lakes, framed by emerald pine forests. Wide and lush glacier-carved valleys make up the rest of the scenery, the preferred territory of grizzly bears who may rear up on their hind legs to watch the train convoy as it cruises past.

| Immense ice sheets flow at a snail's pace into teal and jade-coloured lakes

BY RAIL
NORTH AMERICA

Each of the train's streamlined and refurbished stainless-steel passenger cars – originally built in the 1950s – offer stunning views of the awe-inspiring scenery, thanks to generously sized picture windows. Special observations cars, with glass-domed roofs, allow for panoramic sightseeing, and the conductor will even slow down the powerful diesel locomotive for extraordinary sights. When not gazing out at turquoise-hued lakes and snow-dusted mountains, passengers can kick back in one of the entertaining cars, and enjoy wine and beer tastings, as well as live musical acts. Throughout the day, delicious, freshly made meals featuring refined regional cuisine are offered in the dining cars. And, as night falls, passengers can choose from an array of accommodation options, from plush seats perfectly suitable for dozing, to roomy and private en suite cabins.

As the train pulls into Toronto, almost 4,500 km (2,800 miles) later, it can feel like journey's end. But the Coast to Coast adventure is not yet over: now it's time to explore the spellbinding natural beauty and cultured cities of Canada's east coast.

another way

For more flexibility and freedom, while still covering all the amazing sights of the Coast to Coast train, drive the Trans-Canada Highway. This route loosely follows the train journey with slight extensions on both coasts, spanning from Victoria in BC all the way to St John's in Newfoundland and Labrador.

Below A bear standing next to the railway tracks as the Canadian snakes past Bottom right Travelling in one of the observation cars Right A musician performing live

199

Left A forest of saguaros stretching into the distance in Arizona
Above The striking façade of Union Station in Los Angeles

Sunset Limited

LOCATION US **START/FINISH** New Orleans/Los Angeles
DISTANCE 3,211 km (1,995 miles) **TIME** 2 days
INFORMATION www.amtrak.com/sunset-limited-train

This remarkable train glides from New Orleans through the sultry bayous of Louisiana, the vast, rolling plains of Texas, and the epic deserts of New Mexico and Arizona on its way to Southern California.

Rattling out of New Orleans, the Sunset Limited soars over the Mississippi River, high above its swirling, muddy waters. On board, passengers can relax in the lounge car, and watch the flat marshlands and flooded forests of rural Louisiana go by, or devour seasonal fare in the cosy dining car. The land remains dead level into Texas, as the carriages grind on past small towns and ramshackle farms. At San Antonio, a long wait gives travellers the chance to head into the city for a meal, stroll along the River Walk or visit the Alamo. Back on board, the train hits the vast, seemingly endless plains of West Texas, where things become dryer, hotter and dustier.

In New Mexico, the train's chain of carriages seem to be swallowed up by a vast, sand-swept landscape, studded with saguaros (tree-like cacti) and spiky yucca. Herds of cattle wander between the flat-topped mountains known as mesas and rugged buttes – narrow pillars of rock. The tall, finger-like saguaros become thicker in Arizona, the desert a reddish brown. The most desolate section of track is through the sun-blasted Sonoran Desert of Southern California, where the train passes the ghostly outlines of long-abandoned stations, mining shacks and ranches, the silence broken only by the rhythmic clacking of the wheels on the tracks.

After Palm Springs it's over quickly – the tracks wriggle through the San Gorgonio Pass and into the LA Basin, a densely populated world of highways and strip malls. The line terminates in Downtown LA at the Mission Revival-style Union Station – an elegant 1930s hold out in a sea of gleaming skyscrapers.

BY RAIL
NORTH AMERICA

③
Coast Starlight

LOCATION US **START/FINISH** Los Angeles/Seattle
DISTANCE 2,216 km (1,377 miles) **TIME** 2 days
INFORMATION www.amtrak.com/coast-starlight-train

This train takes in some of the US's most dazzling scenery, from the sun-drenched Southern California shoreline to the snowy peaks of the Cascade Range.

Leaving LA behind, the Coast Starlight traces the Pacific coastline for some 563 km (350 miles), passing by the mist-swathed piers of Santa Barbara, and remote beaches at Gaviota and Jalama. Inland, between Paso Robles and Salinas, the track skirts neatly planted fields of lettuce and strawberries, with vineyards spread over the low-lying slopes. At Oakland, you get a tantalizing glimpse of San Francisco across the bay, before the train drives inland once more.

   North of Redding, pine forests and snowy mountains fill the horizon, among them the giant cone of Mount Shasta. After a brief stop in the town of Klamath Falls, the train winds around the mirror-like rim of Upper Klamath Lake, before twisting its way through densely wooded Willamette Pass at the heart of the Cascade Mountains. On the final stretch, it feels as if you're floating on Puget Sound, the inlet that connects Seattle to the ocean. Finally, fir trees fall away and the skyscrapers of Washington's "Emerald City" rise up ahead.

> It feels as if you're floating on Puget Sound, the inlet that connects Seattle to the ocean

The Coast Starlight speeding across a bridge on the Southern California coast

201

A train skirting the mountains near White Pass on the US–Canada border

④ White Pass and Yukon Route

LOCATION US to Canada **START/FINISH** Skagway/Carcross **DISTANCE** 109 km (68 miles) **TIME** 1 day **INFORMATION** www.wpyr.com; passports required; open May–Sep

Blasted out of solid rock with dynamite, this narrow-gauge railroad forges a historic route through North America's wild northern frontier. It was built at the height of the Klondike Gold Rush to ease the journey for American prospectors heading to the gold fields in the Yukon. Before the railway, travellers took their lives in their hands along the treacherous Chilkoot Trail, a pack-horse route that ascended up the steep White Pass.

The train's comfortable vintage cars tightly track the mountainside, snaking through dark tunnels, over high wooden trestle bridges and past a pristine natural landscape. Through the window, misty waterfalls can be seen streaming down the cliffsides, while blankets of wildflowers bloom brightly across the meadows and deer forage around the edges of mineral-blue lakes.

⑤ Empire Builder

LOCATION US **START/FINISH** Chicago/Seattle **DISTANCE** 3,550 km (2,206 miles) **TIME** 2 days **INFORMATION** www.amtrak.com

Follow in the footsteps of explorers Lewis and Clark on this journey across the American West, from the Great Plains to the evergreen forests of the Pacific Northwest.

Leaving Chicago in the late afternoon, the Empire Builder charges into the Midwest. While passengers sleep through the twin cities of St Paul and Minneapolis, the train speeds on through Minnesota. Early light illuminates the pancake-flat plains of North Dakota, where the horizon is punctured only by red barns and weathered grain elevators. If this bucolic scene wasn't enough of a wake-up call, the sound of the wheels clacking over rickety old bridges, such as the Gassman Coulee Trestle, is bound to rouse snoozing passengers.

In the evening, waves of mountains rise up in Western Montana, where the rails circle Glacier National Park and twist through a bewildering labyrinth of razor-edged peaks and valleys into Idaho. The train splits late at night in Spokane, sending sleeping railriders to either Portland or Seattle, where you'll arrive in time for brunch.

LEWIS AND CLARK

The Empire Builder shadows the Lewis and Clark Expedition of 1804–1806, which set out to chart the vast new lands acquired by the Louisiana Purchase in 1803. Starting in St Louis, Meriwether Lewis and William Clark, aided by their indispensable guide Sacagawea – a Lemhi Shoshone woman – and countless volunteers, traversed the continent to the Pacific.

BY RAIL
NORTH AMERICA

⑥ Rupert Rocket

LOCATION Canada **START/FINISH** Jasper/Prince Rupert **DISTANCE** 1,160 km (720 miles) **TIME** 2 days **INFORMATION** www.viarail.ca

Inching out of Jasper station, Rupert Rocket's gleaming steel-sided carriages soon curve round Moose Lake into breathtaking backcountry. This is a region of snow-dusted peaks and silvery lakes, crashing rivers and forests that brim with wildlife. Passengers lurch between windows for a glimpse of roaming black bears and longhorn sheep, which are unerringly picked out by cheery train attendants and local travellers who still marvel at the neck-craning views. Those lucky enough to bagsy a seat on the top deck of the glass-ceilinged Park Car can spot eagles soaring overhead and moose eyeing the passing train with elegant indifference.

After piling out at Prince George to overnight, travellers greet each other back on board the juggernaut the next morning as if old friends. Ahead, the craggy Coast Mountains loom in anticipation; by mid-afternoon, sheer rock suddenly rises up against the windows. Salmon hatcheries and sawmill settlements whip past until the Skeena River shimmers into view and, beyond it, the sun sets over Prince Rupert.

⑦ Adirondack

LOCATION US to Canada **START/FINISH** New York City/Montréal **DISTANCE** 613 km (381 miles) **TIME** 11 hours **INFORMATION** www.amtrak.com; sit on left-hand side for best views

Amtrak's once daily Adirondack service winds its way through the awe-inspiring scenery of both the Hudson Valley and the Lake Champlain region. This epic journey is at its best in October, when the blazing autumn leaves become brighter and more vibrant as the train speeds further north.

Leaving New York City, the train runs along the wide Hudson River all the way to Albany, where the forests become denser, with deep reds, ambers and golds smothering the hills. The tracks eventually snake between the Adirondack Mountains themselves and the shore of Lake Champlain. Here, bald eagles' nests sit high in the trees and deer run swiftly through the undergrowth. Look out for the hefty battlements of Fort Ticonderoga, scene of a famous American victory in the War of Independence. With Lake Champlain now behind, the train trundles over miles of flat Canadian farmland and into Montréal, Canada's cultural capital.

The Hudson Valley, on the Adirondack route, covered in a riotous carpet of orange, yellow and red leaves in autumn

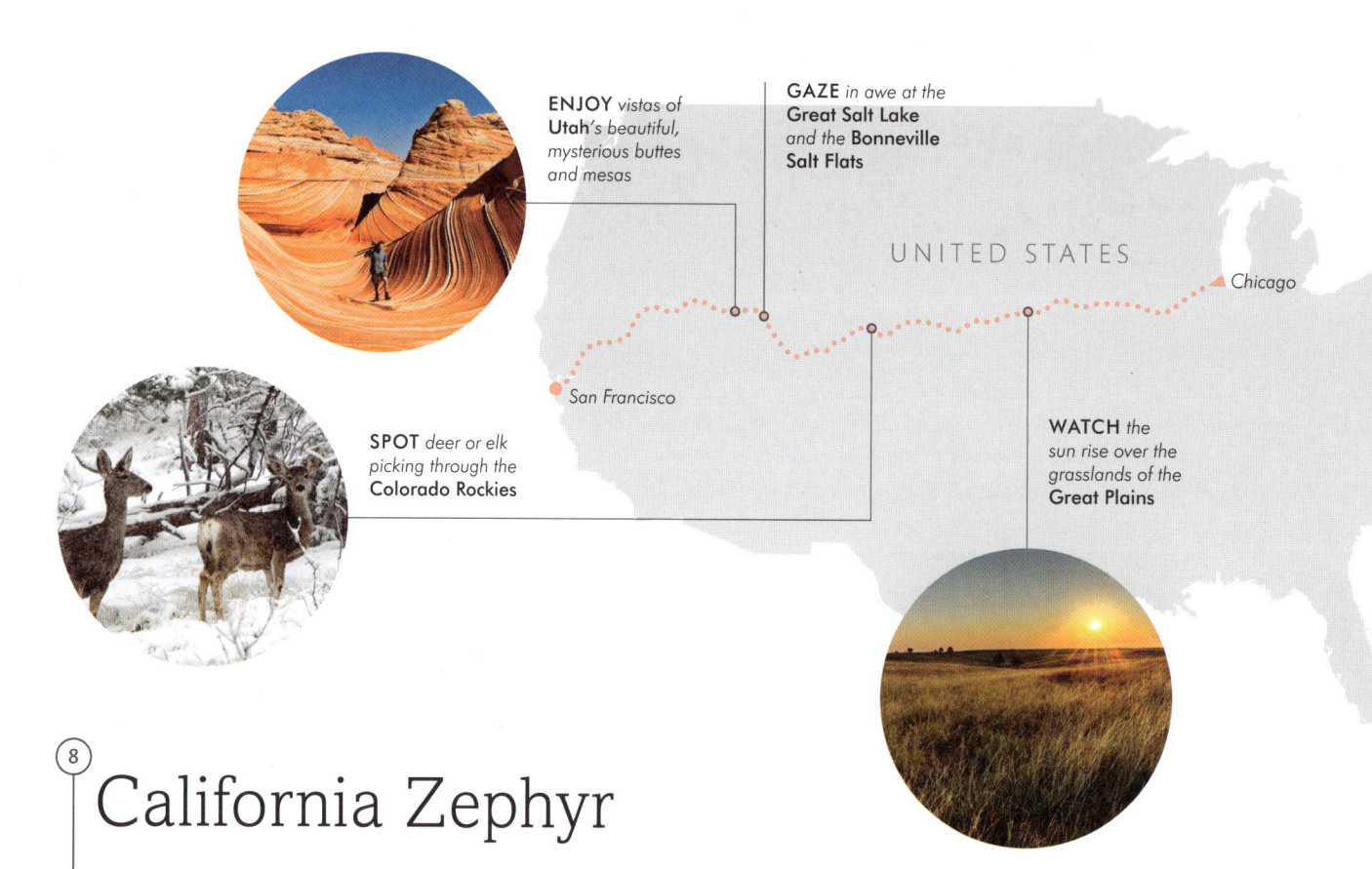

ENJOY vistas of **Utah**'s beautiful, mysterious buttes and mesas

GAZE in awe at the **Great Salt Lake** and the **Bonneville Salt Flats**

SPOT deer or elk picking through the **Colorado Rockies**

WATCH the sun rise over the grasslands of the **Great Plains**

California Zephyr

LOCATION US **START/FINISH** Chicago/San Francisco
DISTANCE 3,924 km (2,438 miles) **TIME** 2 days
INFORMATION www.amtrak.com/california-zephyr-train

Slicing through the mythic landscapes of the American West, the California Zephyr is the classic transcontinental railway journey, linking Chicago and San Francisco by way of the awe-inspiring Colorado Rockies and the snow-capped High Sierras.

Few train rides offer such natural beauty as the California Zephyr – almost every landscape is represented on its course through the heart of America. First rattling over the Great Plains and on to Iowa and Nebraska, the train ploughs through an ocean of neat farmland dotted with tiny barns and tractors, the wheatfields flushed with an occasional burst of pink clover. There are mighty rivers too – the train crosses the Mississippi on a rusty red bridge south of Burlington, and the swirling Missouri at Omaha. But the mountain sections are the route's most memorable. Past Denver, the train ratchets up the Big Ten Curve, and dives under snowy ridges in the Moffat Tunnel, snaking through dizzying Colorado canyons, spruce forest and cascading rapids. The Zephyr's path through the Sierra Nevada is equally spectacular, traversing the vast, sun-baked deserts of Nevada before cresting the mountains at wind-blown Donner Pass, with a glint of the ocean on the horizon. On the final approach to Oakland, the track edges around the glistening San Francisco Bay, the Golden Gate heralding the Pacific beyond.

HELL ON WHEELS

Completed in 1869, the California Zephyr was America's first transcontinental railroad. Its tracks were laid by a crew of emigrants, Civil War veterans and formerly enslaved labourers, who worked in terrible conditions. Hundreds died, and mobile camps on the route were soon dubbed "Hell on Wheels".

BY RAIL
NORTH AMERICA

| But the mountain sections are the route's most memorable

Right *Union Station in Denver*
Below *Colorado's striking landscape, beautifully illuminated at sunset*

Belmond Andean Explorer

The blue-and-white Belmond Andean Explorer travelling through the high plains of the Andes

LOCATION Peru **START/FINISH** Cusco/Arequipa **DISTANCE** 734 km (456 miles) **TIME** 3 days **INFORMATION** www.belmond.com

Nothing promises more romance than crossing the high plains of the Andes aboard South America's most luxurious sleeper train. With five-star service and comfort, this elegant mode of transport is fit for the Inca emperor himself.

The marks of civilization melt away as the Belmond Andean Explorer trundles out of Cusco, moving at a speed of just 11 km/h (7 mph). Gradually, as the train rolls onwards, roads and rooftops are replaced by scenes of wild natural beauty. There's a reason rows of wide windows line the walls of each and every carriage: they're there to frame the stunning, ever-transforming Andean landscapes.

The best views are captured from the wrought-iron railings of the open observation carriage at the train's rear. One moment, the midnight-blue-and-ivory train curls around the bank of a thunderous river, hemmed in by ragged peaks that are jet black but for a fine dusting of snow. The next, the carriages rumble across a sweeping valley plain, the tracks lined with wind-blasted stems of *ichu* grass nibbled by wild vicuña – close cousin of the llama.

But one view crowns them all: sunrise on the shoreline of resplendent Lake Titicaca. At these high altitudes, the distinction between water and sky becomes flimsy and indistinguishable. Excursions from the train to the lake's floating islands, made of reeds, introduce passengers to a place that the Incas believed was the birthplace of the sun.

BY RAIL
CENTRAL AND SOUTH AMERICA

◀ ▶

THE UROS ISLANDS

Lake Titicaca is home to the Uros people, who live on 100 or so floating islands built from *totora* reeds. The Uros's buoyant villages contain *totora* houses, furniture and a watchtower. Fresh *totora* must be constantly added to the islands, as the cut reeds quickly rot when in contact with the water.

WATCH day breaking over **Lake Titicaca**

MAKE an excursion to **Sumbay Cave** and learn about its 7,000-year-old cave paintings

TAKE a boat tour of the **Uros and Taquile Islands** in Lake Titicaca

Cusco

PERU

Arequipa

Even on board the train, where sumptuous decor reflects the magnificence of the surrounding landscape, the outside world feels close at hand. Belle-époque cabins are fitted with mahogany panelling and crisp linens, and the Chakana cross – an Inca motif symbolizing the juncture of the heavens, earth and the underworld – is etched into everything from wine glasses to staff uniforms.

As the train begins its final descent, the journey offers up one last spectacular vista. Stretching across the landscape below, the white-stone colonial city of Arequipa – the train's last stop – shimmers in the afternoon sunlight, watched over by a triumvirate of looming volcanoes.

Traditionally dressed performers dancing on a station platform next to the Belmond Andean Explorer

BY RAIL
CENTRAL AND SOUTH AMERICA

10 Chepe Train

LOCATION Mexico **START/FINISH** Los Mochis/Divisadero **DISTANCE** 312 km (194 miles) **TIME** 2 days **INFORMATION** www.chepe.com.mx

Leading you into the very heart of Mexico, this route snakes through the forested mountain valleys of the Copper Canyon. Boarding El Chepe and leaving Los Mochis and the west coast behind, you ascend into the Sierra Madre. Here, it won't take long for you to understand how the canyon got its name – the landscape transforms into a maze of show-stopping valleys, their slopes a copper-green riot of mountain and tree. This is train travel on a Hollywood scale: viaducts span yawning chasms, tunnels burrow through immovable mountains, and cougars and wolves prowl the dark forests beyond.

Jump off at the city of El Fuerte to experience a synthesis of indigenous and colonial culture: roam Jesuit ruins, then listen to traditional music, played on gourds and accompanied by enchanting dances. Back on board, it's cameras at the ready in the Terrace Car, as plunging valleys and hanging bridges pass by on the approach to the Divisadero viewpoint. Nearby, meet the Rarámuri – an indigenous group famed for their long-distance running – and look out on the canyons they call home, where the Río Urique snakes to the horizon.

> **another way**
> *Ride the Regional Chepe train between Chihuahua and Creel to experience a different stretch of the Copper Canyon Railway. This route offers epic scenery and, once you reach Creel, you can explore the pretty waterfalls and bizarre rock formations outside the town.*

The green-and-white Hershey Train pulling in at the station in Havana Casablanca

11 Hershey Train

LOCATION Cuba **START/FINISH** Havana Casablanca/Matanzas **DISTANCE** 92 km (57 miles) **TIME** 4 hours **INFORMATION** www.infotur.cu; runs three times a day

Built to transport sugar from American chocolate baron Milton Hershey's sprawling factory, this route connects isolated hamlets to big port cities. The rickety carriages lope through Cuba's rolling rural north, making their leisurely way through a patchwork of sugarcane fields and palm groves, past clusters of houses fronted by banana fronds and trees heavy with red-tinged mango.

When the train stops – at clapboard stations, occasionally flagged down by hopeful pedestrians, and just as often because the train has wheezed to a mysterious halt – commuters and day trippers load and unload, lugging bags, wilting produce, perhaps a pair of chickens. In these pauses, water is passed around, seatmates strike up conversations and hand-held fans flap to life. By the time Matanzas appears, everyone has given a blast of the horn and tried out the controls, and you will have half a dozen recommendations for the best *congri* (red beans and rice) in town.

BY RAIL
CENTRAL AND SOUTH AMERICA

12 Tren de la Costa

LOCATION Argentina **START/FINISH** Avenida de Maipú/Tigre **DISTANCE** 16 km (10 miles) **TIME** 30 minutes **INFORMATION** www.trendelacosta.com.ar

The leafy suburbs of Buenos Aires are thrown into focus as the Tren de la Costa rolls along the coast from Avenida de Maipú station. As it moves northwards, the train – popular with both locals and travellers – pauses at a string of eleven historic stations. Many date to the late 19th century and were built in a quaint, antique style of architecture that mimics old train stations in England. Tickets allow passengers to hop on and off; the track-side café at Borges is an opportune coffee stop, while the Fería de Anticuarios at Barrancas is packed to the rafters with bric-a-brac for browsing.

Between stops, glimpses of the Río de la Plata flicker past, the river's metallic gleam refracting shards of sunlight. One of the most spectacular views spreads out from the station of Anchorena, where open vistas of the river to the east and Buenos Aires to the south are revealed. Too quickly, the town of Tigre appears, where passengers are discharged and, without ceremony, the train hurtles back towards Buenos Aires.

13 La Trochita

LOCATION Argentina **START/FINISH** Esquel (loop) **DISTANCE** 38 km (22 miles) **TIME** 3 hours **INFORMATION** www.latrochita.org.ar

Once upon a time, La Trochita rattled for 402 km (250 miles) between remote Argentine ranches, and was immortalized in American author Paul Theroux's 1979 travelogue, *The Old Patagonia Express*. Nowadays, "the Little Gauge" may be truncated to 38 km (24 miles), but the steam train remains an ode to the easy pace of Patagonia.

Hauling itself sluggishly out of Esquel's elderly wooden station, the locomotive grinds into boundless arid steppe, jumbled with thorny bushes. Forty-six broad bends punctuate the route. The most striking is Curva del Huevo (Egg Bend), where the vastness of the scrubland is thrown into relief by the solitary, snaking length of antique wooden carriages and jet-black steel.

Stalls selling handicrafts signal the end of the line at Nahuel Pan, where there's an hour's pause before the train rumbles stoically back to Esquel.

La Trochita emitting billowing steam as it rumbles along the tracks between Esquel and Nahuel Pan

Above The Serra Verde Express chugging through lush tropical hills
Left Bright green parrots chattering on a branch in the Atlantic Rainforest canopy

| Glimpse fluttering parrots and hummingbirds among the clusters of bromeliad plants |

BY RAIL
CENTRAL AND SOUTH AMERICA

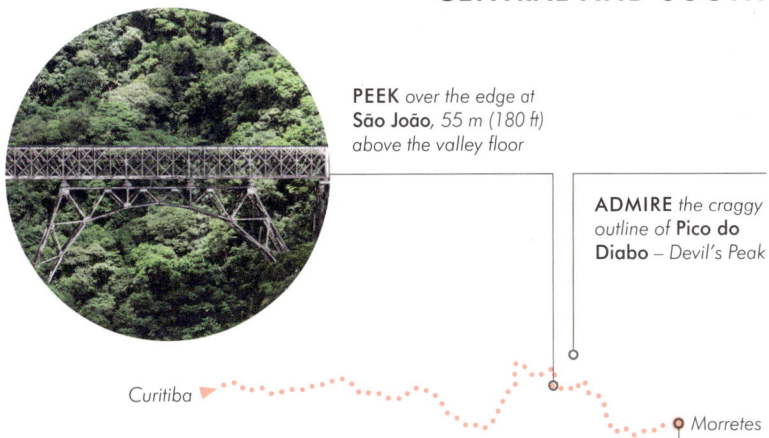

PEEK over the edge at **São João**, 55 m (180 ft) above the valley floor

ADMIRE the craggy outline of **Pico do Diabo** – Devil's Peak

Curitiba ▶ .... ○ Morretes

SAVOUR a sumptuous lunch of Barreado beef stew, a local speciality of **Morretes**

⑭ Serra Verde Express

LOCATION Brazil **START/FINISH** Curitiba/Morretes **DISTANCE** 110 km (69 miles) **TIME** 4 hours **INFORMATION** www.serraverdeexpress.com.br

Encapsulating all of South America's scenic splendour, the Serra Verde Express winds through the Atlantic Rainforest from the mountains to the sea. Clinging to cliffsides dripping with foliage, the gleaming train offers jaw-dropping views of granite peaks, jungle-clad gorges and sparkling waterfalls.

Inaugurated in 1884, this route was hailed as one of Brazil's greatest engineering marvels, its 14 tunnels and 30 bridges spanning once inaccessible terrain. Originally made to transport the region's rich farm produce to the port of Paranaguá, it is now one of the continent's last great rail journeys. Setting out from Curitiba, today the morning train rumbles past crumbling suburban villas, as humid mountain air filters through the carriages' open windows. Soon, the buildings drift away as the rails roll across pastures grazed by hump-backed Zebu cattle, with bottle-brush Paraná pines dotting the horizon. The gleaming carriages emerge from the first tunnel into a different world. Chugging through tropical forest hillsides, you'll glimpse fluttering parrots and hummingbirds among the clusters of bromeliad plants, liana creepers and blue hydrangeas, and catch the cries of distant howler monkeys. Few passengers alight at the sleepy stations along the way, but many hop off at Santuário de Nossa Senhora do Cadeado viewpoint, to photograph the plunging mountain gorges. Arriving four hours later at Morretes, everyone spills out of the train, ready – after all that adventure – for a blow-out lunch.

THE ATLANTIC RAINFOREST

This vast forest is incredibly biodiverse, home to an estimated 20,000 plant and 2,315 animal species. From orchids to golden-lion tamarins many species are unique. Less than 8 per cent of the original forest remains, but local environmental groups are campaigning to save it from extinction.

BY RAIL
EUROPE

⑮ Interrailing

LOCATION France to Italy **START/FINISH** Paris/Rome **DISTANCE** 1,250 km (776 miles) **TIME** 5 days **INFORMATION** www.interrail.eu; passports required

With an Interrail Pass, the whole of Europe is your oyster: zoom from one world-famous city to the next, switching from cutting-edge culture to crumbling ancient ruins at the wave of a ticket. The route options are practically limitless, but this journey from France to Italy is undoubtedly one of the continent's finest.

BY RAIL
EUROPE

For an introduction to the joys of Interrailing, this route through France and Italy is the perfect package. Featuring many of the world's most famous icons of art and architecture – not to mention some of the world's most celebrated cuisine – it offers an enticing glimpse into the pass's potential that will leave you wanting more.

Paris – the City of Lights, Love and the Louvre – is an unbeatable place to start an Interrail adventure. See the Eiffel Tower, look deep into the eyes of *Mona Lisa* and lose yourself in Montmartre's tangle of streets – and all before you've even boarded a train. When you do, you'll find a sleek and comfortable carriage waiting to whisk you south to the culinary city of Lyon. To be food capital of France is no small feat, but it's a moniker that sits easily in this part of the world.

Heading east on a speeding train bound for Italy, you'll soon reach Milan, where yet more transcendent works of art await: Leonardo's *Last Supper*, the startling Gothic spires of the Duomo, and the Titians and Tintorettos that grace the corridors of the Pinacoteca di Brera.

> To be food capital of France is no small feat, but it's a moniker that sits easily

Left Passy, a station on the Paris metro
Below Alfresco dining at a traditional restaurant in Lyon **Right** The towering spires of Milan's Duomo

Above left The sun setting over Florence **Left** A train travelling over a bridge in Tuscany **Above** Looking across at Rome's Colosseum

Leaving Milan behind, you'll whizz south through the Emilia-Romagna countryside to Bologna – just like Lyon, this is the cuisine capital of a country world-famous for its food. Take home some of its secrets with a cookery class – learn to fold the perfect tortellini or whip up a mean ragù that would make any Italian *nonna* proud.

Grab a window seat for the next leg of the journey, which wends its way through romantic Tuscany. Here, rolling vineyards and cypress trees unfold outside your window, the landscape dotted with grand villas in varying stages of elegant decay. Disembark in Florence, the Cradle of the Renaissance, and dive into an Aladdin's cave of artistic treasures. Michelangelo's *David* is the star resident at the Galleria dell'Accademia, while untold masterpieces by Botticelli, Raphael and Caravaggio line the walls of the Uffizi. Taking in all that culture is hungry work, so be sure to refuel with some of Florence's famous wild boar *pappardelle* pasta, accompanied by a glass of fine Chianti.

THE HISTORY OF INTERRAILING

Interrail was introduced in 1972, to celebrate the 50th birthday of the UIC (International Union of Railways). Initially intended as a one-time offer covering 21 countries, the idea of a multi-country rail pass proved such a hit that it was rolled out full time, with more European countries joining to make up the present-day total of 33.

BY RAIL
EUROPE

Journey south, past the pretty medieval city of Siena and clay moonscapes of the Crete Senesi, to the ultimate Italian city: the capital, Rome. No prizes for guessing why they call this place the Eternal City – echoes of its ancient and colourful past are everywhere, from the ruins of the Colosseum to the pagan temple-turned-church that is the Pantheon, via the Baroque excesses of the Trevi Fountain. Toss in a coin for good luck, then head north on foot up the famous Spanish Steps to the Villa Borghese, where landscaped gardens are peppered with Neo-Classical temples and follies, and grand mansions have housed both popes and emperors. Looking out west to the River Tiber and Vatican City beyond, this is one of the most photogenic spots in Rome to catch the sunset. Wander through the gardens, taking in the view and reflecting on your journey, or – if time allows – boarding another sleeper train into the Italian night.

another way
The beauty of Interrail lies in its flexibility, with vast swathes of Europe yours to explore. A northern route, for example, might take in Brussels, Amsterdam, Berlin and Warsaw.

TRAWL the bars and bistros of **Paris**

LEARN to cook the Italian way with a cookery class in **Bologna**

GAZE at world-famous masterworks like The Last Supper in **Milan**

TASTE the wine of Chianti and famous foods of **Tuscany**

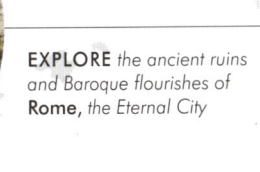

EXPLORE the ancient ruins and Baroque flourishes of **Rome**, the Eternal City

215

BY RAIL
EUROPE

⑯
Glacier Express

LOCATION Switzerland **START/FINISH** St Moritz/Zermatt **DISTANCE** 290 km (180 miles) **TIME** 8 hours
INFORMATION www.glacierexpress.ch

The Switzerland of storybooks, chocolate boxes and souvenir tea towels is alive and well on this once-in-a-lifetime, high mountain rail route, which marries the super-rich alpine playgrounds of Zermatt and St Moritz.

Dairy farmers shepherd cattle to time-stopped mountain refuges. Snaggletooth peaks rise above frosted-over lakes. Grazing cows pose for portraits amid emerald pastures. Rattling through a series of only-in-Switzerland scenes, chugging year-round through winter snows and across summer pastures, the Glacier Express has been wowing passengers since 1930. It's Europe's slowest express train (at an average speed of 39 km/h or 24 mph), but the journey through the cantons of Graubünden, Uri and Valais is one you won't find nearly long enough.

Window-seat highlights from panoramic carriages include glimpses of the Rhine Gorge, affectionately dubbed Switzerland's Grand Canyon; the narrow-gauge Albula Line, with its historic viaducts and spiral tunnels; and the natural spectacle of the Toblerone-shaped Matterhorn, the undisputed star of the Swiss Alps. When you emerge from the darkness of each tunnel (count 91 in total), you'll find yourself not only in another realm, but seeing the world in a new light, more sharply than before.

another way

A similarly scenic day tour can be found in Scotland, courtesy of the slow-motion Jacobite Steam Train. In summer, the seasonal tourist train stops for photos along the West Highland Line running north from Fort William, with Harry Potter fans thrilled to ride the same rails as the Hogwarts Express. The highlight? The cinematic Glenfinnan Viaduct, of course.

The Glacier Express crossing the jaw-dropping Landwasser Viaduct

Oslo to Bergen

LOCATION Norway **START/FINISH** Oslo/Bergen
DISTANCE 496 km (308 miles) **TIME** 6.5 hours
INFORMATION www.vy.no

This ride is most beautiful in autumn, when snowfall has already reached Norway's high mountains. The track traverses tunnels and passes fjords, finally reaching a wild, white-out landscape of roadless infinity.

As you chug north from Oslo, the busy capital soon gives way to sprawling domesticity around Dramsfjord. Farms thin and passengers board bound for famous resorts at Gol, Geilo and Ustaoset, laiden with ski gear. Frosted autumn colours fade into white, as sugar-iced mountains rush by. Shuttling onward, Haugastøl's old-fashioned, red wooden station reminds you that trains have run here since 1908. The effort it took to harness nature is palpable – over 180 tunnels had to be carved through thick mountain gneiss. But today this past struggle seems far away, as you wipe steam from the window and watch the train roll up through the frosted Hallingdal Valley. Climbing to Finse, the highest train station in Norway, there's a sudden shock of emptiness. The great white expanse of the Hardangervidda plateau ripples, a never-ending blank slate. Just as your ears pop, you're shuttling down to Myrdal station, heading back to sea level. Away from the swirling snow, the world comes back into focus as the train clatters into Norway's former capital city, Bergen.

The view out of the window en route from Oslo to Bergen

> Autumn colours fade into white, as sugar-iced mountains rush by

Train stewards preparing for departure from a snowy platform

(18) Venice Simplon-Orient-Express

LOCATION UK to Italy **START/FINISH** London/Venice **DISTANCE** 1,556 km (967 miles) **TIME** 2 days **INFORMATION** www.belmond.com; runs Mar–Nov

The world's most famous train journey is as romantic as it ever was: climb aboard to immerse yourself in the golden age of travel, to mingle with fellow passengers and see western Europe in style.

Few trains are preceded by a reputation like that of the Venice Simplon-Orient-Express. Just its name conjures the old-fashioned glamour of rail travel, brought so vividly to life in novels like Agatha Christie's *Murder on the Orient Express* and Ian Fleming's *From Russia with Love*, as well as countless movies. Instantly recognizable by its polished blue sleeping cars, this train is synonymous with unrefined luxury.

When you arrive on the platform at London Victoria, the gleaming carriages stand cloaked in an aura of mystery and ceremony. But they soon transform into a hive of activity, as cabin stewards in royal-blue

> On board, the compartment is welcoming, the silver fixtures gleaming

BY RAIL
EUROPE

IMMERSE yourself in the legacy of Agatha Christie by reading her whodunit Murder on the Orient Express

UK
London

WINE AND DINE in the glamorous restaurant car

CHUG across the grasslands of **Lombardy** and the **Veneto**

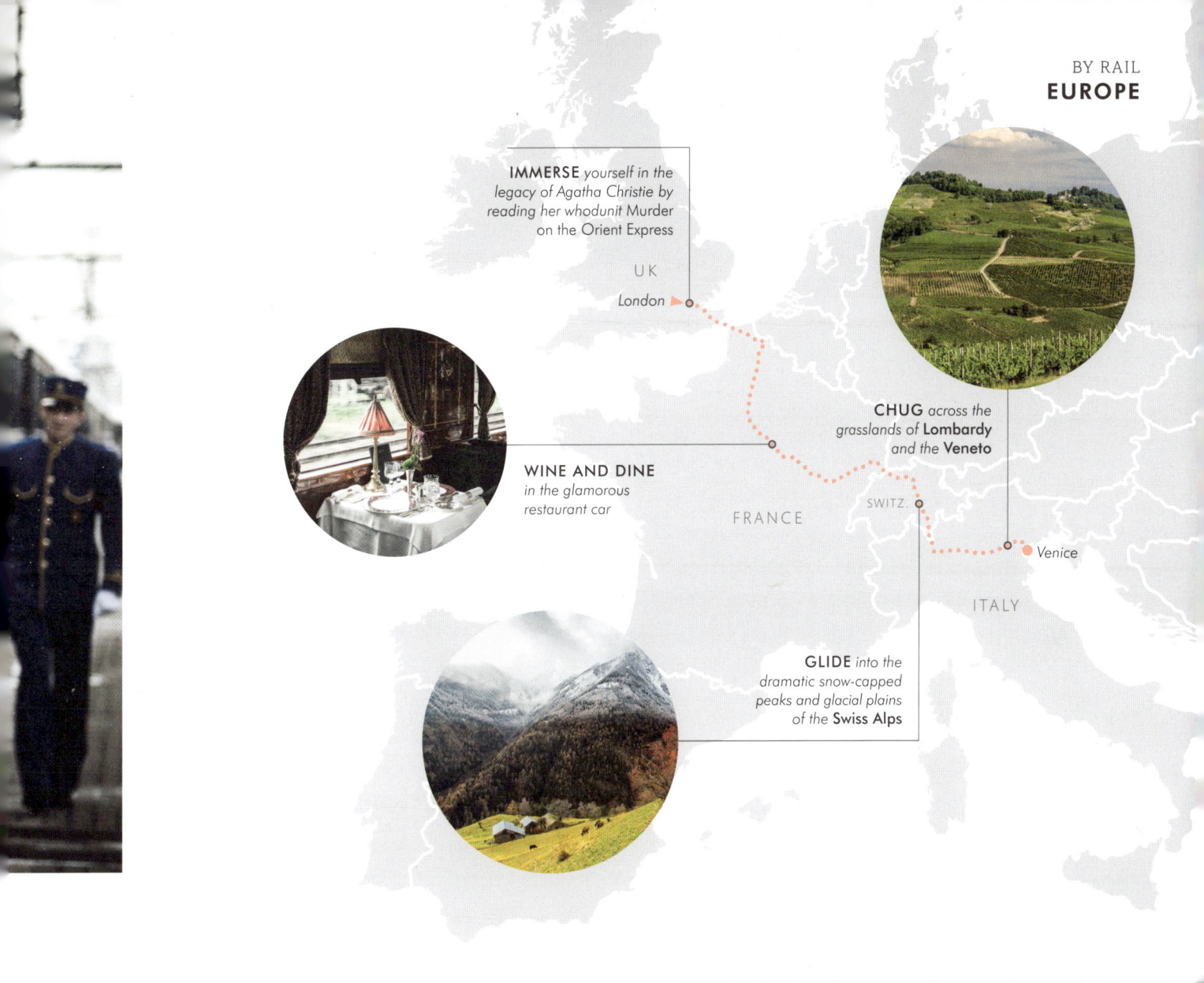

FRANCE

SWITZ.

Venice

ITALY

GLIDE into the dramatic snow-capped peaks and glacial plains of the **Swiss Alps**

uniforms leap out to greet their guests. Commuters and tourists look on from the sidelines, forgetting their own trains to marvel at this apparition from another age.

As you climb the stairs into your carriage under lamplight, the fantasy becomes a reality. You're on your way to Venice on a 24-hour journey that'll take in southern England, France and Switzerland, before slowly gliding across the grasslands of Lombardy and the Veneto in time for tea overlooking Venice's Grand Canal. On board, the compartment is welcoming, the silver fixtures gleaming from a hard-knuckle polish; out of the corner of your eye you spot a bottle of champagne waiting on ice. The cabin steward, now dressed in a gold buttoned tunic, appears and with an effortless smile pops the cork. Steady now: you're in for the trip of a lifetime and there's a three-course meal with matching wines waiting for you in the brocaded piano lounge.

A waiter serving cocktails on board the Venice Simplon-Orient-Express

BY RAIL
AFRICA AND THE MIDDLE EAST

A lonely windmill standing in the sprawling semi-desert of the Great Karoo

The Blue Train

LOCATION South Africa **START/FINISH** Pretoria/Cape Town
DISTANCE 1,600 km (995 miles) **TIME** 2 days
INFORMATION www.bluetrain.co.za

Africa's answer to the Orient Express, the Blue Train cuts a swathe across South Africa in sumptuous style. It's slow travel at its best, two days of elegance and indulgence as you glide through the golden desert and lush winelands of this beautiful country.

The Blue Train takes its name from the shining royal-blue carriages that await you. Inside lies a world of genteel opulence that will become your home for the next two days. It's more than a means of travel: life on board is as much a part of the journey as the route itself.

The wood-panelled cabins come complete with fresh flowers, a bottle of South African sparkling wine and a marble bathroom with gold-plated fittings. Comfortable armchairs (transformed into beds at night by your butler) create a cosy private sitting room, furnished with a huge picture window that invites you to while away the hours surveying the views. And what spectacular views they are. After leaving the urban centres of Johannesburg and Gauteng, south of Pretoria, you'll cross the Vaal River then reach the arid wilderness of the Kalahari Thornveld as the sun sets, giving this vast green desert a golden glow.

> Life on board is as much a part of the journey as the route itself

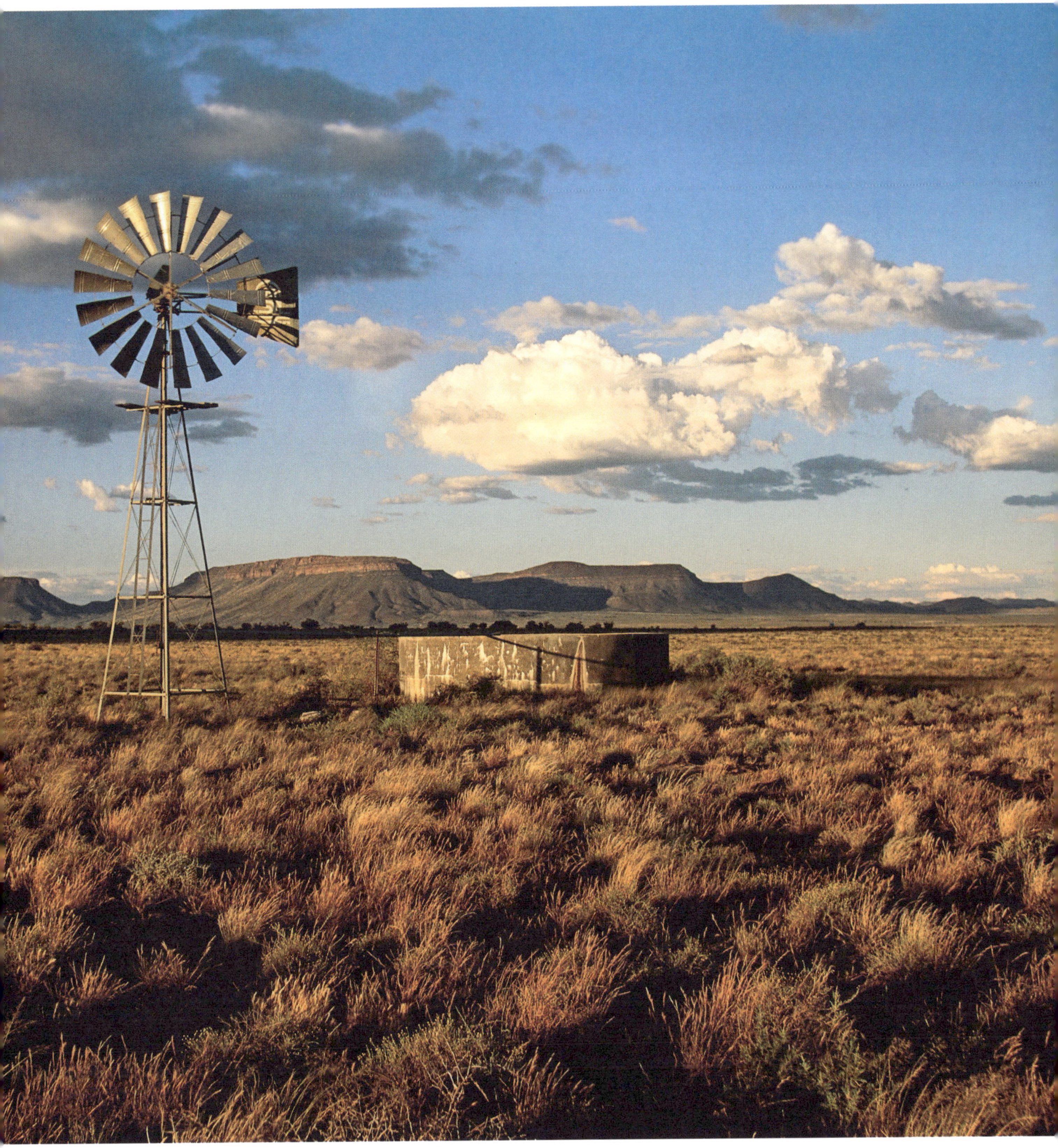

BY RAIL
AFRICA AND THE MIDDLE EAST

THE "CAPE TO CAIRO" RAILWAY

The Blue Train runs on the "Cape to Cairo" railway – the ambitious colonial dream of British mining magnate Cecil Rhodes, who planned to link all of the British Empire's African territories by rail. Work began in the late 19th century, but the two world wars prevented construction and as the empire diminished, so too did the need and desire to finish the line. It was never completed.

As evening draws in, dress up for dinner (the dress code is "elegant", as befits the ambience) and head to the lounge car for cocktails followed by an exquisite four-course meal, with fine South African wines, in the dining car. Think crisp white linens and crystal glassware, and menus of seared scallops, beef fillet with biltong dust, and desserts to die for. Later, chill in the club car, perhaps with a Cognac and a Cuban cigar, or enjoy some mellow jazz or soul music in the bar, as the train rolls on into the night.

Dawn brings expansive vistas of open plains as you travel south to the Great Karoo, a semi-desert hinterland characterized by flat-topped hills, known as Karoo Koppies. Wander to the observation car at the end of the train on the approach to the town of Kimberley in time to see Kamfers Dam, where thousands of flamingos cover the water in a blanket of pink. After a decadent breakfast, take an off-train excursion to the fascinating Kimberley Open Mine Museum, known as "The Big Hole". This is where the famous

Left The Blue Train on its way to Pretoria *Below left* The train's insignia *Below right* A red hartebeest

222

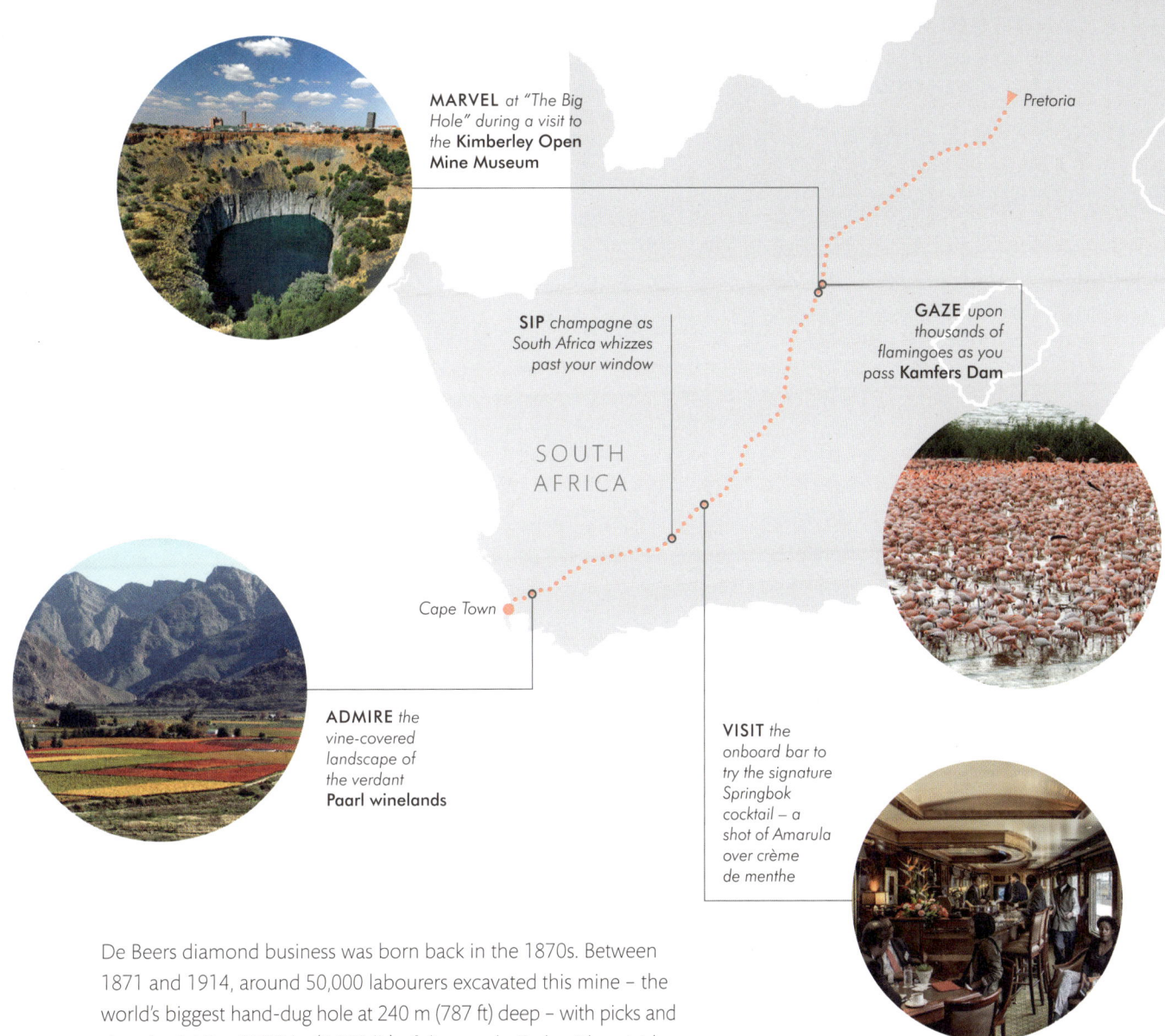

MARVEL at "The Big Hole" during a visit to the **Kimberley Open Mine Museum**

SIP champagne as South Africa whizzes past your window

GAZE upon thousands of flamingoes as you pass **Kamfers Dam**

ADMIRE the vine-covered landscape of the verdant **Paarl winelands**

VISIT the onboard bar to try the signature Springbok cocktail – a shot of Amarula over crème de menthe

De Beers diamond business was born back in the 1870s. Between 1871 and 1914, around 50,000 labourers excavated this mine – the world's biggest hand-dug hole at 240 m (787 ft) deep – with picks and shovels, yielding 2,720 kg (6,000 lb) of diamonds. Today, it's a vivid turquoise lake. Learn about the fascinating history of the mine, check out the museum's exquisite collection of cut and uncut diamonds, and then maybe buy your own gem in the specialist shops nearby.

Back on the Blue Train in time for lunch, you return to the rhythm of life on the rails. Wallow in the joys of slow travel, maybe read a book or simply watch nature go by. Keep an eye out for gazelle, oryx and ostriches as you trundle through Karoo National Park and its vast open spaces dotted with windmills and fringed by distant mountains.

After your last night on board, you arrive in Cape Town having passed South Africa's famous Paarl winelands, with row after row of neat green vines. It's a tough ask to leave the Blue Train, but the country's beloved "Mother City" is waiting to be explored.

another way

Combine a trip on the Blue Train with a day in the renowned Kruger National Park from Pretoria. You'll enjoy game drives, a bush breakfast and dinner with cultural entertainment.

BY RAIL
AFRICA AND THE MIDDLE EAST

(20)

Rovos Rail

LOCATION South Africa to Zimbabwe **START/FINISH** Pretoria/Victoria Falls
DISTANCE 1,400 km (870 miles) **TIME** 4 days **INFORMATION** www.rovos.com

Safari in style on board this Rovos Rail service. The luxury train rolls through the wildlife and wilderness of Hwange, Zimbabwe's biggest and best national park, en route to the world's largest curtain of falling water.

Rovos Rail's vintage carriages exude glamour and grace, with mahogany-panelled cabins, leather couches and shiny brass fittings. Simply sit back and enjoy all the onboard indulgence, fine dining and fabulous scenery.

The train takes in rugged plains, high escarpments and the towns of Warmbaths (named for its mineral waters) and Nylstroom (once believed to be the source of the Nile), all before crossing the Tropic of Capricorn. The highlight of the journey, however, is when you rattle along 114 km (71 miles) of track through the vast game-rich plains bordering Hwange National Park. The Big Five (elephants, buffalo, lions, leopards and rhino) all roam this golden savannah, along with cheetahs, zebras, giraffe and painted wolves. It's something to spot wildlife from the open balcony of the observation car, but it's hard to resist taking a break from the train to embark on a game drive in the park.

The journey ends at Victoria Falls station, a short drive from the majestic waterfall itself, a roaring torrent known locally – and aptly – as Mosi oa Tunya, "the smoke that thunders".

> **Sit back and enjoy all the onboard indulgence, fine dining and fabulous scenery**

A Rovos Rail train stopped at the ornate Matjiesfontein station

224

BY RAIL
AFRICA AND THE MIDDLE EAST

Left The TAZARA Railway curving along a bridge in Tanzania's hills *Above* Selling bananas to passengers

(21)
TAZARA Railway

LOCATION Tanzania to Zambia **START/FINISH** Dar es-Salaam/Kapiri Mposhi
DISTANCE 1,865 km (1,159 miles) **TIME** 2 days **INFORMATION** www.tazarasite.com

Connecting the Tanzanian coast with the Copperbelt in Zambia's interior, the TAZARA Railway makes a relentless march across some of Africa's wildest country.

Starting in the coastal city of Dar es-Salaam – buzzing with impromptu markets and football games, hairdressing salons and music stores – the TAZARA Railway soon leaves the clamour and colour of urban life far behind. The railway was built in the 1970s so that Zambian trade could reach a port without the need to cross Rhodesia (now Zimbabwe) or South Africa, which were both ruled by white-minority governments at the time. The longest railway south of the Sahara, it stops only – if often – at small rural stations. These pauses bring brief reminders of the bustle of daily life, at platforms clustered with fruit sellers and passengers.

When not pulling into villages, the train crosses long stretches of uninhabited country, including Selous Game Reserve, one of Africa's largest protected wilderness areas. While wheeling through this land, watch for elephants and lions – this vast reserve claims to protect Africa's largest lion population – as well as giraffe, zebra, wildebeest and impala. Elsewhere, there are mountains to contend with, the deep-green Kilombero Valley to traverse and the Kibasira Swamp to navigate, before the short stretch down through Zambia – a land of mud-walled villages and a terrain that gets drier by degrees the further south you travel.

Gradually, the Lizard trundles out into the sun-baked desert

Above Passing through dusty canyons on the way to the Fhelja iron mine *Right* Snaking along a section of single track through the Selja Gorge

BY RAIL
AFRICA AND THE MIDDLE EAST

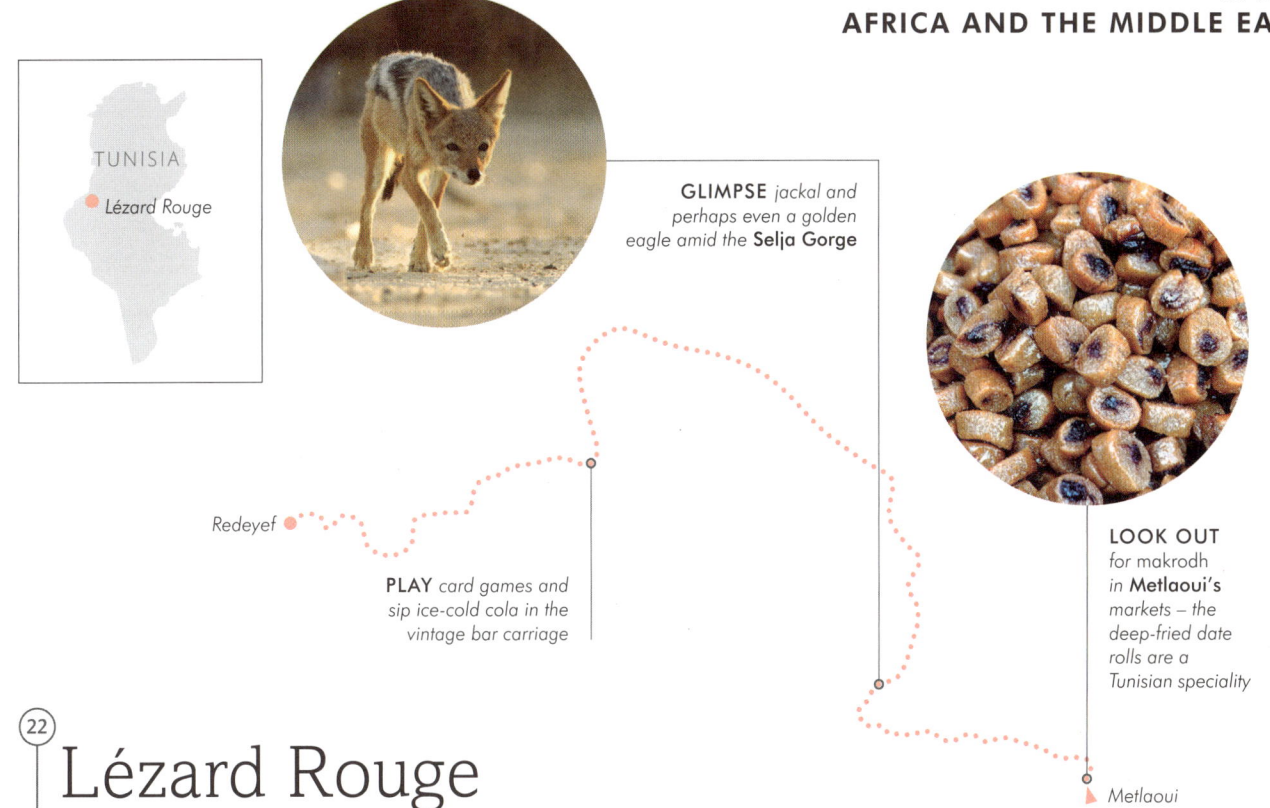

TUNISIA
Lézard Rouge

GLIMPSE *jackal and perhaps even a golden eagle amid the* **Selja Gorge**

Redeyef

PLAY *card games and sip ice-cold cola in the vintage bar carriage*

LOOK OUT *for makrodh in* **Metlaoui's** *markets – the deep-fried date rolls are a Tunisian speciality*

Metlaoui

22 Lézard Rouge

LOCATION Tunisia **START/FINISH** Metlaoui/Redeyef **DISTANCE** 50 km (31 miles) **TIME** 2 hours **INFORMATION** www.lezard-rouge.com

Board the Red Lizard – a century-old former royal train – and trundle through the northern fringes of the sandy seas of the Sahara. This rickety ride through southwestern Tunisia brings the charms of the Maghreb region roaring back to life.

The bordeaux-coloured Lézard Rouge is a grand dame of an antique train gifted by the King of France to the Bey of Tunis in 1911. Once a symbol of Europe's colonial oppression of North Africa, the train was retired in 1957 when Tunisia was declared independent from France. Reborn in 1984 as a tourist train, its six vintage carriages are fitted with wood panels, deep studded armchairs and brass light fittings. Today, the Lézard Rouge still trundles along a 14-km (9-mile) track through the Selja Gorge, originally laid to transport mined phosphates.

As the train pulls out of the sleepy town of Metlaoui, snag a window seat and watch life unfold: see pavement cafés crowded with customers nursing cigarettes and cups of syrupy coffee; baguettes stacked in pyramids outside bakeries; and jagged, half-built houses. Accompanying it all is the constant rattle of motorbikes pootling past. Gradually, the Lizard trundles out into the sun-baked desert, snaking between rust-red canyons and through mountain tunnels that snap you into obsidian darkness, before emerging into the blinding Saharan sunlight once more. At the canyon-side terminus, there's just enough time to explore before jumping back aboard for the return journey.

TATOOINE

Tunisia's desert moonscapes play a starring role as the planet Tatooine in the *Star Wars* films, named after the Berber village of Tataouine. Nearest to the Lézard Rouge route is Mos Espa, Anakin Skywalker's hometown in *Star Wars: Episode I – The Phantom Menace*.

The Palace on Wheels

LOCATION India **START/FINISH** New Delhi (loop) **DISTANCE** 3,000 km (1,850 miles) **TIME** 8 days **INFORMATION** www.thepalaceonwheels.com; tours operate Apr–Oct, departing on Wed only

From the moment you step aboard the Indian Railways' Palace on Wheels, you're transported to a world of old-fashioned luxury. This heritage train is an opulent way to explore the remarkable hinterland of northwest India, with its lush landscapes and awe-inspiring architecture.

Operating in its current guise since the early 1980s, the Palace on Wheels is no longer the dominion of princes and viceroys, but a place where ordinary people are treated like royalty. The week-long round trip between New Delhi and Jaisalmer covers 3,000 km (1,850 miles), travelling mostly at night while passengers snooze in their deluxe air-conditioned cabins. Each cabin is named after a famous palace in Rajasthan and is decked out with polished teak furniture, colourful wall hangings and silk curtains. There's no escaping the fact that this is a nostalgia trip, but it's all part of the charm.

BY RAIL
ASIA

Left *Jaipur's impressive Amber Fort, reflected in Maota Lake*
Above *Staff members posing next to the Palace on Wheels* **Right** *View of Jaisalmer's epic fort*

The Palace on Wheels departs Safdarjung station in New Delhi on Wednesday afternoon, in time for a silver-service evening meal and a talk on the history and heritage of the train. The next day you arrive at Jaipur, known as the "Pink City" for its distinctive terracotta-hued old quarter. A guided tour takes in Jaipur's abundance of UNESCO World Heritage Sites, including the walled city and its eye-catching palaces, the surreal 18th-century astronomical observatory at Jantar Mantar and the dazzling Amber Fort.

The following morning, passengers are woken at dawn to seek out prowling Bengal tigers in the early morning chill of Ranthambore National Park, before chugging along to Chittorgarh for a tour of the city's magnificent hill fort. The train then sweeps onwards through the countryside to reach the romantic lakeside city of Udaipur, from where it snakes through the desert to Jaisalmer. With its vast honey-coloured fort and finely decorated *havelis* (traditional townhouses), Jaisalmer is the most westerly point on your Indian railway adventure.

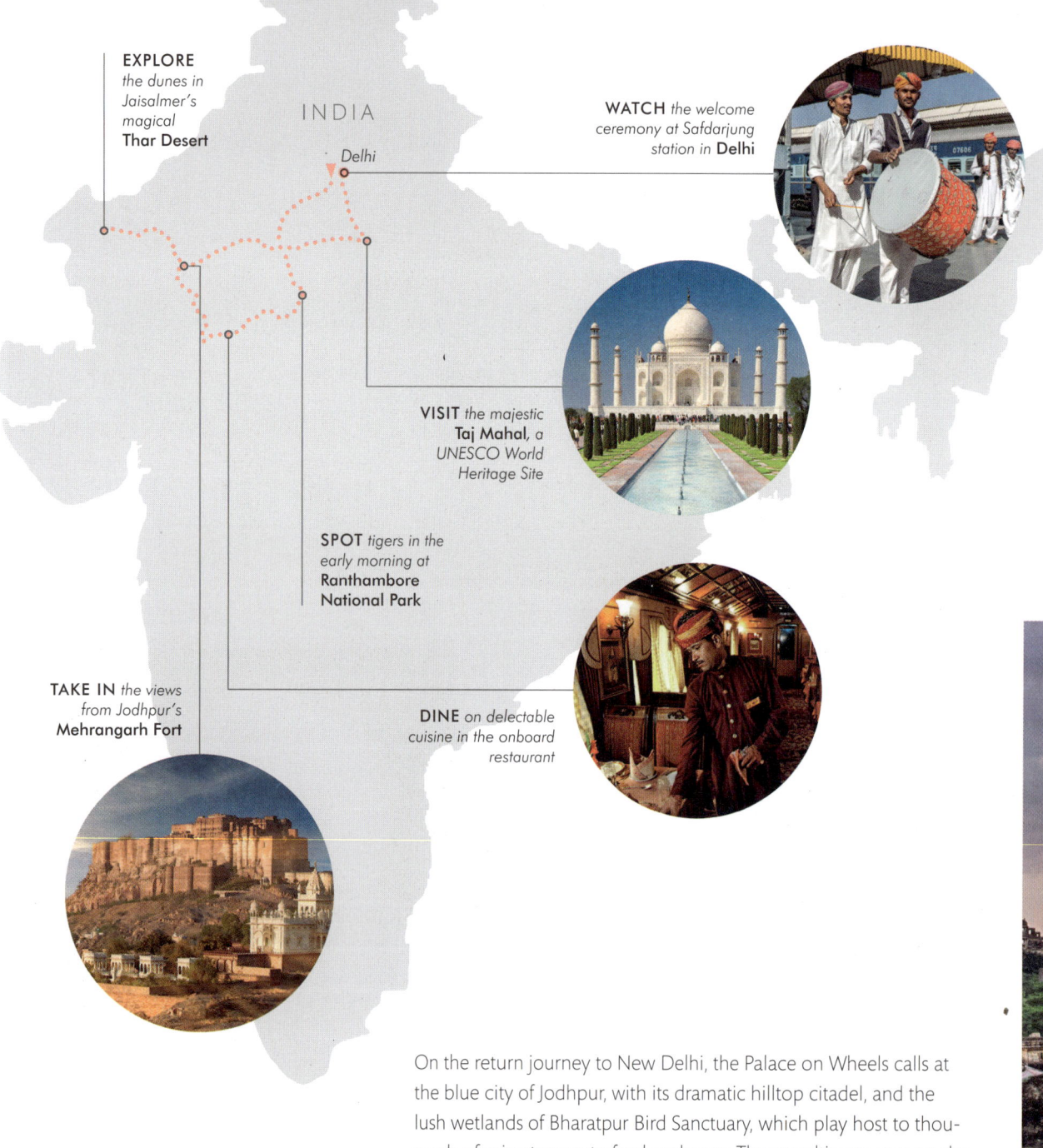

EXPLORE the dunes in Jaisalmer's magical **Thar Desert**

INDIA

Delhi

WATCH the welcome ceremony at Safdarjung station in **Delhi**

VISIT the majestic **Taj Mahal**, a UNESCO World Heritage Site

SPOT tigers in the early morning at **Ranthambore National Park**

TAKE IN the views from Jodhpur's **Mehrangarh Fort**

DINE on delectable cuisine in the onboard restaurant

On the return journey to New Delhi, the Palace on Wheels calls at the blue city of Jodhpur, with its dramatic hilltop citadel, and the lush wetlands of Bharatpur Bird Sanctuary, which play host to thousands of migratory waterfowl each year. The penultimate stop on the tour is the sprawling city of Agra, where arguably the best has been saved for last. Here, on the bank of the Yamuna River, stands the ivory-white Taj Mahal – one of the seven modern wonders of the world – built by Mughal emperor Shah Jahan in memory of his favourite wife.

After a week of life on the Palace, you'll be quite used to special treatment. At every stop, passengers are swept to the front of the queue. You won't have to deal with touts or negotiate with auto-rickshaw drivers, and the restaurants that you visit during

> Here, on the bank of the Yamuna River, stands the ivory-white Taj Mahal

BY RAIL
ASIA

excursions are among India's finest. On board, you'll dine on decadent Rajasthani dishes like dal Mahkani and paneer tikka, rich with ghee and aromatic spices. The morning wake-up call comes with a steaming cup of tea or coffee served by the *khidmatgar*, an indispensable personal waiter-cum-concierge on hand in every carriage. And, of course, there's an onboard Ayurvedic Spa offering massages and other treatments. It's only on Wednesday morning, as the Palace on Wheels rolls back into Delhi at first light, that you must consider how to fend for yourself again. Happily, there's time for a final decadent breakfast before you have to re-enter the real world.

Below *The stunning Samadhisvara temple located in Chittorgarh Fort*
Below right *The distinctive blue architecture of Jodhpur*

THE TAJ MAHAL: A MONUMENT TO LOVE

Arguably one of the world's most recognizable buildings, and surely one of its most beautiful, the Taj Mahal was built by Mughal emperor Shah Jahan as a mausoleum for his second wife, Mumtaz Mahal ("Chosen One of the Palace"). Construction began in 1632, shortly after she died giving birth to their fourteenth child: Shah Jahan's hair was said to have turned grey overnight through grief. Built from white marble and decorated in semi-precious stones, construction of the complex spanned 22 years.

BY RAIL
ASIA

Above Tea pickers at work
Right Snaking through Sri Lanka's scenic Hill Country

The Hill Country Railway

LOCATION Sri Lanka **START/FINISH** Kandy/Badulla **DISTANCE** 183 km (114 miles) **TIME** 7 hours **INFORMATION** www.railway.gov.lk; reserve seats as far in advance as possible

The trip from Kandy to Badulla is one of Asia's great railway journeys, traversing the uplands of Sri Lanka and rolling through a spectacular tapestry of misty hills, tumbling waterfalls and endless acres of vivid green tea fields.

Starting at the historic capital of Kandy, Sri Lanka's hill country railway was constructed during the colonial era to service the burgeoning tea industry and connect the island's upcountry towns and villages. Cutting a memorable path across Sri Lanka's uplands, the ride serves up a heady brew of breathtaking scenery and colonial charm.

The most spectacular section of the route stretches between Hatton and Ella, with delicate waterfalls cascading out of clefts in the hills and sweeping views unfolding in every direction as the train grinds its way ever higher. Vast swathes of tea blanket the hills, dotted with the distant outlines of Tamil tea pickers toiling among the bushes.

Punctuating the journey are regular halts at a series of toytown stations, complete with original platform signs and time-warped architecture. Hawkers rush aboard at every stop, armed with baskets of fresh samosas, bundles of bananas and steaming pots of coffee and tea – a unique opportunity to taste the landscape through which you're riding. The town of Badulla marks the end of the line, but the scenery doesn't stop with it: tea-lined hills stretch endlessly on, as far as the eye can see.

BY RAIL
ASIA

Death Railway

LOCATION Thailand **START/FINISH** Bangkok/Nam Tok
DISTANCE 115 km (71 miles) **TIME** 4.5–6 hours **INFORMATION** The train from Bangkok departs twice daily; book tickets in person at the station

The spectre of war haunts this storied stretch of railway, immortalized in the 1957 movie The Bridge on the River Kwai. *Ride from Bangkok to Nam Tok, taking in spectacular landscapes and harrowing history en route.*

No longer running all the way to Yangon in Myanmar (formerly Burma), the notorious Death Railway lives on between Thailand's capital and the town of Nam Tok, traversing dramatic viaducts, photogenic riverbanks and harsh mountain passes. Taking in the scene from the comfortable carriage, it's hard to imagine that more than 100,000 people lost their lives building this track, condemned to forced labour by the Japanese during World War II.

Alight at Kanchanaburi, where you can walk across the famous bridge over the Khwae Yai River and learn about the human cost of its construction at the Thailand–Burma Railway Centre. Further up the line, the train makes the most spectacular leg of its journey across the Wampo Viaduct, hugging cave-peppered cliffs and defying gravity as it snakes along the river. Beyond Nam Tok, the track runs out – walk on to see the hand-hewn Hellfire Pass, which continued through the jungle into Myanmar.

THE DEATH RAILWAY ARTISTS

Despite the risk, artists such as Ashley George Old and Jack Chalker documented the horrors of life as prisoners of war in the Death Railway camps. Many of their works – created with brushes of human hair and paints made from animal and plant fluids – are today housed in the Australian War Memorial in Canberra.

The Death Railway running alongside the Khwae Yai River at Kanchanaburi

BY RAIL
ASIS

㉖ Yangon to Bagan

LOCATION Myanmar **START/FINISH** Yangon/Bagan **DISTANCE** 500 km (311 miles) **TIME** 2 days **INFORMATION** http://myanmartrainticket.com; it is advisable to book tickets in advance

Ride this atmospheric rail route, from the dazzling gilded pagodas of Myanmar's capital to the breathtaking plains of Bagan, home to thousands upon thousands of ancient Buddhist temples.

Sunrise over the plains of Bagan, strewn with Buddhist temples

MYANMAR

Bagan

EXPLORE *the unqiue legacy of Buddhist art and architecture in the ancient city of* **Bagan**

Yangon

ADMIRE *the glittering Shwedagon Pagoda in* **Yangon***, which stands 99 m (325 ft) tall*

another way
Consider extending your trip by a couple of days and boarding an onward train from Bagan to the evocatively named city of Mandalay, considered the cultural capital of Myanmar.

Myanmar – the very name conjures evocative images of timeless temples, standing steadfast amid the ever-shifting sands of history. And this is just what you'll see on the rustic Yangon–Bagan railway, which offers an authentic glimpse of local life as you travel to some of the country's most incredible sacred sights.

It begins in the capital, Yangon, where the skyline is crowned by the unmistakable form of the gold Shwedagon Pagoda: a sanctuary of tranquillity in an often ravaged city. On board the train, the urban soundscape is replaced by the rattle of decades-old rolling stock, the racket of vendors hawking beer and tea, and the contented murmur of conversation with fellow passengers – your roommates for the night, in a small but comfortable sleeper car. Outside the window, scenes of rural Myanmarese life steadily roll past – farmers tilling fields, people washing in streams and children cycling to school – with the occasional flash of a gilded stupa reminding you that you're in the Land of Shwe (gold).

Even by Myanmarese standards, your destination is spectacular. The plains of Bagan are home to thousands of centuries-old temples, relics of the Pagan Empire. Walk or cycle among them freely – you'll find many completely deserted – or take a sunrise hot-air balloon ride above the plains, when their red-brick walls are bathed in a pink and gold glow.

Strolling through the magnificent Shwedagon Pagoda complex

BY RAIL
ASIA

A steam "toy train" making its ascent to the Himalayan city of Darjeeling

(27) Trans-Mongolian Express

LOCATION Russia to China **START/FINISH** Ulan-Ude/Beijing **DISTANCE** 1,486 km (923 miles) **TIME** 3 days **INFORMATION** www.transsiberianexpress.net

A spur of the famed Trans-Siberian Railway, this three-day journey between Russia and China follows an ancient tea caravan route across Mongolia. The trip can be taken in either direction, though most passengers travel west to east, en route from Moscow to Beijing. Going this way, the train sets out from Ulan-Ude in Russia, passing through pine forest and tundra before steaming south. After a stop in Sukhbaatar for Monglian border formalities, you continue southwards across arid flatlands to the capital city, Ulaanbaatar. The train trundles on across the desolate rust-brown landscape of the Gobi Desert, as passengers make friends over card games and shared snacks. At the Chinese border, there's a stop for several hours (usually at night) as the carriages are raised by huge hydraulic lifts to change gauges. Dawn breaks over the dusty reaches of Inner Mongolia, and as the train snakes on into the mountains above Beijing, passengers catch a first glimpse of the iconic Great Wall over breakfast.

(28) Darjeeling Himalayan Railway

LOCATION India **START/FINISH** New Jalpaiguri/Darjeeling **DISTANCE** 87 km (54 miles) **TIME** 1 day **INFORMATION** www.dhr.in.net

American author Mark Twain described his 1896 journey on the Darjeeling Himalayan Railway as "the most enjoyable day I have spent on earth". It is a sentiment that has been echoed by countless other passengers.

The narrow-gauge line was launched in 1881 to improve access to Darjeeling, a tea-growing hill station and popular summer retreat for Raj officials and their families. Today, diesel and steam "toy trains" ply the railway, which uses an ingenious series of loops and zigzags to ascend 2,100 m (6,890 ft) in just 87 km (54 miles). Progress is slow – the full journey takes over seven hours – but this gives plenty of time to soak up the views. The standout moment comes just before the village of Ghoom, when the world's third-highest mountain, towering Kanchenjunga, appears suddenly on the horizon.

| "Toy trains" ply the railway, which uses an ingenious series of loops and zigzags |

BY RAIL
ASSIA

29 Shimla Toy Train

LOCATION India **START/FINISH** Kalka/Shimla
DISTANCE 96 km (60 miles) **TIME** 4–6 hours
INFORMATION www.irctctourism.com

Shimla, "Queen of the Hills", has been a popular Himalayan retreat since the mid-19th century. The best way to get here is on the narrow-gauge Kalka-Shimla "toy train", via 102 tunnels and 864 bridges and viaducts – a remarkable feat of engineering for the terrain. Climbing 1,463 m (4,800 ft), continual switchbacks offer panoramic views of the Shivalik Hills from both sides, with lush green terraces extending in every direction.

The train passes through 18 historic stations, occasionally stopping to allow passengers a break. It's a romantic but very slow journey, so it's worth booking a more comfortable seat on one of the "tourist trains". Come prepared to chat to well-to-do Delhiites, excited about seeing Shimla's towering, snow-dusted peaks.

30 Reunification Express

LOCATION Vietnam **START/FINISH** Hanoi/Ho Chi Minh City **DISTANCE** 1,726 km (1,072 miles)
TIME 3 days **INFORMATION** http://12go.asia

An inspiring symbol of Vietnam's recovery from the ravages of war, the Reunification Express is the most atmospheric way to travel from Hanoi to Ho Chi Minh City. Hawkers make their rounds through air-conditioned sleeper cars and rows of wooden pews, selling potent Vietnamese coffee and cans of Saigon Beer to fuel conversations with new friends and fellow travellers. In the bacchanalian restaurant car, steaming bowls of beef pho, fried chicken feet and blood soup are all available, depending on how adventurous you're feeling. All the while, green oceans of rice paddies flash past your window, in an impressionistic blur of rural Vietnamese life. Stop en route at Hue, to roam the tombs of ancient emperors, or relax on the sun-drenched sands of party town Nha Trang, before the train barrels on to gleaming Ho Chi Minh City – a modern emblem of Vietnam's present and future.

The picturesque mountain city of Shimla, dusted with winter snow

NORTH-SOUTH RAILWAY

Officially known as the North-South Railway, the line between Hanoi and Ho Chi Minh City was built in the early 20th century. Much of it was destroyed by war, but it became a key artery after the reunification of Vietnam in 1976.

BY RAIL
ASIA

EXPLORE Tokyo station, *a vast underground warren of shops, cafés and souvenir stands*

JAPAN

Tokyo

Nagoya

ENJOY *an eki-ben (train lunch box) as you whizz through the countryside*

WATCH Mount Fuji *from the train; be sure to ask for a yama-gawa ("mountain side") seat*

(31)

Tokyo to Nagoya Shinkansen

LOCATION Japan **START/FINISH** Tokyo/Nagoya **DISTANCE** 370 km (230 miles)
TIME 1 hour 40 minutes to 3 hours **INFORMATION** A Japan Rail Pass covers the journey on any shinkansen except Nozomi services

Japan's record-breaking shinkansen are some of the fastest – and most punctual – trains in the world. Sit back in the comfort of one of these iconic bullet trains and watch Mount Fuji sailing serenely past your window.

Pulling out of the station, the sleek and pristine shinkansen gradually picks up speed until the neon signs and high-rises of Tokyo are whipping past the window; then – quick as a flash – it bursts into the countryside at 443 km (275 miles) per hour.

On board, all is peaceful in spite of the breakneck speed, the seats spacious. A smiling member of staff enters the carriage, pushing a trolley groaning with *eki-ben*, or "train lunch boxes". But there are no sad sandwiches and anaemic cups of tea here – expect elegant dishes like breaded chicken on rice or a bright selection of sushi.

More than the creature comforts, though, train travel in Japan is remarkable for the landscapes which unfurl like a painted scroll past your window. The lush swell of tea fields, brightly tiled roofs on wooden farmhouses, and mysterious torii (shrine gates) half hidden by trees all flash past, while cartoon-daubed billboards blur as you zoom through towns.

Finally, it's time for the journey's most iconic sight: proud Mount Fuji, rising in beautiful symmetry above a landscape dotted with lakes and rice paddies. From tourists to commuters, first-time visitors to old hands, all are transfixed by this ancient symbol of Japan.

A shinkansen speeding through lush fields past Mount Fuji, Japan

Qinghai-Tibet Railway

One of the trains on the Qinghai-Tibet Railway, passing through the bleak yet beautiful Himalayan landscape

LOCATION China **START/FINISH** Xining/Lhasa **DISTANCE** 1,956 km (1,215 miles)
TIME 2 days **INFORMATION** www.chinahighlights.com/china-trains/tibet-train.htm

Crossing some of the most beautiful but unforgiving terrain on earth, the world's highest train route runs from China's Qinghai province up over the semi-frozen Tibetan Plateau and into the soaring Himalayas.

Though this line can be accessed via a connection from Beijing, most travellers join the route from Xining, the capital of Qinghai province. At 2,500 m (8,200 ft), the city is a good place to acclimatize before heading to high-altitude Tibet.

Setting off from Xining's sparkling, modern railway station, the train carves alongside the arid banks of the Yellow River before reaching Qinghai Lake – China's largest – which lingers like a vast mirage outside the window for nearly an hour. As the carriages climb higher, passengers gobble pots of instant noodles before settling in for the night in sleeper berths. Soon, conversation from the rows of bunks falls to whispers, the atmosphere crackling with the anticipation of reaching the mighty Himalayas. Overnight, the train creeps higher and higher, rolling along tracks laid ingeniously over permafrost, and through the highest tunnels in the world. Sleep is fitful from the high altitude and the heat of the carriage, but the view from your window of a spangled veil of stars makes for a constant companion.

Wake early enough and you'll catch the first rays of dawn stretching over the giant, barren peaks of the Himalayan mountains. A glacier trundles by, and soon you'll alight in Lhasa, one of the planet's highest cities, on the "Roof of the World".

BY RAIL
ASIA

Golden Eagle Luxury Train

LOCATION China to Russia **START/FINISH** Beijing/Moscow **DISTANCE** 6,400 km (4,000 miles) **TIME** 21 days **INFORMATION** www.goldeneagleluxurytrains.com

Whether by car, bike or train, journeying along the Silk Road is an epic experience. But to do it in style, there's no better way than on this sumptuous rail ride.

Starting in Beijing, the carriages speed across China, making it hard to imagine that it once took months to go the same distance on foot or by caravan. From the windows, it's easy to appreciate the scale of the impenetrable Gobi Desert and the importance of oases, such as Dunhuang. Soon sand gives way to mountains, beyond which lie Central Asia: the heart of the Silk Road, where the UNESCO World Heritage Sites of Samarkand, Bukhara and Khiva dazzle even the most world-weary travellers.

The journey continues into Turkmenistan, where the ancient ruins of Merv contrast sharply with the white marble buildings and golden statues of Ashgabat, nicknamed "Las Vegas of the Karakum". The desert sands turn to Eurasian steppe as the Golden Eagle makes its way north to Volgograd (formerly the infamous Stalingrad) before reaching its final destination: the spiralling onion domes and Stalinist Gothic monuments of Moscow.

DARVAZA GAS CRATER

This crater – also known as The Gates of Hell – is the highlight of the Golden Eagle's stops in Turkmenistan. Measuring 69 m (226 ft) across and 30 m (98 ft) deep, the crater formed when a natural gas field collapsed in the 1970s. Engineers set light to the gas, thinking it would quickly burn off, but nearly 20 years later it is still on fire.

Left *The oasis at Dunhuang, home to the shimmering Crescent Lake* **Below** *Dining on board a Golden Eagle Luxury Train*

BY RAIL
ASIA

㉞ Trans-Siberian Railway

LOCATION Russia **START/FINISH** Moscow/Vladivostok
DISTANCE 9,289 km (5,772 miles) **TIME** Minimum 8 days
INFORMATION Train availability, facilities and itineraries vary

The world's longest train ride slices through the forests, cities and perma-frosted steppes of Eurasia, from megacity Moscow in the west to Vladivostok on the Pacific Ocean. An engineering masterpiece, this route is at its most dramatic in winter.

The Trans-Siberian Railway, tracking the edge of the frozen Lake Baikal

SIZE UP the 42-tonne (46-ton) head of Lenin – the biggest in the world – in **Ulan Ude**

LOOK OUT for native irises, pansies and oriental poppies growing wild alongside the tracks

CLIMB aboard historic steam trains at the Museum of Railway Technology in **Novosibirsk**

ADMIRE the grand station buildings in cities such as **Khabarovsk** and **Novosibirsk**

RUSSIA
Moscow
Vladivostok

The eye-catching façade of Vladivostok station

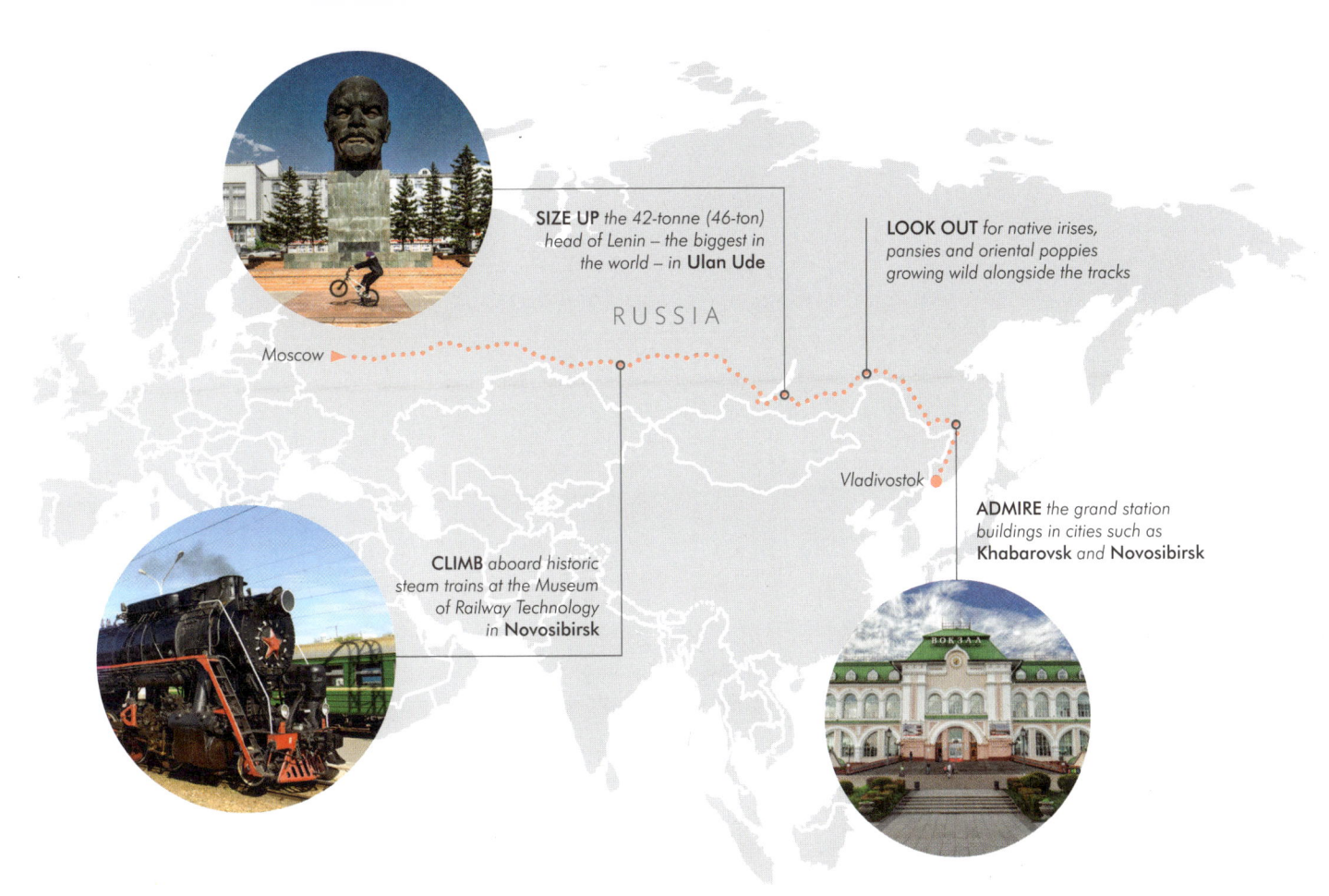

Riding the Trans-Siberian Railway from end to end is an adventure of epic proportions: this iconic route traverses eight time zones and goes nearly a quarter of the way around the world. The train's carriages roll steadily through the so-called wastelands of Siberia which – as you'll soon discover – are far from empty. Here, the landscapes change day by day, season by season, and pioneering communities have established unexpectedly vibrant cities in the Russian hinterland.

> The train's carriages roll steadily through the so-called wastelands of Siberia

Travelling on the Trans-Siberian is an immersive Russian cultural experience. The characters you meet on board – miners and engineers, housewives and pensioners, salesmen and students – might as well populate the pages of a classic Russian novel. In the restaurant car, delicate dishes of red caviar are on offer alongside plainer fare such as boiled eggs and smoked sausage. As you travel onwards, the rumbling of the wheels becomes a lullaby, the swaying of the carriages a cradle to rock you to sleep.

Without doubt, the most striking part of the line is the Circum-Baikal Railway around Lake Baikal. The world's largest body of freshwater, the lake glitters in the summer sun but freezes solid in winter. The track hugs the shoreline, and when the train stops at Baikal's pretty wooden station, summertime passengers dive into the water for a swim. In colder months, a mouthful of fish straight from the ice is preferred, washed down with a shot of warming vodka and a cheer of "Na Zdorovie!".

244

BY RAIL
AUSTRALASIA

The Ghan travelling through the vast expanse of the Australian Outback

The Ghan

LOCATION Australia **START/FINISH** Adelaide/Darwin
DISTANCE 2,979 km (1,851 miles) **TIME** 3 days
INFORMATION www.journeybeyondrail.com.au/journeys/the-ghan/

Australia's most storied rail journey, The Ghan crosses the continent from south to north, from the Great Australian Bight to the Timor Sea.

European explorers took more than a century to make the first land crossing of Australia. They brought back tales of great hardship, convinced of the impossibility of their task. Today, you can do the same journey these intrepid explorers did – but in style, riding the rails in a luxury carriage.

Flying between Adelaide and Darwin may be quicker – it takes just under four hours – but the three days you spend on The Ghan serve as a reminder that it's the getting there, and not the destination, that really matters. There is something authentic about taking the slow route: in an age when you can board an aeroplane and arrive at your destination without any time for adjustment, The Ghan luxuriates in the transition between the chilly south and the tropical north. Australia's diverse colour palette is beautifully showcased en route, from the pale yellows of the Outback and the blood-red sands of the Red Centre to the dull greens and piercing blue skies of the tropics. Along the way, three stop-off points provide the opportunity to delve into Australia's spellbinding landscapes and rich culture.

ARRIVE in **Darwin**, the tropical capital of Australia's Top End

DRIFT between the sheer red cliffs of **Nitmiluk Gorge** in a boat

AUSTRALIA

VISIT the Aboriginal art galleries and shops of **Alice Springs**

EXPERIENCE the big horizons of Outback life at **Marla**

Adelaide

EXPLORE cultured **Adelaide**, one of Australia's most underrated cities

> There is no more beautiful, nor soulful, way to experience the Outback

WHAT'S IN THE NAME?

"The Ghan" was named in honour of some of Australia's earliest immigrants, Afghan cameleers who arrived in the country during the 19th century. Initially, they aided exploration parties in opening up routes into Australia's interior; later, they helped with the construction of the The Ghan railway itself by carrying supplies into the interior.

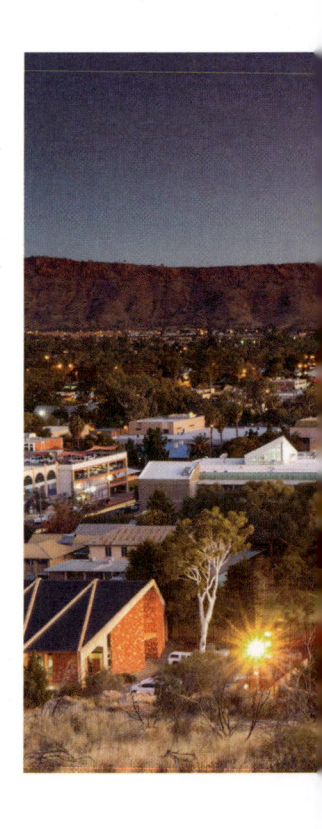

246

BY RAIL
AUSTRALASIA

The first stop is at the Outback road station of Marla, where passengers step out of the train and into the pure, unnerving silence of the deep desert – for countless travellers, this moment is a highlight. Next stop is Alice Springs, the self-declared capital of the Outback and centre for Aboriginal culture, home to art galleries and museums. Last stop is the town of Katherine, where you can cruise down spectacular Nitmiluk Gorge by boat in the company of a Jawoyn guide, from the Aboriginal community whose land this is; there is no more beautiful, nor soulful, way to experience the Outback.

Life on board is all about luxury, with private cabins combining old-world glamour with modern comforts. High-end dining, too, is a part of the package, reinventing the whole experience of a railway dining car by pairing respected chefs with impeccable service and quality local wines. But the real highlight is watching the Australian Outback go by through The Ghan's big glass windows, as the thrum of train on track marks with metronomic pulse each passing kilometre. For many, this is how a journey across a continent should feel.

another way
It's possible to take a shorter version of The Ghan, from Adelaide to Alice Springs, or between Alice Springs and Darwin. While cheaper, you'll still need to fly home from wherever you finish the journey.

Below *Sunset in the town of Alice Springs* **Bottom right** *The Ghan stopping near a railway crossing* **Right** *Serving a meal in The Ghan's restaurant car*

247

BY RAIL
AUSTRALASIA

Great Southern

LOCATION Australia **START/FINISH** Brisbane/Adelaide
DISTANCE 2,100 km (1,305 miles) **TIME** 3–4 days
INFORMATION www.journeybeyondrail.com.au

Added to Australia's portfolio of long haul rail epics in 2019, the Great Southern from Brisbane to Adelaide is already an Australian classic.

This is no ordinary train journey. For a start, the train is as much a destination in itself as it is a means of transport. Expect luxury accommodation in beautifully appointed wood-panelled carriages and fine dining with impeccable service and contemporary Australian cuisine. The whole experience harks back to the golden age of rail touring, when trains were considered an exclusive means of travel and the journey was as important as the train's arrival.

Leaving Brisbane, the train passes through the dense rainforest and rolling hills of the coastal hinterland – it's a glorious introduction to the diverse charms of east coast Australia. The first stop is the seaside city of Coffs Harbour, for beach dining under a spray of stars, followed by a guided tour of the Hunter Valley, one of Australia's premier wine regions. Next up is the buzzing cultural hub of Melbourne, with the chance for a scenic side trip to the Twelve Apostles, one of the most dramatic rock formations on Victoria's famed coastline. And then it's time to wind up northwest, gliding through rolling green farmland into Adelaide. This sedate "City of Churches" makes a suitably stately end to such a refined journey.

> The whole experience harks back to a golden age of rail touring

HUNTER VALLEY WINES

Lying north of Sydney, the Hunter Valley is one of Australia's oldest wine-producing regions; the first grapes were planted here early in the 19th century. Semillon is the areas's signature wine, but arguably Chardonnay is its most iconic. Chardonnay grapes were first grown here in the 1960s, and today they make up 70 per cent of the crop in the Upper Hunter.

Curving through rural bushland on the outskirts of Adelaide

TranzAlpine

Gliding across a bridge in the Canterbury Plains

LOCATION New Zealand **START/FINISH** Christchurch/Greymouth **DISTANCE** 223 km (139 miles) **TIME** 4.5 hours **INFORMATION** www.greatjourneysofnz.co.nz

The TranzAlpine passenger train runs daily between Christchurch and Greymouth on New Zealand's scenic South Island, cutting through the dramatic Southern Alps via Arthur's Pass and the Otira viaduct.

The TranzAlpine train has to be one of the most relaxing ways to experience New Zealand's legendary landscape. As the train eases out of Christchurch towards the bucolic Canterbury Plains, travellers get comfy in their reclining seats, ready for an unhurried climb through the spectacular Southern Alps. The carriage windows are panoramic, but it's well worth braving the frigid open-air viewing-car to gaze at the snow-cloaked folds of the looming mountains.

Passengers often alight to stretch their legs at the beautiful Arthur's Pass; it's also possible to break your journey here (or elsewhere en route) and spend more time roaming this stunning region. Beyond the pass, the train descends through lush rainforest, past pretty Lake Brunner, and on to Greymouth. If you're on the same-day return trip, you have just one hour to explore the historic west coast town before climbing back on board to enjoy it all in reverse.

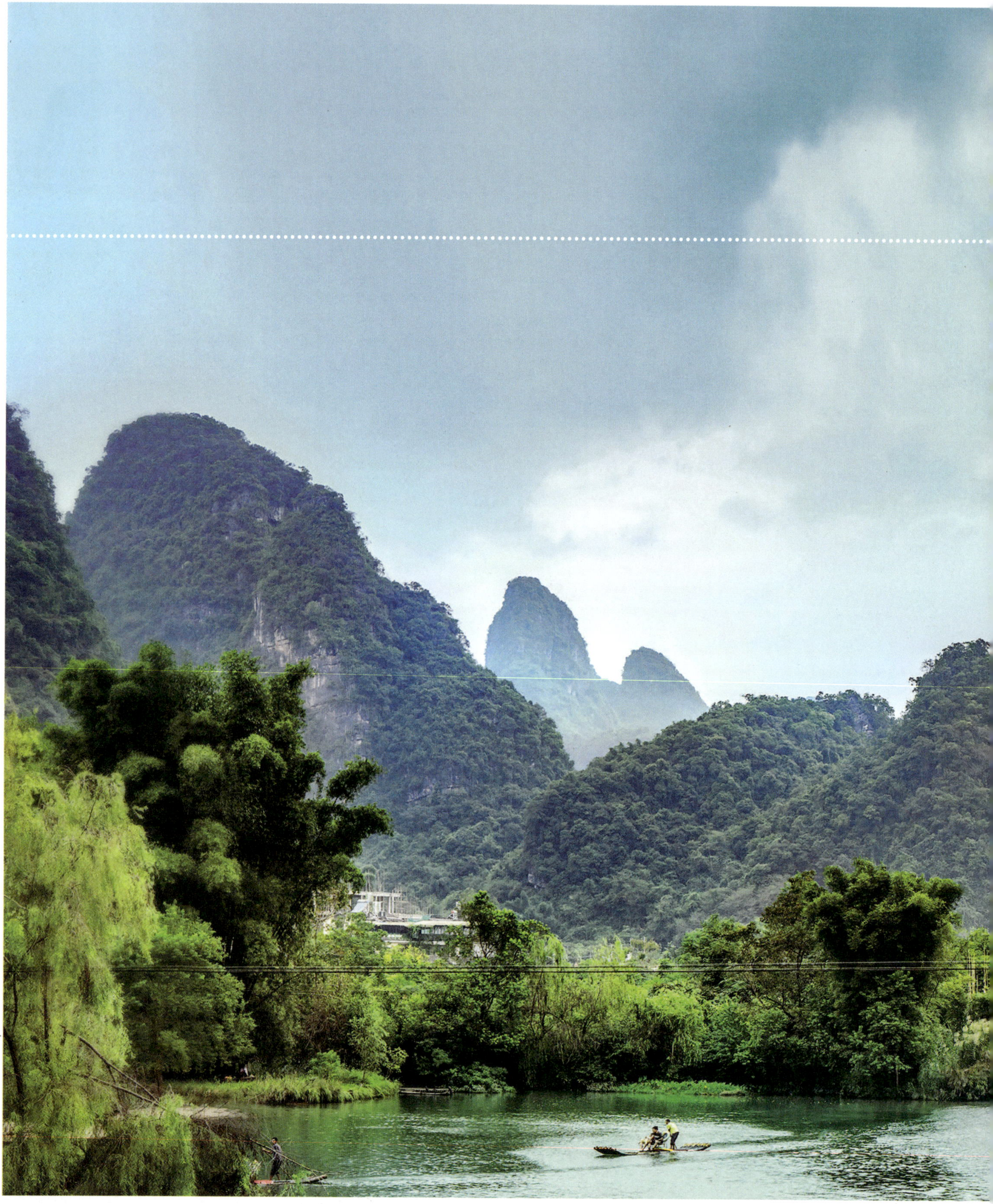

BY WATER

Salted air, lapping waves and the lullabying rock of your boat – travelling on water feels completely different to journeying by land. And there are countless ways to do it, from cruising aboard a luxury ship to kayaking around a windswept archipelago. Whatever you choose, time seems to move slower when you're travelling by water and it's the ultimate way to disconnect from your earthly concerns.

AT A GLANCE
BY WATER

NORTH AMERICA pp254–263
This continent offers countless on-the-water adventures – sail between sandy islands in the Caribbean or cruise past icy glaciers in Alaska.

CENTRAL AND SOUTH AMERICA pp264–271
Dart in and out of Patagonia's majestic fjords, float along the Amazon to the hooting call of howler monkeys or cruise into the icy silence of Antarctica.

KEY TO MAP
- .... Long route
- • End point

Previous page *China's shimmering Li River, winding between soaring karst peaks*

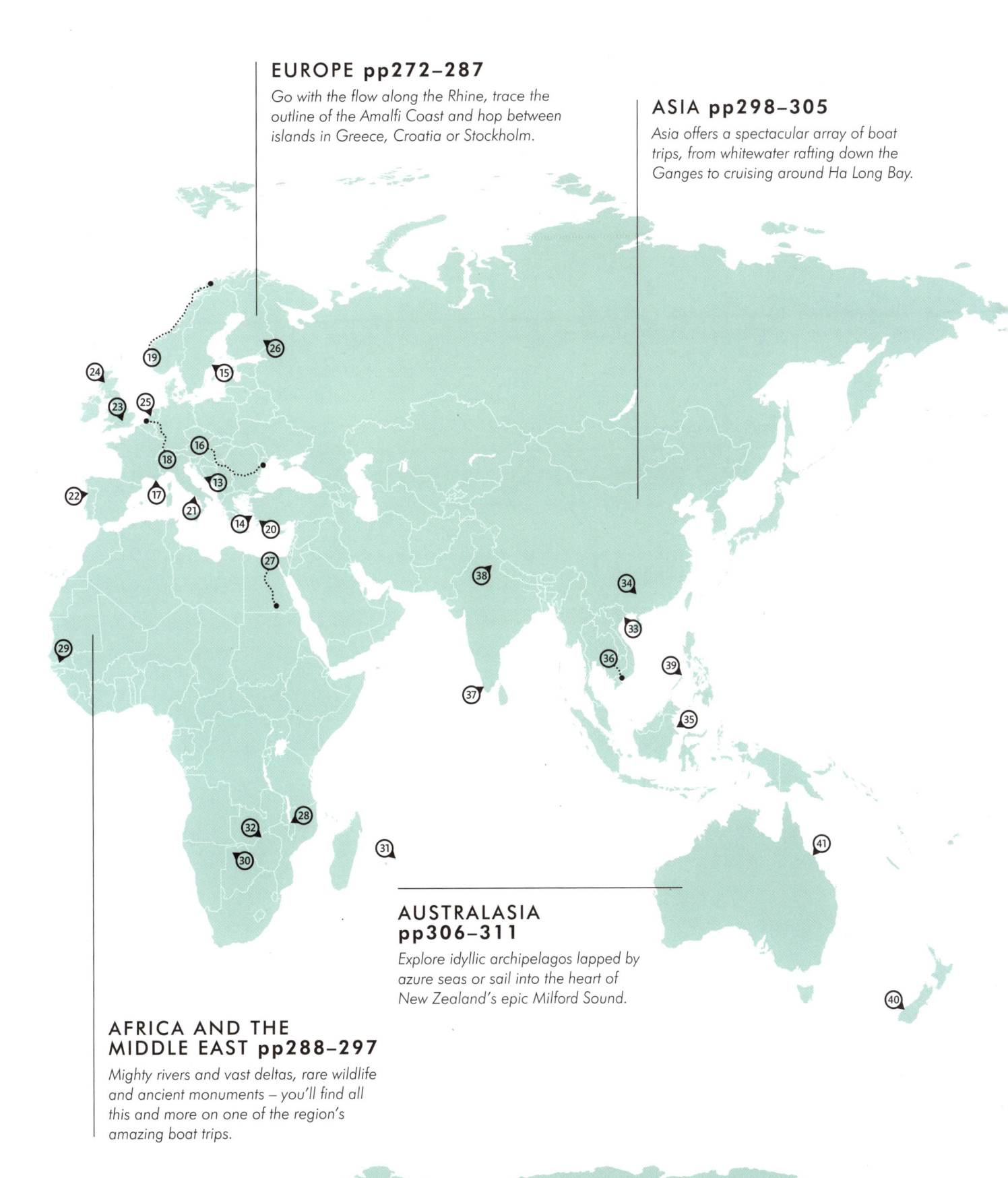

EUROPE pp272–287
Go with the flow along the Rhine, trace the outline of the Amalfi Coast and hop between islands in Greece, Croatia or Stockholm.

ASIA pp298–305
Asia offers a spectacular array of boat trips, from whitewater rafting down the Ganges to cruising around Ha Long Bay.

AUSTRALASIA pp306–311
Explore idyllic archipelagos lapped by azure seas or sail into the heart of New Zealand's epic Milford Sound.

AFRICA AND THE MIDDLE EAST pp288–297
Mighty rivers and vast deltas, rare wildlife and ancient monuments – you'll find all this and more on one of the region's amazing boat trips.

BY WATER
NORTH AMERICA

Alaska and Inside Passage

LOCATION Canada to US **START/FINISH** Vancouver/Seward **DISTANCE** 2,787 km (1,732 miles) **TIME** 11 days **INFORMATION** www.travelalaska.com

Rich in culture, wildlife and awe-inspiring landscapes, much of Alaska's Inside Passage remains untouched wilderness, its small ports and harbours cut off from the rest of North America. One of the only ways to experience it is by cruise – but what better way to revel in nature at its most spectacular?

Cruising through tranquil Glacier Bay National Park

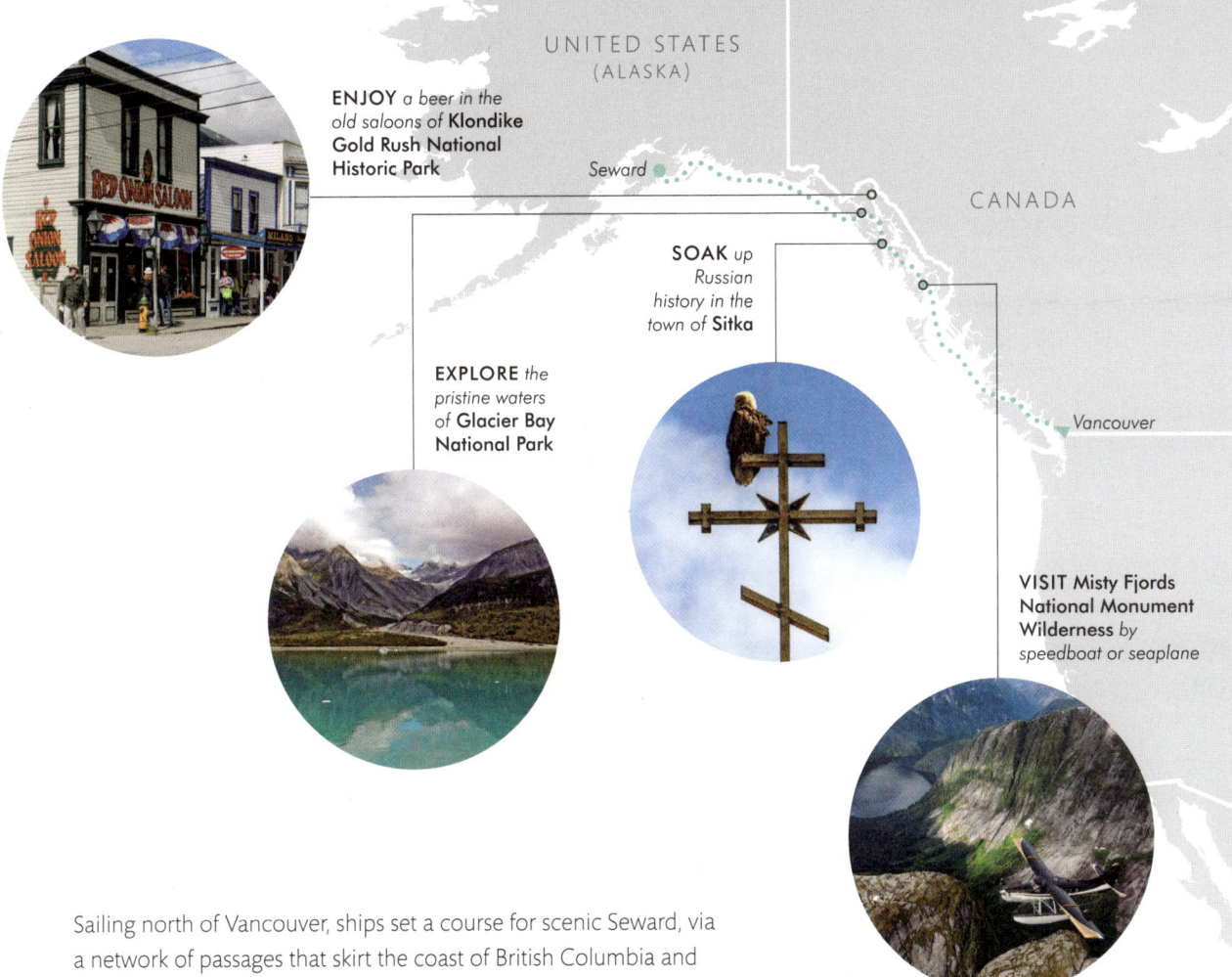

ENJOY *a beer in the old saloons of* **Klondike Gold Rush National Historic Park**

SOAK *up Russian history in the town of* **Sitka**

EXPLORE *the pristine waters of* **Glacier Bay National Park**

VISIT Misty Fjords National Monument Wilderness *by speedboat or seaplane*

Sailing north of Vancouver, ships set a course for scenic Seward, via a network of passages that skirt the coast of British Columbia and south Alaska. For over a week, days are spent weaving in and out of islands, gazing at superlative scenery and wildlife-watching from the deck. As the ship noses along you'll spy whales as they breach the surface, comical otters play and bald eagles wheel overhead – and perhaps a brown bear plodding along the coastline.

Shore excursions are frequent and well-rewarded. Disembark for the old frontier town of Ketchikan and the extraordinary Misty Fjords National Monument Wilderness, a preserve of craggy, spruce-smothered peaks and plunging waterfalls. Pop into pocket-sized Juneau and set off on an expedition to the startling Mendenhall glacier. Stroll the weathered boardwalks of Skagway, poking your nose into the creaky timber saloons preserved as part of the Klondike Gold Rush National Historic Park.

It's hard to pick a highlight, but Glacier Bay National Park, with its abundance of wildlife, snow-capped peaks and tidewater glaciers, is surely up there. Here, it's not uncommon for peaceful moments to be interrupted by a thunderous clap of breaking ice, as a glacier calves into the still waters below – a violent reminder that this popular route is still very much Mother Nature's backyard.

KLONDIKE GOLD RUSH

At the height of the Klondike Gold Rush, in 1898, the now tiny hamlet of Skagway was booming. It was here that miners assembled their gear and supplies before trekking up over the Chilkoot Pass into Canada, lured by the prospect of gold. The Canadian authorities didn't try to prevent the countless numbers from entering, but they did insist that each miner bring one full ton of supplies, enough to keep himself alive for a year.

BY WATER
NORTH AMERICA

Bowron Lakes Circuit

LOCATION Canada **START/FINISH** Registration Centre, Bowron Lake (loop) **DISTANCE** 116 km (72 miles) **TIME** 6–10 days **DIFFICULTY** Challenging **INFORMATION** www.bcparks.ca; open May–Oct for a set number of canoes per day (advance reservations are recommended)

The challenge and beauty of the Bowron Lakes Circuit draws enthusiastic paddlers from across the globe to this mountain wilderness chain of shimmering lakes and rushing waterways.

Tucked between the serrated ridges of the Cariboo Mountain Range to the east and the soft rolling hills of the Quesnel Highlands to the west, the Bowron Lakes Circuit lies in British Columbia's Bowron Lake Provincial Park. It encompasses more than a dozen lakes, several fast-flowing rivers, and a series of portages that provide safe paths around the rapids and waterfalls en route. Lakes brim with trout and salmon, while the wild blueberry-lined shore attracts grizzly and black bears. In the evenings, paddlers can dock up on the beach of their choice and peruse the water's edge for ancient First Nations arrowheads, before being lulled to sleep by the chatter of loons.

Intermediate and advanced paddlers can complete the full route within a week; beginners should only attempt the calmer West Side section, which takes two to four days to finish. Each new day brings a unique set of challenges and – with fickle waters and capricious weather to contend with – ample camping gear is essential. If the weather is truly unruly, rustic log cabins promise temporary sanctuary in this untamed Canadian landscape.

Canoeing through a serene stretch of water on the rugged Bowron Lakes Circuit

A riverboat docked at the bank of the Mississippi in New Orleans

Mississippi River

LOCATION US **START/FINISH** New Orleans/St Paul
DISTANCE 1,931 km (1,200 miles) **TIME** 15–22 days
INFORMATION Cruise availability, facilities and itineraries vary

This cruise takes in the best of the mighty Mississippi, from the jazz bands and languid bayous of Louisiana to the high plains and pine forests of Minnesota.

Cruising the Mississippi is as much about life on the river as the places you'll visit along the way. The "Big Muddy" has been eulogized in literature since American author Mark Twain hopped paddle steamers here in the 1850s. Though the boats have changed, the scenery remains the same – wide bends and meanders through swamp, wetland and dense forest alive with chirping birds, crickets and humming cicadas. White-tailed deer watch from the banks, while otters duck beneath the boat's wake and eagles soar overhead.

The journey through this timeless world is broken up by countless sights and stops en route. North of New Orleans, the checkered history of the Deep South unfolds in the grand plantations and stately antebellum houses built close to the river. Vicksburg, with its historic parks, captures the spirit of the Civil War; barbecue and blues rule in Memphis; and the gleaming Gateway Arch soars high above the river in St Louis. Finally, meadows give way to evergreen forests as the river slices between Wisconsin and Minnesota – the boat docks at St Paul, but the river flows on.

MARK TWAIN'S MISSISSIPPI

Novelist Mark Twain, born Samuel Clemens, spent most of his youth in Hannibal, a small port on the Mississippi River. This experience influenced his famous novels about Tom Sawyer and Huckleberry Finn, but his best book about the "Big Muddy" is *Life on the Mississippi* – part travelogue, part memoir (and part tall tales).

BY WATER
NORTH AMERICA

4. Athabasca River

LOCATION Canada **START/FINISH** Jasper/Whitecourt **DISTANCE** 292 km (181 miles) **TIME** 3 days **DIFFICULTY** Challenging **INFORMATION** www.jasper.travel

Originating from the Columbia Glacier, part of the massive Columbia Icefield in Jasper National Park, the Athabasca River flows northeast for over 1,500 km (930 miles), eventually draining into the Arctic Ocean. Once prime hunting ground for First Nations tribes, then a busy trading route, the river today is a spectacular outdoor adventure corridor, with paddling routes suitable for beginners and experts alike.

Popular with canoeists is the stretch between Jasper and Whitecourt, a winding route through the foothills of the Canadian Rocky Mountains. As paddles glide through teal-coloured waters, milky with glacial silt, all eyes are on the passing surroundings: inland, herds of bison graze prairies; overhead, ospreys soar, scanning tall grasses for their next morsel. Come evening, the shores of uninhabited sandy islands are ideal for a snug campfire and well-earned respite. Keep those eyes peeled: the aurora borealis might appear to round off a truly brilliant day.

The Athabasca River, snaking through the Canadian Rockies

> **WHAT'S IN A NAME?**
> It was once assumed that the name Quetico was derived from the Quebec Timber Company. Today, however, it is commonly accepted that the park's name comes from the Ojibwe word *gwetaming*. For the Lac La Croix First Nation, this means to have sacred respect for the living spirits that dwell in Quetico Lake.

5. Quetico Provincial Park

LOCATION Canada **START/FINISH** Dawson Trail (loop) **DISTANCE** Varies **TIME** Varies **DIFFICULTY** Moderate **INFORMATION** www.ontarioparks.com

Drifting across any of the pristine Quetico Provincial Park's 2,000 lakes, it's easy to imagine what it might have been like when the Ojibwe first powered their birch bark canoes across the surface centuries ago. This is canoeing paradise, so vast the only sounds to be heard are birdsong and the quiet slap of the paddle.

From the head of the Dawson Trail, canoeists must portage through pine-scented terrain to the lakeshore. Once on the water, the lake opens, cool and glassy, fringed with soaring boreal forest. There's plenty of time to dive into the water, then laze on the pink-streaked rocks bulging along the banks. The lake provides an easy menu, too: cast a line and wait for fish to nibble; later you'll be dining on barbecued lake trout as the final flare of the sun skims across the trees. When you're ready to move on the next morning, all you'll leave behind will be footsteps in the earth and a ripple on the water.

BY WATER
NORTH AMERICA

Paddling down the forest-fringed Nahanni River on fast-flowing waters

⑥ Nahanni River

LOCATION Canada **START/FINISH** Virginia Falls/Nahanni Butte **DISTANCE** 240 km (150 miles) **TIME** 1 week **DIFFICULTY** Challenging **INFORMATION** www.pc.gc.ca; guided trips are strongly recommended

An ancient river of legend and lore, the Nahanni is a mecca for adventure-seekers looking to tackle this wilderness's whitewaters. Flowing with an immense force long before the surrounding peaks rose around it some 200 million years ago, the river forges east through Canada's deepest canyons, past the tremendous Virginia Falls, and eventually empties into the wide plains of the Liard River Valley. Concealed amid the fossil-rich karst landscapes that confine the river, hot springs bubble up from the depths of the earth's core, and unexplored cave systems extend for miles around. In this rugged dreamscape, myths of headless skeletons and great gold deposits are plentiful. And possible sightings of lynx, wood bison and grizzly bears will add more tales for paddlers to take back home with them.

⑦ Churchill River

LOCATION Canada **START/FINISH** Churchill/Prince of Wales Fort **DISTANCE** 1.5 km (1 mile) **TIME** 1 day **DIFFICULTY** Moderate **INFORMATION** www.everythingchurchill.com

On the fringes of the Canadian Arctic, the isolated town of Churchill is the starting point for a kayak journey that features a historic fort, stark landscapes, beluga whales and – with a bit of luck – polar bears.

Timing is everything: the summer months see thousands of beluga whales arrive to feed, mate and give birth, so come between June and September to secure a sighting. As you paddle across the icy waters of the Churchill River, and the small low-rise town slowly fades from view, it won't be long before pods of whales come out to play. These small, white, surprisingly vocal cetaceans are highly inquisitive, and you could easily while away hours watching them dart around your kayak, arc above the surface and expel spray from their blowholes.

But they aren't the only notable sight in this remote stretch of Manitoba province. This is polar bear country and, though more common in October and November, summer sightings of the world's biggest land-based predator are known along the rocky shoreline of the river. Bears and whales in one day? That surely makes the journey more than worth it.

another way
The town of Churchill has no road connections with the rest of Manitoba and can only be reached by plane or – perhaps much more memorably – a 45-hour sleeper train from provincial capital Winnipeg.

Island-Hopping in the Grenadines

LOCATION St Vincent to Grenada **START/FINISH** St Vincent/Grenada
DISTANCE 150 km (93 miles) **TIME** 10 days **INFORMATION** Tours can be arranged by local charter companies; cruise availability, facilities and itineraries vary

Few places embody Caribbean charm more than the Grenadines, an idyllic archipelago. Each tropical island here is topped with dreamy palms and dazzling white sands that shelve into sapphire waters teeming with kaleidoscopic fish. Without doubt, the best way to experience the chain is on a sailboat cruise.

Of volcanic origin, the Grenadines form a necklace of over 30 islands, islets and sun-drenched cays stretching between St Vincent and Grenada. For many years a magnet for savvy yachties, they are now accessible to even the most novice sailor via a luxury crewed sailboat cruise. Imagine waking to the sound of lapping waves and slipping straight into the warm sea, paddling by kayak to secluded coves, and sipping cocktails on deck at sunset, and you're there.

BY WATER
NORTH AMERICA

Left Sailboats moored off the uninhabited Tobago Cays
Above Diving into the turquoise waters of the Caribbean

A short sail from St Vincent's bustling capital, Kingstown, to the first anchorage at Bequia – pronounced "Beck-way" – transports you to another world. The latter's mellow vibe pervades the picturesque village-capital, Port Elizabeth, which is fringed with quaint pastel-hued houses and casual waterside restaurants. Here, Jack's Bar is a choice spot to linger over a daiquiri, while watching the glowing sun sink over the gorgeous Princess Margaret Beach.

Glamorous Mustique is the next port of call, where ranks of lofty palms greet new arrivals. Beloved of royalty and celebrities, this A-lister retreat is surprisingly welcoming – provided residents' privacy is respected. While gawping at the opulent villas sprinkled over the hillside, look out for the ubiquitous tortoises tottering across manicured lawns. On the west of the island, a stroll down the sugar-soft shoreline of Britannia Bay leads to the lagoon. The archipelago's most protected wetland, hidden amid a tangle of mangroves and mudflats, it is rich with birdlife – keep your eyes peeled for the red-throated magnificent frigatebird and elegant yellow-crowned night heron.

BEQUIA'S BOATS

Possessing a proud maritime history, Bequia was once the boat-building capital of the West Indies. These days the island is more famous for its hand-crafted miniature sailboats. They range from simple vessels fashioned out of coconut shells to intricate wooden replicas that can take months to complete, such as the model HMY *Britannia*, which was presented to Queen Elizabeth on her state visit here in 1985.

261

ST VINCENT

Kingstown

RELAX *by soaking up the sunshine on deck*

STROLL *along Port Elizabeth's waterfront in* **Bequia**

SPOT *turtles swimming in the* **Tobago Cays**

SIP *cocktails on deck at sunset*

HIKE *along the rainforested ridge of* **Union Island**

Carriacou

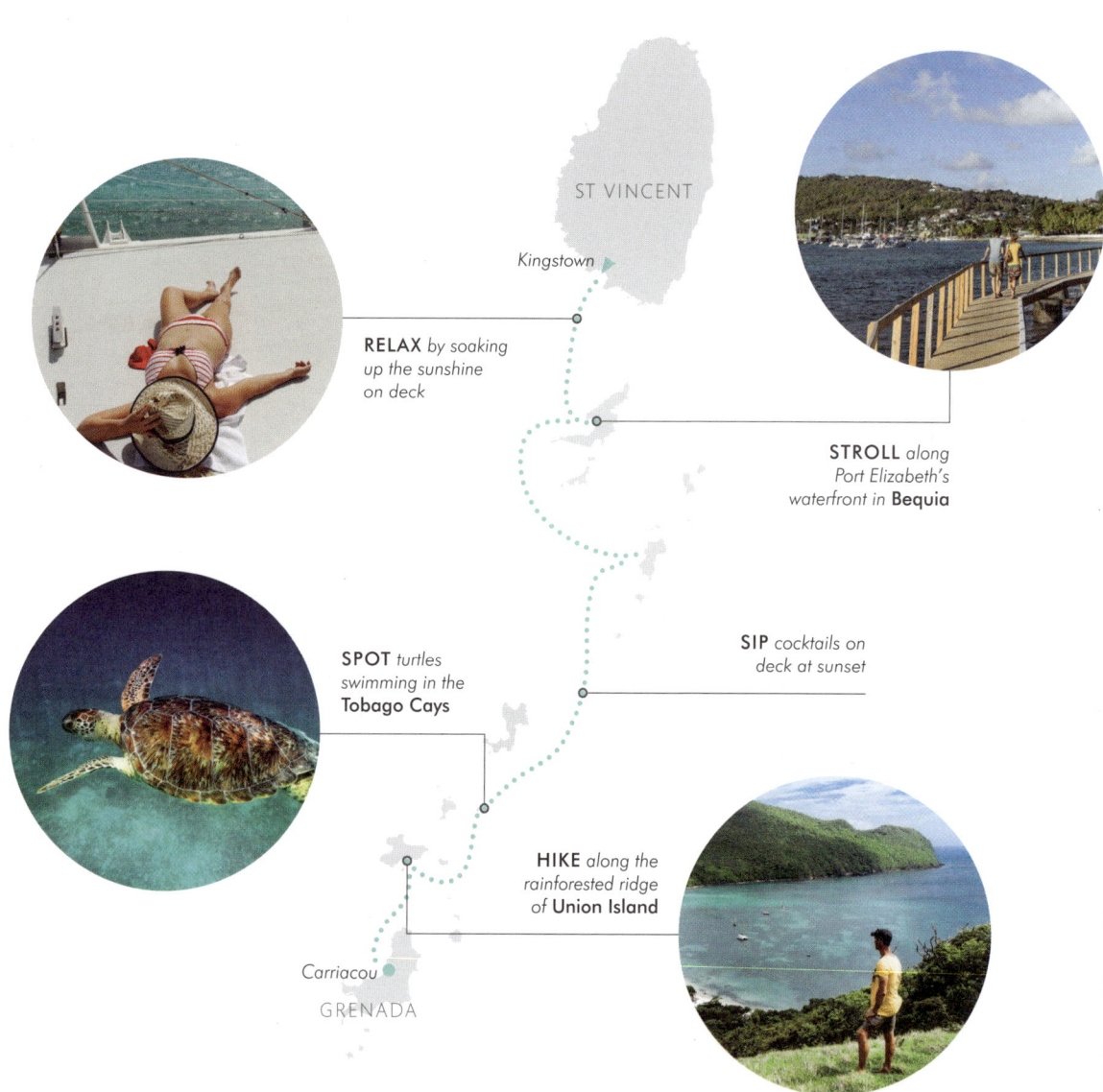

GRENADA

Awaiting you next are the Grenadines' undisputed crown jewels: the Tobago Cays. These five magical islets, fringed with bright white sand, are set within a protected marine park overflowing with wildlife. Here, there's chance to snorkel with green turtles as they forage in the translucent shallows; further out, at coral-encrusted Horseshoe Reef, you'll find vibrant sponges and shoals of rainbow-coloured fish. Back on land, a meander through cacti, agaves and flowering shrubs brings encounters with basking iguanas and skittish lizards. Invigorated by all this activity, there's no better way to round off the day than with a beach barbecue on Petit Tabac, savouring succulent lobster under the glittering night sky, on the very isle where Johnny Depp and Keira Knightley were stranded in the first *Pirates of the Caribbean* movie.

The following stop on the tour could not be more of a contrast: in Union Island's secluded Chatham Bay, jagged volcanic peaks rise out of dark, blue-green waters. Cloaked in luxuriant rainforest, the

| Jagged volcanic peaks rise out of dark, blue-green waters

BY WATER
NORTH AMERICA

mountainous skyline rewards energetic hikers with breathtaking panoramas. Less touristy than many Caribbean isles, it still offers plenty to do – such as heading over to the breezy east coast for an exhilarating kitesurfing lesson before weighing anchor.

As you sail steadily southwards, the crinkly coastline of Carriacou looms into view. Meaning "land of reefs" in Amerindian, the island is surrounded by an underwater paradise, inviting thrilling encounters with nurse sharks, stingrays and fearsome barracuda. Ashore, communities steeped in African heritage come alive during "maroons" – spirited festivals featuring traditional drumming and dancing, tasty "smoke food" and, of course, lashings of rum. This vibrant culture extends across the waves to neighbouring Grenada, where the lush green hills are rich with the scents of nutmeg and cinnamon. The "Spice Island" may be the last stop on your voyage, but its wealth of pristine white-sand beaches and rainforest hiking trails mean that this doesn't yet have to be the end of your Caribbean adventure.

another way

If money is no object and ten days under sail seems daunting, consider unwinding at an exclusive villa on Mustique, Canouan or Petit Saint Vincent. Each has its own airstrip, so you can island-hop by plane and take day cruises out to the cays.

Below Princess Margaret Beach on Bequia Bottom right Snorkelling in the crystal-clear Caribbean Sea Right A local fisherman with a freshly caught puffer fish

263

The Amazon

LOCATION Peru **START/FINISH** Iquitos (loop) **DISTANCE** 82 km (51 miles)
TIME 4 days **INFORMATION** Cruise availability, facilities and itineraries vary

A safari riverboat cruise along the Amazon is a spectacular adventure through the rainforest's natural beauty and diversity. Navigating the world's greatest waterway, your boat drifts through vine-draped side creeks, alive with iridescent butterflies, parrots and monkeys.

Above A boat cruising along a tributary of the Amazon River
Below A bright-beaked toucan perching on the branch of a tree

The Amazon River rises high in the Peruvian Andes; joined by its tributaries, it flows through six countries before disgorging into the Atlantic Ocean in northeastern Brazil. To explore this mighty river and its treasured wildlife, venture deep into the Amazon Basin on a four-day trip through the Reserva Nacional Pacaya-Samiri. This vast protected reserve shelters over a third of the entire basin's known animal species. It is also home to some 100,000 indigenous people, among the few remaining undisturbed cultures on earth.

Setting off from the bustling harbourside of Iquitos, your elegant wooden craft glides along the river's swiftly moving water, past the thatch-roofed settlements of local communities.

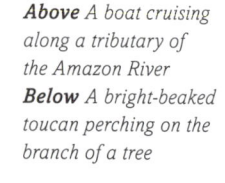

BY WATER
CENTRAL AND SOUTH AMERICA

The shallow-bottomed riverboat grants easy access along smaller channels, where curtains of creepers fringe the river, toucans bob between ceiba trees and alligators bask on sunny sandbanks.

Each morning, from the comfort of your cabin, wake to an Amazonian dawn chorus. Expert onboard naturalists lead the day's adventures: in the cool early morning, hop into a canoe and paddle up a side creek lined with tangled foliage, where eye-catching blue morpho butterflies flit and howler monkeys boom from the treetops. In the heat of midday, though, nothing stirs. A cooling dip in the river may reward swimmers with sightings of giant otters, or – if luck is on your side – rare pink Amazonian dolphins. Later, once the equatorial dusk has swiftly descended, a night safari into the forest unveils a treescape dotted with fireflies and the reflections of watchful eyes. Back on board, loll in a hammock under the stars and dream of tomorrow's wildlife waiting around the next river bend.

THE CEIBA

A giant of the Amazon Basin, the ceiba tree grows up to 60 m (200 ft) tall. It harbours a plethora of animals, which in turn keep it alive. Frogs, snakes and birds live in its branches, eating harmful insects, and bats feed on its nectar, pollinating the flowers of neighbouring trees. The ceiba is also valued by indigenous peoples: its wood is light and durable, ideal for making dugout canoes, and its seeds are used in traditional medicine. Considered the portal to their spirit world, the tree was sacred to the ancient Maya.

VISIT indigenous communities in **Puerto Miguel** as part of your trip to learn about their daily life

CLIMB treetop walkways at the **Amazon Natural Park** and come eye to eye with iguanas and monkeys

Reserva Nacional Pacaya-Samiri

GO FISHING In **Yanayaquillo** for a piranha, the Amazon's toothiest resident

PERU

265

BY WATER
CENTRAL AND SOUTH AMERICA

Panama Canal

LOCATION Panama **START/FINISH** Colón/Panama City **DISTANCE** 82 km (51 miles)
TIME 10 hours **INFORMATION** Cruise availability, facilities and itineraries vary

Wending across a sliver of the Central American isthmus, the Panama Canal is a marvel of engineering. At the locks, container vessels jostle with cruise ships and tiny Panamanian tugs, while jungles teeming with wildlife skirt the edges.

Belying its clockwork precision, the Panama Canal is a lesson in patience. There is no overtaking in the long stretches between each of the three locks: each vessel must wait its turn to drift passively from the Atlantic coast to the Pacific, driven by enormous quantities of water up and down between levels.

The journey begins in the natural deepwater port at Colón aboard a towering passenger vessel, which churns across the bay to the mouth of the canal. On the approach to Gatún Locks, passengers edge along the railings at the prow for a bird's-eye view of ships shimmying into position. A Panamanian pilot skilfully noses the vessel into the chamber, before a crash of water propels it up 26 m (85 ft). Passengers bask on the upper decks as the canal pours into Lago di Gatún, a vast artificial lake fed by the Chagres River. Beyond the lake, the boat follows the Culebra Cut as it bites into the rugged flank of a mountain ridge.

As the boat slips over the Continental Divide, there are plenty of chances to spot white-faced capuchin monkeys squabbling at the edge of the dense green jungle or cackling toucans on the hunt for nuts. Along the water's edge, caimans lie log-like in the sunshine and green iguanas loll about on the rocks. Two more locks and suddenly there you are, the setting sun glinting on Panama City as you wait for the huge metal doors of the Bridge of the Americas to usher you through to the Pacific.

Ships passing through Gatún Locks on the Panama Canal

BY WATER
CENTRAL AND SOUTH AMERICA

Left The tranquil waters of the Beagle Channel stretching into the distance *Above* The Yaghan ferry waiting at Puerto Williams

Patagonian Fjords

LOCATION Chile **START/FINISH** Punta Arenas/Puerto Williams **DISTANCE** 560 km (303 miles) **TIME** 2 days **INFORMATION** www.tabsa.cl

Hulking glaciers and waters teeming with aquatic life are the constant companions on this passenger ferry through the Patagonian fjords. An unsung highlight of the region, the journey follows in the wake of early explorers as it strikes out towards the very ends of the earth.

The orange hues of Punta Arenas evaporate into the evening darkness as the Yaghan ferry sets sail for the south. Between now and Puerto Williams, the world's southernmost settlement, there is nothing but wilderness.

Hours later, the veil of night lifts to reveal the raw nature of the fjords: Magellanic penguins bob on the icy water, while sea lions raise their fins in greeting, sunbathing beneath cobalt skies. Through endless channels stitched together by low, sculpted islands, the ocean stretches out as an unblemished mirror.

> The veil of night lifts to reveal the raw nature of the fjords

The final eight hours are simply magical. Entering the Beagle Channel – named after British vessel HMS *Beagle* – lumps of ice as large as cars splinter from tidewater glaciers, staining the ocean a milky blue. If luck prevails, humpback whales breach the water, their tails slapping the surface as they bid the boat adieu.

When night falls once again, just hours from Puerto Williams, a profound darkness and silence engulf the ship. The explorers of yesteryear may be long gone, but the world here, at the ends of the earth, remains unchanged.

267

Passengers looking out over ice-covered waters in Antarctica

BY WATER
CENTRAL AND SOUTH AMERICA

Antarctica

LOCATION Argentina to Antarctica **START/FINISH** Ushuaia (loop) **DISTANCE** 2,500–4,000 km (1,555–2,485 miles) depending on the itinerary **TIME** 10–23 days **INFORMATION** Cruise availability, facilities and itineraries vary

Inhospitable, otherworldly and unfathomably beautiful, Antarctica is the greatest wilderness on earth. It's fitting then that this journey from the southern edge of South America to the "white continent" is a once-in-a-lifetime experience.

Hundreds of thousands of penguins huddling together against bitter, sub-zero temperatures. Looming icebergs the size of small countries drifting slowly by. Pods of whales breaking the surface of the water and raising their flukes to the sky. Great walls of snow that appear to have been sculpted by a surrealist. Travelling to Antarctica is perhaps the ultimate journey available on earth. Modern cruises are very comfortable, but as you cross the choppy Southern Ocean to the seventh continent it is easy to imagine yourself in the snow-shoes of great polar explorers like Amundsen, Scott and Shackleton.

Although it is possible to travel to Antarctica from Australia, New Zealand and Chile, most cruises depart from the remote Argentine city of Ushuaia. Located in Tierra del Fuego, Ushuaia is just 1,000 km (620 miles) north of the Antarctic peninsula, a finger of land that curls northeast out of the rest of the continent. From the port, ships travel along the Beagle Channel before making the two-day crossing of the Drake Passage, a notoriously rough stretch of ocean between Cape Horn, the southernmost tip of South America, and the South Shetland Islands, an archipelago that lies just north of the Antarctic peninsula.

A group of Adélie penguins resting on stony ground

Weather conditions in this part of the world are – to put it mildly – challenging and ever-changing. As a result, itineraries are prone to alteration at short notice and no two cruises are ever quite the same. But whichever route the ship ends up sailing, the experience is mesmerizing, even life-altering. Travellers encounter places like Elephant Island, a rocky, ice-packed member of the South Shetlands where Ernest Shackleton and his hardy band of men were stranded during their ill-fated *Endurance* expedition. To the south lie the rarely visited and ominously named Danger Islands, which are home to a cacophonous "super colony" of 1.5 million curious and often comical Adélie penguins.

Many cruises will later stop at Mikkelsen Harbour, home to a tiny island teeming with gentoo penguins, and nearby Cierva Cove,

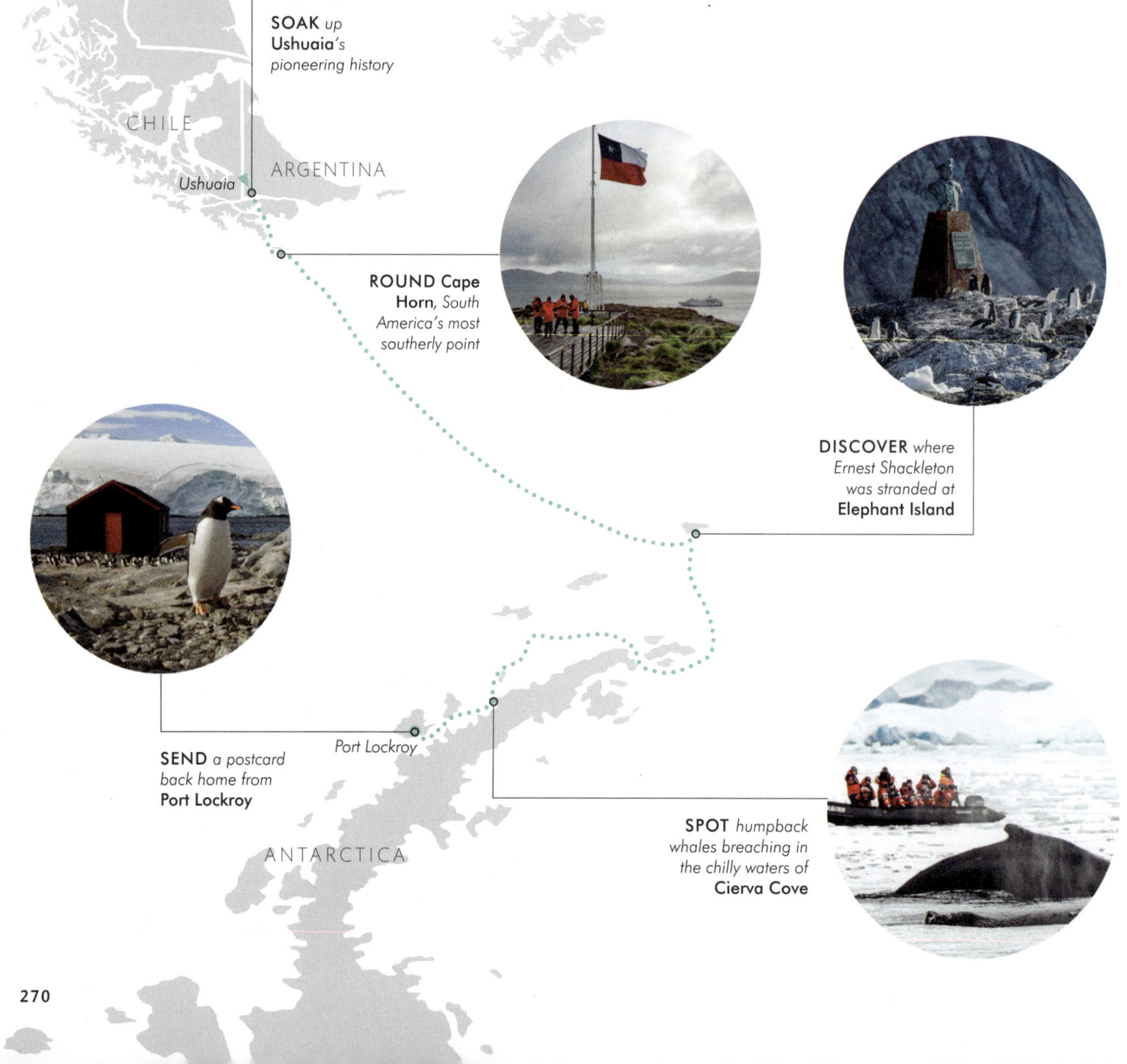

SOAK up **Ushuaia**'s *pioneering history*

ROUND Cape Horn, *South America's most southerly point*

DISCOVER *where Ernest Shackleton was stranded at* **Elephant Island**

SEND *a postcard back home from* **Port Lockroy**

SPOT *humpback whales breaching in the chilly waters of* **Cierva Cove**

BY WATER
CENTRAL AND SOUTH AMERICA

Left Observing a sea lion colony near Ushuaia *Top* A glassy blue iceberg floating in Cierva Cove *Above* A humpback whale raising its flukes

a sweeping bay dotted with mini icebergs. Here, passengers wrap up warm in layer upon layer of thermals, disembark their ships and clamber into Zodiacs (rigid inflatable boats) to search for fur and leopard seals, and minke and humpback whales. Meanwhile, Brown Bluff is where many people take their first steps on the Antarctic continent itself, crunching over a snow-covered beach in the company of countless besuited Adélies and gentoos. Wiencke Island is another popular stop-off, home to isolated Port Lockroy: once a British scientific base, it's now a museum and site of the most southerly post office on earth.

En route back to Ushuaia, many cruises pause at the doughnut-shaped Deception Island, passing through a narrow channel known as Neptune's Bellows and mooring in a huge flooded caldera in the centre. Intrepid travellers have the opportunity to hike across the island's active volcanic craters before ending their Antarctic expedition in style with what's known as a "polar plunge" – a brief, bracing dip in the frigid Southern Ocean.

another way

Some longer cruises from Argentina travel to/from Antarctica via the Falkland Islands and South Georgia, both of which are incredibly rich in wildlife, feature dramatic scenery and have fascinating histories. Another option is to add on a cruise through the iceberg-filled southern Chilean fjords.

BY WATER
EUROPE

Above Looking out over the leafy island of Hvar and the sparkling Adriatic Sea
Left A couple standing on a sailboat off the coast of Split

| This golden crescent of a bay is only accessible by sailboats

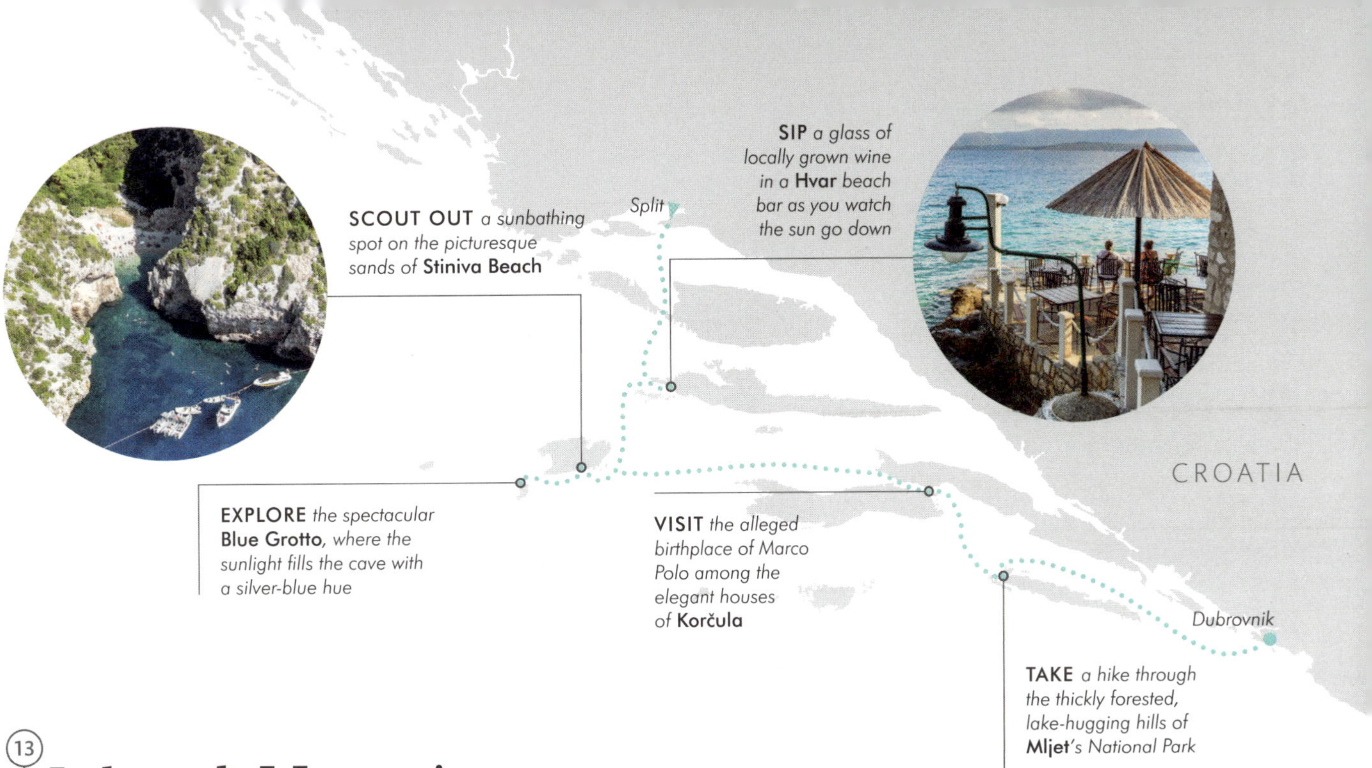

SCOUT OUT a sunbathing spot on the picturesque sands of **Stiniva Beach**

SIP a glass of locally grown wine in a **Hvar** beach bar as you watch the sun go down

Split

EXPLORE the spectacular **Blue Grotto**, where the sunlight fills the cave with a silver-blue hue

VISIT the alleged birthplace of Marco Polo among the elegant houses of **Korčula**

CROATIA

Dubrovnik

TAKE a hike through the thickly forested, lake-hugging hills of **Mljet**'s National Park

Island-Hopping in Croatia

LOCATION Croatia **START/FINISH** Split/Dubrovnik **DISTANCE** 365 km (235 miles) **TIME** 3–5 days **INFORMATION** Cruise availability, facilities and itineraries vary

Scattered around Croatia's sun-drenched coastline are more than 1,000 idyllic islands and islets. Take to the water on this laid-back voyage to explore five of the prettiest by chartered yacht.

This Adriatic adventure begins as you push off from Split, the cultural hub of the Dalmatian Coast, and plot a course for Hvar. It may have a reputation as Croatia's party island, bur Hvar is also home to dramatic Gothic palaces, hilltop fortresses and lavender fields, so save the beachside cocktail until sunset.

Next up is Vis, where Stiniva Beach, one of Europe's most beautiful stretches of sand, awaits. Almost entirely enclosed by a curtain of sheer rock, this golden crescent of a bay is only accessible by sailboats. Hidden nearby is Biševo island's Blue Grotto, a rocky cavern that shimmers a silvery blue in the sunlight.

Skidding over aquamarine seas, the boat reaches Korčula. While known for its old town – a merry tangle of medieval squares and Venetian-style terracotta roofs – a trip inland reveals hidden sandy coves, verdant vineyards and abundant olive groves. From Korčula, it's not far to unassuming, forest-sheathed Mljet, where rolling hills rich in Mediterranean vegetation swaddle two sparkling saltwater lagoons. Ancient ruins are complemented by gentle sandy shores and crystal-clear water, revealing an abundant underwater world. A small hop takes you back to the mainland, where Dubrovnik's ancient city walls lie in wait.

another way

Instead of going south from Split, head north to explore the Komati Islands, an archipelago of around 100 rocky isles blessed with rugged cliffs, hidden caves and grottos, and startling rock formations.

BY WATER
EUROPE

Yachting Around the Greek Islands

LOCATION Greece **START/FINISH** Samos/Mykonos
DISTANCE 320 km (200 miles) **TIME** 2 weeks
INFORMATION Cruise availability, facilities and itineraries vary

A lifetime could be spent exploring Greece's many islands – after all, Homer's wandering hero Odysseus took ten years to make his way home to Ithaka from Troy – so take your time on this yachting odyssey.

The red-tiled rooftops of Pythagoreio slip astern as you set sail from Samos aboard a chartered yacht, heading off into the mystical stretch of the Aegean known as the Ikarian Sea. As you travel south, the tawny hillsides of Agathonisi – "thorny island" – come into sight, the scent of wild herbs wafting from the slopes. Clumps of juniper, thistle and prickly pear festoon the island, which is covered with walking trails that invite leisurely exploration. From here, dolphins and flying fish may accompany you as you set sail again.

The islands along the way are shrouded in history and myth. According to some, Lipsi – your next anchorage point – was the original Ogygia, home of the nymph Calypso, who charmed Odysseus into lingering here for seven years. You'll soon see why he would have stayed – gullies filled with flowering oleander cut vivid pink rivers through the island's ochre-coloured slopes and rainbow-coloured wrasse swim in its glass-clear harbour.

While you sail unhurriedly onwards, the islands will regularly lure you away from the water, whether it's the quayside tavernas of Fourni or the cool nightspots of Mykonos. But some of the best times are those spent at anchor in a deserted bay, lazily listening to the gentle lapping of waves against the hull.

> Some of the best times are those spent at anchor in a deserted bay

An elegant yacht anchoring in calm, deep-blue waters, just off the island of Lipsi

Sailboats nestling on the edge of Hallskär, one of the many islands in the Stockholm archipelago

Stockholm Archipelago

LOCATION Sweden **START/FINISH** Stockholm (loop) **DISTANCE** Varies **TIME** Varies **INFORMATION** www.visitstockholm.com

Dip your toes in the water, eat your weight in crayfish, then set a course to your next destination. This is an average day sailing Stockholm's archipelago of 24,000 islands – a place of rugged, spellbinding beauty.

Sustainability is a buzz word in Sweden and no-fly holidays have made Stockholm's verdant archipelago a go-to for guilt-free breaks. But even before this, many Swedes were devoted to sailing among these salt-tanged islands – and it's easy to see why. Here, from the froth-lapped prow of a boat, beach-fringed atolls, uninhabited skerries and forested islands dotted with copper-coloured summer houses unfurl in front of you.

The sailing is easy, with soft winds and few tides to worry about; the only problem is deciding where to sail to next. Should you visit Vaxholm and Malma Kvarn, with their well-preserved wooden houses? Or how about Hallskär and Sandhamn, with sand dunes and world-renowned sailing reputations? There is one risk, however – staying an extra week to see it all. But in Sweden they'll tell you to just do it: here, the freedom and desire to venture into nature — *allemansrätten* — is a human right.

Copper-coloured summer houses overlooking the water on the Stockholm archipelago

another way

Jump in a sea kayak to explore the Stockholm archipelago under your own steam. Paddling around the islands, you'll pass by craggy coves and forested islets, pristine beaches and cute-as-a-button fishing villages.

BY WATER
EUROPE

(16) # The Danube

LOCATION Germany to Ukraine **START/FINISH** Bavaria/Black Sea **DISTANCE** 1,850 km (1,150 miles) **TIME** 10–15 days **INFORMATION** Cruise availability, facilities and itineraries vary

A shortcut to seeing the best of the continent begins on the deck of a river cruiser, sailing through the heartlands of Central and Eastern Europe. One day you're breakfasting in Budapest, the next you're wining and dining in Bucharest – what's not to like?

Budapest's striking Parliament building, standing beside the Danube

MARVEL at **Vienna's** opulent Schönbrunn Palace, former home of the Habsburgs

MINGLE with new friends as you hop from ruin bar to ruin bar on an evening out in **Budapest**

TASTE vintage wines while exploring **Villány**, one of Hungary's finest wine regions

TAKE a tour of **Vukovar**, a town ravaged during Croatia's 1991–1995 War of Independence

Bratislava Castle and the Danube in Slovakia

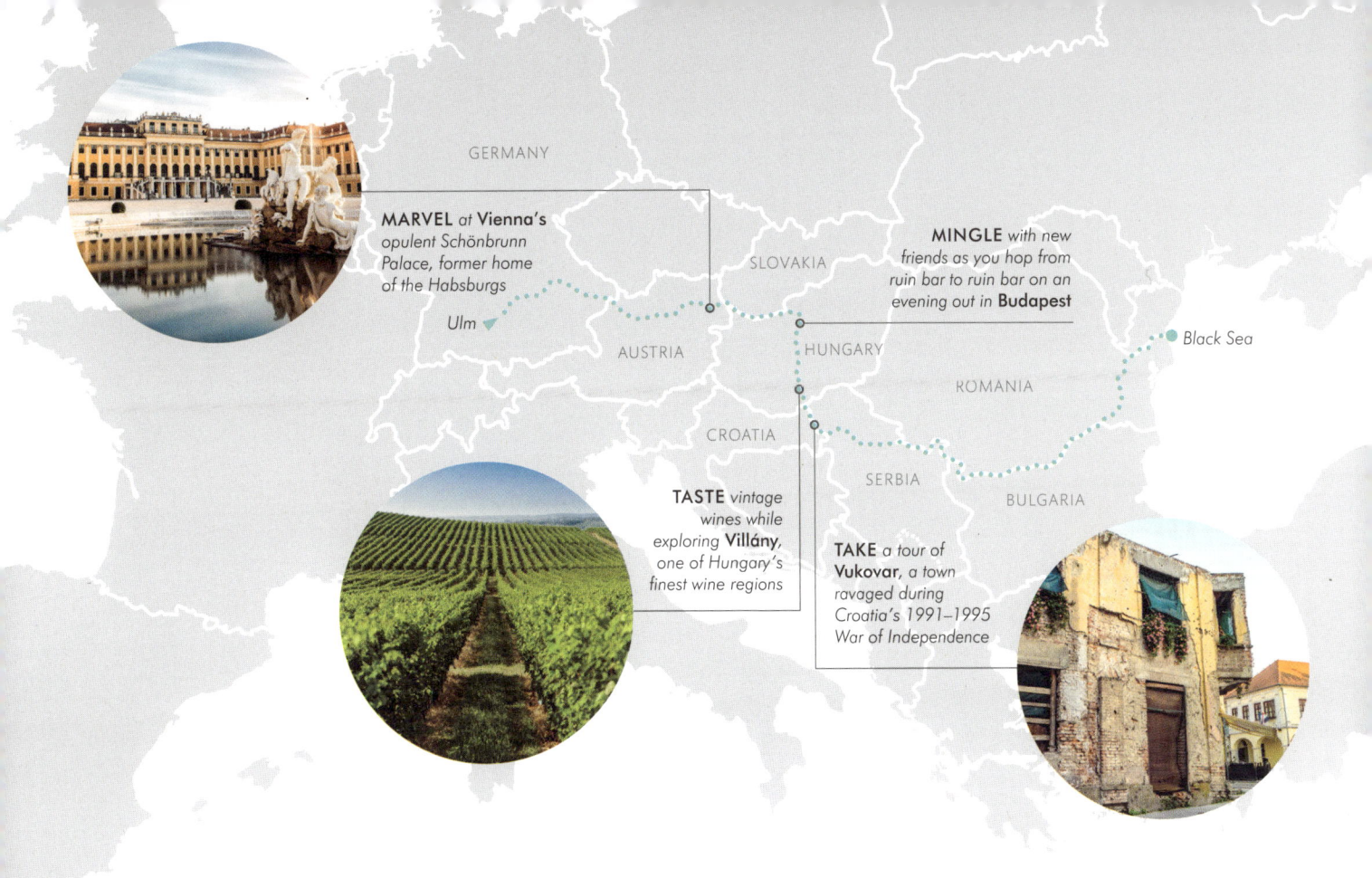

The day begins in a haze of pre-dawn light, as the boat weighs anchor and begins its slow putter to the next port. From the prow, the spires and silhouettes of Budapest slide into soft focus, at once majestic, yet mysterious. Like many stops on the Danube, the Hungarian capital is a spectacular wonder, a thrilling symbiosis of two

> Sailing on Europe's most storied river is nothing if not an out-and-out crowd-pleaser

halves: modern, momentous Buda; historic, higgledy-piggledy Pest. Tonight, the river journey continues south towards Serbia, but for now the day promises a gloriously decadent thermal bath and a whistle-stop tour of Hungarian history.

Sailing on Europe's most storied – and second-longest – river is nothing if not an out-and-out crowd-pleaser. With an almost unfathomable choice of itineraries to choose from, a journey can take in any one of ten countries, and begin at the source in Bavaria or at a port along the river's journey to the Black Sea, 2,850 km (1,770 miles) away. Highlights include Regensburg, the Danube's oldest city; the Baroque architecture and coffee and cake culture of Linz in Austria; time-warped Bratislava Castle in Slovakia; and Budapest's toe-wrinkling Szechenyi Thermal Baths. As for history? The empires of Persia, Greece, Rome, Turkey and Austro-Hungary have all enjoyed these river lands. Now it's your turn.

French Riviera

Above Looking out over the charming houses and sparkling harbour of St Tropez *Below* Striped deck chairs lining the shore in Nice

LOCATION France **START/FINISH** Hyères/Monaco **DISTANCE** 200 km (130 miles) **TIME** 1 week **INFORMATION** www.france.fr/en

Dotted with ports where superyachts moor, the Riviera has been a playground for the rich and famous for over a century. You may not be able to afford a plutocrat's mega-cruiser, but even aboard a more modest vessel, you can enjoy a dream voyage along this gorgeous Mediterranean shore.

Settling off from the seaside town of Hyères, cruise along the hazy coastline of the Massif des Maures to the Baie de Pampelonne. Sojourn amid turquoise waters and white sands here before rounding Cap de St Tropez to a port that has been a byword for glamour since the 1950s. Big spenders hang out in chic clubs, while locals lunch in the cafés around the plane-tree-shaded Place des Lices.

Further up the coast, the scent of sun-warmed pine and eucalyptus wafts from the tiny Îles de Lérin, where the chance to swim in crystalline waters and sip Lérina liqueur, distilled by local monks, lures boats to anchor. Beyond this island idyll, the fleshpots of Cannes beckon; in May, this glamorous city is the setting for the legendary Festival International du Film.

It's on around Cap d'Antibes to Nice, where a stroll along the palm-lined Promenade des Anglais to the palatial Hotel Negresco for cocktails is mandatory. From here, follow the near-vertical coastline until you spy Monaco's bright lights – perhaps a celebratory visit to the tables of the famed Casino de Monte Carlo is in order. Who knows? You might win enough to buy your own superyacht.

BY WATER
EUROPE

The Rhine

LOCATION Switzerland to the Netherlands **START/FINISH** The Rhine flows from Vorderrhein to the Hook of Holland; itineraries vary along its course **DISTANCE** Varies **TIME** Varies **INFORMATION** Cruise availability, facilities and itineraries vary

Follow this ancient river route as it unfurls through the very heart of Europe, looping past tree-shrouded valleys, castle-topped border towns and vineyard-backed meadows along the way.

Europe's largest river has shaped the course of history, flowing onwards as empires have fallen and the lines of the continent have been redrawn. There is much to explore here: to the north and west lie the seaside Hook of Holland and the culinary riches of France, while to the south and east sit Germany's UNESCO-rated Rhine Valley and the alpine landscapes of Switzerland. Countless painters (Turner, van Gogh), musicians (Beethoven, Wagner), poets, philosophers and authors (Byron, Goethe, Shelley) have been inspired by its ever-variegated seasonal beauty. Indeed, a Rhine cruise offers everything you'd want from a European break in one neatly packaged sitting. It's a trip designed to appeal to those whose travel instincts run the gamut from chocolate in Basel to architecture in Cologne, wine in Strasbourg to art in Amsterdam. But more than that, the Rhine represents an idea: of how connected people and places prosper, and why Europe is all the better for it.

PATRICK LEIGH FERMOR

In 1933, Patrick Leigh Fermor set out on an ambitious journey across Europe, from the Hook of Holland to Istanbul, loosely following the meandering Rhine. He wrote a memoir of his journey 40 years later, which became a trilogy of celebrated classics: his first book, *A Time of Gifts*, traces his journey as far as Hungary.

Cruising past the German town of Rüdesheim am Rhein and Ehrenfels Castle

Above *The breathtaking beauty of the Lofoten archipelago* **Left** *The Hurtigruten cruising up the Geirangerfjord*

BY WATER
EUROPE

Norway's Fjords

LOCATION Norway **START/FINISH** Bergen/Tromsø **DISTANCE** 1,623 km (1,008 miles) **TIME** 5 days **INFORMATION** www.hurtigruten.co.uk

A cruise through Norway's legendary fjords and across the Arctic Circle shines brightest in summer, when the midnight sun paints the dramatic landscapes a dazzling rose gold.

There are few experiences more authentically Norwegian than dipping in and out of the fjord-cracked coastline on an unhurried Hurtigruten cruise ship. These iconic black-and-red-striped boats have been the lifeblood of Norway's northern coastal communities since 1893, carrying family, mail and supplies to far-flung islets and archipelagos.

Starting from the brightly painted shipping offices of Bryggen in Bergen, the ship slices through blue-and-green sea, past skerries and tiny islands, towards the resplendent Geirangerfjord. Coasting beneath the 800-m (2,625-ft) cliffs towards the gushing torrents of De Syv Søstrene (the Seven Sisters Waterfall), it's easy to see why local legend claims that these falls are petrified troll women shaking their tresses. From here, the ship pauses at Norway's charming former capital, Trondheim, on its eponymous fjord.

The beauty of the days before is eclipsed on the final stretch of the ship's voyage, on the other side of the Arctic Circle. Between black granite cliffs and white-sand beaches lie the pearls of the Lofoten archipelago. Tiny red rorbuer – fisherman's cabins – frame sheltered bays. Sheep-dotted green pastures nudge craggy mountains. And the endless water reflects the mystical rosy glow of the never-ending midnight sun.

END your journey in the city of **Tromsø**, located inside the Arctic Circle

○ Tromsø

VISIT Nidaros Domkirke in **Trondheim**, where Christianity replaced Norse mythology

KICK back in charming **Molde** ("Town of Roses") at the mouth of Romsdalfjord

MARVEL at **Geirangerfjord**, where steep-sided rock walls and frosted mountain peaks rise high above

DISCOVER secret passageways and tiny shops in **Bryggen**

○ Bergen

NORWAY

281

BY WATER
EUROPE

The Turkish Coast

LOCATION Turkey **START/FINISH** Marmaris/Fethiye
DISTANCE 120 km (75 miles) **TIME** 4 days
INFORMATION Cruise availability, facilities and itineraries vary

Sailing the rugged coast of the eastern Mediterranean aboard a traditional Turkish gulet is a chance to explore secret coves, deserted islands and historical relics.

The sleek, twin-masted sailboat slips out of Marmaris' bustling harbour. Soon, the white buildings of the town are replaced by olive-coloured hillsides that drop away into the water; then, at the mouth of the bay, the glittering expanse of the Mediterranean opens.

Ahead lies a four-day voyage aboard a gulet (pronounced "goo-let"), a traditionally designed Turkish yacht that holds around 16 passengers. On this gently paced odyssey, the boat glides between lively harbour towns, stony islets and quiet anchorages in sheltered bays. At times, the slender gulet noses its way into narrow inlets – utterly inaccessible to larger vessels – where passengers can leap straight from deck into the warm, glass-clear sea.

Skimming onwards, the gulet reaches the shimmering azure waters of the Gulf of Göcek, one of the most mesmerizing stages on the voyage. Here, rugged islands offer the chance to swim, snorkel or explore archaeological remains – this whole coast is marked with traces of the eastern Mediterranean's many ancient states and kingdoms. Back on board, after a traditional Turkish dinner prepared by your crew, you'll fall asleep to the soft sound of lapping water.

TURKISH GULETS

The name "gulet" comes from the Italian word for "schooner", *goletta* – an indication of Italian influence on maritime technology in ancient times. Most contemporary gulets are built around Bodrum, following an old design pattern that had fallen almost entirely out of use – it wasn't until the 1970s that the arrival of tourism kick-started a revival of traditional boatbuilding skills.

A traditional Turkish gulet bobbing on the Mediterranean, just off the coast of Turkey

The Amalfi Coast

The pastel-coloured houses of the town of Amalfi, tumbling down the coast towards the sea

LOCATION Italy **START/FINISH** Amalfi (loop) **DISTANCE** 5 km (3 miles)
TIME 1 hour 30 minutes **INFORMATION** www.gruppobattellieriamalfi.com

Starting in the cliffside town of Amalfi, this journey traces the jagged coastline before finally reaching the dreamy Grotta dello Smeraldo, a striking emerald-green cave where thick stands of moon-coloured stalactites protrude from the ceiling.

As the boat plies the deep-blue waters of the Amalfi Coast, the shimmering Mediterranean stretches out before you. Amalfi slowly recedes from view, snugly nestled in a ravine, its pastel-coloured houses looking out towards the sea's azure waters. Increasingly dramatic vistas unfold as you head west, with vertiginous cliffs carpeted with greenery, topped here and there with ancient hamlets. Ahead lies the super-stylish island resort of Capri, its dramatic Faraglioni – three towering rock formations – visible in the distance. In no time at all the boat passes the rocky headland of Conca dei Marini, harbouring one of Italy's most beautiful beaches, before reaching the jetty of Grotta dello Smeraldo. Here, smaller boats take visitors into a spectacular emerald-green grotto partly filled with sea water. Roofed with a riot of stalactites, the grotto's stalagmites rise in a myriad of contorted shapes, some protruding above the water. Scattered along the bed of the cave are a number of ceramic figures, part of an underwater Nativity scene placed here in 1956. A quick change of boats and you're once again in the blinding sunlight, travelling along the ragged coast back to the treasure town of Amalfi.

The Rio Douro passing gently by the terraced hills of the Douro Valley

22 Douro Valley

LOCATION Portugal **START/FINISH** Vila Nova de Gaia/Porto **DISTANCE** 100 km (62 miles) **TIME** 1 day **INFORMATION** Cruise availability, facilities and itineraries vary

Winding down the Rio Douro on a traditional riverboat, a glass of port in hand, drinking in the view of rolling vineyards and historic wine lodges – what a splendid way to spend a day.

From the pleasingly ramshackle riverfront of Vila Nova de Gaia, your boat passes under the looming girders of Dom Luís I Bridge and out east, into the lush green Douro Valley. This is the heartland of port wine – a fact not lost on the British, who set up innumerable lodges here. Look out for elegantly crumbling quintas, with names like Cockburn, Taylor and Yeatman, in between the vineyards. In the town of Pinhão, disembark to visit one such estate: Symington's Quinta do Bomfim. Taste the wines that have been made here since 1896, and learn about the process with a factory tour. Back on board, wind lazily back towards Porto, as the sun sets on the vineyards of the valley walls. It'll soon be clear why it's named the Rio Douro, the River of Gold.

23 River Thames

LOCATION UK **START/FINISH** Oxford/Windsor **DISTANCE** 100 km (62 miles) **TIME** 4 days **INFORMATION** www.visitthames.co.uk

Winding its way from the Cotswold Hills through water meadows, market towns and, finally, London on its way to the sea, no waterway is more symbolic of England than the Thames. To see it at its finest, set up home on a canal barge and plot a leisurely course through this sliver of quintessential English countryside.

Bidding farewell to Oxford's dreamy college spires, the prow of your barge slips between weeping-willow-fringed banks, and pootles on past thatched cottages, rolling chalk hills and centuries-old riverside inns that simply insist you moor nearby. Progress is slow but that's the joy; meandering down the river offers glimpes of everyday life that are otherwise so easily missed.

As the river flows on, reminders of modernity interrupt the tranquility. Here, Clifton Hampden's splendid six-arched bridge; there, the steel-and-glass office towers of Reading. Finally, as your bow turns eastward towards the outskirts of London, the turrets of Windsor Castle come into view – a fitting finale to this very English journey.

> Plot a leisurely course through this sliver of quintessential English countryside

BY WATER
EUROPE

24 Great Glen Canoe Trail

LOCATION UK **START/FINISH** Corpach/Clachnaharry **DISTANCE** 96 km (60 miles) **TIME** 5 days **DIFFICULTY** Challenging **INFORMATION** www.greatglencanoetrail.info

Slicing diagonally across Scotland, the Caledonian Canal connects the four silvery lochs of the Great Glen: Lochy, Oich, Ness and Dochfour, where the canal wiggles its way round Inverness to meet the sea at Clachnaharry. But don't let pictures of mirror-flat waters deceive you; conditions on lochs Lochy and Ness can be as severe as at sea, with high waves buffeting your vessel. Weary arms must also portage crafts over the canal's numerous locks. And, of course, there are the rumours to contend with. Scotland's famous Loch Ness prompts even the bold to take a deep breath before pushing off. Are the stories true? Does a monster really lurk beneath its steely-dark? Few can resist keeping an eye open for a glimpse of a serpentine neck as they plough the loch's 37-km (23-mile) length.

25 Holland's Canals

LOCATION The Netherlands **START/FINISH** Amsterdam (loop) **DISTANCE** 170 km (105 miles) **TIME** 1 week **INFORMATION** www.holland.com

Created to reclaim a waterlogged hinterland, Holland's canals and rivers are a tribute to Dutch ingenuity, and an ideal way to see the country.

The Amstel River sweeps boats out of the capital, beneath bridges and past tall, tilted houses. Before long, suburban sprawl yields to countryside where dairy cattle graze in the waterside meadows of cheese-making country; farmers still sell great rounds of their yellow gold in central Gouda, which is hemmed in by a medieval maze of canals. Red-brick townhouses flank the waterside as you putter on through pretty Oudewater en route to Utrecht, a lively city of broad quays and waterside café-bars. The mood changes as you emerge from narrow channels into the Loosdrecht. The open waters, big skies and wildfowl-haunted islets of this inland sea serve up a welcome taste of the natural world before you cruise back towards Amsterdam.

The shimmering Amstel River flowing through the centre of Amsterdam

BY WATER
EUROPE

PICNIC in lush Linnansaari National Park

DISCOVER traditional farming methods at Linnansaari Croft

Oravi

FINLAND

SPOT the world's most endangered seal, the ringed seal, in the waters of Lake Saimaa

RELAX in a snug, wood-fired sauna, a favourite pastime of Finnish locals

26 Finnish Lakeland

LOCATION Finland **START/FINISH** Oravi (loop) **DISTANCE** 12 km (7.5 miles) **TIME** 1 day **DIFFICULTY** Moderate **INFORMATION** www.nationalparks.fi; best to book a guide

Kayaking on the immense Lake Saimaa is best in high summer, when temperatures are balmy and near-perpetual daylight illuminates this placid body of water and its thousands of verdant islands.

Paddling over the calm waters of Linnansaari National Park

As you paddle away from the village of Oravi, the first thing you'll notice is the quiet. At 4,400 sq km (1,700 sq miles), Lake Saimaa – the most immense lake in Europe's largest lake district – is a place where your thoughts can be the loudest thing for miles.

It's not just the solitude and still waters that attract kayakers here; the lake is home to some 13,700 islands. Breaking through the calm surface, these forested green splinters of land create an understated, watery maze of beauty, making it easy to see why the Finnish often equate paradise with Lakeland. One such cluster of islands comprises the vast Linnansaari National Park, a haven for wildlife and the home of Linnansaari Croft, a traditional farm from the 1930s. It'll take more than a day's paddle to circumnavigate the 40-km (25-mile) coastline of the park's main island, so choose a section and take it slow, dragging your craft onto the shore to picnic along the way. In summer, blueberries and chanterelle pepper the island's greenery, inviting foragers seeking a tasty titbit.

Back on the water, keep a lookout. Navigating these straits is the rarest of creatures: Finland's much-loved and endangered Saimaa ringed seal. Watch to see these protected creatures break the water and wriggle onto nearby rocks, their chocolatey-brown, barnacled fur immediately camouflaging. Thankful for the silence of your craft, the scene is undisturbed.

Looking out over the tranquil waters and forested islands of the vast Lake Saimaa

BY WATER
AFRICA AND THE MIDDLE EAST

The Nile

LOCATION Egypt **START/FINISH** Cairo/Aswan **DISTANCE** 878 km (546 miles) **TIME** 10 days **INFORMATION** Cruise availability, facilities and itineraries vary

Visitors to Egypt have been cruising the Nile for pleasure since antiquity, when the Egyptian queen Cleopatra took Roman emperor Julius Caesar upriver on her royal barge around 47 BC. More than 2,000 years later, the journey has lost none of its appeal.

Traditionally, voyages along the Nile begin in Cairo, Egypt's capital, which lies in the north of the country. Not particularly old by Egyptian standards, this clamorous and over-crowded city dates only to the 10th century. It was founded near the site of a much earlier capital, Memphis – a city long since erased by time except for the funerary monuments of its kings, including the famous Pyramids at Giza. The spectacle of these towering yet geometrically precise piles of stone is just a taster for what's to come.

| Onboard Egyptologists give stimulating talks on pharaohs and gods

Some of the Nile cruisers can accommodate hundreds of passengers but the best have only about 20 or fewer cabins. Among the most atmospheric options are vintage steamers dating back to the early 20th century and traditional-style sailboats known as a *dahabiyyas*. Most of the big-ticket attractions on a Nile cruise are clustered in the south of the country, so the first few days are spent simply enjoying the languid rhythms of life on the river. As the boat gently chugs against the current, leaving Cairo ever further behind, the hours drift by in a blissful haze of relaxing on deck and observing life in the palm-fringed villages along the riverbanks. In the evenings, onboard Egyptologists give stimulating talks on pharaohs and gods, fuelling your imagination in readiness for exploring the ancient wonders upriver.

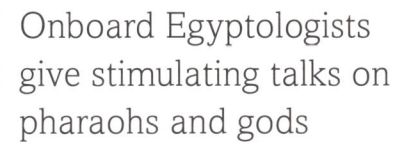

Left *Traditional Egyptian sailboats on the Nile* **Below** *A vintage steamboat cruising up the river* **Right** *Relaxing with refreshments on deck*

BY WATER
AFRICA AND THE MIDDLE EAST

After several lazy days, you arrive in the south of the country – a region known as Upper Egypt, because it is from here that the Nile flows downriver to the Mediterranean Sea in the north. Your first expeditions ashore are to the grand temples of Abydos and Dendera. The former is famed for its King List – a hieroglyphic table that lists the names of 76 kings of ancient Egypt – while the latter is one of the best-preserved temple complexes in Egypt and features a colourful blue ceiling painting in its striking hypostyle hall.

The following day the boat arrives at Luxor. Once known as Thebes, this was the capital of ancient Egypt in its prime. Pharaohs who ruled from here extended their dominion down into Africa and north around the Eastern Mediterranean basin, and used their wealth to fund vast building projects. The greatest of these is undoubtedly Karnak – even today, its main hypostyle hall, filled with columns the size of giant sequoia trees, renders visitors speechless. Opposite the temple, on the west bank of the Nile, is the Valley of the Kings, where the pharaohs and nobles were buried in tombs

AGATHA CHRISTIE ON THE NILE

As the wife of an archaeologist, Agatha Christie spent a lot of time in the Middle East. Her husband's work was mainly in eastern Syria and Iraq, but in 1933 the couple visited Egypt and took a Nile cruise. The isolated, desert-edged stretch of the river from Aswan to Abu Simbel provided a suitably claustrophobic setting for her 1937 novel *Death on the Nile*.

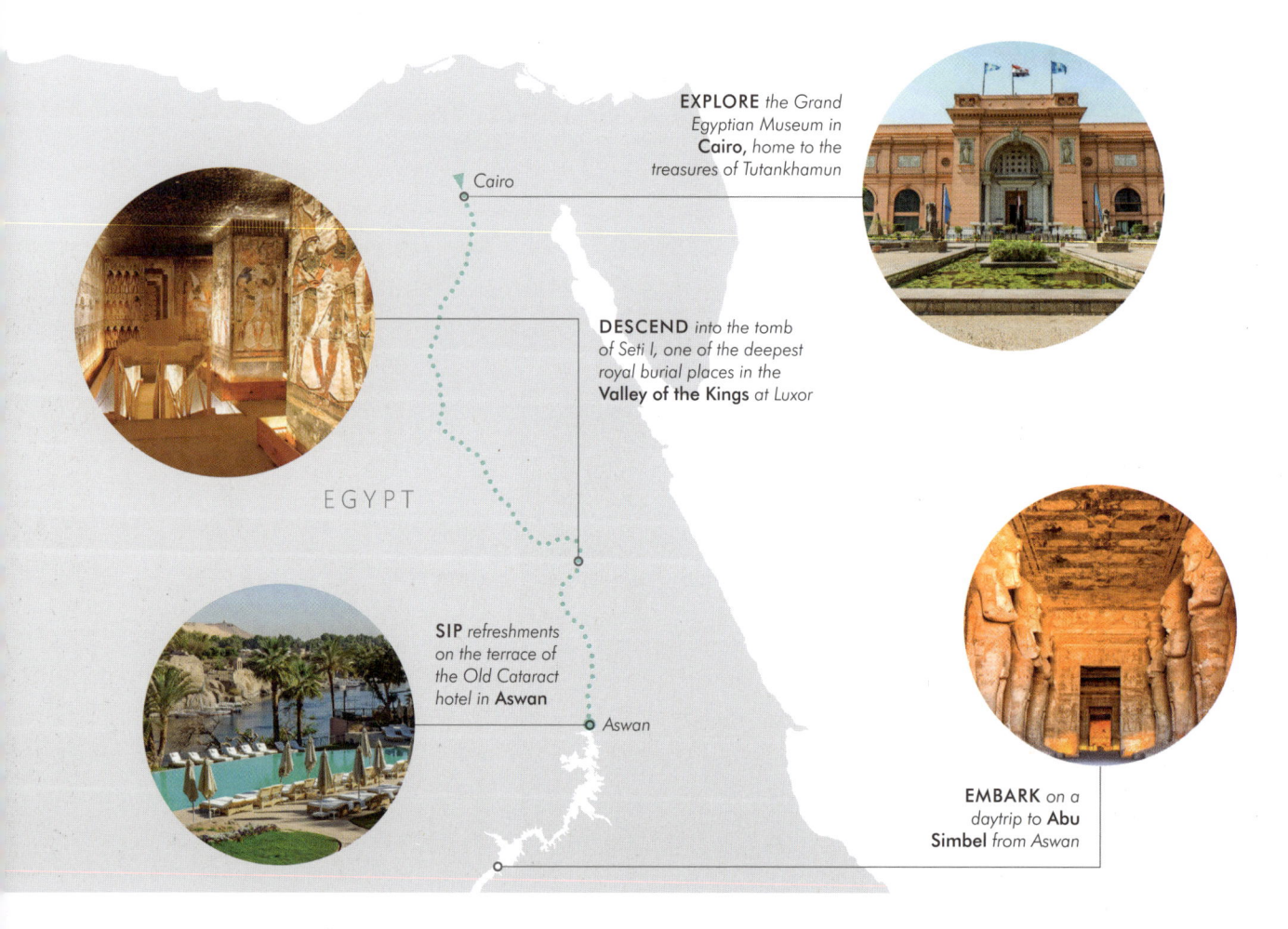

EXPLORE the Grand Egyptian Museum in **Cairo,** home to the treasures of Tutankhamun

Cairo

DESCEND into the tomb of Seti I, one of the deepest royal burial places in the **Valley of the Kings** at Luxor

EGYPT

SIP refreshments on the terrace of the Old Cataract hotel in **Aswan**

Aswan

EMBARK on a daytrip to **Abu Simbel** from Aswan

Left *Gazing up at the huge stone pillars of Karnak Temple* **Above** *A stall selling spices in Aswan's souk*

tunnelled deep into the dusty Theban Hills. It's here where the gold-filled burial chamber of the "Boy King" Tutankhamun was uncovered in 1922.

After Luxor, there are three more days of sailing, punctuated by visits to more magnificent riverside temples, before the journey comes to an end at Aswan, a low-rise market town that feels more African than Arabic – we're not that far here from the border with Sudan. The dam at Aswan prevents further progress on the river, but there are coach excursions south to Philae, a small island crowned with a temple to the river goddess Isis. While Philae is ancient, with its oldest parts dating to about 380 BC, it is sobering to realize that it is nearer in age to us today than it is to the Pyramids at Giza, which were built over 2,100 years earlier. It's a fitting reminder that a Nile cruise is not just a journey up a river, but a voyage through time.

another way

If time is short, make the journey by land via the deluxe sleeper train that connects Cairo with both Luxor and Aswan. Leaving Cairo in the evening, it follows the Nile south to arrive in Luxor or Aswan in time for breakfast the following day.

BY WATER
AFRICA AND THE MIDDLE EAST

The Ilala Ferry

Above The deck of the Ilala Ferry
Above right The turquoise waters of Nkhata Bay

LOCATION Malawi **START/FINISH** Monkey Bay/Chilumba **DISTANCE** 480 km (300 miles) **TIME** 3 days **INFORMATION** www.malawitourism.com

Travelling on the MV Ilala *takes you on a voyage of discovery to the remotest corners of Malawi, affording you a glimpse of genuine local life on the scenic shores of the "Lake of Stars".*

Every week since 1951, the *Ilala* ferry has been plying its way across the vast Lake Malawi, one of the largest lakes in Africa. Don't expect glitz or glamour – this boat is a workhorse, a lifeline to local people, but there's plenty of enjoyment to be found in the ship's abundant character and beautiful shabby dignity.

Starting from the frenetic southern port of Monkey Bay and ending at Chilumba, near the Tanzanian border in the north, the complete trip takes at least three days. Embarking is chaotic, with throngs of passengers heaving all manner of baggage and cargo on board – including live goats and chickens – and the ferry very rarely sets sail on time. Once aboard, however, life on the MV *Ilala* is surprisingly peaceful, as the ferry drifts across the "inland sea" that's mostly calm and as smooth as glass – although the occasional wild storm does pass through here. Sandy bays, rocky promontories and verdant hills line the shore, and dramatic sunsets turn the waters a vivid red. Although a handful of cosy cabins are available, the best views are had by buying a first-class ticket and sleeping on deck (bring a blanket). There's a bar and small restaurant on board, but take water with you as they often sell out.

Pandemonium reappears with each port of call, exacerbated by crowds of dugouts and small boats if the ferry anchors offshore. Seven ports and two days into the journey, most travellers jump ship at the friendly fishing village of Nkhata Bay, and chill on the pretty shore of the lake until the *Ilala* returns.

BY WATER
AFRICA AND THE MIDDLE EAST

(29)

River Gambia

LOCATION The Gambia **START/FINISH** Bao Bolong Wetland Reserve and Kiang West National Park/Banjul **DISTANCE** 100 km (60 miles) **TIME** 3 days **INFORMATION** There are no regular ferry services, but tour operators run boats along the river

To travel down the River Gambia is to return to the Africa of old, with beautiful riverside villages and forests teeming with wildlife.

Few rivers define a nation quite like the eponymous river of The Gambia. Nowhere in the country are you more than 40 km (25 miles) from its banks, and its waters are key to local livelihoods, both as a source of fish and as a trade route. A boat journey here offers an immersive insight into life along the forest-fringed river, as you drift slowly from the neighbouring national parks of Bao Bolong and Kiang West to Banjul, the busy capital, on the coast. Along the way you slide softly past a string of sleepy thatched villages and solitary fishermen in dugout canoes, silhouetted at sunset against a blazing crimson sky.

But it's not just human scenes that animate this journey. Wildlife found almost nowhere else in West Africa thrives in the jungle along the riverbank, with chimpanzees in the canopy, antelopes such as sitatunga in the shallows, and a remarkable 560 species of birds sprinkled throughout. The Gambia may be the smallest country in mainland Africa, but it's definitely big on natural beauty.

THE GAMBIA

English-speaking The Gambia is one of only two countries that officially have "The" attached to their name. (The other is The Bahamas.) The origins of the name Gambia date back to the 15th century; the "The" was added in 1970, post-independence, in part to prevent the country from being confused with Zambia.

A fisherman casting his net from a dugout canoe on the River Gambia

Above *An African elephant standing on the bank of the delta* **Left** *Visitors being guided through a papyrus-lined channel on a* mokoro *safari*

BY WATER
AFRICA AND THE MIDDLE EAST

The Okavango Delta

LOCATION Botswana **START/FINISH** Okavango Delta (loop) **DISTANCE** Varies **TIME** Varies **INFORMATION** www.botswanatourism.co.bw; the best time for *mokoro* safaris is in the dry season from Apr–Oct

Gliding along a lily-strewn waterway in a traditional dugout canoe, with dragonflies fluttering around and wild animals coming to drink as you watch in awed silence – exploring the Okavango Delta by mokoro *is pure bliss.*

A UNESCO World Heritage Site, the Okavango in northern Botswana is the largest inland delta on the planet. Between May and August, floodwaters from the Okavango River fan out over the dry Kalahari sands to produce this massive oasis, creating a temporary wetland sanctuary home to myriad wild animals and birds.

The best way to explore the delta's waterways is by *mokoro* – a wooden canoe poled by a local boatman who knows his way around the maze of channels. *Mokoro* safaris can take anything from three hours to three days. Many lodges and camps in the Okavango offer morning or afternoon excursions, but for a truly wild experience you can't beat a guided camping trip. Days are spent leisurely searching for wildlife by *mokoro* or on foot, while nights bring star-filled skies and the sounds of whooping hyena and laughing hippos.

The experience is magical, whichever option you choose. All around are magnificent African fish eagles perched high up in the trees, tiny Malachite kingfishers darting above the water and jewel-hued dragonflies dancing around the papyrus. On the banks, you might spot familiar creatures such as elephants. If you look carefully, you'll also find tiny painted frogs balancing on reeds, or perhaps even spy rare antelopes such as sitatungas and red lechwe. All that's left to do is to sit back and relax, and listen to the rhythmic swooshing of the water as you glide through this unique natural paradise.

ENJOY a refreshing sundowner as you watch the sun set over the Delta

FEEL a connection with nature while camping out in the bush

Okavango Delta

WATCH wildlife almost at eye level from your low vantage point

BOTSWANA

Mauritius

Picture-perfect Flic En Flac Beach on the west coast of Mauritius

LOCATION Mauritius **START/FINISH** Port Louis (loop) **DISTANCE** 330 km (205 miles) **TIME** 3–5 days **INFORMATION** www.tourism-mauritius.mu

Heaven, according to American author Mark Twain, was modelled on Mauritius. As you circumnavigate the island you'll soon understand what he meant about this tropical idyll, with its near-perfect beaches, cobalt-blue sea and palm trees at every turn.

Mauritius is green and blue and every shade in between. The mountainous interior rises abruptly from the coastal hinterland in deep tones of bottle green, while the coast is fringed with brilliant yellow- and white-sand beaches. Offshore, a shallow reef creates a stunning ring of vivid turquoise sea – from above, it almost looks as if a halo encircles the island.

As you sail around Mauritius – on either your own yacht or a crewed charter – this gorgeous natural canvas provides plenty of inspiring sights. UNESCO-listed Le Morne mountain vies with the curiously shaped Lion Mountain for sheer drama, while the stirring profile of Coin de Mire – an abrupt outcrop off Mauritius' north coast – rises serenely from the ocean like a wave frozen in time. Then there's Île aux Aigrettes, a perfectly preserved island where endangered wildlife, such as giant tortoises and pink pigeons, live in ebony forests that have stood quietly for centuries. As if that's not enough, this is one paradise where what you do – swimming and snorkelling off the back of the boat, kayaking in the shallows, fishing for your dinner – is every bit as rewarding as what you see.

BY WATER
AFRICA AND THE MIDDLE EAST

The Zambezi River

LOCATION Zambia and Zimbabwe **START/FINISH** Kariba (loop)
DISTANCE 130 km (80 miles) **TIME** 6 days **DIFFICULTY** Moderate
INFORMATION www.wildzambezi.com; the best months for canoeing are Aug–Nov

Canoeing the mighty Zambezi is truly one of Africa's greatest adventures. Picture elephants wading across the water as you row, hippos bobbing up and down, and vivid kingfishers darting to the shores – all this awaits when you immerse yourself in the rhythm of the river.

Marking the border between Zambia and Zimbabwe, the Zambezi forges its way from the tumultuous Victoria Falls to the iridescent Indian Ocean on the shores of Mozambique. En route it passes through Lake Kariba, once the world's largest man-made reservoir, which is where your adventure begins. From Kariba Gorge, you head east downriver in sturdy open canoes, letting the current coax you to the floodplains on both the Zambian and Zimbabwean shores. You'll drift alongside the renowned national parks of Lower Zambezi and then Mana Pools, both home to prolific wildlife. Keep an eye out for sly crocs and harrumphing hippos in the water, as well as herds of elephants, impalas and waterbucks coming to drink at the shore. You might even spot predators such as leopards, lions and rare painted wolves as they prowl the floodplains for food. With early starts and long lunches, you'll rest during the heat of the day before finally stopping at small islands to set up camp each night under a sky full of stars.

another way
If canoeing isn't your thing, opt for a safari cruise instead. Itineraries usually include a three-day voyage around the lake on a luxury houseboat, followed by a stay on the shores of the Zambezi at a safari lodge.

Canoeing through Mana Pools National Park on the Zimbabwean side of the river

BY WATER
ASIA

Traditional junks floating on the shimmering waters of Ha Long Bay

(33)

Ha Long Bay

LOCATION Vietnam **START/FINISH** Ha Long City (loop)
DISTANCE 90 km (56 miles) **TIME** 2 days **INFORMATION**
Cruise availability, facilities and itineraries vary

Jagged shards of forest-topped limestone shatter the turquoise calm of Vietnam's Ha Long Bay. This scene – possibly the most breathtaking sight in Southeast Asia – is best enjoyed from the deck of a traditional junk boat.

The Vietnamese name Ha Long Bay translates as "descending dragon". Legend has it that, in the distant past, a family of these mythical creatures was sent from the gods to protect the land from invaders. Spying enemy ships circling the bay, the dragons spat out stones of jade, which destroyed the interlopers and came to rest in the water. When you see the forested tops of the limestone islands glittering in the sun like green jewels, you might just start to believe the story.

Happily, both invading enemies and mythical beasts have long since deserted this peaceful corner of the earth. There are some 1,600 islands peppering this sprawling bay, with climbing, caving and kayaking among the ways to explore them. The most unforgettable adventure, though, has to be a multi-day trip on board a traditional junk. These majestic wooden boats snake among the bay's ancient emerald islets – home to mysterious caves and wildlife-rich jungles – and past floating fishing villages which have abided here, largely unchanged, for millennia.

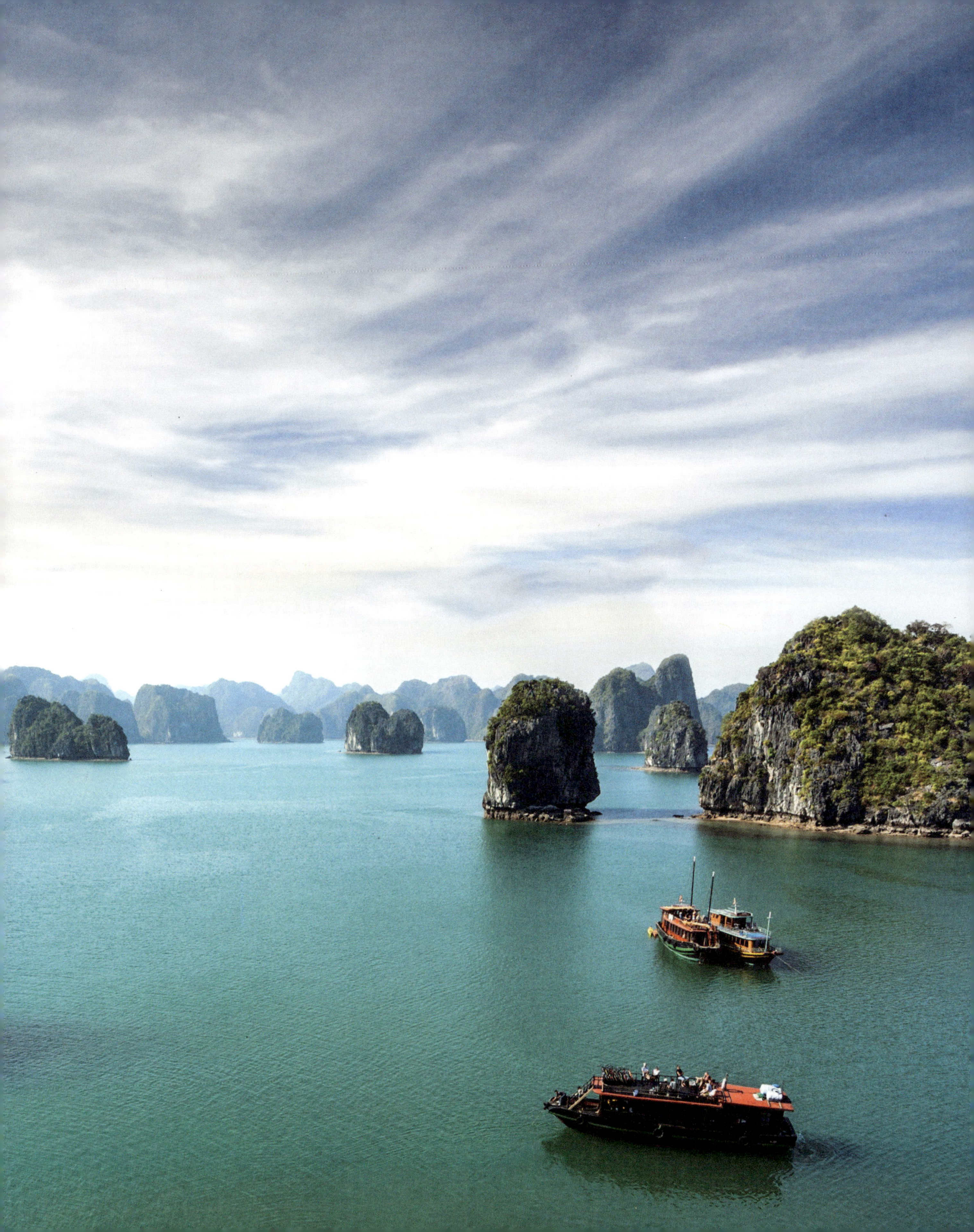

VIETNAM

Ha Long City

FISH for squid and enjoy the bounty in a seafood barbecue

BORROW a kayak and explore the thousands of islands and islets up close

VISIT the floating fishing village of **Cua Van**

SPOT the rare golden langur in the jungles of **Cat Ba**

EXPLORE the ancient caves of **Thieng Cun** and **Sung Sot**, steeped in legend

Wild adventures await once you disembark the junk and explore the islands. Trekking through the emerald jungles of Cat Ba, you might be lucky enough to glimpse the golden head of one of the world's rarest monkeys, the Cat Ba langur, flitting through the treetops. Back on the junk, another scenic journey takes you to Ti Top Island; ascend through the forests to the peak and you'll be rewarded with views of the jungle tumbling down limestone hills into the island-studded bay below.

As unlikely as it sounds, Ha Long Bay is just as beautiful below ground as above. Disembark at Bon Hon Island to explore the winding depths of the Sung Sot Cave, marvelling at atmospherically lit rock formations which have been worshipped by locals as images of the Buddha, animals and fertility symbols. Thieng Cun ("the Celestial Palace") is another cave worth exploring. Legend holds that the bay's dragon guardians made their home here, amid the stalactites which

HOSPITAL CAVE

Famed for their ingenuity in carving out subterranean tunnels during the Vietnam War, the Communist Viet Cong turned the unique topography of Ha Long Bay to their advantage. Hospital Cave on Cat Ba was turned into a three-storey medical complex, which even had its own swimming pool – today, guided tours bring this engineering marvel to life.

300

BY WATER
ASIA

drip like icing from the walls of the cave. Overgrown by jungle, Thieng Cun was abandoned for centuries, only to be rediscovered in 1993 by fishermen seeking shelter from a storm – today, you feel like you're discovering a lost world as you navigate its labyrinthine corridors.

Ha Long Bay's charms transcend the realms of myth, however. Humans have made their homes here for thousands of years, and continue to live in traditional floating fishing villages, houses swaying on wooden stilts above the water. Sail on to Cua Van and learn how the locals make a living from the area, farming pearls, and fishing for squid and grouper – which make for a delectable barbecue lunch. Then, jump in a kayak and explore the bay at your own pace, admiring the craggy karsts and discovering the hidden coves up close.

another way

If you're not sure that you have the sea legs for two days on a boat, get a different perspective on Ha Long Bay by taking a scenic seaplane sightseeing tour. You'll get a spectacular bird's-eye view over the sparkling bay, dotted with thousands of emerald islets.

Left *Junks harbouring in Ha Long Bay* **Below** *A local man rowing over the water*

BY WATER
ASIA

(34) Li River

LOCATION China **START/FINISH** Guilin/Yangshuo
DISTANCE 86 km (53 miles) **TIME** 5 hours
INFORMATION Cruise availability, facilities and itineraries vary

This relaxing river cruise floats through some of China's most ethereal scenery. Here, mystical karst peaks shrouded in cloud soar above the winding Li River.

Green karst mountains rising like crooked dragon's teeth, reflected in misty waters of the winding Li River: the landscapes around Guilin could be taken straight from a classical Chinese scroll painting. This serene cruise downriver from Guilin to its little sister city, Yangshuo, is a pocket-sized journey through picture-perfect scenery.

A variety of double-decker boats make the five-hour one-way trip. Settle in to an open-air deck seat and watch jade-green mountains slide by as the boat cuts through the still humidity. Before you know it, you're passing Elephant Trunk Hill, a perfectly formed cliff arch that's become one of the journey's landmarks. Further along, the names of the elaborate peaks become more and more imaginative as the river twists and turns around them – you float past "Dragons Playing in the Water" and "Five Tigers Catch a Goat" before reaching Yangdi village. Here, the scenery is at its most jaw-dropping, the karst peaks complemented by bamboo groves fixed in improbable contortions. At last, the river curves around Yellow Cloth Shoal, named for the blonde stone here that colours the shallow water yellow. This scene of soaring mountains rising from a looping emerald river is so perfect that it is featured on the back of the Chinese twenty-yuan banknote.

The Li River winding through a dramatic landscape of karst peaks

Boats sprinkling the sparkling turquoise sea next to the island of Derawan

Derawan Islands

LOCATION Borneo **START/FINISH** Tanjung Batu (loop) **DISTANCE** 90 km (56 miles) **TIME** 2 days
INFORMATION Cruise availability, facilities and itineraries vary

This heavenly boat tour takes you to a pristine water wonderland off the coast of Borneo, where you can dive, snorkel and spot turtles.

Nowhere evokes images of pristine, untamed wilderness quite like Borneo. But while many people's minds will jump straight to fluffy-headed orangutans swinging through dense jungles, Borneo's beauty extends far beyond its rugged interior to the outer fringes of its offshore islets – of which the Derawan Islands are the pick of the bunch.

From the town of Tanjung Batu on Borneo's east coast, it's a white-knuckle speedboat ride to the archipelago. As the azure sea melts into the cloudless sky, jewel-like islands come into view. The largest, Maratua, is a great place to snorkel or dive – the waters here are thought to be the third most biodiverse in the world, home to everything from tiny rainbow-hued nudibranchs to vast manta rays.

Back above the waves, your boat motors on to the eponymous island of Derawan. See out the day here at one of the beach lodges: laze on the sand, feast on fresh seafood and spend the night in a hammock beneath the stars.

THE BAJAU

The ocean in this region has long been home to an enigmatic indigenous group called the Bajau. Spending much of their lives at sea or in wooden-stilt fishing villages, the Bajau are remarkable for their fishing and pearling abilities, as well as their incredible capacity to swim underwater; some are able to hold their breath for up to 13 minutes.

303

BY WATER
ASIA

㊱ The Mekong

LOCATION Cambodia to Vietnam
START/FINISH Siem Reap/Ho Chi Minh City
DISTANCE 700 km (435 miles) **TIME** 4–10 days
INFORMATION Cruise availability, facilities and itineraries vary

Southeast Asia reveals its best side from the river. Villages raised on bamboo stilts slip past at a gentle pace; the breeze carries a faint scent of rumduol blossoms; small boats cut back and forth across the flow; and the vast green expanse of the countryside rolls out in all directions.

The Mekong is the great connecting thread of the region, and travelling its lower reaches offers total immersion in complex cultures and lavish landscapes. The classic Mekong itinerary begins close to the great temple complex of Angkor. From here, your boat – an old-style wooden-decked river cruiser – heads out across Tonlé Sap, the vast lake at the heart of Cambodia, to join the main flow of the Mekong at Phnom Penh. Beyond the busy Cambodian capital, with its dignified French architecture and clamorous markets, the journey continues downstream, across the Vietnamese frontier to end in the myriad channels and backwaters of the delta near Ho Chi Minh City.

another way

For dry-land adventurers, the countryside around the Mekong – between the towns of Stung Treng and Kratie, north of Phnom Penh – is home to a network of biking and hiking routes known as the Mekong Discovery Trail.

A kettuvallam punting laungidly along the backwaters of Kerala

㊲ Kerala Backwaters

LOCATION India **START/FINISH** Kollam/Alappuzha **DISTANCE** 90 km (56 miles) **TIME** 2 days **INFORMATION** www.keralatourism.org

In southwest Kerala, wedged between the Arabian Sea and the fertile hills of the Western Ghats, is a 900-km (560-mile) labyrinth of rivers, canals, channels, lakes and lagoons. The most atmospheric way to travel through these "backwaters" is on a *kettuvallam*, a traditional rice barge that has been converted into a houseboat. They range from basic options aimed at backpackers to luxury versions kitted out with hot tubs and air conditioning.

From the bustling town of Kollam, your *kettuvallam* either chugs or is punted along at a gentle pace. On the banks are tangled forests and rice paddies, coconut groves and sleepy villages. In the evening, after mooring for the night, a traditional Keralan thali, a multi-dish meal laid out on a banana leaf, is served. Tomorrow you'll reach the canal-lined city of Alappuzha, known as the "Venice of the east".

BY WATER
ASIA

㊳ The Ganges

LOCATION India **START/FINISH** Marine Drive/Lakshman Jhula, Rishikesh **DISTANCE** 24 km (15 miles) **TIME** 4–5 hours **DIFFICULTY** Easy to challenging **INFORMATION** Always book with a reputable and regulated tour operator

The north Indian city of Rishikesh has traditionally been a spiritual retreat on the banks of the holy Ganges. These days the city also styles itself as a major whitewater rafting destination, where rafters flow down the choppy waters of India's most sacred river on an adrenaline-fuelled course.

Rafts push off from the green foothills above the city. Armed with a helmet, lifejacket and paddle, you'll spend a short while drifting in the languid waters before being propelled through consecutive broiling rapids with names like "roller coaster", "crossfire" and "return to sender". On the way you're rewarded with a unique perspective of ashrams (religious retreats), ghats (steps leading down to the water), brightly painted temples and the landmark Lakshman Jhula suspension bridge.

Whitewater rafting down the Ganges near Rishikesh

㊴ Palawan Archipelago

LOCATION Philippines **START/FINISH** El Nido/Coron City **DISTANCE** 150 km (93 miles) **TIME** 3 days **INFORMATION** Cruise availability, facilities and itineraries vary

Turquoise waters filled with clownfish and basking turtles. Rusty wrecks smothered in brightly hued coral. Empty white-sand beaches shaded by swaying palms. Soak up the languid island life of the Philippines by sea, cruising through the Palawan archipelago in a *bangka* – a traditional outrigger boat used for thousands of years in the Philippines.

On a leisurely cruise around Palawan, from El Nido to Coron, you'll land on isolated islands with little more than bone-white beaches and palms, spending the night on the wooden boat deck and feasting on tuna served adobo-style (the traditional Philippine marinade). Out in the channels lie numerous World War II shipwrecks, now havens for sea life, their rusty hulls wrapped with coral – the perfect sites for diving. Back on board, turtles paddle beside the boat by day, while fruit bats fill the sky at dusk. By the time you reach Coron, the gently rocking boat, caressed by the salty air and warm sea breezes, will feel like home.

THE UNDERWATER LIFE

Palawan's reefs harbour a phenomenal range of marine life. Corals attract parrotfish, angelfish and many others. Five types of turtle bask here, along with manta rays, blacktip reef shark and – those gentle sea giants – whale sharks.

BY WATER
AUSTRALASIA

Travelling over the inky blue waters of Milford Sound, surrounded by waterfall-clad cliffs

Milford Sound

LOCATION New Zealand **START/FINISH** Milford Sound Visitor Terminal (loop) **DISTANCE** 16 km (10 miles) **TIME** 1 hour 45 minutes to overnight **INFORMATION** www.newzealand.com

A place where glacier-carved sheer cliffs plunge steeply into a watery expanse, this pristine slice of Fiordland always looks spectacular, whether shrouded in mist or gleaming in sunlight.

In Māori, this sacred place is known as Piopiotahi, for the single thrush said to have flown here to mourn the death of legendary hero Māui. The long narrow body of water, found on the southwestern coast of New Zealand's South Island, was later renamed Milford Sound by European settlers, after an inlet of the Celtic Sea on the Welsh coast. But they got the geology wrong – while sounds are formed when a river valley is flooded by the sea, Milford Sound was carved out by glaciers, making it a fjord.

For hundreds of years, Māori have traversed the fjord to collect precious pounamu (greenstone), picking their way along traditional tracks, including what is now known as Mackinnon Pass. Today, visitors venture into the heart of Milford Sound by boat, setting off from the wharf in the tiny namesake village. Adventure beckons as the boat glides into the kilometre-wide valley, floating over the sound's mirror-like waters and sailing alongside near-vertical cliffs. Around each bend lie unusual geological features like Lion Mountain, the Elephant and, looming above all else, the mile-high Mitre Peak/Rahotu, named by the Europeans for its resemblance to a bishop's ceremonial headdress.

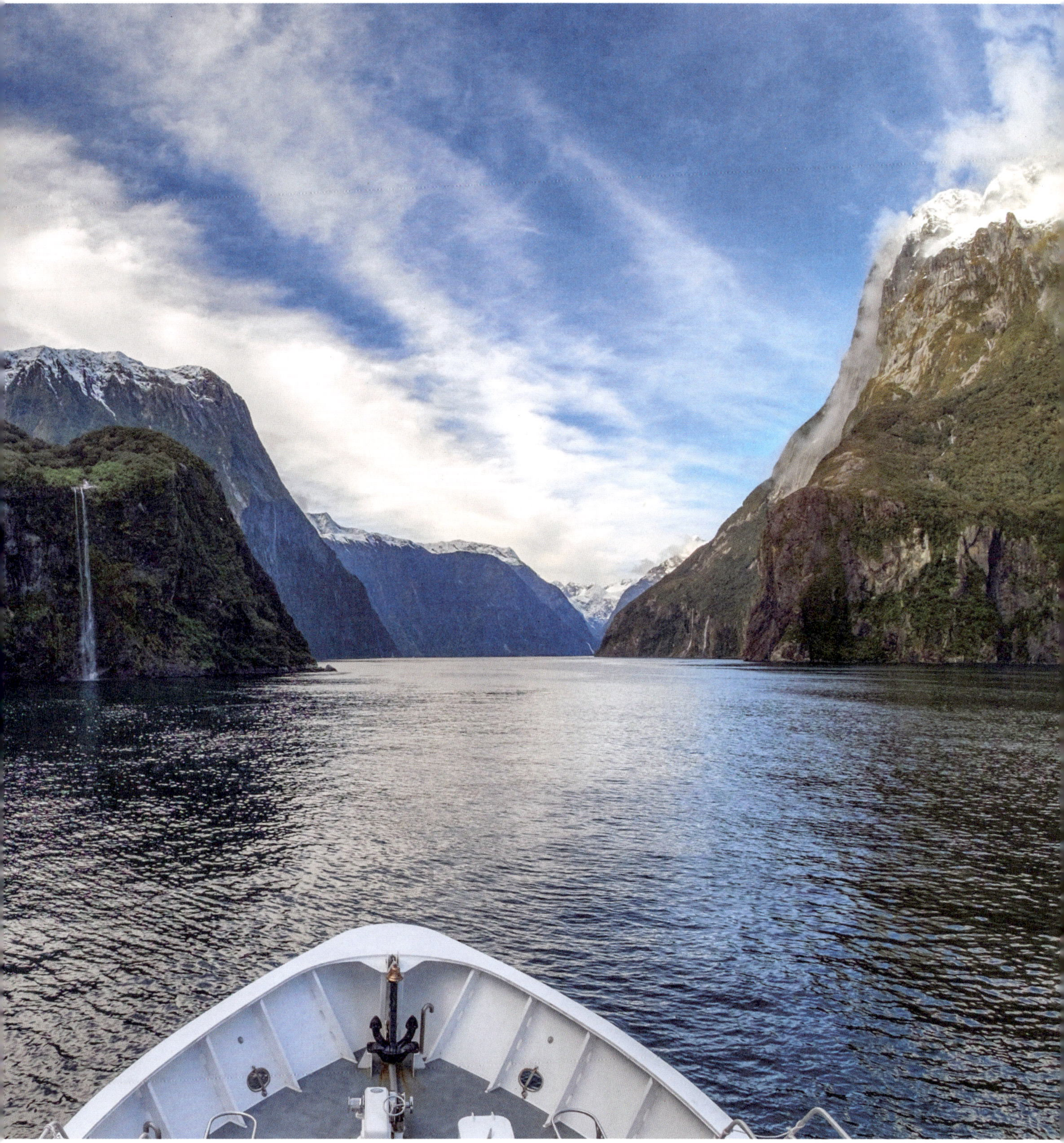

BY WATER
AUSTRALASIA

Above Silky fur seals sunbathing on a rock
Right Mitre Peak looming over Milford Sound at sunset

As the boat glides onwards, misty waterfalls thunder down from the overhanging rock faces, disturbing the glassy surface of the fjord with countless ripples. These majestic cascades are best appreciated during or after rainfall – luckily, it rains here an astounding 182 days of the year. Cruises pause to allow time for passengers to behold the staggeringly high 160-m (530-ft) Lady Bowen Falls and 146-m (480-ft) Stirling Falls – here, the captain might nudge the boat closer for a glacial dunking of brave top-deck volunteers.

Passengers will almost certainly spot fur seals lazily sunbathing on Seal Rock, their bodies looking like velvety commas against the stone, and maybe even curious bottlenose dolphins riding the waves in the wake of the boat. Those who venture through the fjord between July and November might be lucky enough to catch a glimpse of rare Fiordland crested penguins – distinctive thanks to their protruding yellow "eyebrows" – nesting on the rocks. Some cruises even offer the chance to stop at the Milford Sound Discovery Centre: here, there's a chance to disembark and peer into the brackish waters by

THE ROAD TO MILFORD SOUND

Most visitors rush from Te Anau to Milford Sound as quickly as possible. Slow down instead and explore the road to Milford – a World Heritage Highway. Take time to discover the lush lakeside forest, rugged mountains and cascading alpine rivers on some of the hiking trails deep within Fiordland National Park (ask at the visitor centre in Te Anau – they can also advise about overnight accommodation in the area).

descending into a tiny glass-walled observatory. Rare black corals lurk in the gloom, along with flashes of colourful fish and even the occasional shark or seal.

Eventually the boat reaches Anita Bay, the untamed mouth of the fjord – it is here that Māori have traditionally gathered *tangiwai* (bowenite), a rare translucent type of pounamu. From the deck of the ship, passengers will get a glimpse of the shimmering Tasman Sea before the boat loops around, heading back into the sheltered waters of the fjord. While most boats return to the wharf from here, overnight cruises linger amid the sound's superlative scenery. There's time to lounge on deck, or kayak and swim in the cold inky waters, before watching untold stars light up the vast night sky and then hunkering down in a gently rocking bunk. The next day, as morning light transforms these tranquil waters, passengers head back to dry land, to explore more of glorious Fiordland National Park on foot.

LOOK *for green* tangiwai *among the boulders and pebbles around* **Anita Bay**

SPOT *pointy-nosed fur seals basking in the sun on* **Seal Rock**

EXPLORE *under the water at the* **Milford Sound Discovery Centre**

PHOTOGRAPH *the iconic summit of* **Mitre Peak** *at sunset*

FEEL *the spray of mist on your face at* **Lady Bowen Falls**

NEW ZEALAND

Milford Sound Visitor Terminal

BY WATER
AUSTRALASIA

(41)

Whitsunday Islands

LOCATION Australia **START/FINISH** Bowen/Muckay
DISTANCE 250 km (155 miles) **TIME** 1 week
INFORMATION www.tourismwhitsundays.com.au

With the Great Barrier Reef below the water and 74 idyllic islands strung out like tropical pearls above, the Whitsundays rival the Caribbean when it comes to sailing trips.

A typical day's sailing around the archipelago goes something like this: drift with the wind from one island to the next, pause for lunch and a swim, then find a pretty cove in which to drop anchor and sleep. Some of the islands you'll pass – such as Hamilton, South Molle and Lindeman – are home to luxury resorts; others are uninhabited outcrops rising from an azure sea. Between the islands, snorkelling takes you within sight of the astonishingly rich marine life of the Great Barrier Reef. Humpback whales calve here between May and September, sharing the waters with 600 kinds of coral, 1,625 fish species, 30 different whales and dolphins, more than 130 types of sharks and stingrays, six of the world's seven marine turtle species, and even saltwater crocodiles.

In the heart of the Whitsundays is Whitehaven Beach, often described as the most beautiful beach in the world – its perfect sand lapped by turquoise waters and fringed with deep forest greens. But locals all have their own favourite strip of sand – be it Catseye, Bettys, Chalkies or Turtle Bay – and it's entirely up to you to decide on yours.

The spectacular Whitehaven Beach on the west coast of Whitsunday Island

Sailing towards Nuku Hiva, with its lush, steep-sided hills

㊷ Marquesas Islands

LOCATION French Polynesia **START/FINISH** Pape'ete, Tahiti (loop) **DISTANCE** 4,500 km (2,800 miles) **TIME** 2 weeks **INFORMATION** www.aranui.com; includes two full days at sea

Island-hop around the Marquesas on a combined cruise and cargo ship, as it brings essential supplies to the lush, far-flung archipelago.

The Marquesas Islands in the Pacific are truly remote, with their nearest continental landmass – Mexico – a dizzying 4,800 km (3,000 miles) away. This archipelago is most definitely a place to get away from it all, but its glorious isolation also leaves it cut off from trade routes. Twice a month, the *Aranui 5* sails from Tahiti to the Marquesas, carrying vital supplies – and tourists – to these beautiful volcanic isles.

Each of the six stops en route have their own unique charms. The northern islands are characterized by dramatic scenery, with the vertiginous slopes of Nuku Hiva, the windswept plains and wild horses of 'Ua Huka, and the monolithic basalt columns of 'Ua Pou. Further south, you'll find a wealth of cultural treasures in the form of Hiva Oa's moss-covered tiki statues, Tahuata's richly scented *mono'i* oil and Fatu Hiva's traditional *tapa* cloth made from bark. Throughout, a world of underwater wonders thrives offshore, with manta rays and melon-headed whales representing a mere fraction of the archipelago's superb biodiversity.

> This archipelago is most definitely a place to get away from it all

INDEX

A

Abel Tasman Coast Track
(New Zealand) 78
Abu Dhabi 128
Adam's Peak (Sri Lanka) 70-71
Adelaide (Australia) 245, 246, 247, 248
Adirondack (US to Canada) 203
Afghanistan, Pamir Highway 137
Agathonisi (Greece) 274
Agra (India) 138, 230
Akureyri (Iceland) 121
Alaska and Inside Passage
(Canada to US) 254-5
Albanian Alps 42
Alice Springs (Australia) 146, 246, 247
Alice Springs to Darwin
(Australia) 146
Alps 2 Ocean Cycle Trail
(New Zealand) 186-7
Alps, The 37, 39, 122
Amalfi Coast (Italy) 36, 283
Amalfi (Italy) 283
Amazon River, safari riverboat cruise
(Peru) 264-5
Amritsar (India) 138
Amsterdam (Netherlands)
215, 279, 285
Andes 26, 28, 105, 112, 161, 206-7, 264
Angkor Wat (Cambodia) 304
by tuk-tuk 139
Anita Bay (New Zealand) 309
Annapurna II (Nepal) 66
Antarctica 268-71
Anti Atlas (Morocco) 53, 54
Aoraki/Mt Cook (New Zealand) 186
Appalachian Mountains (US)
12-15, 98
Appalachian Trail (US) 12-15
Appenzell Whisky Trek
(Switzerland) 38
Arctic Circle 102, 103, 104, 281
Arequipa (Peru) 207
Argentina
Antarctica cruise 268-71
La Trochita 209
Pan-American Highway 104-7
Route of the Seven Lakes 162
Tren de la Costa 209
Arles (France) 119
Artists, Death Railway 233
Aswan (Egypt) 290, 291
Atacama Desert (Chile) 104, 105
Athabasca River (Canada) 258
Atlantic Forest (Brazil) 210-11
Atlantic Ocean Road (Norway) 119
Atlas Mountains (Morocco)
52-5, 129
Aupouri Peninsula
(New Zealand) 81

Australia
Alice Springs to Darwin 146
Coral Coast 146
Cowaramup to Margaret River 188
The Ghan 244-7
Grand Canyon Track, Blue
Mountains 84
Great Ocean Road 142
Great Southern 248
Heysen Trail 84
Mount Sorrow Ridge Trail 85
MS Sydney to Gong 188
Murray Valley Trail 80
Queensland Coast 143
Tasmanian Trail 82-3
Whitsunday Islands 310
Wild West Coast 191
Australian Alps 80
Austria
The Danube 276-7
Grossglockner High Alpine
Road 122
Trans-Alpine Crossing 37
Avalon Peninsula (Canada) 21
Avenue of the Volcanoes
(Ecuador) 104, 105, 161

B

Badulla (Sri Lanka) 232
Bagan (Myanmar) 234-5
Baikal, Lake (Russia) 242, 243
Bajau people 303
Baltic Sea 43, 124
Baltic Trail (Estonia to Lithuania) 124-5
Bangkok (Thailand) 233
Banjul (The Gambia) 293
Barossa Valley (Australia) 84
Basque Circuit (Spain) 118
Beagle Channel (Chile/Argentina)
107, 112, 267, 269
Beijing (China) 236, 241
Belgium, Flanders 173
Bellamy, Mount
(Papua New Guinea) 85
Belmond Andean Explorer
(Peru) 206-7
Ben Nevis (UK) 116, 165
Bequia 261, 262
Berbers 52-5, 179
Bergen (Norway) 217, 281
Berlin (Germany) 215
Bhutan, Rigsum Gompa Trek 75
Big Sur (US) 92-3
Bilbao (Spain) 118
Biševo (Croatia) 273
Black Sea 277
Bled, Lake (Slovenia) 46-7
Blue Mountains (Australia) 84
Blue Ridge Mountains (US) 13, 98
Blue Ridge Parkway (US) 98
Blue Train, The (South Africa) 220-23
Bodensee to the Königsee
(Germany) 173

Bolivia
Che Trail 110
Death Road 162
Bollenstreek (Netherlands) 170-71
Bologna (Italy) 118, 214, 215
Bon Hon (Vietnam) 300
Bonneville Salt Flats (US) 204
Borneo
Derawan Islands 303
Headhunter's Trail 67
Bornholm (Denmark) 172
Bosnia and Herzegovina, Via Dinarica
(Slovenia to Macedonia) 42
Botswana
Botswana Circuit 178
Nairobi to Cape Town
(Kenya to South Africa) 132-3
Okavango Delta 294-5
Tour d'Afrique
(Egypt to South Africa) 174-7
Zambezi River 297
Bowron Lakes Circuit (Canada) 256
Bratislava (Slovakia) 277
Brazil
Chapada Diamantina Trek 27
Costa Verde 111
Pan-American Highway
(US to Argentina) 105
Serra Verde Express 210-11
Bright Angel Trail (US) 23
Brijuni Islands (Croatia) 164
Brisbane (Australia) 248
Brussels (Belgium) 215
Bryson, Bill 15
Bucharest (Romania) 276
Budapest (Hungary) 276, 277
Buenos Aires (Argentina)
103, 104, 105, 209
Bukhara (Uzbekistan) 137, 241
Burren, the (Ireland) 115
Busan (South Korea) 138, 182

C

Cabot, John 154
Cabot Trail (Canada) 152-3
Cairo (Egypt) 174, 289, 291
Caledonian Canal (UK) 285
California Zephyr (US) 204-5
Camargue (France) 119
Cambodia
Angkor Wat by tuk-tuk 139
The Mekong 304
Camino de Santiago
(Portugal/Spain) 32-3
Canada
Adirondack 203
Alaska and Inside Passage 254-5
Athabasca River 258
Bowron Lakes Circuit 256
Cabot Trail 152-3
Churchill River 259
Coastal Hiking Trail 22
Coast to Coast 196-9

Canada (cont.)
Dempster Highway 103
East Coast Trail 21
Icefields Parkway 100-101
La Route Verte 159
Nahanni River 259
Pan-American Highway
(US to Argentina) 104-7
Rupert Rocket 203
Sea to Sky Highway 102
Trans-Canada Highway 199
Underground Railroad 157
Waterfront Trail 158
West Coast Trail 20
White Pass and Yukon Route 202
Cannes (France) 278
Canouan 263
Cape Breton Island (Canada) 153
Cape Horn (Chile) 269, 270
Cape to Cairo railway 216
Cape Town (South Africa)
132, 174, 223
Cape Tribulation (Australia) 85, 143
Capri (Italy) 283
Caribbean, Island-Hopping in the
Grenadines 260-63
Carpathian Mountains (Romania) 41
Carretera Austral (Chile) 105, 112
Carriacou 263
Cascade Mountains (US) 19, 201
Castles and fortifications
Amber Fort (India) 229
Bran Castle (Romania) 41
Bratislava Castle (Slovakia) 277
Chittorgarh Fort (India) 229, 231
Loire Valley (France) 166
Rhine castles (Germany) 270
Schloss Neuschwanstein
(Germany) 123
Slot Teylingen (Netherlands) 171
Windsor Castle (UK) 284
Cat Ba (Vietnam) 300
Cathedrals
Duomo (Milan) 213
Nidaros Domkirche
(Trondheim) 281
Causeway Coast Way (UK) 50
Caves
Bingling Caves (China) 185
Grotta dello Smeraldo (Italy) 283
Hospital Cave (Vietnam) 300
Mogao Caves (China) 136, 137
Sambay Cave (Peru) 207
Sung Sot Cave (Vietnam) 300
Thieng Cun (Vietnam) 300-301
Ceiba trees 265
Central Highlands (Tasmania) 82, 83
Champlain, Lake (US/Canada) 203
Chapada Diamantina Trek (Brazil) 27
Chefchaouen (Morocco) 179
Chepe Train (Mexico) 208
Che Trail (Bolivia) 110
Chianti region (Italy) 167
Chicago (US) 95, 202, 204

Chile
 Antarctic cruises 271
 O Circuit 24-5
 Pan-American Highway
  (US to Argentina) 104-7
 Patagonian Fjords 267
 Ruta de los Parques 112-13
Chilumba (Malawi) 292
China
 Golden Eagle Train 241
 Huanghuacheng 69
 Karakorum Highway 139
 Li River 302
 Qinghai-Tibet Railway 240
 Silk Road 134-7, 184-5
 Tea Horse Road 183
 Trans-Mongolian Express 236
Choquequirao (Peru) 28
Christchurch (New Zealand) 249
Christie, Agatha 218, 219, 290
Christmas markets (Germany) 123
Churchill (Canada) 259
Cierva Cove (Antarctica) 270-71
Circum-Baikal Railway (Russia) 243
Civil War Battlefields (US) 108
Clark, William 202
Cliffs of Moher (Ireland) 115
Coastal Hiking Trail (Canada) 22
Coast Starlight (US) 93, 201
Coast to Coast (Canada) 196-9
Colombia
 Lost City Trek 30
 Pan-American Highway
  (US to Argentina) 104-7
Colón (Panama) 266
Colorado Trail (US) 18
Columbia Icefield (Canada) 100, 258
Copper Canyon (Mexico) 208
Coral Coast (Australia) 146
Coron (Philippines) 305
Costa Rica
 Nicoya Peninsula 160
 Pan-American Highway
  (US to Argentina) 104-7
Costa Verde (Brazil) 111
Cotopaxi, Volcán (Ecuador) 161
Cotswolds (UK) 117, 284
Cowaramup to Margaret River
 (Australia) 188
Craters of the Moon National
 Monument (US) 97
Croatia
 The Danube
  (Germany to Ukraine) 276-7
 Island Hopping 272-3
 Istrian Coast 166
 Via Dinarica (Slovenia
  to Macedonia) 42
Cua Van (Vietnam) 300, 301
Cuba
 Cuban Drive 109
 Hershey Train 208
 Santiago to Marea del Portillo 163
 Valle de Viñales 163

Củ Chi Tunnels (Vietnam) 140
Cueca (Ecuador) 161
Cusco (Peru) 206

D
—
Dali (China) 183
Danube, The (Germany
 to Ukraine) 276-7
Dar es-Salaam (Tanzania) 225
Darjeeling Himalayan Railway
 (India) 236
Darvaza Gas Crater (Turkmenistan) 241
Darwin (Australia) 146, 245, 246, 247
Dayet Srij, Lac (Morocco) 129
Death Railway (Thailand) 233
Death Road (Bolivia) 162
Dempster Highway (Canada) 103
Denali Highway (US) 157
Denmark, Around Bornholm 172
Derawan Islands (Borneo) 303
Dinaric Alps 42
Dingle Way (Ireland) 50
Dolomites (Italy) 37, 38
Douro Valley (Portugal) 284
Dover (Tasmania) 82
Dracula 41, 169
Drake Passage 269
Dubrovnik (Croatia) 273
Dunedin (New Zealand) 190
Dunhuang (China) 185, 241

E
—
East Coast Trail (Canada) 21
Ecuador
 Avenue of the Volcanoes
  104, 105, 161
 Pan-American Highway
  (US to Argentina) 104-7
 Quilotoa Traverse 26
Egypt
 The Nile 288-91
 Tour d'Afrique 174-7
Eiger Trail, The (Switzerland) 39
El Nido (Philippines) 305
El Salvador, Pan-American Highway
 (US to Argentina) 104-7
Empire Builder (US) 202
England see United Kingdom
Erfoud (Morocco) 129
Esquel (Argentina) 209
Estonia, Baltic Trail 124-5
Ethiopia
 Simien Mountains 56
 Tour d'Afrique
  (Egypt to South Africa) 174-7

F
—
Falkland Islands
 (UK Overseas Territory) 271
Fatu Hiva (French Polynesia) 311
Fès Southwards (Morocco) 129

Fethiye (Turkey) 282
Finland, Finnish Lakeland 286-7
Fjords, Norway's 280-81
Flanders (Belgium) 173
Flinders Ranges (Australia) 84
Florence (Italy) 167, 214
Florida Keys (US) 94
Food and drink
 Appenzell Whisky Trek
  (Switzerland) 38
 Cowaramup to Margaret River
  (Australia) 188
 Douro Valley (Portugal) 284
 Hunter Valley wines (Australia) 248
 Kentucky Bourbon Trail (US) 108
 Korean cuisine 138
 Napa Valley Tour (US) 109
 Route 62 (South Africa) 131
 Route des Grands Crus (France) 167
Forgotten World Highway
 (New Zealand) 147
Fort William (UK) 165, 216
Four Rivers Path (South Korea) 182
France
 Camino de Santiago 35
 French Riviera 278
 Interrailing 212-15
 La Loire à Velo 166
 Provence 119
 The Rhine (Switzerland to
  the Netherlands) 279
 Route des Grands Crus 167
 Venice Simplon-Orient-Express
  (UK to Italy) 218-19
French Polynesia, Marquesas
 Islands 311
Friday Harbor (US) 156
Fuji, Mount (Japan) 73, 238
Funaoriseto Strait (Japan) 181
Füssen (Germany) 123

G
—
Gaborone (Botswana) 178
Gaelic 168
Galway (Ireland) 115
Gambia, The, River Gambia 293
Ganges, The (India) 305
Garden Route (South Africa) 130
Gatún, Lago de (Panama) 266
Geirangerfjord (Norway) 281
Germany
 Bodensee to the Königsee 173
 The Danube (Germany
  to Ukraine) 276-7
 Rennsteig Trail 39
 The Rhine (Switzerland to
  the Netherlands) 279
 Romantic Road 123
 Trans-Alpine Crossing 37
Geysir Geothermal Area (Iceland) 121
Ghan, The (Australia) 244-7
Ghost Lake (New Zealand) 189
Giant's Causeway (Northern Ireland) 50

Glacier Express (Switzerland) 216
Glacier Grey (Chile) 25
Glencoe (UK) 116
Gobi Desert 184, 185, 236, 241
Gold Coast (Australia) 143
Golden Circle loop (Iceland) 121
Golden Eagle Train (China/Russia) 241
Gorilla trekking (Rwanda) 58-9
Gouda (Netherlands) 285
Grand Canyon Track, Blue Mountains
 (Australia) 84
Grand Canyon (US) 23
Grand Trunk Road (India) 138
Great Australian Bight 80, 245
Great Barrier Reef (Australia) 143, 310
Great Glen Canoe Trail (UK) 285
Great Karoo (South Africa) 222
Great Ocean Road (Australia) 142
Great Plains (US) 97, 204
"Great Rides" (New Zealand) 190
Great Rift Valley 176, 177
Great Salt Lake (US) 204
Great Smoky Mountains (US) 13, 97
Great Southern (Australia) 248
Great Walks (New Zealand) 76, 78, 189
Great Wall (China) 69, 184, 185, 236
Greece, Yachting around the Greek
 Islands 274
Grenada 260, 263
Grenadines, Island-Hopping
 (St Vincent to Grenada) 260-63
Greylock, Mount (US) 15
Greymouth (New Zealand) 249
Grossglockner High Alpine Road
 (Austria) 122
Guatemala
 Pan-American Highway
  (US to Argentina) 104-7
 La Ruta de Maya 26
Guevara, Ernesto "Che" 110
Guilin (China) 302
Gulf of Gocek (Turkey) 282
Gullets, Turkish 282
Guyana, Kaieteur Falls Trek 27

H
—
Hadrian's Wall Path (UK) 48
Hai Van Pass (Vietnam) 140, 141
Half Dome (US) 22
Halifax (Canada) 197, 198
Hallskär (Sweden) 275
Ha Long Bay (Vietnam) 298-301
Hana Highway (US) 99
Hanoi (Vietnam) 140, 237
Harry Potter films 216
Havana (Cuba) 109
Hawaii (US)
 Hana Highway 99
 Kalalau Trail 19
Headhunter's Trail (Borneo) 67
Heaphy Track (New Zealand) 78, 189
Hebridean Way (UK) 168
Hershey Train (Cuba) 208

Heysen Trail (Australia) 84
High Atlas (Morocco) 53, 55
High Coast Trail (Sweden) 43
Hill Country Railway (Sri Lanka) 232
Himalayas 66, 139, 183, 236, 238
Hindu Kush 139
Hiva Oa (French Polynesia) 311
Ho Chi Minh City (Vietnam) 140, 237, 304
Holland's Canals (Netherlands) 285
Honduras, Pan-American Highway (US to Argentina) 104-7
Hong Kong, MacLehose Trail 68
Hook of Holland (Netherlands) 279
Horseshoe Reef (Tobago Cays) 262
Huanghuacheng (China) 69
Hudson River Valley (US) 203
Hungary, The Danube (Germany to Ukraine) 276-7
Hunter Valley (Australia) 248
Huron, Lake (Canada/US) 158
Húsavik (Iceland) 121
Hvar (Croatia) 272, 273
Hyères (France) 278

I

Icefields Parkway (Canada) 100-101
Iceland
   Golden Circle loop 121
   Iceland's Ring Road 120-21
   Laugavegur Trail 51
Ilala Ferry (Malawi) 292
Île aux Aigrettes (Mauritius) 296
Îles de Lérin (France) 278
Il Sentiero degli Dei (Italy) 36
Imet Gogo (Ethiopia) 56
Inca civilization 28
India
   Darjeeling Himalayan Railway 236
   The Ganges 305
   Grand Trunk Road 138
   Maharajas Express 229
   The Palace on Wheels 228-31
   Shimla Toy Train 237
Inside Passage (US/Canada) 254-5
Interrailing (France to Italy) 212-15
Inverness (UK) 116
Iquitos (Peru) 264
Iran, Silk Road (Italy to China) 134-7
Ireland
   Dingle Way 50
   Wild Atlantic Way 114-15
Isfahan (Iran) 135, 137
Island-hopping
   in Croatia 272-3
   in the Greek Islands 274
   in the Grenadines (St Vincent to Grenada) 260-63
Issyk Kul (Kyrgyzstan) 74
Istanbul (Turkey) 137
Istrian Coast (Italy to Croatia) 166

Italy
   Amalfi Coast 283
   Il Sentiero degli Dei 36
   Interrailing 212-15
   Istrian Coast 166
   Silk Road 134-7
   Trans-Alpine Crossing 37
   Tre Cime di Lavaredo 38
   Tuscany 167
   Via Emilia 118

J

Jacobite Steam Train (UK) 216
Jaipur (India) 229
Jaisalmer (India) 228, 229
Japan
   Kumano Kodo 72
   Michinoku Coastal Trail 72
   Mount Fuji 73
   Shikoku Henro 73
   Shimanami Kaido 180-81
   Tokyo to Nagoya Shinkansen 238-9
Jasper (Canada) 198, 203
Jebel Hafeet (UAE) 128
Jenny Lake Trail (US) 23
Jodhpur (India) 230
John Muir Trail (US) 17
John O'Groats (UK) 164-5
Jordan Trail 62-3
Julian Alps (Slovenia) 42
   Peak Walk 46-7

K

Kahurangi (New Zealand) 189
Kaieteur Falls Trek (Guyana) 27
Kalahari Desert 178, 220, 295
Kalalau Trail (Hawaii) 19
Kamfers Dam (South Africa) 222, 223
Kamloops (Canada) 198
Kanchanaburi (Thailand) 233
Kanchenjunga, Mount (India) 236
Kandy (Sri Lanka) 232
Karakorum Highway (Pakistan to China) 139
Kariba, Lake 297
Karlu Karlu (Australia) 146
Katahdin, Mount (US) 13, 15
Kayan warriors 67
Kentucky Bourbon Trail (US) 108
Kenya
   Nairobi to Cape Town 132-3
   Tour d'Afrique (Egypt to South Africa) 174-7
Keukenhof (Netherlands) 171
Key Largo (US) 94
Khabarovsk (Russia) 243
Khiva (Uzbekistan) 241
Khwae Yai River (Thailand) 233
Kilarney (Ireland) 115
Kilimanjaro, Mount (Tanzania) 60, 132, 133
Kimberley (South Africa) 222

Kinsale (Ireland) 115
Klondike Gold Rush 103, 202, 255
Kokoda Trail (Papua New Guinea) 85
Komati Islands (Croatia) 273
Königsee (Germany) 173
Korčula (Croatia) 273
Kratie (Cambodia) 304
Kumano Kodo (Japan) 72
Kungsleden Trail (Sweden) 43
Kurushima Strait (Japan) 181
Kyrgyzstan
   Pamir Highway 137
   South Shore Panorama Trail 74

L

La Higuera (Bolivia) 110
Lake District (UK) 165
Lalibela (Ethiopia) 176
Land's End to John O'Groats (UK) 164-5
La Paz (Bolivia) 162
Larkya La Pass (Nepal) 66
La Route Verte (Canada) 159
La Ruta de Maya (Guatemala) 26
La Trochita (Argentina) 209
Latvia, Baltic Trail (Estonia to Lithuania) 124-5
Laugavegur Trail (Iceland) 51
legends
   Greek 274
   Nāpali 19
   Tis-sa-ack 22
Leigh Fermor, Patrick 279
Le Morne mountain (Mauritius) 296
Lewis, Meriwether 202
Lézard Rouge (Tunisia) 226-7
Lhasa (Tibet) 240
Linz (Austria) 277
Lipsi (Greece) 274
Li River (China) 302
Lisse (Netherlands) 171
Lithuania, Baltic Trail 124-5
Liunnansaari Croft (Finland) 286
Loch Ard Gorge (Australia) 140
Lochy, Loch (UK) 285
Lofoten Archipelago (Norway) 280
Loire River (France) 166
London, Jack 103
London (UK) 218, 284
Los Angeles (US) 91, 95, 103, 200, 201
Lost City Trek (Colombia) 30
Luxor (Egypt) 176, 290-91
Lycian Way (Turkey) 42
Lyell (New Zealand) 189
Lyon (France) 213

M

Macedonia, Via Dinarica 42
Machu Picchu (Peru) 28-9
Mackinnon Pass (New Zealand) 79, 306
MacLehose, Murray 68
MacLehose Trail (Hong Kong) 68
Mae Hong Son (Thailand) 68

Mafate (Réunion) 61
Maharajas Express (India) 229
Malawi
   The Ilala Ferry 292
   Tour d'Afrique (Egypt to South Africa) 174-7
Malawi, Lake 292
Malin Head (Ireland) 115
Malma Kvarn (Sweden) 275
Manaslu Circuit (Nepal) 66
Mandalay (Myanmar) 235
Maps
   by bike 150-51
   by rail 194-5
   by road 88-9
   by water 252-3
   on foot 10-11
Marea del Portillo (Cuba) 163
Margaret River (Australia) 188
Marla (Australia) 246, 247
Marmaris (Turkey) 282
Marquesas Islands (French Polynesia) 311
Matterhorn (Switzerland/Italy) 216
Maui (Hawaii, US) 99
Mauritius 296
Maya civilization 26
McKinley Bar Trail (US) 18
Mekong, The (Cambodia to Vietnam) 304
Melbourne (Australia) 248
Merzouga (Morocco) 129
Metlaoui (Tunisia) 227
Mexico
   Chepe Train 208
   Pan-American Highway (US to Argentina) 104-7
Mexico City 103, 104
Michinoku Coastal Trail (Japan) 72
Middle Atlas (Morocco) 53, 54
Mikkelsen Harbour (Antarctica) 270
Milan (Italy) 213, 215
Milford Sound (New Zealand) 77, 79, 306-9
Milford Track (New Zealand) 76-9
Missions, California's Spanish 93, 109
Mississippi River (US) 257
Mitre Peak (New Zealand) 308, 309
Mljet (Croatia) 273
Modena (Italy) 118
Mogotes 163
Mojave Desert 19, 95
Mokihinui Valley (New Zealand) 189
Molde (Norway) 281
Monaco 278
Monasteries
   Dechen Phodrang (Bhutan) 75
   Mu Gompa (Nepal) 66
Mongolia, Trans-Mongolian Express 236
Monkey Bay (Malawi) 292
Monte Carlo (Monaco) 278
Montenegro, Via Dinarica (Slovenia to Macedonia) 42

Monterrey Peninsula (US) 93
Montréal (Canada) 158, 197, 203
Morocco
   Atlas Mountains 52–5
   Fès Southwards 129
   Rif Mountains 179
Morretes (Brazil) 211
Moscow (Russia) 241, 243
Mossel Bay (South Africa) 130
Motorbikes
   TransAmerica Trail (US) 96–7
   in Vietnam 140–41
Mount Sorrow Ridge Trail (Australia) 85
Mozambique, Zambezi River 297
MS Sydney to Gong (Australia) 188
Muir, John 17
Murray Valley Trail (Australia) 80
Museums and galleries
   Galleria dell'Accademia
      (Florence, Italy) 214
   Grand Egyptian Museum (Cairo) 290
   Hirayama Ikuo Museum of Art
      (Japan) 181
   Kimberley Open Mine
      Museum (The Big Hole)
      (South Africa) 222–3
   Museum of Railway Technology
      (Novosibirsk, Russia) 243
   Pinacoteca di Brera
      (Milan, Italy) 213
Mustique 261, 263
Myanmar
   Thailand-Burma Railway 233
   Yangon to Bagan 234–5
Mykonos (Greece) 274

N

Nabatean civilization 63
Nagoya (Japan) 238
Nahanni River (Canada) 259
Nairobi to Cape Town
   (Kenya to South Africa) 132–3
Namaqualand Flower Route (N7)
   (South Africa) 131
Namibia
   Nairobi to Cape Town
      (Kenya to South Africa) 132–3
   Skeleton Coast 126–7
   Tour d'Afrique (Egypt
      to South Africa) 174–7
   Zambezi River 297
Nam Tok (Thailand) 233
Napa Valley Tour (US) 109
Napa Valley Vine Trail 109
Narrows, The (US) 16
Nashville (US) 156
Natchez Trace Parkway (US) 156
National parks
   Amboseli (Kenya) 132, 176, 177
   Aukstaitija (Lithuania) 124, 125
   Banff (Canada) 100
   Cape Breton Highlands
      (Canada) 155

National parks (cont.)
   Chapada Diamantina (Brazil) 27
   Cotopaxi (Ecuador) 161
   Denali (US) 18, 157
   Dorob (Namibia) 127
   Fiordland (New Zealand)
      77, 308, 309
   Glacier Bay (US) 254, 255
   Grand Teton (US) 23
   Gunung Mulu (Borneo) 67
   Gyeryongsan (South Korea) 138
   Hoang Lien (Vietnam) 69
   Hohe Tauern (Austria) 122
   Hwange (Zimbabwe) 224
   Ifrane (Morocco) 54, 55
   Jasper (Canada) 100, 198, 258
   Karoo (South Africa) 223
   Kiang West (The Gambia) 293
   Klondike Gold Rush (US) 255
   Kruger (South Africa) 132, 223
   Linnansaari (Finland) 286
   Lower Zambezi (Zambia) 65
   Mana Pools (Zimbabwe) 297
   Mljet (Croatia) 273
   Nambung (Australia) 146
   North Luangwa (Zambia) 65
   Phong Nha Khe Bang (Vietnam) 140
   Piatra Craiului (Romania) 41
   Þingvellir (Iceland) 121
   Pukaskwa (Canada) 22
   Queulat (Chile) 112
   Ranthambore (India) 229, 230
   Richtersveld (South Africa) 131
   Royal (Australia) 188
   Serengeti (Tanzania) 130, 132
   Setonaikai (Japan) 181
   Simien Mountains (Ethiopia) 56
   Skeleton Coast (Namibia) 127
   Skuleskogen (Sweden) 43
   South Luangwa (Zambia) 64–5
   Sutjeska (Bosnia and
      Herzegovina) 42
   Tarangire (Tanzania) 124
   Torres del Paine (Chile) 25, 112
   Triglav (Slovenia) 46–7
   Tsitsikamma (South Africa) 130
   Valle de Viñales (Cuba) 163
   Volcanoes (Rwanda) 58, 59
   West Coast (South Africa) 131
   Yosemite (US) 17, 22
   Zuid-Kemmerland
      (Netherlands) 170
Nature reserves
   Amazon Natural Park (Peru) 265
   Amsterdamse Waterleinduinen
      (Netherlands) 171
   Bao Bolong Wetland Reserve
      (The Gambia) 293
   Bharatpur Bird Sanctuary
      (India) 230
   Misty Fjords National Monument
      Wilderness (US) 255
   Point Lobos State Natural
      Reserve (US) 93

Nature reserves (cont.)
   Þórsmörk nature reserve
      (Iceland) 51
   Riserva Nacional Pacaya-Samiri
      (Peru) 264
   Selous Game Reserve
      (Tanzania) 225
   Skilpad Wildflower Reserve
      (South Africa) 131
Navoi (Uzbekistan) 136–7
Nazca Lines (Peru) 102
Nepal, Manaslu Circuit 66
Ness, Loch (UK) 285
Netherlands
   Bollenstreek 170–71
   Holland's Canals 285
   The Rhine 279
New Delhi (India) 228, 229, 231
New Orleans (US) 200, 257
New York City (US) 203
New Zealand
   Alps 2 Ocean Cycle Trail 186–7
   Forgotten World Highway 147
   Great Walks 78
   Heaphy Track 189
   Milford Sound 306–9
   Milford Track 76–9
   Old Ghost Road 189
   Otago Central Rail Trail 190
   Te Araroa - The Long Pathway 81
   TranzAlpine 249
   West Coast Drive 147
Nicaragua, Pan-American Highway
   (US to Argentina) 104–7
Nice (France) 278
Nicoya Peninsula (Costa Rica) 160
Nikhata Bay (Malawi) 292
Nile Valley (Egypt) 174, 176
Nile cruise 288–91
Nitmiluk Gorge (Australia) 146, 246, 247
Northern Ireland *see* United Kingdom
Northern Lights 44, 104
North Kaibab Trail (US) 23
North-South Railway (Vietnam) 237
Norway
   Atlantic Ocean Road 119
   Fjords 280–81
   Oslo to Bergen 217
   Trollsteinen 44
   Trollstigen 172
Novosibirsk (Russia) 243
Nuku Hiva (French Polynesia) 311

O

Oahu, Lake (New Zealand) 186, 187
O Circuit (Chile) 24–5
Okavango Delta (Botswana) 294–5
Old Ghost Road (New Zealand) 189
Ontario, Lake 158
Oravi (Finland) 286
Orderville Canyon (US) 16
Orient Express *see* Venice Simplon-
   Orient-Express

Oslo to Bergen (Norway) 217
Otago Central Rail Trail
   (New Zealand) 190
Outer Hebrides (UK) 168
Overseas Highway (US) 94
Owen Stanley Range
   (Papua New Guinea) 85
Oxford (UK) 284

P

Paarl winelands (South Africa) 223
Pacific Coast Highway (US) 90–93
Pacific Crest Trail (US) 19
Paine Massif (Chile) 25
Pakistan, Karakorum Highway 139
Palace on Wheels, The (India) 228–31
Palawan Archipelago (Philippines) 305
Pamir Highway 137
Pamplona (Spain) 118
Panama
   Panama Canal 102, 266
   Pan-American Highway
      (US to Argentina) 104–7
Panama City (Panama) 266
Pan-American Highway
   (US to Argentina) 104–7
Paparoa Track (New Zealand) 78
Papua New Guinea, Kokoda Trail 85
Paraty (Brazil) 111
Paris (France) 213, 215
Parma (Italy) 118
Patagonia (Argentina/Chile)
   24–5, 103, 104, 112, 162
Patagonian Fjords (Chile) 267
Pennine Way (UK) 48
Perth (UK) 116
Peru
   The Amazon 264–5
   Belmond Andean Explorer 206–7
   Pan-American Highway
      (US to Argentina) 104–7
   Salkantay Trek 28–9
Petit Saint Vincent 263
Petit Tabac (Tobago Cays) 262
Petra (Jordan) 62–3
Philippines, Palawan Archipelago 305
Phnom Penh (Cambodia) 304
Pilgrimages
   Adam's Peak (Sri Lanka) 70–71
   Camino de Santiago
      (Portugal/Spain) 32–5
   Kokoda Trail (Papua
      New Guinea) 85
   Kumano Kodo (Japan) 72
   Shikoku Henro (Japan) 73
Poland, Tatra Mountains 40
Poolburn Gorge (New Zealand) 190
Port Lockroy (Antarctica) 270, 271
Port Louis (Mauritius) 296
Porto (Portugal) 33, 284
Portugal
   Camino de Santiago 32–5
   Douro Valley 284

Pretoria (South Africa) 220, 223
Prince Rupert (Canada) 203
Provence (France) 119
Provincial parks
   Bowron Lake (Canada) 256
   Porteau Cove (Canada) 102
   Quetico (Canada) 258
Ptolemy 57
Pueblos Blancos drive (Spain) 119
Puerto Miguel (Peru) 265
Puerto Montt (Chile) 112
Puerto Williams (Chile) 112, 267
Pula (Croatia) 166
Punta Arenas (Chile) 112, 267
Pyramids of Giza (Egypt) 289, 291
Pyramids of Meroe (Sudan) 176

Q

Qinghai-Tibet Railway (China) 240
Queensland Coast (Australia) 143
Quilotoa Traverse (Ecuador) 26

R

Rainbow eucalyptus 99
Rajasthan (India) 228–31
Ras Dashen (Ethiopia) 56
Ratnapura (Sri Lanka) 71
Ravenna (Italy) 118
Red Sea 63
Regensburg (Germany) 277
Reykjavik (Iceland) 121
Rennsteig Trail (Germany) 39
Reunification Express (Vietnam) 237
Réunion, Tour des Cirques 61
Rhine Gorge 216
Rhine, The (Switzerland to
   the Netherlands) 279
Rif Mountains (Morocco) 179
Riga (Latvia) 124, 125
Rinpoche, Guru 75
Rio de Janeiro (Brazil) 111
Rishikesh (India) 305
Rob Roy Way (UK) 45
Rocky Mountains (Canada/US)
   18, 100–101, 198, 204, 258
Romania
   Carpathian Mountains 41
   The Danube (Germany
      to Ukraine) 276–7
   Transylvania 169
Romantic Road (Germany) 123
Rome (Italy) 214
Rothenburg (Germany) 123
Route 62 (South Africa) 131
Route 66 (US) 95
Route des Grands Crus (France) 167
Route of the Seven Lakes
   (Argentina) 162
Rovinj (Croatia) 166
Rovos Rail (South Africa
   to Zimbabwe) 224
Rupert Rocket (Canada) 203

Russia
   Golden Eagle Train 241
   Trans-Mongolian Express 236
   Trans-Siberian railway 242–3
Ruta de los Parques (Chile) 112–13
Rwanda, gorilla trekking 58–9
Rwenzori Mountains (Uganda) 57

S

Safaris
   Amazon (Peru) 264–5
   safety 65
   Zambia 64–5
Saguenay Fjord (Canada) 159
Sahara Desert 174, 227
Saimaa, Lake (Finland) 286
Saint Vincent 260, 261
Salamanca (Spain) 284
Salkantay Trek (Peru) 28–9
Samarkand (Uzbekistan) 135, 137, 241
Samos (Greece) 274
San Antonio (US) 200
Sandhamn (Sweden) 275
San Francisco (US) 93, 201, 204
San Juan Islands Scenic Byway
   (US) 156
San Juan Mountains (US) 18
San Sebastian (Spain) 118
Santa Clara (Cuba) 109
Santiago (Chile) 103, 105
Santiago de Compostela (Spain) 32–5
Santiago de Cuba 109, 163
Santiago to Marea del Portillo
   (Cuba) 163
Santos (Brazil) 111
Sa Pa (Vietnam) 69
Scotland see United Kingdom
Sea to Sky Highway (Canada) 102
Seattle (US) 201, 202
Selja Gorge (Tunisia) 226, 227
Seoul (South Korea) 132, 182
Seoul to Busan (South Korea) 138
Serengeti (Tanzania) 130, 132
Serra Verde Express (Brazil) 210–11
Seto Inland Sea (Japan) 180, 181
Seward (US) 255
Shackleton Crossing, The
   (South Georgia) 31
Shackleton, Sir Ernest 31, 270
Shangri-la (China) 183
Shikoku Henro (Japan) 73
Shimanami Kaido (Japan) 180–81
Shimla Toy Train (India) 237
Siberia (Russia) 242–3
Siem Reap (Cambodia) 304
Sierra Madre (Mexico) 208
Sierra Nevada (US) 17, 19, 204
Silk Road
   cycle route (China) 184–5
   Golden Eagle Luxury Train
      (China/Russia) 241
   Italy to China by road 134–7, 139
Simien Mountains (Ethiopia) 56

Sitka (US) 255
Skagway (US) 255
Skeleton Coast (Namibia) 126–7
Slavery 157
Slovakia
   The Danube (Germany
      to Ukraine) 276–7
   Tatra Mountains 40
Slovenia
   Istrian Coast (Italy to Croatia) 166
   Julian Alps Peak Walk 46–7
   Via Dinarica 42
Sonoran Desert (US) 200
Sorrow, Mount (Australia) 85
South Africa
   The Blue Train 220–23
   Garden Route 130
   N7 Namaqualand
      Flower Route 131
   Nairobi to Cape Town 132–3
   Route 62 131
   Rovos Rail 224
   Tour d'Afrique 174–7
South Georgia
   Antarctic cruises 271
   Shackleton Crossing 31
South Korea
   Four Rivers Path 182
   Seoul to Busan 138
South Shetland Islands
   (Antarctica) 269, 270
South Shore Panorama Trail
   (Kyrgyzstan) 74
South Sudan, Tour d'Afrique
   (Egypt to South Africa) 177
Spain
   Basque Circuit 118
   Camino de Santiago 32–5
   Pueblos Blancos drive 119
   Rio Douro 284
Split (Croatia) 272, 273
Sri Lanka
   Adam's Peak 70–71
   Hill Country Railway 232
Stanley, Mount (Uganda) 57
Stanley (Tasmania) 191
Star Wars films 227
State parks
   Custer (US) 97
   Harriman (US) 14
   Lime Kiln Point (US) 156
Stirling (UK) 116
St James 34
St John's (Canada) 199
St Lawrence River 158, 159
St Louis (US) 257
St Moritz (Switzerland) 216
Stockholm Archipelago (Sweden) 275
St Paul (US) 257
Strahan (Tasmania) 191
Strait of Magellan (Chile) 103, 112
Strasbourg (France) 279
Stratford upon Avon (UK) 117
St Tropez (France) 278

Stung Treng (Cambodia) 304
Sudan, Tour d'Afrique
   (Egypt to South Africa) 174–7
Sunset Limited (US) 200
Superior, Lake (Canada/US) 22
Svalbard (Norway) 44
Sweden
   High Coast Trail 43
   Kungsleden Trail 43
   Stockholm Archipelago 275
Switzerland
   Appenzell Whisky Trek 38
   The Eiger Trail 39
   Glacier Express 216
   The Rhine 279
   Venice Simplon-Orient-Express
      (UK to Italy) 218–19
Sydney (Australia) 188

T

Table Mountain (South Africa) 176
Tahiti (French Polynesia) 311
Tahuata (French Polynesia) 311
Taieri Gorge Railway (New Zealand) 190
Tajikistan, Pamir Highway 137
Taj Mahal (India) 138, 230, 231
Taklamakan Desert 185
Tallinn (Estonia) 124, 125
Tanganyika, Lake (Zambia) 132
Tanjung Batu (Borneo) 303
Tanzania
   Mount Kilimanjaro 60
   Nairobi to Cape Town
      (Kenya to South Africa) 124–5
   The Serengeti 130
   TAZARA Railway 225
   Tour d'Afrique (Egypt to
      South Africa) 174–7
Taquile Islands (Peru) 207
Taroudant (Morocco) 54, 55
Tasmania (Australia) 191
Tasmanian Trail 82–3
Tasman Sea 189, 309
Tatooine 227
Tatra Mountains (Poland to Slovakia) 40
TAZARA Railway (Tanzania to
   Zambia) 225
Tea Horse Road (China) 183
Te Anau (New Zealand)
   77, 308, 309
Te Araroa - The Long Pathway
   (New Zealand) 81
Temples
   Abu Simbel (Egypt) 290
   Abydos (Egypt) 290
   Angkor Wat (Cambodia) 139, 304
   Bagan (Myanmar) 234–5
   Dendera (Egypt) 290
   Golden Temple (Amritsar) 138
   Karnak (Egypt) 291
   Luxor (Egypt) 290
   Philae (Egypt) 291
   Rigsum Gompa (Bhutan) 75

Teotihuacán (Mexico) 102
Terracotta Warriors (China) 137, 185
Tetouan (Morocco) 179
Teyuna (Colombia) 30
Thailand
    Death Railway 233
    Mae Hong Son 68
Thames River (UK) 284
Tibet, Qinghai-Tibet Railway 240
Tierra del Fuego (Argentina/Chile) 103, 104, 112, 269
Tikal (Guatemala) 26
Timor Sea 245
Titicaca, Lake (Peru) 206, 207
Tizi-n-Test pass (Morocco) 55
Tobago Cays 262
Tokyo to Nagoya Shinkansen (Japan) 238–9
Tongariro Alpine Crossing (New Zealand) 81
Tonlé Sap (Cambodia) 304
Toronto (Canada) 197, 198, 199
Toubkal, Mount (Morocco) 55
Tour d'Afrique (Egypt to South Africa) 174–7
Tour des Cirques (Réunion) 61
Trans-Alpine Crossing (Germany to Italy) 37
TransAmerica Trail (US) 96–7
Trans-Canada Highway 199
Trans-Mongolian Express (Russia to China) 236
Trans-Siberian Railway (Russia) 236, 242–3
Transylvania (Romania) 169
TranzAlpine (New Zealand) 249
Tre Cime di Lavaredo (Italy) 38
Tren de la Costa (Argentina) 209
Trieste (Italy) 166
Trollsteinen (Norway) 44
Trollstigen (Norway) 172
Tromsø (Norway) 281
Trondheim (Norway) 281
Tsum Valley (Nepal) 66
Tunisia, Lézard Rouge 226–7
Turkey
    Lycian Way 42
    Turkish Coast 282
Turkmenistan, Golden Eagle Luxury Train (China/Russia) 241
Tuscany (Italy) 167
Twain, Mark 236, 257, 296
Twelve Apostles (Australia) 140
Two Moors Way (UK) 51

U

UAE, Jebel Hafeet 128
'Ua Hukas (French Polynesia) 311
'Ua Pous (French Polynesia) 311
Udaipur (India) 229
Ugab River Trail (Namibia) 127
Uganda
    Rwenzori Mountains 57
    Tour d' Afrique (Egypt to South Africa) 177
Ukraine, The Danube 276–7
Ulaanbaatar (Mongolia) 236
Ulan Ude (Russia) 236, 243
Ulug Beg, Emperor 136
Um Qais (Jordan) 63
Underground Railroad (US/Canada) 157
Union Island 262–3
United Kingdom
    Causeway Coast Way 50
    Cotswolds 117
    Great Glen Canoe Trail 285
    Hadrian's Wall Path 48
    Hebridean Way 168
    Jacobite Steam Train 216
    Land's End to John O'Groats 164–5
    Pennine Way 48
    Rob Roy Way 45
    Scottish Highlands 116
    Thames River 284
    Two Moors Way 51
    Wales Coast Path 49
    West Highland Way 45
United States
    Adirondack 203
    Alaska and Inside Passage 254–5
    Appalachian Trail 12–15
    Blue Ridge Parkway 98
    Bright Angel Trail 23
    California Zephyr 204–5
    Civil War Battlefields 108
    Coast Starlight 93, 201
    Colorado Trail 18
    Denali Highway 157
    Empire Builder 202
    Half Dome 22
    Hana Highway 99
    Jenny Lake Trail 23
    John Muir Trail 17
    Kalalau Trail 19
    Kentucky Bourbon Trail 108
    McKinley Bar Trail 18
    Mississippi River 257
    Napa Valley Tour 109
    Napa Valley Vine Trail 109
    The Narrows 16
    Natchez Trace Parkway 156
    North Kaibab Trail 23
    Overseas Highway 94
    Pacific Coast Highway 90–3
    Pacific Crest Trail 19
    Pan-American Highway 104–7
    Route 66 95
    San Juan Islands Scenic Byway 156
    Sunset Limited 200
    TransAmerica Trail 96–7
    Underground Railroad 157
Uros Islands (Peru) 207
Uruguay, Pan-American Highway (US to Argentina) 105
Ushuaia (Argentina) 107, 269, 270, 271
Utrecht (Netherlands) 285
Uzbekistan
    Golden Eagle Luxury Train (China/Russia) 241
    Pamir Highway 137
    Silk Road (Italy to China) 134–7

V

Valle de Viñales (Cuba) 163
Valley of the Kings (Egypt) 290
Vancouver (Canada) 102, 156, 197, 255
Vancouver Island (Canada) 20
Vaxholm (Sweden) 275
Venice (Italy) 135, 136, 219
Venice Simplon-Orient-Express (UK to Italy) 218–19
Via Dinarica (Slovenia to Macedonia) 42
Via Emilia (Italy) 118
Vicksburg (US) 257
Victoria (Canada) 199
Vienna (Austria) 277
Vietnam
    Ha Long Bay 298–301
    The Mekong 304
    motorcycling in 140–41
    Reunification Express 237
    Sa Pa 69
Vila Nova de Gaia (Portugal) 284
Villány (Hungary) 277
Vilnius (Lithuania) 124, 125
Vintgar Gorge (Slovenia) 47
Virunga Mountains (Rwanda) 59
Vis (Croatia) 273
Vladivostok (Russia) 242
Volgograd (Russia) 241
Vukovar (Croatia) 277

W

Wadi Rum (Jordan) 63
Wakhan Corridor (Afghanistan) 137
Wales Coast Path (UK) 49
Warsaw (Poland) 215
Waterfalls
    De Syv Søstrene (Norway) 281
    Dettifoss (Iceland) 120
    Gullfoss (Iceland) 121
    Kaieteur Falls Trek (Guyana) 27
    Lady Bowen Falls (New Zealand) 308, 309
    Mackay Falls (New Zealand) 79
    Niagara Falls (Canada/US) 158
    Savica Waterfall (Slovenia) 47
    Stirling Falls (New Zealand) 308
    Sutherland Falls (New Zealand) 78
    Upper Waikani Falls (US) 99
    Victoria Falls (Zambia/Zimbabwe) 176, 224, 297
    Virginia Falls (Canada) 259
Waterfront Trail (Canada) 158
West Coast Drive (New Zealand) 147
West Coast Trail (Canada) 20
West Highland Way (UK) 45
Whistler (Canada) 102
White Mountains (US) 15
White Pass and Yukon Route (Canada) 202
Whitney, Mount (US) 17
Whitsunday Islands (Australia) 310
Wild Atlantic Way (Ireland) 114–15
Wildlife
    Amazon safari riverboat cruise (Peru) 264–5
    Atlantic Forest (Brazil) 211
    birds on the Old Ghost Road (New Zealand) 189
    cassowaries (Australia) 85
    Fungie the Dolphin (Ireland) 50
    gorilla trekking (Rwanda) 58–9
    Okavango Delta *mokoro* safaris (Botswana) 294–5
    Palawan Archipelago coral reefs (Philippines) 305
    Serengeti (Tanzania) 130
    Zambian safari 64–5
Wild West Coast (Australia) 191
Winnipeg (Canada) 259
Wollongong (Australia) 188
World War I 173
World War II 233
Würzburg (Germany) 123

X

Xi'an (China) 135, 137, 185
Xining (China) 240

Y

Yachting around the Greek Islands 274
Yanayaquillo (Peru) 265
Yangon to Bagan (Myanmar) 234–5
Yangshuo (China) 302
Yoshida Trail (Japan) 73

Z

Zambezi River (Zambia/Zimbabwe) 297
Zambia
    Nairobi to Cape Town (Kenya to South Africa) 132–3
    safari 64–5
    TAZARA Railway 225
    Tour d'Afrique (Egypt to South Africa) 174–7
    Zambezi River 297
Zermatt (Switzerland) 216
Zimbabwe
    Nairobi to Cape Town (Kenya to South Africa) 132
    Rovos Rail 224
    Tour d'Afrique (Egypt to South Africa) 174–7
    Zambezi River 297
Zion Canyon (US) 16
Zion National Park (US) 16

ACKNOWLEDGMENTS

Dorling Kindersley would like to thank the following authors for their contribution to this book: Andrew Humphreys, Anthony Ham, Becca Hallett, Daniel Stables, Danielle Watt, Emma Grundy Haigh, Emma Thomson, Gavin Thomas, Huw Hennessy, Joseph Reaney, Kiki Deere, Leon McCarron, Lisa Voormeij, Mary Novakovich, Megan Eaves, Mike MacEacheran, Patricia Harris & David Lyon, Rachel Mills, Rachel Thompson, Robin Gauldie, Rudolf Abraham, Sara Humphreys, Sarah Hedley Hymers, Shafik Meghji, Sophie Ibbotson (Maximum Exposure Ltd), Steph Dyson, Stephen Keeling, Sue Watt, Taraneh Jerven, Tim Hannigan

The publisher would like to thank the following for their kind permission to reproduce their photographs:

(Key: a-above; b-below/bottom; c-centre; f-far; l-left; r-right; t-top)

123RF.com: Duncan Andison 48tl; mihtiander 282b; nakedking 42tl.

4Corners: Kav Dadfar 68tl; Design Pics / Ian Cumming 65br; Reinhard Schmid 21br.

Alamy Stock Photo: 22DigiTal 100ca; agefotostock / Braden Gunem 79br; Colin Monteath 190bl, 249t; Rubens Alarcon 105tr; Jerónimo Alba 34tl; All Canada Photos / Barrett & MacKay 154-55tl; Claude Robidoux 196-97, 199bl; TJ Watt 20t; Ambling Images 263cr; Andia / Darrault 166bl; Arctic Images / Ragnar Th Sigurdsson 121tc; Art Kowalsky 290br; Arterra Picture Library / Arndt Sven-Erik 121cla; van der Meer Marica 163bl; Zoltan Bagosi 107br; Andrew Bain 82cla, 186cl; John Bentley 190cr; Gabi Berger 63ca; Russ Bishop 187t; Blackout Concepts / Mark Owen 165cla; blickwinkel / M. Woike 223tl; Brent Beach 100tl; James Brunker 35c; Edgar Bullon 102tr; Robert Bush 271tr; Susan Candelario 14tr; Peter Carey 255ca; Carmen K. Sisson / Cloudybright 156tl; Michael DeFreitas Caribbean 261br; Cavan / Aurora Photos / Jake Norton 55tl; Chris Schmid Photography 210t; Christian Kober 1 102tl; Chromorange / Günter Fischer 131bl; Chronicle 103cr; Chuck Place 92br; Gary Cook 295cb; Matjaz Corel 47cra, 115tc; CPA Media Pte Ltd / Pictures From History 183br; Cultura Creative (RF) / Guido Cavallini 63tc; George Karbus Photography 115cla; Ian Dagnall 125bl; Danita Delimont / Ralph H. Bendjebar 59br; Adam Jones 14cr, 229tr; David L. Moore - NZL 78bl, 309cl; Design Pics Inc / Alaska Stock / Harry M. Walker 255tl; Axiom / Susan Dykstra 22bl; Henry Huntington 31bl; NULL 255cr; Donna Dietrich 255cla; dpa picture alliance 230c; eye35 291tr; Mark Ferguson 168tl; Jürgen Feuerer 280bl; David Foster 247bl; Larry Geddis 99cr; Eddie Gerald 185clb; Robert Gilhooly 181cra; Godong 141bl; Ben Goode 80-81t; Tim Graham 185crb; Granger Historical Picture Archive / NYC 17br; Greatstock / Horst Klemm 220-21; Jeffrey Isaac Greenberg 7 161tr; Martin Harvey 267tl; Hemis / Bertrand Gardel 304tr; Francis Leroy 140tc; Hemis.fr / Franck Charton 30tr, 297bl; Gil Giuglio 243tl; Franck Guiziou 231bl, 234b; Philippe Renault 199cr; Guillaume Soularue 289bc, 289br; Arnaud Spani 61br; James Hodgson 277cr; i4images rm 123bc; Image Professionals GmbH / Franz Marc Frei 61bl; Thomas Roetting 172tl; Konrad Wothe 270c; imageBROKER / Christian Handl 124-25t; Moritz Wolf 23tl, 76-77b, 308rt; ImageDB 305bl; Ivoha 35bc; Alun John 208tr; John Warburton-Lee Photography 176crb; Jon Arnold Images Ltd 285br, 266b; John Coletti 161tc; Theodore Kaye 137tr; Pawel Kazmierczak 273tr; Andreas Keuchel 55cla; Daniel Korzeniewski 265cl; Eric Lafforgue 59cla; Look Up! 213br; Ilene MacDonald 108tl; Iacob Madaci 227cra; William Manning 132tr; mauritius images GmbH / ClickAlps 115ca; Reinhard Dirscherl 145crb; Nicolas Marino 175tr, 178tl, 185tr; Rene Mattes 127tl; Novarc Images / Dennis Schmelz 242b; Marco Simoni 25cla, 308tl; Angus McComiskey 127cla; Mikel Bilbao Gorostiaga- Travels 135br; Minden Pictures / Larry Minden 103b; Tim Moore 198cl, 199br; Tuul and Bruno Morandi 232tl; National Geographic Image Collection / Jonathan Irish 28cr; Todd Gipstein 264t; Alex Saberi 210bl; Natrow Images 165c; Nature Picture Library / Will Burrard-Lucas 65tr; Naturepix 265bc; Roberto Nistri 177br; M. Timothy O'Keefe 290bl; Ingo Oeland 145clb; Aboriginal art exhibited in the Albert Namatjira Gallery at the Araluen Arts Centre / Samantha Ohlsen 246cra; Oneworld Picture / Viviane Wild 286bl; Efrain Padro 205b; Paul Mayall Australia 244-45; Matteo Pessini 112tc; Photononstop / Severine Baur 262crb; PhotoStock-Israel / Ilan D Rosen 137cl; Prisma by Dukas Presseagentur GmbH / Raga Jose Fuste 41br; Pulsar Imagens 211cr; Sergi Reboredo 224bl; Edwin Remsberg 176cra; Robert Preston Photography 137cr; Robertharding / Neale Clark 84tr; Dallas & John Heaton 226br; James Hager 222br; Matthew Williams-Ellis 47bl, 271tl; Louise Murray 223cra; Michael Nolan 271cra; Michael Runkel 97tl, 176-77bl; Julia Rogers 207c; Ian Rutherford 116bl; scott sady / tahoelight.com 16-17, 19bl; eter Schickert 246tc; Ivan Sebborn 290clb; Leonid Serebrennikov 141t; Robert Smith 168tr; dave stamboulis 71br; Bob Stanton 93tl; Simon Stapley 51bl; Steve Taylor ARPS 309clb; Stockimo / khair mispan 303br; Paul Strawson 129tr; Stephen Sykes 309cra; Tom Till 27bl; Pete Titmuss 222bl; UrbanZone 139bl; Lucas Vallecillos 72tr, 238tc, 281br; Tom Walker 157bl; David Wall 186tc; wanderluster 69bl; Sebastian Wasek 49t; Westend61 GmbH / Fotofeeling 204tl; Stefan Schurr 112c; Karin De Winter 235ca; Jan Wlodarczyk 215cl, 230ca; Ariadne Van Zandbergen 292tl; Zoonar GmbH / zhu difeng 184t; ZUMA Press, Inc. 300cl.

AWL Images: Aurora Photos 67tr; Jan Christopher Becke 5bc, 192-93; Marco Bottigelli 50tl; ClickAlps 283t; Danita Delimont Stock 186cra; Niels van Gijn 300tr; Hemis 247tc; Christian Kober 106clb; Karol Kozlowski 209br; Nigel Pavitt 228-29; Doug Pearson 231br; Richard Stanley 144; Jane Sweeney 236t, 262tr; Emily Wilson 284tl.

Belmond Ltd.: 206t, 207br, 218t, 219cla, 219br.

Depositphotos Inc: sergeyonas 112cla; travelmaid 286tl.

Dreamstime.com: Artushfoto 127crb; Kushnirov Avraham 113; Avstraliavasin 243cla; Awhelin 138tl; Bereczki Barna 41tr; Bennymarty 200tr, 215clb; Lukas Bischoff 134-35b; Paul Brady 198tc; Byheaven87 74t, 229cr; Candy1812 125tr; Jerome Cid 213bl; Sorin Colac 311tr; Luis Costa 35clb; Florea Paul Daniel 132clb; Daniloalarconlopez 267tr; Digitalsignal 214cl; Mikhail Dudarev 71tr; Dwnld777 140cra; Rusty Elliott 153br; Erectus 44t; Esmehelit 84bl; Evgeniy Fesenko 136cr; Augustin Florian 181br; Giovanni Gagliardi 246bl; Janos Gaspar 39bl; Craig Hastings 165tc; Menno Van Der Haven 170t; Jia He 18tl; Henryturner 201bl; Aagje De Jong 187br; David Knibbs 117b; Shalender Kumar 237bl; Steve Lagreca 60; Lcc54613 238ca; Pierre Leclerc 98t; Sungbok Lee 182-83; Jennifer Lobo 275cr; Kattiya Loukobkul 241bl; Sergey Mayorov 75cr; Aliaksandr Mazurkevich 230tr; MNStudio 173bl; Luciano Mortula 136br; MrLis 295cr; Marketa Novakova 128-29s; Nuvisage 181c; Sean Pavone 235cr; Pipa100 171bc; Grobler Du Preez 130tr; Ronniechua 100cr; Rosshelen 118bl; Saiko3p 243cra, 243bl; Richard Semik 277c; Hans Slegers 169; Slidezero 281cra; Calin Stan 288-89b; Phoonperm Suwannarattaphoom 265bl; Ranulph Thorpe 139tr; Peter Titmuss 222cl; Tomas1111 125ca; Tommyandone 277tl; Torjrtrx 183tr; Aleksandr Vorobev 106bl; Petr Vrchovsky 207cl; Rattapon Wannaphat 78clb; Yanyanyan881 306-07; Chang Jung Yu 185c; Yurataranik 230clb.

Getty Images: 500px / Steve Baker 293cr; Thomas Bronner 262cl; Jaroslaw Rufer 40; Seppo Ulmanen 286ca; Marcus Visic 178tr; VGM 128b; 500px Prime / Angeles Antolin Hoyos 155cr; Eric Lai 191t; Guilherme Mesquita 24b; AFP / Gianluigi Guercia 223crb; Aizar Raldes 110bl; Chris Bennett 12-13b; Bettmann 257cr; Cavan Images 143tr; Corbis / Atlantide Phototravel 274-75; Reinhard Dirscherl 126bl; Maremagnum 111tr; Paul Panayiotou 176tc; Henrik Trygg 275tr; De Agostini / DEA / BIBLIOTECA AMBROSIANA 282cr; DigitalVision / Christian Ender 270cla; Justin Paget 176bc, 177cr; Paul Souders 294t; James Strachan 55crb; EyeEm / Ilona Ait 132cra; Emily Deltetto 214tr; / Mark Fitzpatrick 310-11; Matthias Kestel 264br; Kayvon Monjezi 159br; Sam Ratcliffe 4-5b, 86-87; Fabian Schmiedlechner 26tl; Gamma-Rapho / Christophe Courteau 58b; Tim Graham 37br; The Image Bank / Peter Adams 235bl; Timothy Allen 56tl; Atlantide Phototravel 226t; Andrew Aylett 83bl; Gonzalo Azumendi 300cr; Marc Dozier 247br; Michael Hall 54br, 77bc; Richard I'Anson 145cb, / Julian Elliott Photography 45bl; Hans-Peter Merten 171clb; Andrew Peacock 85br, 270br; Pawel Toczynski 154br, 260-61t, 262-63b; ImaZinS / TERAN 239; Kyodo News 180b; The LIFE Picture Collection / Joseph Scherschel 110cr; LightRocket / SOPA Images / Ana Fernandez 34tr; Moment / 7cero / Enrique Díaz 32-33b; Igor Alecsander 107bl; Emad aljumah 56tr; Nuttapoom Amornpashara 73b; Audun Bakke Andersen 281clb; Eduardo Fonseca Arraes 115br; Marco Bottigelli 114b, 119tr, 167tl; Carlos Carreno 25tl; Noppawat Tom Charoensinphon 104-05b; Ed Cheung 258bl; Manuel Breva Colmeiro 54bl; Artur Debat 94-95; Diana Robinson Photography 174-75b; Chantip Ditcharoen 280t; Jon Douglas 116t; Verónica Paradinas Duro 292tr; by Jonathan D. Goforth 257tr; Chris Griffiths 179b; Hou 158-59t; Greg Jaggears 17tr; / Harri Jarvelainen Photography 154ca; John Crux Photography 71cr; kittisun kittayacharoenpong 240t; Alexandre Morin-Laprise 30tr; Laura BC 109br; Lightvision, LLC 205tr;Ali Majdfar 15bl; Sasipa Muennuch 133; Nora Carol Photography 142-43; M.Omair 217tr;

Ozkan Ozmen 227tc; Anton Petrus 120t; Posnov 82ca, 83t; RICOWde 212b; Manuel Romaris 59tl; Teradat Santivivut 147b; Alex Saurel 225tr; Steve Daggar Photography 82crb; Pintai Suchachaisri 207tl; Suttipong Sutiratanachai 214tl; Punnawit Suwuttananun 4bl, 8-9, 62, 66-67; Ignatius Tan 270cr; Christoph Wagner 37bl; wiratgasem 69tr; xia yuan 135bc; Moment Open / Chasing Light Photography Thomas Vela 154cl; Matteo Colombo 160b; Francisco Goncalves 293bl; Patrick McMullan / Joe Schildhorn 262cla; PitGreenwood 303tr; Laszlo Podor 153bc; Photography by Deb Snelson 155tr; Gabriel Sperandio 211tc; Bill Swindaman 13bc; by Geof Wilson 223cl; Sky Noir Photography by Bill Dickinson 95tr; Photodisc / , Tim Bieber 97cl; James Osmond 5ca, 148-49; George Rose 92bl, 93ca; Michel Setboun 270clb; Stone / Peter Adams 126t; Gonzalo Azumendi 301bl; Matteo Colombo 279bl; Jorg Greuel 215bc; Andrew Peacock 268-69; Peter Unger 152-53b; Kuni Takahashi 75bl; Universal Images Group / REDA&CO 125clb; Visual China Group / Wang Jianmin 2-3.

Golden Eagle Luxury Trains Limited: 241br.

iStockphoto.com: nazar_ab 81b; anothersteph 79t; aphotostory 5cra, 250-51; BeyondImages 248br; brytta 294bl; cesa53rone 287; chameleonseye 78crb; danilovi 70t; dchadwick 189tl; E+ / adamkaz 90-91; bchelovi 46t; benedek 200tl; borchee 130bl; chinaface 101; DavorLovincic 273cr; David_creative 261tr; dchadwick 164b; deimagine 106tc, / DieterMeyrl 6-7, 38tl; DoraDalton 25c; ferrantraite 286cra; FG Trade 272t; FilippoBacci 159; KenCanning 204cr; Lya_Cattel 171cb; nicolamargaret 25bl; Nikada 64t, 65ca; pidjoe 95br; powerofforever 29; simonbradfield 146tr; Spanic 272bl; Starcevic 52-53b; Flavio Vallenari 263br; vuk8691 273tl; AJ_Watt 295clb; wilpunt 53bc; Yiming Li 302-03; Zuki 96-97b; filrom 162t; GiorgioMorara 215cr; guenterguni 57bl; helovi 74bl; holgs 28ca; karp85 36t; Michelinedesgroseilliers 198c; Martin Schütz 33br; Iuliia Serova 28tc; SWKrullImaging 204cla; tbradford 298-99; urbanglimpses 202tl, 254b; xenotar 171tl; yes-thats-it 43br.

Rex by Shutterstock: Daily Mail / Graham Trott 279cr; The Independent / David Sandison 233cr.

Robert Harding Picture Library: Gavin Hellier 291tl.

Shutterstock.com: arkanto 99bl; Fabien Astre 246cb; Diego Bonacina 216-17; Burak Budak 290crb; Alex Cimbal 121tr; Eve Wheeler Photography 98bl; Food Via Lenses 97cr; Geza Kurka Photos 276b; GROGL 259tl; kirstylee152 278bl; Janelle Lugge 188bl; Carl Milner 48tr; Mountain Man Photos 203br; Wanangwe Muchika 225tl; s4svisuals 278t; Dmitrii Sakharov 123t; Roberto Lo Savio 219tr; Renata Sedmakova 277bl; SL-Photography 106cr; Marcin Szymczak 136bl; TAMVISUT 233b; Tsuguliev 219c; VQHPicture 122-23; wtondossantos 111tl.

Unsplash: Teodor Kuduschiev / @teodorpk 296t; Simon Migaj / @simonmigaj 121br; Anup Mishra / @oxanup 232tr; Gabrielle Mustapich / @gmustapich 256-57; Hubert Neufeld / @hltn_films 269br; Taylor Simpson / @taylorgsimpson 301br; Kirk Thornton / @kirkthornton 15crb; Jon Tyson / @jontyson 33bc.

Cover images:
Front: iStockphoto.com: E+ / franckreporter main.
Back: Alamy Stock Photo: mauritius images GmbH / Nicolas Marino cr; Dreamstime.com: Calin Stan cb; Getty Images: 500px Prime / Guilherme Mesquita c; Unsplash: Anup Mishra / @oxanup cl

For further information see: www.dkimages.com

DK | Penguin Random House

Senior Editor Alison McGill
Senior Designer Tania Gomes
Project Editor Rebecca Flynn
Project Designer William Robinson
Designers Van Anh Le, Javana Boothe, Jordan Lambley, Sarah Snelling
Editor Lucy Sienkowska
Additional Editors Elspeth Beidas, Rachel Laidler, Rada Radojicic, Zoë Rutland
Proofreader Susanne Hillen
Indexer Helen Peters
Senior Picture Researcher Ellen Root
Picture Research Flora Spens, Sumita Khatwani, Vagisha Pushp
Senior Cartographic Editor Casper Morris
Jacket Designer Tania Gomes
Jacket Picture Research Tania Gomes
Senior DTP Designer Jason Little
Technical Prepress Manager Tom Morse
Image Retouching Steve Crozier
Senior Production Controller Stephanie McConnell
Managing Editor Hollie Teague
Managing Art Editor Bess Daly
Art Director Maxine Pedliham
Publishing Director Georgina Dee

First edition 2020
Published in Great Britain by
Dorling Kindersley Limited,
DK, One Embassy Gardens, 8 Viaduct Gardens,
London, SW11 7BW
The authorised representative in the EEA is
Dorling Kindersley Verlag GmbH. Arnulfstr. 124,
80636 Munich, Germany
Copyright © 2020 Dorling Kindersley Limited
A Penguin Random House Company
24 25 26 27 10 9 8
All rights reserved.
No part of this publication may be reproduced, stored in or introduced into a retrieval system, or transmitted, in any form, or by any means (electronic, mechanical, photocopying, recording, or otherwise), without the prior written permission of the copyright owner.
A CIP catalog record for this book
is available from the British Library.
ISSN: 1542 1554
ISBN: 978 0 2414 2616 6
Printed and bound in Malaysia.
www.dk.com

MIX
Paper | Supporting responsible forestry
FSC™ C018179

Every effort has been made to ensure that this book is as up-to-date as possible at the time of going to press. Some details, however, such as websites and travel information, are liable to change. The publishers cannot accept responsibility for any consequences arising from the use of this book, nor for any material on third party websites, and cannot guarantee that any website address in this book will be a suitable source of travel information. We value the views and suggestions of our readers very highly. Please write to: Publisher, DK Eyewitness Travel Guides, One Embassy Gardens, 8 Viaduct Gardens, London SW11 7BW or email: travelguides@uk.dk.com